Pearson
BTEC National

Travel and Tourism

Student Book

Gillian Dale

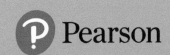 Pearson

Published by Pearson Education Limited, 80 Strand, London, WC2R 0RL.

www.pearsonschoolsandfecolleges.co.uk

Copies of official specifications for all Edexcel qualifications may be found on the website: www.edexcel.com

Text © Gillian Dale, 2019
Typeset by PDQ Media
Original illustrations © Pearson Education Ltd
Cover design by Pearson Education Limited
Cover photo/illustration © Stefano Garau, Triff / Shutterstock.com

The rights of Gillian Dale to be identified as author of this work have been asserted by her in accordance with the Copyright, Designs and Patents Act 1988.

First published 2019

22 21 20

10 9 8 7 6 5 4

British Library Cataloguing in Publication Data
A catalogue record for this book is available from the British Library

ISBN 978 1 292 18775 4

Acknowledgements

We would like to thank Sonia Bailey and Carol Spencer for their invaluable help in reviewing this book.

Gillian Dale thanks the following for their contributions: Jo Quincy, Nick Garcia, Cathy Farrell, Hollie Rae Brader, Caroline Robinson, Simon Godfrey and Ben Butler.

The authors and publisher would like to thank the following individuals and organisations for permission to reproduce materials:

p.83 13 Of The Best Spas For Mind And Body by Grazia. © Copyright 2016 Bauer Consumer Media Limited. Used with permission of The Bauer Consumer Media. http://lifestyle.one/grazia/diet-body/health-fitness/spa-retreats-uk-mindfulness-meditation-detox/; **p.97** © Used with permission of The Jules Verne. https://www.vjv.com/europe-tours/russia/treasures-of-the-hermitage-1/#itinerary; **pp.137, 277, 338** BTEC Level 3 National Travel and Tourism: Teaching Resource Pack, Gillian Dale, Pearson Education Limited. © 2010, Pearson Education, Inc.; **p.160, 161** BTEC Level 3 National Travel and Tourism. Student Book 2, Gillian Dale, Pearson Education Limited. © 2010, Pearson Education, Inc.; **p.225** ©Telegraph Media Group Limited 2017. Used with permission of The Telegraph. http://www.telegraph.co.uk/business/2016/10/02/even-corporate-away-days-like-to-be-beside-the-seaside-says-butl/; **p. 124** Easyjet plc: Easyjet plc, http://corporate.easyjet.com/~/media/Files/E/Easyjet/pdf/investors/results-centre/2018/2018-annual-report-and-accounts.pdf; **p. 126** Easyjet plc, https://www.easyjet.com/en/terms-and-conditions; **p. 124** UNIGLOBE Travel International Limited: https://www.uniglobe.com/about-uniglobe; **p. 124** Norwegian Air Shuttle ASA: https://www.norwegian.com/uk/about/our-story/vision-and-values/; **p. 125** Insure & Go Insurance Services Limited: Insure & Go Insurance Services Limited, https://www.insureandgo.com/about-us; **p. 125** Trailfinders Ltd: Trailfinders Ltd,https://www.trailfinders.com/aboutus; **p. 131** Association of British Travel Agents (ABTA): https://www.abta.com/sites/default/files/2019-01/Code%20of%20Conduct%20Jan%202019%20ii.pdf; **p. 141** The Chartered Institute of Marketing (CIM): The Chartered Institute of Marketing (CIM), https://www.cim.co.uk/media/4772/7ps.pdf; p. 138 Thomas Cook Group plc: https://www.thomascookgroup.com/investors/insight_external_assest/Thomas_Cook_AR_2018_web.pdf; **p. 168** VisitBritain: https://www.visitbritain.org/annual-review/annual-review-2016-17/who-we-are-and-what-we-do; **p. 140** Historic Royal Palaces: https://secure.thebiggive.org.uk/charity/view/5206/historic-royal-palaces; **p. 144** NATS Limited: https://www.nats.aero/; **p. 142** Travelweekly: HYPERLINK "http://www.travelweekly.co.uk/articles/54160/tui-outlines-plan-for-global-rebrand"Travel Weekly Group, Tui outlines plan for global rebrand, May 13th 2015, http://www.travelweekly.co.uk/articles/54160/tui-outlines-plan-for-global-rebrand, **p. 146** HYPERLINK "http://www.travelweekly.co.uk/articles/320900/the-cruise-village-targets-po-cruises-sales-with-revamped-site"Travel Weekly Group, Jan 9th 2019, Harry Kemble, http://www.travelweekly.co.uk/articles/320900/the-cruise-village-targets-po-cruises-sales-with-revamped-site, **p. 138** HYPERLINK "http://www.travelweekly.co.uk/articles/320789/virgin-atlantic-flightstores-10-week-giveaway"Virgin Atlantic Flightstore's 10-week giveaway!, Travel Weekly Group, Jan 8th 2019, http://www.travelweekly.co.uk/articles/320789/virgin-atlantic-flightstores-10-week-giveaway, **p. 139** HYPERLINK "https://travolution.com/articles/110006/on-the-beach-agrees-emirates-distribution-deal"On the Beach agrees Emirates distribution deal, Phil Davies on Jan 15th, 2019,Travel Weekly Group, https://travolution.com/articles/110006/on-the-beach-agrees-emirates-distribution-deal; **p. 147** STA Travel: https://www.statravel.co.th/social-responsibility.htm; **p. 151** TUI group: https://www.tuigroup.com/en-en/about-us/about-tui-group, HYPERLINK "https://urldefense.proofpoint.com/v2/url?u=https-3A__www.tui.co.uk_destinations_deals_premium-2Dhotel-2Ddeals&d=DwMGaQ&c=0YLnzTkWOdJJub_y7qAx8Q&r=S2SctWMl72kfrM68ewEa_cQqpS5Pxjiys7fPMB0JJew&m=q9MPDeAzIAkWASPWBs7_rxrYCq4ZX5Zcxmdc IvoiQHs&s=1U5LXPUQlodlH41hzIoZ7IHnx0H-diMJeItUZgsWZY4&e="https://www.tui.co.uk/destinations/deals/premium-hotel-deals; **p. 131** The Beth Chatto Gardens: https://www.bethchatto.co.uk/gardens/about.htm; **p. 133** Kuoni: https://www.kuoni.co.uk/all-inclusive-holidays; **p. 135** Whitbread Plc: Annual Report and Accounts 2017/18, Whitbread Plc; **p. 176** VISIT FAROE ISLANDS: PETITION: WE WANT GOOGLE STREET VIEW!, JUL 2016, Durita, VISIT FAROE ISLANDS; **p. 178** Ryanair DAC: Ryanair Unveils 2018 "Always Getting Better" Plan including 5 Year Plan To Eliminate Plastics, Jan 2018, Ryanair DAC; **p. 147** Crown copyright: Office for National Statistics (ONS), 2017 26; **p. 134, p. 136, p. 137, p. 142, p. 147, p. 161, p. 167** Pearson Education: © Pearson Education

The publisher would like to thank the following for their kind permission to reproduce their photographs:

(Key: b-bottom; c-centre; l-left; r-right; t-top)

123RF.com: 194tl; © **Alamy Stock Photo:** Paul Adams - North West Images 10, B.O'Kane 264, Imaginechina Limited 149, Stuart Black 76t, Elsie Kibue 273, M. Timothy O'Keefe 263, Reuters 1; **The American Institute of Graphic Arts (AIGA):** 14; **Aspire; Hollie-Ray Brader:** Matt Sprake 62; **Cathy Farrell:** 231; **Department of Transport:** Crown Copyright 13; **easyJet:** 128; **easyJet:** Jan H. Andersen 256, Chrisdorney 257, devilkae 240, G.C. photo 280, Imran's Photography 257, Lucky Images 62, Dmitri Maruta 183, Dirk Vonten 45; **Getty Images:** leezsnow 65, Jetlinterimages 139, Ullstein bild 191, **Lake District, Cumbria Tourism:** 220; **Let's Go Cambridge Ltd:** Caroline Robinson 279; **National Readership Survey:** 264b; **Nicholas Garcia:** 117; **Rail Delivery Group:** 26tr, 26l, 26br; **Shutterstock.com:** 138, 172, achinthamb 79, Djomas 232, FocusDzign 194bl, PathDoc 194br, pudi studio 205, Sorbis 85, zahorec 113; **STA Travel:** 75; **Edward Thorpe:** Edward Thorpe 111; **Trivago:** 49; **VisitEngland:** 40, 104, 245; **VisitScotland:** 42

123RF: Oleksandr Nebrat 146; **Alamy Stock Photo:** Stephen Barnes/Northern Ireland 140, ZUMA Press, Inc. 150, WENN Rights Ltd 169, Karine Aigner/National Geographic Image Collection 171; **Getty Images:** Jetlinerimages/iStock 169; **Shutterstock:** hektoR 121, Roman Samborskyi 169, voloshin311 169, AboutLife 176, AstroStar 176

All other images © Pearson Education

Websites

Pearson Education Limited is not responsible for the content of any external internet sites. It is essential for tutors to preview each website before using it in class so as to ensure that the URL is still accurate, relevant and appropriate. We suggest that tutors bookmark useful websites and consider enabling students to access them through the school/college intranet.

A note from the publisher

In order to ensure that this resource offers high-quality support for the associated Pearson qualification, it has been through a review process by the awarding body. This process confirms that this resource fully covers the teaching and learning content of the specification or part of a specification at which it is aimed. It also confirms that it demonstrates an appropriate balance between the development of subject skills, knowledge and understanding, in addition to preparation for assessment.

Endorsement does not cover any guidance on assessment activities or processes (e.g. practice questions or advice on how to answer assessment questions) included in the resource nor does it prescribe any particular approach to the teaching or delivery of a related course.

While the publishers have made every attempt to ensure that advice on the qualification and its assessment is accurate, the official specification and associated assessment guidance materials are the only authoritative source of information and should always be referred to for definitive guidance.

Pearson examiners have not contributed to any sections in this resource relevant to examination papers for which they have responsibility.

Examiners will not use endorsed resources as a source of material for any assessment set by Pearson.

Endorsement of a resource does not mean that the resource is required to achieve this Pearson qualification, nor does it mean that it is the only suitable material available to support the qualification, and any resource lists produced by the awarding body shall include this and other appropriate resources.

Contents

How to use this book

Welcome to your BTEC National Travel and Tourism course!

Choosing to study a BTEC National in Travel and Tourism is a great decision for a number of reasons. This qualification will help you to create a path of progression towards eventually working in this industry.

The qualification will help you to gain knowledge and experience that will help you to prepare for university or employment in a range of different job roles. You may be interested in tour operations or working in tourism development. Or you may be interested in working in transportation or accommodation and catering. Whatever career path in this sector you are interested in, this course will help you build and develop the skills you need to make a success of higher education, employment or both.

Readers will find that much of the Managing Customer Experience unit is replicated in the Principles of Marketing unit so that students have all the material required to complete the marketing unit in one place with no need to study the Customer Experience unit unless they wish to explore this further.

This publication can also be used for those students studying the 2010 BTEC National specification. A mapping grid is provided as an appendix on page 281 to show how this book can be mapped to that qualification.

How your BTEC is structured

Your BTEC National is divided into **mandatory units** (the ones you must do) and **optional units** (the ones you can choose to do). The number of mandatory and optional units will vary depending on the type of BTEC National you are doing.

This book supports all the mandatory units for the Certificate, Extended Certificate and Foundation Diploma.

You will also need to complete a range of optional units for this qualification at every size, except the Certificate.

Your learning experience

You may not realise it but you are always learning. Your educational and life experiences are constantly shaping your ideas and thinking, and how you view and engage with the world around you.

You are the person most responsible for your own learning experience so you must understand what you are learning, why you are learning it and why it is important both to your course and to your personal development. Your learning can be seen as a journey with four phases.

Phase 1	Phase 2	Phase 3	Phase 4
You are introduced to a topic or concept and you start to develop an awareness of what learning is required.	You explore the topic or concept through different methods (e.g. research, questioning, analysis, deep thinking, critical evaluation) and form your own understanding.	You apply your knowledge and skills to a task designed to test your understanding.	You reflect on your learning, evaluate your efforts, identify gaps in your knowledge and look for ways to improve.

During each phase, you will use different learning strategies to secure the core knowledge and skills you need. This student book has been written using similar learning principles, strategies and tools. It has been designed to support your learning journey, to give you control over your own learning, and to equip you with the knowledge, understanding and tools you need to be successful in your future studies or career.

Features of this book

This student book contains many different features. They are there to help you learn about key topics in different ways and understand them from multiple perspectives. Together, these features:

▶ explain what your learning is about
▶ help you to build your knowledge
▶ help you to understand how to succeed in your assessment
▶ help you to reflect on and evaluate your learning
▶ help you to link your learning to the workplace.

Each individual feature has a specific purpose, designed to support important learning strategies. For example, some features will:

▶ encourage you to question assumptions about what you are learning
▶ help you to think beyond what you are reading about
▶ help you to make connections between different areas of your learning and across units
▶ draw comparisons between your own learning and real-world workplace environments
▶ help you to develop some of the important skills you will need for the workplace, including teamwork, effective communication and problem solving.

Features that explain what your learning is about

Getting to know your unit

This section introduces the unit and explains how you will be assessed. It gives an overview of what will be covered and will help you to understand why you are doing the things you are asked to do in this unit.

Getting started

This is designed to get you thinking about the unit and what it involves. This feature will also help you to identify what you may already know about some of the topics in the unit and act as a starting point for understanding the skills and knowledge you will need to develop to complete the unit.

Features that help you to build your knowledge

Research

This asks you to research a topic in greater depth. These features will help to expand your understanding of a topic and develop your research and investigation skills. All of this will be invaluable for your future progression, both professionally and academically.

Theory into practice

In this feature you are asked to consider the workplace or industry implications of a topic or concept from the unit. This will help you to understand the close links between what you are learning in the classroom and the effects it will have on a future career in your chosen sector.

Discussion

Discussion features encourage you to talk to other students about a topic, working together to increase your understanding of the topic and to understand other people's perspectives on an issue. These features will also help to build your teamworking skills, which will be invaluable in your future professional and academic career.

Key terms

Concise and simple definitions are provided for key words, phrases and concepts, giving you, at a glance, a clear understanding of the key ideas in each unit.

Link

Link features show any links between units or within the same unit, helping you to identify knowledge you have learned elsewhere that will help you to achieve the requirements of the unit. Remember, although your BTEC National is made up of several units, there are common themes that are explored from different perspectives across the whole of your course.

Further reading and resources

This contains a list of other resources – such as books, journals, articles or websites – you can use to expand your knowledge of the unit content. This is a good opportunity for you to take responsibility for your own learning, as well as preparing you for research tasks you may need to do academically or professionally.

Features connected to your assessment

Your course is made up of mandatory and optional units. There are two different types of mandatory unit:

▶ externally assessed
▶ internally assessed.

Externally assessed units

These units will give you the opportunity to demonstrate your knowledge and understanding, or your skills, in a direct way. For these units you will complete a task, set directly by Pearson, in controlled conditions. This could take the form of an exam or it could be another type of task. You may have the opportunity to prepare in advance, to research and make notes about a topic which can be used when completing the assessment.

Internally assessed units

Most of your units will be internally assessed and will involve you completing a series of assignments, set and marked by your tutor. The assignments you complete will allow you to demonstrate your learning in a number of different ways, from a written report to a presentation to a video recording and observation statements of you completing a practical task. Whatever the method, you will need to make sure you have clear evidence of what you have achieved and how you did it.

Assessment activity

These features give you the opportunity to practise some of the skills you will need during the unit assessment. They do not fully reflect the actual assessment tasks but will help you to prepare for them.

Plan – Do – Review

You will also find handy advice on how to plan, complete and evaluate your work. This is designed to get you thinking about the best way to complete your work and to build your skills and experience before doing the actual assessment. These questions will prompt you to think about the way you work and why particular tasks are relevant.

Getting ready for assessment

For internally assessed units, this is a case study of a BTEC National student, talking about how they planned and carried out their assignment work and what they would do differently if they were to do it again. It will give you advice on preparing for your internal assessments, including Think about it points for you to consider for your own development.

Getting ready for assessment

This section will help you to prepare for external assessment. It gives practical advice on preparing for and sitting exams or a set task. It provides a series of sample answers for the types of question you will need to answer in your external assessment, including guidance on the good points of these answers and ways in which they could be improved.

Features to help you reflect on and evaluate your learning

Ⅱ PAUSE POINT

Pause Points appear regularly throughout the book and provide opportunities to review and reflect on your learning. The ability to reflect on your own performance is a key skill you will need to develop and use throughout your life, and will be essential whatever your future plans are.

Hint
Extend

These also give you suggestions to help cement your knowledge and indicate other areas you can look at to expand it.

Features that link your learning with the workplace

Case study

Case studies are used throughout the book to allow you to apply the learning and knowledge from the unit to a scenario from the workplace or the industry. Case studies include questions to help you consider the wider context of a topic. This is an opportunity to see how the unit's content is reflected in the real world, and for you to build familiarity with issues you may find in a real-world workplace.

THINK ▶FUTURE

This is a case study in which someone working in the industry talks about their job role and the skills they need. The *Focusing your skills* section suggests ways for you to develop the employability skills and experiences you will need to be successful in a career in your chosen sector. This will help you to identify what you could do, inside and outside your BTEC National studies, to build up your employability skills.

The World of Travel and Tourism

1

Getting to know your unit

Assessment
This unit is assessed by an examination that is set and marked by Pearson.

The travel and tourism industry is extremely important to the UK economy. There are many different influences on the industry and these change continually in response to developments economically, socially and politically around the world. This unit introduces you to the scope of the industry and its key components. You will find out about the many different examples of organisations within the industry and the ways in which they react to new developments. You will learn how organisations work together to benefit their customers. You will also discover where to find statistics about travel and tourism, and how to analyse these statistics.

How you will be assessed

This unit will be assessed by an examination set by Pearson. You will be assessed on your understanding of the following topics:

▶ types of travel and tourism, and types of customers
▶ travel and tourism organisations and their roles, and the products and services they offer to customers
▶ the scale of the travel and tourism industry, and its importance to the economy and to employment
▶ factors affecting the travel and tourism industry, and organisations' responses to these factors.

Throughout this unit you will find assessment activities to help you prepare for the examination. Completing these activities will give you an insight into the types of questions you will be asked and how to answer them.

As the guidelines for assessment can change, you should refer to the official guidance on the Pearson Qualifications website for the latest definitive guidance.

Unit 1 has five assessment outcomes (AOs), which will be included in the external examination. Certain command words are associated with each assessment outcome. Table 1.1 explains what these command words are asking you to do.

Here are the assessment outcomes for the unit.

▶ **AO1** Demonstrate knowledge and understanding of the travel and tourism industry, types of tourism and organisations involved.
  • Command words: complete, describe, give, identify, outline.
  • Marks: ranges from 2 to 4 marks.
▶ **AO2** Apply knowledge and understanding of the travel and tourism industry and factors affecting the industry to real-life travel and tourism scenarios.
  • Command words: analyse, assess, calculate, describe, discuss, evaluate, explain.
  • Marks: ranges from 4 to 12 marks.
▶ **AO3** Analyse information and data from the travel and tourism industry, identifying trends and the potential impact of different factors on the industry and its customers.
  • Command words: analyse, assess, discuss, evaluate.
  • Marks: ranges from 6 to 12 marks.

▶ **AO4** Evaluate how information and data can be used by the travel and tourism industry to make decisions that affect organisations and customers.
  - Command words: analyse, assess, discuss, evaluate.
  - Marks: ranges from 6 to 12 marks.

▶ **AO5** Make connections between the factors that influence the travel and tourism industry and how the industry responds to minimise the potential impact on organisations and customers.
  - Command words: analyse, assess, discuss, evaluate.
  - Marks: ranges from 6 to 12 marks.

▶ **Table 1.1:** Command words used in this unit

Command word	Definition – what it is asking you to do
Analyse	Identify several relevant facts of a topic, demonstrate how they are linked and then explain the importance of each, often in relation to the other facts
Assess	Evaluate or estimate the nature, ability or quality of something, identifying the most important or relevant factors and arriving at a conclusion
Calculate	Work out an answer. Usually this will be by adding, multiplying, subtracting or dividing but sometimes you may need to use a formula
Complete	Add relevant information or data to a table or diagram
Describe	Give a full account of all the information, including all the relevant details of any features, of a topic
Discuss	Write about the topic in detail, taking into account different ideas and opinions, considering different aspects, how they are linked and the extent to which they are important
Evaluate	Bring all the relevant information you have on a topic together and make a judgement on it (for example, on its success or importance). Your judgement should be clearly supported by the information you have gathered
Explain	Make an idea, situation or problem clear to your reader by describing it in detail, including any relevant data or facts, showing how any conclusions have been reached. You will need to show you fully understand the topic you are writing about
Give	Provide examples, justifications and/or reasons
Identify	State the key fact(s) about a topic or subject
Outline	Give a summary or overview, or a brief description of something

Getting started

How many people do you know who work in the travel and tourism industry? Write down the names of the organisations they work for. Try to decide which sector of travel and tourism they work in. For example, if they work in a hotel, then they work in the accommodation sector, whereas someone who works for an airline works in the transport sector. Compare your list with others in your group. As you work through this unit, you will be able to check your knowledge of travel and tourism sectors and find out more about them.

A   Types of travel and tourism

Key terms

Tourism – the movement of people to countries or places outside their usual environment for either personal or business reasons.

United Nations World Tourism Organization (UNWTO) – the agency for world tourism, responsible for the promotion of responsible, sustainable and universally accessible tourism.

Domestic tourist – someone travelling within their own country and staying away from home for at least one night.

Day visitor – someone taking a day trip with no overnight stay.

Inbound tourist – someone entering a country for the purpose of tourism.

Outbound tourist – someone leaving their own country to travel to another country for the purpose of tourism.

Before you can study the scope of the travel and tourism industry, you need to know some key terminology relating to **tourism**. Definitions of tourism can vary. According to the **United Nations World Tourism Organization (UNWTO)**, tourism is the movement of people to countries or places outside their usual environment for either personal or business reasons.

Types of tourism

Domestic tourism

Domestic tourists are tourists travelling within their own country. To be considered a tourist, you have to stay somewhere away from home for at least one night. People who take day trips are also important to travel and tourism businesses because they spend money and make an important contribution to the economy of the area that they visit. However, they are not counted as tourists but are known as **day visitors**.

Inbound tourism

Inbound tourists are people who enter a country to visit for the purposes of tourism, such as for a holiday. A Spanish tourist travelling from Spain to the UK for a holiday is an inbound tourist to the UK. According to the International Passenger Survey, there are 36.8 million inbound trips to the UK forecast for 2019. This inbound tourism is worth £25 billion to the British economy.

Outbound tourism

Outbound tourists are people leaving their own country and travelling to a different one for the purposes of tourism. For example, the Spanish tourist who was an inbound tourist to the UK was also an outbound tourist from Spain. Similarly, if you leave the UK to spend a few weeks with your extended family in another country, you are an outbound tourist from the UK.

Types of travel

Leisure travel

Tourists who partake in leisure travel are travelling for their own pleasure and enjoyment or to take a relaxing holiday. They may also travel for a special interest or to attend a special event. For example, they might attend a football match in another city or country, or take a residential course in painting or writing.

Holidays such as package holidays, holidays planned by tourists themselves and cruises are all classed as leisure travel. Some leisure travellers attend seasonal events like festivals or sporting events like the FIFA World Cup and extend the trip into a holiday.

One common form of leisure travel is the **short break**. This includes city breaks to destinations such as London or Paris, or a countryside break in a rural location such as the Peak District. **Stag and hen parties** are also a form of popular leisure travel.

Corporate travel

There are several reasons why someone might travel for business, such as:

▶ to attend a conference
▶ to go to a meeting
▶ to attend training or to deliver training for other people
▶ to work in another geographical location for a while to work on a short-term contract, either in their country of residence or in another country.

A particularly interesting form of corporate travel is known as **incentive travel**.

Specialist travel

Tourists partaking in specialist travel are travelling for a particular reason, such as to participate in a particular sport or to go on a specific kind of holiday like a honeymoon. Some travel and tourism organisations operate in highly specific markets to provide for some of these specialist customers. For example, a tourist who wants to go on holiday to go rock climbing may choose to use a particular tour operator who specialises in adventure holidays.

Specialist travel includes travelling for:

▶ adventure, such as trekking in the Himalayas
▶ health, such as going abroad to have dental treatment
▶ education, such as attending a language course in Spain
▶ heritage or culture, such as visiting temples in Asia
▶ a gap year, such as young people taking a break between school and higher education
▶ conservation, such as helping to maintain walking trails through volunteer work
▶ sustainable tourism or responsible travel, such as to provide education to local communities in less developed countries
▶ special interests, hobbies or sports, such as birdwatching in Madagascar
▶ weddings and honeymoons, such as getting married in St Lucia.

Visiting friends and relatives (VFR)

Tourists who are visiting friends and relatives are usually leisure travellers staying overnight with a friend or a member of their family. However, these tourists might be visiting the area for business purposes and choosing to stay with friends or relatives to save money or to meet up with people they may not see frequently.

VFR tourists can be domestic, inbound or outbound tourists, depending on their place of departure and arrival. In 2017, inbound VFR tourists made over 12 million visits (up 4 per cent on the previous year) and spent £5.8 billion in Britain (up 15 per cent on the previous year). VFR tourists tend to stay quite a long time in comparison with other types of tourists, with their stays averaging ten nights.

> ### Key terms
>
> **Short break** – two or three days' holiday, often at a weekend.
>
> **Stag or hen party** – a group of men or women celebrating the marriage of their friend, usually shortly before the wedding takes place.
>
> **Incentive travel** – a trip or holiday that is given to an employee for reaching their targets or for extremely good performance in their job.

PAUSE POINT In 2017, the average spend per visit for an inbound VFR tourist was only £486. What kind of things do you think these tourists spend their money on?

Hint Look at the Great Britain Tourism Survey.

Extend Find out what the current average spend is and see how much it has increased or decreased since 2017. Calculate the percentage change.

Day trips

Day trips are trips that do not include an overnight stay. Some reasons to go on day trips include:

▶ visiting a city to go shopping or to visit an event such as the Great North Run
▶ going to a visitor attraction, such as Warwick Castle or Alton Towers
▶ going to the countryside for relaxation or for activities such as hillwalking.

Remember that people on day trips are not counted as tourists as they are not staying away from home. Instead, information about the number, value and types of day visitor trips is given in the Great Britain Day Visits Survey. In comparison, the Great Britain Tourism Survey measures the volume and value of domestic overnight tourism in the UK.

Types of travel and tourism customer

There are different types of travel and tourism customer. Travel and tourism organisations need to know who their customers are and understand the purpose of their trips to be able to meet their customers' needs.

Individuals and couples

An individual is someone who is not in a large group. They may be travelling alone or with another person, for example, with a partner as a couple. An individual travelling alone may require a single room and might have to pay a supplement for this. Individuals may want the possibility of joining tours or activities with other people at some point in their holiday, or they may prefer to enjoy their own company and have their own table in a restaurant.

Families

Families come in different shapes and sizes, and this has an effect on what they do on holiday. For example, a single-parent family with young children has different requirements to an extended family group that includes teenagers. Different generations of a family may go on holiday together, so a family can include people with many different interests. Families may need entertainment that is suitable for them all to enjoy, babysitting or children's clubs, or special mealtimes.

Groups

Groups can include educational groups such as school groups, special interest groups and friendship groups. Some groups may all know each other and have similar needs, such as a group of young men travelling together for a stag party. However, it is best to remember that a group is always made up of many individuals with different needs. For example, senior citizens on a group trip to a stately home may share an interest in history and be of a similar age, but they are all still individuals.

Corporate travellers

Corporate customers can be profitable customers. They are often travelling at peak times, and require convenience and comfort so that they are ready to go to work when they reach their destination. Also, the expenses of corporate travel are usually paid by the customer's company, not by the individual, so the traveller will probably be less concerned about getting the best possible value for money. Many organisations use approved corporate travel providers to ensure that they get the best deal. Corporate travellers expect business services on transport and in hotels, for example, power supply for laptops on trains and planes, and Wi-Fi in hotel rooms.

Customers with specific requirements

Some customers may have special requirements, for which travel and tourism organisations are expected to offer different or additional products and services, such as:

▶ different languages and cultures – providing maps and tourist guides in a variety of languages

▶ mobility problems – providing a wheelchair-accessible coach or minibus

▶ a hearing impairment – providing induction loops

▶ a visual impairment – providing large print menus

▶ a medical condition – allocating a ground floor room to a guest with a heart condition.

Theory into practice

Study each of the examples in Table 1.2, then decide what kind of tourist they are and what type of travel they are undertaking. Use the information in the text to help you. Some of the examples might fit into more than one category.

▶ **Table 1.2:** Different types of tourist and travel

Example	Type of tourist	Type of travel
Marianne lives in Austria but is going on a holiday in the UK		
Raj lives in Birmingham but is going to Bournemouth to see his cousin for the weekend		
Suzie is a travel agent in London and is going to a three-day conference in Barcelona		
Sinead travels from Bristol to Dublin every year to see her dad		
Aart is visiting the UK from the Netherlands to take a scuba-diving course		
Marta and her friends live in Lincoln and are going on a hen party weekend in Paris		
Travel and tourism learners from Canterbury College are taking a day trip to Stonehenge		

Travel Green Holidays is a specialist tour operator offering holidays around the world to groups and travellers who are interested in sustainable travel and holidays. The company is based in the UK, marketing to UK residents.

1   Give a definition of outbound tourism.
(1 mark)

2   Give an example of outbound tourism.
(1 mark)

3   Explain **one** special service requirement that a wheelchair user might require.
(2 marks)

Plan
- What is the question asking me to do? Do I need to give examples?
- What are the key words that I will need to include relating to inbound and outbound tourism?

Do
- I will write down the key terms that need to be included in each answer.
- I will ensure that I have given sufficient examples relating to the number of marks available.

Review
- I will check my answer. Is it clear? Have I given suitable examples?

B The types of travel and tourism organisations, their roles and the products and services they offer to customers

Ownership and operating aims

In the UK, travel and tourism organisations can be private businesses, public or government-run organisations and voluntary organisations or charities. Often these different types of organisations work in partnership with one another.

Private businesses

Most tourism businesses are part of the private sector. This means that they make up part of the economy that is not under government control but is owned by private individuals or companies. Private businesses aim to make a profit and are commercial companies that are staffed by paid employees. When they fail to make a profit over a period of time, they are likely to stop trading.

Examples of private businesses include:
▶ tour operators such as TUI and travel agents such as STA Travel
▶ transport organisations and hubs such as LHR Airports, which operates Heathrow Airport
▶ large visitor attractions such as Longleat Safari Park
▶ accommodation providers such as Premier Inn.

The size of the organisation is also important. Private businesses can range in size from small or medium-sized businesses to huge multi-national corporations operating across the world, such as International Airlines Group, which operates British Airways (BA).

There are different types of private business ownership, including:
▶ individual or sole trader
▶ private limited company
▶ public limited company.

A **sole trader** is a business that is run by one self-employed individual. A sole trader does not have **limited liability**, which means that if their company goes **bankrupt** they are **liable** to pay its debts themselves.

Key terms

Sole trader – a business run by a self-employed individual.

Limited liability – responsibility that is limited to some extent (such as up to a maximum amount of money).

Bankrupt – when a company is unable to pay its debts.

Liable – legally responsible for something.

A **private limited company** is owned by **shareholders** who own **shares** that can only be bought and sold with the permission of the company's board of directors. In some cases of small companies, there may only be one director. If the company goes bankrupt, each shareholder's liability to pay the company's debts is limited to the amount of company shares that they own. This means that they cannot be asked to put any further money into paying the company's debts. Shareholders are usually the company directors and they do not offer shares to the general public. Accounts have to be reported to Companies House but do not have to be published to the public.

A **public limited company (PLC)** is also owned by its shareholders. Unlike a private limited company, PLCs are listed on the **stock exchange** so their shares can be bought and sold publicly by members of the public. Shareholders are also paid a **dividend** every year that the business makes a profit. The size of the dividend depends on how much money the company has made and how many shares an individual shareholder owns. A PLC must have at least two directors.

Avoid confusing public limited companies with organisations that are in the public sector – a public limited company is still part of the private sector. Examples of PLCs in travel and tourism are easyJet and the Thomas Cook Group.

The aims of a private business are usually to make a profit by increasing market share, increasing turnover by raising prices, or selling more products or services. A business might also aim to diversify by offering new products or services. Another aim could be to improve the public image of the business.

Public organisations

Public sector organisations are owned and funded by the government. Funds for public sector tourism organisations come from:

▶ central government through the Department for Digital, Culture, Media & Sport (DCMS)
▶ lottery funding
▶ local governments, such as county councils.

Many public sector organisations are staffed by paid employees, including civil servants in the DCMS. Other organisations have a core staff of paid employees but are also supported by volunteers, such as the Imperial War Museum.

The overarching aim of all public sector organisations is to provide value for the funding that they receive. Within this, organisations will have aims that include:

▶ providing the best possible quality service to the public
▶ using their funding appropriately and in a cost-effective way
▶ making enough money to continue to operate (known as **breaking even**)
▶ reinvesting profits into their services and activities.

Public sector organisations can be national or local.

The DCMS is a national public sector organisation. It is also responsible for the national tourist agency, VisitBritain, and national tourist boards such as VisitWales and VisitScotland. The DCMS is also responsible for some of Britain's famous tourist attractions, such as the Victoria and Albert Museum in London. Other national public sector organisations can also have a large impact on tourism. For example, the Department for Transport influences tourism because transport is used by tourists to get around when sightseeing and travelling.

Local public sector organisations involved in tourism and travel include:

▶ local tourist information centres, which are usually run by local councils
▶ local visitor attractions
▶ local transport organisations.

Research

Choose a travel and tourism organisation in your local area – a small business, a hotel, a tourist attraction or transport company. Find out what type of business it is, for example, sole trader, private limited company or PLC. What are the advantages and disadvantages of this type of ownership to the organisation? Discuss your findings with your group.

Case study

Visit Manchester

Visit Manchester is the tourist board for the city of Manchester and is run as a public–private sector partnership. It is a tourism organisation with more than 400 members, such as hotels, tourist attractions, restaurants, bars and other services. It is part of a larger organisation called Marketing Manchester, which promotes the city of Manchester both within the UK and also internationally.

Members of Visit Manchester pay an annual membership fee. In exchange for this, Visit Manchester provides them with guidance and advice, and helps them to deliver the services that attract and cater for tourists visiting

Manchester. Members also receive marketing benefits, such as being featured on Visit Manchester's tourist website and listed in publications such as the city's official tourist map.

Check your knowledge

1 What type of organisation is Visit Manchester?

2 How does it receive its funding?

3 What benefits do its members receive?

4 What disadvantages do you think there might be for members?

5 Register for free to take the Visit Manchester online training module.

Voluntary sector

Many voluntary sector organisations are charities. They receive funding from a variety of sources, such as:

▶ government grants
▶ donations from the public, including **legacies**
▶ entry fees paid by visitors to their attractions and purchases made in their visitor shops.

Larger voluntary sector organisations usually have paid staff but also rely on many volunteers who enjoy promoting the values of the organisation or sharing their love of heritage in their spare time. Smaller voluntary sector organisations may have no paid staff at all and are staffed only by volunteers.

Voluntary organisations that are registered as charities are regulated by the Charity Commission and exist for the benefit of others rather than for profit. Their aims are to provide a service for others and to reinvest any profits back into the charity. They will also have other aims that are specific to that particular organisation. These may include:

▶ promoting the arts, culture, heritage or science
▶ preserving or protecting the environment, buildings or features of the landscape, such as conservation work on historical buildings
▶ ensuring sustainability, such as preventing damage to the environment or attractions caused by large numbers of visitors
▶ campaigning against threats such as inappropriate housing developments in an area of natural beauty that attracts tourists
▶ educating visitors
▶ preventing or relieving poverty in tourist destinations and promoting community development.

Examples of voluntary sector organisations include charities such as the National Trust, some visitor attractions such as the Severn Valley Heritage Steam Railway, and some transport organisations such as community transport organised to support older people.

> **Key term**
>
> **Legacy** – a gift of money or property given away by the owner after their death.

> **Research**
>
> Choose one of the following voluntary tourism organisations and find its website.
> • Friends of Conservation
> • Tourism Concern
> • The Travel Foundation
> • Trees for Cities
>
> Identify the organisation's aims and its sources of funding, then evaluate its success against its aims.

 **PAUSE POINT**   Can you describe the different types of travel and tourism organisations?

Hint   Think about the public, private and voluntary sectors and some examples of organisations in each sector.

Extend   Explain the aims of each type of organisation, giving examples.

The key sectors of the travel and tourism industry

Different sectors of the travel and tourism industry provide different products and services, as shown in Figure 1.1. These sectors work together because each sector relies on one or more of the other sectors to operate. For example, an airline cannot operate without airports, but airlines and airports are parts of different sectors within travel and tourism. In this section you will examine the different sectors, find examples of each and look at what they provide. You will also find that the products and services they offer can be:

▶ **tangible** – something that can be handled and touched, such as reserving a seat on a bus

▶ **intangible** – something that is not a physical object and cannot be handled, such as a safe and enjoyable journey.

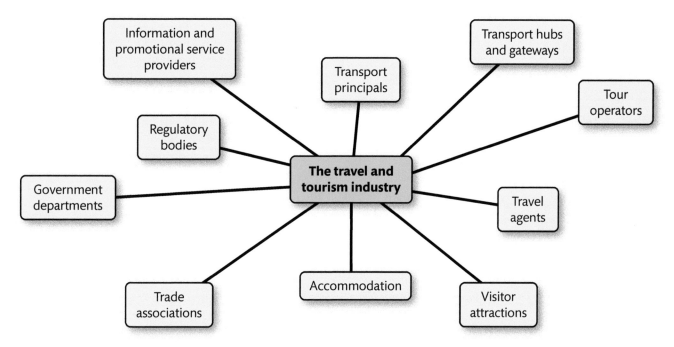

▶ **Figure 1.1:** Different sectors in the travel and tourism industry

Transport principals

The role of these organisations is to provide customers with transport between destinations in a safe and efficient manner.

Airlines

The main service provided by airlines is safe transport from one airport to another. Airlines differ in their definitions of short, medium and long haul; some define long haul as more than 7 hours to complete and short haul as taking less than 3 hours. Low-cost airlines in the UK travel mainly within Europe and usually operate short-haul flights, although some have expanded their operations to include the Canary Islands and Greece, with flights taking between 4 and 5 hours.

The Civil Aviation Authority (CAA) defines short, medium and long haul by distance.

▶ Short-haul flights under 1500 km – for instance, Edinburgh to Dublin.

▶ Medium-haul flights between 1500 km–3500 km – for instance, Manchester to Marrakesh.

▶ Long-haul flights over 3500 km – for instance, London to New York.

Theory into practice

In the summer you are planning to fly to Athens from Gatwick Airport. You would like to leave on 17 July and return on 20 July.

1 Find out how much this will cost, comparing at least two different airlines. You could either find out which airlines operate between Gatwick and Athens and visit their websites, or use a consolidator website such as Skyscanner.

2 Would it be cheaper to leave from a different airport?

Key term

Low-cost airlines – scheduled airlines that offer low prices and basic comfort by keeping costs low.

There are two main types of airline: scheduled and charter. It can be difficult to distinguish between the two as traditional charter operators may also operate scheduled routes.

▸ Scheduled airlines run to a regular timetable that is changed only for the winter and summer seasons. The flights depart even if not all the seats have been booked.

▸ Charter airlines own and operate aircraft that are rented by other organisations such as tour operators. They may be contracted for a specific holiday season and run to a timetable set by the operator. For example, each major tour operator needs seats for its summer passengers flying to the Mediterranean. They aim to fill every seat on the contracted aircraft and each seat forms part of the customer's holiday package. Many major tour operators own their own charter airlines. For example, TUI Group owns TUI Airways.

All UK airlines are privately owned. BA is one of the world's most famous airlines and runs a large number of international and long-haul scheduled services. Virgin Atlantic is the UK's other large long-haul operator. However, hundreds of other airlines from all over the world also fly into and out of UK airports.

Many airlines offer different types of service on the same flight, and which service you receive will depend on how much you paid for your ticket. For example, if you travel on a long-haul BA flight, you may buy a ticket in one of the following categories.

▸ Economy – this includes a baggage allowance included in the price of the ticket.

▸ Premium economy – this is similar to economy, but also includes wider seats with more legroom, a cushion and a blanket.

▸ Business – this includes a wider seat that converts into a flat bed, private departure lounges at airports and priority boarding.

▸ First – this includes a personal 'suite' with a seat that converts into a luxury bed, as well as luxury dining, pyjamas and toiletries.

Low-cost airlines (formerly known as 'no frills') are scheduled airlines that do not offer different types of service on their flights. These airlines aim to keep their costs as low as possible so that they can offer cheap fares. The biggest low-cost airlines operating in the UK are easyJet and the Irish airline Ryanair. A low-cost airline will not offer the kind of luxury offered by BA, but offers extra services at additional cost to the customer, such as seats with extra legroom, priority boarding, and food and drinks.

Ferries

The UK is made up of a number of islands, meaning that sea transport has always been important. Like airlines, ferry operators provide safe transport for customers and their luggage between ports or ferry terminals. Ferry operators in the English Channel include DFDS Seaways and P&O Ferries. Brittany Ferries operates longer routes to France and Spain, such as Poole to Cherbourg, Plymouth to Santander and Portsmouth to Caen. Other important ferry routes connect the UK with countries such as Ireland, the Netherlands and Belgium. Ferries also operate between the British mainland and islands off the coast, such as the Hebrides in Scotland, the Isle of Man and the Isle of Wight, and the Channel Islands.

Link

The Channel Tunnel is a rail tunnel between the UK and France and competes with ferry operators. You will learn more about rail transport later in this section.

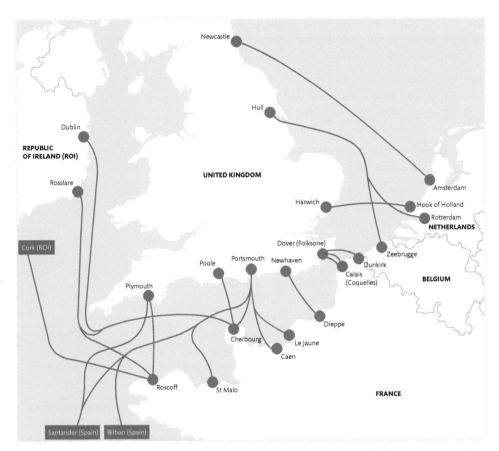

Research

The Department for Transport (DfT) map shows all of the ferry routes operating between the Continent and the UK and Ireland. Find the interactive version online by doing an internet search for 'DfT cross-channel services'.

▶ The Department for Transport's map of ferry crossings between the UK and other European nations

Cruises

Cruises are journeys taken by ship for pleasure and relaxation, rather than as a method of transport from one specific port to another. The holiday destination is the cruise ship itself, which provides on-board entertainment and activities as well as all food and drink, usually on an **all-inclusive** basis. In addition, cruise ships usually stop at several different ports so that passengers can go on day trips in different coastal towns and cities. On a week's cruise, passengers can expect to visit six different ports.

Here are examples of cruise companies, offering different types of cruise.

▶ Cunard operates three ships – Queen Elizabeth, Queen Victoria and Queen Mary 2. Its cruises and cruise ships have a traditional elegant theme. It is owned by an American company called Carnival.

▶ P&O Cruises operates eight ships and are based in Southampton. It offers themed cruises, such as 'Strictly Come Dancing' cruises or 'Food Hero' cruises catered for by top chefs.

▶ TUI operates six cruise ships under the brand Marbella. Its all-inclusive cruises are targeted at the family market.

▶ Fred Olsen operates four small and medium-sized ships. It departs from different UK ports, including Liverpool and Bristol, making it more attractive to people who live outside the south-east of England.

▶ Saga cruises operates four ships. It provides holidays only for the over-50s, so its cruises are targeted at older travellers who want to holiday in an adult-only environment.

Cruises are becoming more popular; in 2016 there were 1.9 million ocean cruise passengers from the UK. This was a record year, up 5.6 per cent on the previous year.

Key term

All-inclusive – a holiday in which the cost of most meals and activities is included in the price, rather than paid for separately.

About a third of passengers tried a cruise for the first time. One of the reasons for the rise in popularity is the growth of cruises starting from ports in the UK. Cruises are sometimes thought to be holidays for older people, but the average age of cruise-goers is falling.

Some passengers take a 'fly cruise', which means flying to a port in another country to start their cruise from there rather than from their home country. River cruises are also growing in popularity; popular destinations include the Rhine, the Moselle, the Danube and the Nile. The river cruise market grew in 2016 by 11 per cent, reaching a total of 166,900 passengers.

PAUSE POINT

Choose one of the cruises operated by P&O. Find out exactly what is included in the price of the cruise.

Hint

You can find information by looking at the P&O website.

Extend

Describe the potential target market for your chosen cruise and explain why it suits this target market.

Buses

Most bus companies in the UK are privately owned. As privately owned companies aim to make a profit, they concentrate on profitable routes, which can mean that they stop operating less popular rural services. Tourists are most likely to use buses for transport within large cities.

Buses can also be used as a convenient way of seeing the sights of a large city or a rural area. Some tourist bus companies, such as City Sightseeing, operate in a number of cities around the world while others focus on rural areas that are popular with tourists, such as minibus tours in the Lake District. These services not only provide transport but inform tourists about the city or the area that they are visiting.

Coaches

Coach operators have adapted their products to meet consumers' changing needs, so coaches today are luxurious. Coaches can be used as transport from one place to another, but they can also be used as an integral part of a holiday. For example, 'fly coach' holidays allow customers to fly to a particular country for their holiday, then transfer onto a coach to tour around the country and see the sights. Popular 'fly coach' holiday destinations include Italy and California.

There are extensive coach networks operating in the UK offering scheduled services between towns and also into Europe. Eurolines is part of National Express and operates to hundreds of European destinations. Its coach services are comfortable, providing on-board toilets, refreshments and DVD facilities, as well as regular stops. Travelling by coach can be extremely affordable: a single trip to Paris from the UK can cost as little as £12.

Hire cars

Major hire-car companies in the UK include Hertz, Avis and Europcar, all of which operate internationally as well. They offer a range of products and services, making car hire easy and convenient for customers. Customers can expect a similar range of services from all hire-car companies, such as:

▶ online booking
▶ airport pick-up and drop-off
▶ a choice of vehicles
▶ varying levels of insurance cover.

Theory into practice

The coach operator National Express uses a set of symbols to indicate what facilities are available at different coach stations.

▶ Symbols used by National Express to indicate facilities at different coach stations

Can you work out what they mean?

Private cars

Car ownership is high in the UK: in 2018 over 38 million cars were registered. This rise in car ownership is partly due to economic prosperity and an increase in population. Most domestic holidays and day trips in the UK are taken by car. The advantages of driving are comfort, a good road network and the ability to take everything you might want on your trip in the car. However, there are disadvantages. For example, traffic congestion can build up at busy periods, such as Friday afternoons and bank holiday weekends, as well as due to roadworks.

Taxis

Taxis are usually only used for short journeys, such as to an airport. They are readily available throughout the UK, although fares vary a lot between different regions. Tourists are most likely to use hackney cabs, which are taxis that they can either flag down or pick up from a taxi rank, such as in a town centre or outside a railway station.

Rail

Railway passengers in the UK can use trains to travel within a small local area, across the country and even into Europe. London contains its own local rail services, such as the London Underground and the Docklands Light Railway, which are run by Transport for London (TfL). In most of the UK, other local and national rail services are provided by train-operating companies (TOCs), such as Virgin Trains and South Western Railway. These TOCs compete with one another to provide rail services and are monitored by the Office of Rail and Road. However, in Northern Ireland the trains are state-owned.

Railways can also transport passengers internationally. Eurostar is the passenger train service through the Channel Tunnel. It operates from St Pancras International in London, and Ashford and Ebbsfleet in Kent, and runs through the Channel Tunnel between Dover and Calais and on to cities in France and Belgium such as Paris, Lille and Brussels. When the Channel Tunnel opened in 1994, it took a substantial share of the cross channel market. From 1998 the share began to fall due to competition from low-cost airlines.

Eurostar runs a high-speed rail line between London and the Channel Tunnel at Dover. This is known as High Speed 1 (HS1) and is the only high-speed rail network in the UK, running trains at 140 miles per hour. It was built specifically to connect to the European high-speed network. There are plans for a High Speed 2 (HS2) line to connect London with the midlands and the north of England.

Tourists in the UK are likely to find planning trips by train quite complex because of the number of different operators and a wide variety of fares. Travelling by train can be expensive, especially at peak times and on long journeys, unless passengers book early to take advantage of cheaper fares, but inbound tourists may struggle to understand how to do this. Railway travel can be made cheaper using a range of railcards that permit cheaper fares for students and older people, but it is unlikely that inbound tourists will have these railcards.

However, there are many heritage and scenic train journeys which are attractive to tourists, such as the Brecon Mountain Railway in Wales. Passengers on this railway travel on vintage steam locomotives alongside the Taf Fechan Reservoir through the Brecon Beacons National Park.

Transport hubs and gateways

Transport hubs and gateways are the places where transport principals start and finish, including airports, rail and coach stations, ferry terminals and ports used by cruise ships. All of these hubs need to provide travellers with safe access to the different forms of transport, as well as catering, toilets and ticketing services. They need to

---

Discussion

Uber is a service that allows taxi drivers to use their own cars to provide taxi rides to Uber users. Customers book through the Uber app when they want a taxi ride, rather than pre-booking in advance. However, Uber has been criticised by traditional taxi drivers and companies. Find out more about Uber, and discuss the advantages and disadvantages for drivers and customers.

Research

Find out about the new Crossrail development in London. What are its aims and when will it start to operate?

Key terms

Gateway – a place where travellers enter or leave a country or destination, including airports, seaports, railway stations and coach and bus stations.

Hub – a central transport facility, such as an airport, from which other transport facilities operate, such as buses, coaches, trains and taxis.

provide information to passengers about the available transport services and also about local and national facilities and attractions.

Airports

Airport terminals are very important to tourism. They provide a gateway for inbound and outbound tourists and have an important role to play in leisure and business travel. The range of facilities in major airports is huge, including check-in desks, lots of eating and drinking establishments, lounge facilities, and shops and services, such as massage, manicures and currency exchange. In addition, many other organisations operate from each airport, such as transport and information services. All these businesses and services pay rent to the airport, providing the airport with important revenue as well as enhancing the experience of customers flying into or out of that particular airport.

Case study

Passenger experience

Glasgow Airport has won several awards including, the Best Airport Award from the Airports Council International Europe in 2016. In the previous year, Glasgow had also won the UK Airport of the Year Award. Reasons for winning these awards included securing almost 30 new routes, such as direct flights to Prague, Nova Scotia and Las Vegas, and investing £25 million to enhance airport facilities and improve passengers' experience.

Check your knowledge

1 Go to Glasgow Airport's website and consider the services that they provide for passengers. How do you think the investment improved these services for passengers?

2 Imagine you had to wait for three hours at Glasgow Airport. Which services would you use to enjoy the time spent waiting? Share your ideas with the rest of the group.

Theory into practice

Find out how much it would cost to buy a day return from your nearest station to London tomorrow. Compare this with how much it would cost if you booked for the same date next month. What is the price difference? Why do you think there is a difference?

Plan a journey for Montse. She is arriving at Heathrow Airport from Spain at 2.30 p.m. next Saturday, and she needs to get to Manchester. How would she get there by train and where would she buy her tickets? She speaks some English but has never been to England before. Explain her itinerary and cost it.

Not all airports in the UK are privately owned – some are in public ownership. For example, Cornwall Airport in Newquay is owned by Cornwall Council. Other airports are in private ownership but are owned by a sole investor or groups of international investors. For example, Ontario Teachers' Pension Plan owns Bristol Airport and also have a large share in Birmingham Airport (in partnership with the Metropolitan Boroughs of the West Midlands).

Rail and coach stations

Rail and coach stations act as gateways to the rest of the UK and, in some cases, to continental Europe. The largest rail and coach stations in London and other major cities may provide facilities similar to those found in an airport, including toilets, food and drink outlets and major high street shops. Other coach and rail stations simply provide toilets and shelter for waiting passengers.

The UK's busiest railway stations are in London, and Waterloo is the busiest station of all. Birmingham New Street is the busiest railway station outside London. The London railway stations act as gateways to the rest of the country. For example, Kings Cross and Euston serve the north of the country, Waterloo and Victoria serve the south and Paddington serves the west and south-west. Most stations are owned by the train operating companies. However, Network Rail, which maintains the rail network, also owns and manages 18 stations, including Birmingham New Street and Manchester Piccadilly.

Ferry terminals and cruise ship ports

Ferries and cruise ships often operate out of separate ports. Some ports service both ferries and cruise ships, although they provide separate facilities for ferry passengers and cruise ship passengers. For example, the Port of Dover is Europe's busiest ferry port, but it also accommodates several large cruise ships. Transport access to the Port of Dover is good, and passengers can arrive by car, taxi, bus or coach.

Facilities available to ferry passengers sailing out of Dover include:

▸ a shuttle bus from terminal to ferry
▸ refreshments
▸ cash and currency services
▸ toilets and showers
▸ shops.

Cruise ship passengers depart and arrive at separate terminals from the ferry passengers. Their facilities are more luxurious than those provided in the ferry terminal. This is because cruise ship passengers may be expected to spend more money. Facilities at Dover for cruise passengers include:

▸ departure lounges
▸ café-bars
▸ washrooms
▸ a greater variety of shops
▸ porters to help with luggage
▸ a bureau de change.

> **Link**
>
> You will find out more about ports, including developments at Tilbury Port, in Section D of this unit.

⏸ **PAUSE POINT**   Compare the facilities at an airport with those at a ferry terminal and a coach station.

    Hint   Check back to the text and think about when you have been travelling and been to these kinds of transport hubs.

    Extend   Explain why you would expect to find a greater range of better quality facilities in an airport.

Tour operators

A tour operator is a business that puts together all the different components that make up a holiday and sells them as complete packages to the customer. They make contracts with **hoteliers**, airlines and other transport companies to put the package together, so that the customer does not have to organise them separately for themselves. All the details about each package, such as information about the resort and prices, are described in a brochure distributed either to travel agents or directly to customers. Modern brochures are usually available online, which saves tour operators the cost of postal distribution and printing, especially as brochures often have to be updated throughout the season to reflect changes in prices.

A new **Package Holiday** Directive was introduced in 2018. This now includes several definitions for package holidays to cover different purchase options.

New regulations were needed as it was often unclear to the customer whether a holiday was or was not a package holiday. Terms such as 'tailor-made' and 'dynamic packaging' meant that the customer actually had separate contracts with different suppliers, even when the holiday had been put together by a business that looked like a tour operator.

For example, a holiday booking made through a supplier such as Teletext Holidays involved separate contracts between the customer and the tourism companies such as the hotel and the airline. The customers might not have understood that this was not a package, therefore not covered by the legislation, leaving customers vulnerable if something went wrong.

> **Key terms**
>
> **Hotelier** – a person who manages a hotel.
>
> **Package holiday** – a pre-arranged combination of transport, accommodation and other tourist services.

> **Link**
>
> You will learn more about travel agents in the next section.

Table 1.3 shows the new definitions of package holidays.

▶ **Table 1.3:** New definitions of package holidays from the Package Holiday Directive

Article from Package Travel Directive	Summary	Example
SINGLE CONTRACT		
Art 3 (2) (a)	Travel services are combined by one trader and sold under a single contract, including packages put together at the traveller's request and sold under a single contract.	Many traditional packages sold by high street travel agents. Bespoke customised packages will also be covered by this.
MULTIPLE CONTRACTS		
Art 3 (2) (b) (i)	A traveller selects from the same point of sale two or more travel services and pays for them.	Websites where a customer selects from a range of travel products related to a single trip to create a package.
Art 3 (2) (b) (ii)	If a selection of travel services for the same trip are sold at an inclusive or total price.	A selection of travel services for the same trip under different contracts are combined and sold for a total price.
Art 3 (2) (b) (iii)	If a combination of travel services are advertised or sold as a 'package' or a similar term.	A travel agent puts together a selection of travel services for the same trip under different contracts, paid for separately, it would be classified as a package if advertised as a 'package deal'.
Art 3 (2) (b) (iv)	A trader sells a product that allows the traveller to pick and choose different travel services after they have concluded the contract.	Package holiday gift boxes fall within this definition. For instance, a 'Tastes of the Region' package that allows you to choose your accommodation and a meal at a gourmet restaurant after you have purchased.
Art 3 (2) (b) (v)	A traveller purchases different travel services for the same trip through a linked online booking process where the traveller's name, payment details *and* email address are sent from the first trader to the second and a contract is concluded with the second trader no longer than 24 hours after the first service was purchased.	A traveller purchases a flight online, the confirmation web page gives the traveller a link to book car hire. The traveller books car hire without re-entering their credit card details. If the car hire was purchased through the link within 24 hours of purchasing the flight, a package would be created.

The first holiday that you might recognise as a package holiday was organised in 1950 by Vladimir Raitz. He took passengers to Corsica on a DC3 aeroplane and he charged them £32.50 each, which covered their accommodation in tents, return flights, transfers and meals. He established a business called Horizon Holidays in the same year, and by the end of the 1950s the company had grown to be one of the UK's major tour operators. Other companies followed Horizon's example and package tours grew in popularity.

The 1970s was a period of major growth in package holidays, as people became wealthier and travel became more affordable. Most of the early package holidays were to Spain and its islands, where hotels were built rapidly to fulfil the demand from British and German tourists in particular.

Mass-market tour operators

Mass-market tour operators have dominated the outbound market for many years. These operators are referred to as 'mass-market' because they sell similar holidays in packages that appeal to the majority of holidaymakers. Examples of mass-market tour operators include TUI and Thomas Cook. TUI also owns the brand First Choice. The aim of mass-market tour operators is to sell large numbers of holidays and make a small amount of profit on each sale.

Research

Find out who Thomas Cook was and why there is a tour operator named after him.

Tailor-made and dynamic packages

A tailor-made or dynamic package is where customers build their own holiday by selecting the different components separately. Any element of the holiday can be customised so the customer can decide which flight, which hotel, whether to include a transfer, airline food or not. It is possible for people to build their holiday online themselves by visiting the website of each supplier and booking, but providing dynamic packages is a service offered by travel agents who will advise on the different components to meet the customer needs. Expedia is an example of an online supplier providing dynamic packaging. Such packages are now covered by the Package Holiday Directive.

Special interest tour operators

Special interest tour operators specialise in selling package holidays to particular destinations or for particular activities, such as safaris. They are often able to tailor-make holidays for individual customers and operate in what are known as **niche markets**. Sometimes specialist tour operators focus on a particular destination, rather than a type of holiday. For example, Olympic Holidays specialises in holidays to Greece.

Specialist tour operators may be small independent businesses. Alternatively, they could be part of one of the large tour operators. Large tour operators often offer specialist products from a brand that is separate from their main brand. For example, TUI Group have specialist brands such as Hayes and Jarvis for tailor-made long-haul holidays and Crystal Ski for skiing holidays.

Some tour operators specialise in premium products for the luxury market. Examples include Abercrombie & Kent and Cox & Kings, which focus on meeting each traveller's individual requirements by tailoring the package to them. Some of the large tour operators also operate luxury brands, such as Sensatori by TUI, which offers five star resorts in a number of destinations with spa facilities and fine dining.

▶ **Table 1.4:** Examples of different tour operators

Example	Aims	Parent company (if any)	Brands offered	Key destinations
HF Holidays				
Kuoni				
First Choice				
Saga Holidays				
Exodus				

Research

There are many different tour operators in the UK. Some are mass market, whereas others are independent with different specialisms. Table 1.4 contains some examples. Research each example, then copy and complete the table.

Travel agents

Travel agents are businesses that arrange the details of a holiday on behalf of customers. They normally specialise in leisure travel such as holidays, but some also cater for business travel customers. Examples include STA Travel, Co-operative Travel and Trailfinders. Many have high street retail shops so that customers are attracted by offers in the windows, but they also sell holidays online through their websites. Some travel agents operate online only. It is often said that high street shops, including travel agents, are declining, but Kuoni opened more outlets in 2016 and 2017, suggesting that they believe it is still worth investing in the high street. Table 1.5 outlines the different types of travel agencies.

▶ **Table 1.5:** Different types of travel agencies

Type of agent	Description
Multiple	Multiples are chains of more than 100 branches on high streets in many towns and cities. They are usually PLCs who prefer, and can afford, prime locations. TUI and Thomas Cook are the major brands and control just over a quarter of high street retail travel agents between them
Miniple	Miniples are small chains. They are usually located in one region where they may be well known and may have developed a good reputation. Premier Travel based in Cambridge is an example of a privately owned miniple with 20 outlets
Independent	Independent retail travel agencies are often owned by a family or partnership. These outlets are more likely to be found in smaller towns, as it is difficult for them to afford the high rents of prime locations in large towns and cities. Often multiple chains buy up independent agencies, but the remaining independents often have a reputation for good personal service
Franchise	Some travel agencies operate as **franchises**. A franchise business gives someone the right to sell their branded products and services in return for a fee or a percentage of profits. The individual franchise shops have to operate according to the rules of the franchise business
Call centre	Some travel agencies, like STA Travel, operate dedicated call centres. Many tour operators and airlines also operate call centres
Online	Some travel agencies trade online only and have no retail shops at all. They sell packages, flights, accommodation and additional products. Examples include Expedia and lastminute.com
Business	Business travel agents specialise in the business travel market and often handle the travel arrangements for large companies. The products that they offer are more likely to be city hotels with business services and scheduled flights at convenient times. Some companies specialise in organising corporate events, such as conferences and incentive travel
Specialist	These travel agents are often independent businesses and offer products and services either in one destination or in one type of product. For example, an agent might just sell holidays to Cuba and develop expertise in holidays in that destination. Alternatively, they might specialise in a special interest such as scuba diving and arrange diving holidays in a variety of different locations

Key terms

Niche market – a small specialist market, unlike a mass market.

Franchise – when someone buys the right to sell a business's products or services under that business's brand name.

PAUSE POINT   What do you think are the advantages of buying into a franchise rather than setting up alone?

> **Hint**   Visit the website of a travel franchise such as www.bepartofsomethingbigger.co.uk.

> **Extend**   Find some other travel franchises. Which one would you choose to join and why?

The role of a travel agent is to give advice and information and sell package holidays for a number of tour operators, although multiples such as Thomas Cook may give preference to their own brands. A travel agent acts as a middleman between the customer and the tour operator. They do not buy the products or services of the tour operators and sell them on, but instead work for a **commission** from the tour operators. The commission varies between tour operators. Alternatively, a customer may pay a fee for a retail travel agent to put together a tailor-made package from components chosen by the customer.

Travel agents provide a range of products and services, including:
▶ information on holidays and travel
▶ booking traditional package holidays
▶ booking specialist holidays such as cruises or coach tours
▶ creating tailor-made and dynamic packages for individual customers, including:
  • booking travel arrangements, such as scheduled flights or ferries
  • booking accommodation
  • booking additional services, such as parking, **excursions** and holiday insurance
  • booking **transfers** in the UK and overseas
  • organising currency exchange
▶ advising on passports, **visas** and health matters such as required vaccinations for particular destinations.

Visitor attractions

Visitor attractions in the UK are important to the domestic tourism market and also to the inbound tourism market. They fulfil a variety of purposes, such as education, entertainment and recreation. There are hundreds of different types of attractions, but they can be broadly divided into the following categories.
▶ Natural areas and features – these include national parks and landscape features such as beaches, mountains, lakes and landscapes. There are ten national parks in England, three in Wales and two in Scotland. Other areas that serve as visitor attractions are Areas of Outstanding Natural Beauty and Heritage Coasts.
▶ Purpose-built or man-made attractions – these include many museums and art galleries, which were built specifically for those purposes. Examples include Tate Britain, the Victoria and Albert Museum, and the National Media Museum in Bradford. Other purpose-built attractions include the London Eye and theme parks such as Alton Towers.
▶ Historical or heritage attractions – the UK has many historic buildings, often owned and maintained by the National Trust or other heritage organisations. These attractions are man-made, but were not purpose-built to be tourist attractions. Figure 1.2 lists some examples.

▶ **Figure 1.2:** Examples of historic or heritage visitor attractions

Key terms

Commission – an amount of money paid to an agent for every sale that they make (often a percentage of the total value of the sale).

Transfer – the transport provided as part of the holiday package from airport or port to accommodation.

Visa – a travel document giving a traveller permission to stay in a country for a certain amount of time.

Excursion – a short trip taken as a leisure activity.

Research

Choose one of the historic attractions in Figure 1.2. Find out how many visitors it has had over the last few years. Have visitor numbers gone up or down, and by how much? Why did the place become a visitor attraction? Who owns it now? What products and services does it offer? Report on your findings to your group.

- Sporting events – large sporting events such as football matches and golf tournaments attract many spectators. For example, when Rio de Janeiro hosted the Olympic Games in 2016, they expected half a million tourists to visit and built an extra 9500 hotel rooms to accommodate them. Other sporting events attract a lot of participants, such as the Great North Run in the North East and the London Marathon. Famous sporting stadiums also attract visitors and offer tours, such as Old Trafford in Manchester.
- Special events – festivals and parades such as the Edinburgh Festival and the Notting Hill Carnival attract many visitors. Music festivals, such as Glastonbury, are also popular; Glastonbury attracted 175,000 people in 2017. Most of these visitors are domestic tourists, with only about half a million inbound tourists visiting British music festivals.

All of the attractions provide their own facilities for visitors, such as:
- parking
- restaurants or cafés
- gift shops
- experiences and entertainments such as dungeon experiences or historical re-enactments at castles
- information about the attraction, including displays and guidebooks, educational talks and tours, leaflets and signs.

Accommodation

Accommodation can be **catered** or it can be **self-catered** or non-catered. Tourists choose their accommodation type according to their needs and their budget. This leads to the provision of lots of different options from the industry.

Hotels

Hotels are an example of catered accommodation. They may be independently owned or part of a large hotel chain. Chain hotels tend to be more impersonal but provide consistency of quality. For example, if you were to stay in a Premier Inn anywhere in the UK, the room would offer the same facilities as any other Premier Inn in the UK. Many hotel chains are global, such as Accor.

The core products of any hotel are rooms, food and drink. The services provided will include housekeeping (room-cleaning service) and a reception, where guests can get information or support. Hotels usually offer a range of products and services to cater for different customers. Prestigious and more expensive hotel brands, like Sofitel, offer greater luxury. A four or five-star rated hotel will offer deluxe rooms and suites as well as standard rooms, and will usually provide facilities such as a restaurant and bar, a swimming pool, a gym and a spa selling services such as massage and beauty treatments. There may even be some form of entertainment, especially if the hotel is in a holiday resort. In comparison, a budget hotel – brands such as Travelodge – offers good value for money and targets people who are travelling or on a short break. There are fewer luxuries and facilities. For example, they rarely provide free toiletries and often just provide a breakfast service rather than a restaurant for evening meals as well.

Hotels cater for both business and leisure customers, so they need to offer a range of products to suit each type. Many hotels offer business conference facilities. Conference customers may come for just a day and will need different services from long-stay tourists. Many golf resorts also include both hotels and these facilities.

Guest houses and bed and breakfasts

Guest houses or bed and breakfasts are another form of catered accommodation. They are often run by homeowners who wish to capitalise on any extra space they have in

---

Research

The national tourist boards of England, Northern Ireland, Wales and Scotland monitor visits to visitor attractions each year through an annual survey. Explore the results of these surveys on their websites.

Key terms

Catered – meals are offered and guests' rooms are cleaned for them.

Self-catered – guests look after themselves and do their own cleaning, shopping and cooking.

their home. Most guest houses are family-run and only have a few rooms, which many tourists consider a charming opportunity to experience local culture. The facilities in a guest house are usually more limited than hotels, often just providing a room and breakfast. Some guest houses may offer meals but not a full restaurant service.

Ski chalets

Ski chalets may be serviced or self-catering. Serviced chalets have staff who live nearby and come in every day to prepare and serve breakfast. While the guests are out skiing, the staff clean the chalets, prepare the guests' dinner and after-ski cake or snacks, before going skiing themselves. They then return to serve dinner.

Youth hostels

Youth hostels offer basic accommodation, often in shared rooms, and usually cater for young people on a limited budget. Hostels appeal to families on a budget too as they offer family rooms at low prices. Their facilities are often even more limited than guest houses. For example, some hostels offer meals, but many do not and guests cook for themselves. Most youth hostels in Britain belong to the Youth Hostel Association (YHA) or Scottish Youth Hostel Association (SYHA). However, youth hostels are available around the world.

Self-catered accommodation

There are many varieties of self-catered accommodation. Cooking facilities are usually provided; examples include:

▶ log cabins and chalets in holiday parks
▶ rented apartments or holiday cottages (gîtes in France)
▶ motels or aparthotels (a hotel with self-catering apartments as well as ordinary hotel facilities)
▶ boats (such as narrowboats on canals)
▶ caravans, either **static** or towed behind a car when touring
▶ tents or luxury alternatives such as **yurts** and **tepees**.

Camping has become more luxurious in recent years. Some people camp in static caravans, which have their own bathrooms and utilities. Luxury camping is known as glamping; people can stay in luxury tents, including yurts or tepees, with amenities such as beds and bathrooms.

Case study

Luxury camping

Fred's Yurts offer luxurious 'glamping' accommodation during festivals. Facilities include:

- beautiful sites and plenty of space between tents
- convenient locations just a short walk from main festival sites
- private parking
- solar-powered and staffed reception tent with device-charging facilities, kitchen, restaurant and bar
- outdoor seating with an open fire for the evenings and a garden
- dry compost toilets (preferable to chemical loos)
- hot showers
- private morning yoga yurt sessions and massage treatments.

Check your knowledge

Plan a visit to a music festival for someone with an unlimited budget. Find the most luxurious and convenient way of getting there and staying for three days. Provide a full itinerary with costings, including transport, festival tickets, accommodation, and food and drinks.

ⅠⅠ   PAUSE POINT

> The MacDonald family (grandmother, mother and three children) are going on holiday to Bournemouth for two weeks in the summer holidays. Advise whether they should stay in a hotel or take an apartment.

> **Hint**   Sum up the advantages and disadvantages of each option, considering the likely needs of this family.

> **Extend**   Find three suitable attractions in Bournemouth or nearby that the MacDonalds could visit, and explain your choice.

Trade associations, government departments and regulatory bodies

These organisations help shape the travel and tourism industry. They determine tourism strategies and industry policies, provide information and support to their members and customers, and **lobby** governments on behalf of their members and tourists. Table 1.6 shows some of the major bodies representing travel and tourism organisations. Organisations that are affiliated to one of these bodies are entitled to use the organisation's logo on their literature so that customers know they have the support of the trade association.

▶ **Table 1.6:** Key travel and tourism organisations

Organisation	Full name	Description
ABTA	Association of British Travel Agents	Represents travel agents and tour operators. Members abide by ABTA Code of Conduct, a charter that requires them to provide accurate advertising, fair terms of trading, changes to bookings and a process to manage customer complaints. ABTA provides an **arbitration** service for customers who might have a dispute with a travel agent or tour operator
ANTOR	Association of National Tourist Office Representatives	Represents and lobbies on behalf of the world's tourist offices, such as VisitBritain. It provides a forum for its members to meet and exchange ideas, and helps them to network with other sectors of the travel industry. The organisation advocates responsible tourism and comments on a wide range of issues affecting worldwide travel and tourism
AITO	Association of Independent Tour Operators	Represents specialist tour operators. It has about 120 independent tour operator members, including Abercrombie & Kent and Cox & Kings. All its members conform to a quality charter. AITO members are financially assessed by the association and are bound by its code of business practice, which requires them to provide clear and accurate descriptions of holidays and to use customer questionnaires to monitor standards
CAA	Civil Aviation Authority	Regulates UK aviation. It is an independent **statutory** body that issues Air Travel Organisers' Licences (ATOLs). Tour operators that offer air-inclusive packages are required by law to be ATOL-protected. These bonds protect air travellers and tourists on package holidays from losing money or being stranded abroad if air travel firms go out of business. The bond goes into a fund, which covers the cost of **repatriation** if a company goes bust and its customers are left in a resort. The cost of this financial protection is included in the price of the holiday
IATA	International Air Transport Association	Represents around 265 of the world's airlines. Its mission is to represent, lead and serve airlines, and it helps to create and enforce industry policy on critical aviation issues such as safety. Travel agents who sell international airline tickets must be accredited by IATA. Accreditation authorises travel agents to sell international and/or domestic tickets on behalf of IATA member airlines
DCMS	Department for Culture, Media and Sport	Responsible for tourism in the UK. It is a government department that aims to protect and promote the UK's cultural heritage, help businesses and communities, and promote Britain as a place to visit
FCO	Foreign and Commonwealth Office	Responsible for the UK's relationship with the rest of the world. It is a government department that advises on where it is safe to travel, giving the current situation on security in countries all over the world. It also repatriates travellers who have been stranded abroad

Key terms

Lobby – try to influence an organisation or government to change something.

Arbitration – the process of settling a dispute through a third party such as an industry regulator.

Statutory – created or required by statute (written law passed by government).

Repatriation – returning something or someone back to its home country.

Research

Divide the different organisations in Table 1.6 on page 23 between everyone in your group. Do some research into the work of your given organisation and then produce a fact sheet that includes:

- the aims
- the type of ownership
- recent activities undertaken and the outcomes
- examples of members (if it has members).

Information and promotional service providers

These organisations serve to develop and promote travel and tourism in order to boost countries' economies and provide employment.

United Nations World Tourism Organization

UNWTO is responsible for the promotion of responsible, sustainable and universally accessible tourism. 158 countries have signed up to it, and it works in the following areas:

▶ promoting tourism as a way of improving economic growth and reducing poverty

▶ educating and training people in the travel and tourism industry to make the most of their tourism

▶ researching and providing information about tourism, such as reports on trends and statistics on international tourism

▶ encouraging the development of sustainable tourism.

VisitBritain

VisitBritain is the national tourist board funded by the DCMS. Its role is to market the UK to the rest of the world as a tourist destination. Its mission is to increase the volume and value of inbound tourism to Britain as a whole and to develop Britain as a tourism 'product'. It advises and supports British tourism organisations, conducts tourism research and promotes Britain as a tourist destination.

VisitEngland, Tourism NI, VisitScotland and VisitWales

Each of the UK's component countries has its own tourist board, each of which reports to the relevant government department in their country. They aim to promote tourism and destinations within their countries. They try to lead strategy for tourism development to get maximum economic benefit for their countries. They also provide marketing materials such as brochures, leaflets and websites to promote their countries as tourist destinations.

Destination management organisations

Destination management organisations (DMOs) co-ordinate the management of the different components that make up a tourist destination, such as visitor attractions, transport, marketing and promotion. DMOs build partnerships between separate tourism organisations within a destination to make the destination more successful.

There are many DMOs in the UK. For example, London & Partners is the official promotional agency for London. Its aim is to promote London as a destination for both leisure and business travellers. It is a non-profit public-private partnership, funded by the Mayor of London and commercial partners.

Regional tourist boards

Each region of the UK has its own tourist board. Originally, these were publicly funded but now form DMOs working with other partners. For example, in Devon, Visit Devon acts as the Devon tourist board, working with local authorities, the local enterprise partnership and VisitEngland.

Local enterprise partnerships

Visit East Anglia is a business-led organisation which promotes tourism across East Anglia. It is supported by some of the most successful tourism businesses in Norfolk and Suffolk, including Adnams, Africa Alive!, Banham Zoo, BeWILDerwood, Dinosaur Adventure, Flying Kiwi Inns, Gough Hotels, Norfolk Broads Direct, Norfolk Country Cottages, Southwold Pier, Suffolk Secrets, T&A Hotel Collection and Wroxham Barns. Consumer, customer and membership focused, Visit East Anglia is managed by experts and brings a unified tourism voice to East Anglia.

Visit East Anglia is working closely with Greater Anglia, the new East Anglian rail franchise operator, and has established links with the major airports, seaports and other gateways in both East Anglia and neighbouring counties. Visit East Anglia is also supported by the New Anglia local enterprise partnership and is therefore fully aligned with the Tourism Strategy for England.

Check your knowledge

1 What is a local enterprise partnership? Do some research and write an explanatory paragraph about it.

2 What is the Tourism Strategy for England? Give some examples of its key points.

3 Find the website for the tourist board in your own area. What are its aims? Give examples of some of its partners from different tourism sectors.

Local tourist information centres

Tourist information centres in towns and cities are funded by local councils. They provide tourists with maps of the town, city or local area, as well as information on local attractions and events, local travel options, places to eat, accommodation and local tours. Most also sell a range of local products and themed merchandise to make extra revenue.

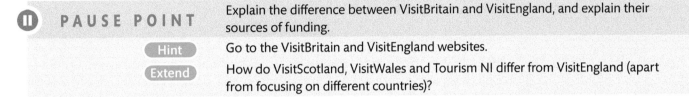

PAUSE POINT   Explain the difference between VisitBritain and VisitEngland, and explain their sources of funding.

Hint   Go to the VisitBritain and VisitEngland websites.

Extend   How do VisitScotland, VisitWales and Tourism NI differ from VisitEngland (apart from focusing on different countries)?

Interrelationships and interdependencies in the travel and tourism industry

As you have already learned, different organisations in the travel and tourism industry cannot work in isolation. Each relies on others for its success.

Distribution channels

Distribution channels are the ways in which businesses and organisations get products to customers. They can either do this directly or through another organisation such as a travel agency. Figure 1.3 shows a traditional distribution channel containing different types of business.

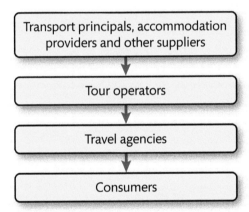

▶ **Figure 1.3:** Traditional distribution channel in travel and tourism

However, due to changes in the industry and the increase in internet use, there are many variations on this channel, as shown in Figure 1.4.

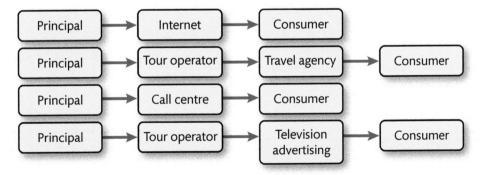

▶ **Figure 1.4:** Variations on distribution channels in travel and tourism

Link

We will look at how people use technology on page 29 of this unit.

These changes have come about because of developments in communication and the customer's desire for immediacy when they buy a product. Customers expect to use any or all of their mobile devices to research and buy products. However, there are still some people who prefer to visit a travel agent and discuss their holiday in person, and some travel agencies are opening more high street branches. Because of these differences in customer behaviour, travel and tourism businesses use all possible channels to get their products and services to market.

Interrelationships

Organisations often choose to work together for mutual benefit; this is an interrelationship. An example is the National Rail Days Out promotion. Anyone travelling by train can pick up a leaflet with two-for-one vouchers to attractions such as the Tower of London, the Edinburgh Dungeon and the Manchester United stadium tour.

Travel and tourism organisations choose to work with organisations outside the industry too. Lots of travel and tourism businesses work with store loyalty schemes such as Tesco Clubcard and Nectar, offering reductions on hotel stays, travel and visitor attractions. This benefits the stores' customers and brings increased business to the travel and tourism organisations that work with the stores.

▶ This deal shows a interrelationship between a rail company and London Zoo

Interdependencies

An interdependency is a relationship between two or more organisations that rely on each other to provide the best possible product or service. For example, if airlines and airports stopped working together, this would harm both organisations. This is because airlines have to depart from and land at airports. The airlines and airports negotiate mutually beneficial terms of business. If an airport decided to raise its airline charges so much that an airline moved to another airport, this would harm the airline because it would take time to move, during which it would have to pay increased fees, and also harm the airport because it would have to find another airline to fill the vacant slots.

Key term

Economies of scale – cost savings made by doing things in larger numbers or volumes, such as buying in bulk.

Table 1.7 lists some of the advantages and disadvantages of interrelationships and interdependencies.

▶ **Table 1.7:** Advantages and disadvantages of interrelationships and interdependencies

Advantages	Disadvantages
Economies of scale achieved by sharing core functions such as administration, call centres and physical offices, or equipment like aircraft	Confusion of identity, which might lead to the customer not knowing which organisation they are dealing with
Joint promotions and shared advertising split the costs of advertising and may make a greater impact on customers	Less personalised service provided when organisations work or merge with other organisations, as they are less likely to have as much knowledge of customers' needs
Increased custom, as satisfied customers from one partner may hear about and try new products from the other organisation	Bad press about partners because if one partner gets negative attention or provides poor service, all partners may be affected
Increased revenue because more customers are likely to hear about and purchase products and services, increasing revenue	Shared commission on sales because commission has to be divided between all parties
Shared expertise, for instance learning more about each other's specialisms, such as knowledge of a niche destination	
Benefits from good publicity about partners because if one partner is known for its good reputation and provides good service, all partners may benefit	
Shared customer bases and mailing lists to increase the number of customers to whom each partner can sell products and services	

Case study

Interdependency – a power struggle?

London Stansted Airport serves London and the south-east of England. Its largest airline customer is Ryanair. Ryanair is an Irish airline which uses airports all over Europe for its services. However, Stansted is its biggest airport base, with many of its 400+ aircraft located there.

Between 2007 and 2012, Stansted lost more than six million passengers. It is thought that this happened because it increased its airport charges. The airport was then taken over by new management, the Manchester Airports Group, which made big changes and renegotiated contracts with airlines. In particular, the new management team made a ten-year agreement with Ryanair, negotiating favourable charges for Ryanair in return for their commitment to Stansted. This helped the airport to recover growth and reach 26 million passengers in 2018.

Manchester Airports has worked to attract new airlines to the airport. They gained agreement from the government to raise the cap of 35 million passengers a year to 43 million. Jet2 is one of the new entrants at Stansted and contributed over 1 million passengers in its first year. Another new entrant for Stansted is Emirates offering long-haul routes, for example to Dubai.

Ryanair only operates short- and medium-haul flights, so most of Stansted's air traffic is travelling to Western Europe. Since the vote to leave the European Union, Ryanair has suggested cutting operations at Stansted and increasing flights at other airports. As Ryanair already uses over 200 airports in Europe and North Africa, with many used as bases for aircraft and crew, they could possibly take their business away from Stansted.

Check your knowledge

1 Explain the advantages and disadvantages of the interdependency to London Stansted Airport.

2 Explain the advantages and disadvantages of the interdependency to Ryanair.

3 What do you think might happen if Stansted raised its charges again?

4 What do you think might happen if Ryanair reduced its flights from Stansted?

5 Who do you think is more powerful in this relationship? Give reasons for your answer.

Horizontal and vertical integration

Integration occurs when two or more businesses or organisations merge together, often because one buys the other. Traditionally, travel and tourism businesses specialise in one area of the industry, working with the businesses that precede or follow them in the distribution channel. For example, hotels work with the tour operators who work with travel agents who reach the customers. Organisations that want to control their distribution channel often buy out or merge with another company.

▸ **Horizontal integration** occurs when a business buys another business at the same level in the distribution channel. It will do this to offer a wider variety of products and services. For example, a hotel chain buys an independent hotel and brings it into the chain with the same branding and facilities.

▸ **Vertical integration** occurs when a business buys or merges with a business at a different level in the distribution channel. It will do this to control more sectors of the travel and tourism industry. This integration may go backwards along the channel, for example a tour operator buying a hotel, or forwards along the channel, for example a tour operator buying a travel agency.

Some tour operators have bought or created airlines, hotels and travel agencies. This means they own all the different components in their distribution channel and control the whole operation. They claim that this gives them economies of scale, which allows them to offer better prices to customers. It can also mean that smaller or independent businesses are forced out of business because they cannot compete on price.

Key terms

Horizontal integration – when a business buys or merges with another business of the same type.

Vertical integration – when a business buys or merges with a business that performs a different role in the same industry to control the distribution channel.

Most of the major tour operators are both vertically and horizontally integrated, owning their own travel agencies, airlines, hotels and, in some cases, different tour-operating businesses.

Theory into practice

Look again at the Ryanair case study on page 27 and the advantages and disadvantages in Table 1.7 on page 26. Which advantages and disadvantages do you think apply to the relationship between Stansted Airport and Ryanair?

Ⅱ PAUSE POINT

A travel agency with 20 shops in north-west England has been approached by a travel agency in a neighbouring region to merge their businesses. What kind of integration is this? Explain the advantages and disadvantages to both parties.

Hint Remember that both businesses operate in the same part of the industry.

Extend What kind of integration would result if the organisation approaching the travel agency was a tour operator?

Case study

Dart Group PLC

Dart Group is the parent company of the tour operator, Jet2 holidays and the airline Jet2.com. The group also owns Fowler Welch, a food distributor. The group's history is available at dartgroup.co.uk.

Jet2 holidays has over 1.5 million customers a year taking package holidays to over 60 destinations. Jet2 holidays employs over 1200 employees in various parts of its operations including IT, finance, marketing and its call centre.

In 2017, Jet Villas, a specialist tour operator was launched. Jet2.com has over 340 routes from nine UK bases including Stansted and Birmingham from 2017. These routes serve 12 million customers each year. Customers can book flights only or a Jet2 holiday with a Jet2.com flight.

Fowler Welch offers food storage, picking and packing and distribution services to food retailers, processors and importers.

As the group owns its own airline, its tour operator business can match all its holiday destinations with its scheduled services. In 2014, a purpose-built training centre was opened with four full flight simulators for pilot training and facilities for cabin crew training.

Engineers are trained to maintain Jet2's aircraft. Jet2.com has maintenance hangars at its bases in Leeds Bradford and Manchester airports.

Check your knowledge

1 What are the advantages to the Dart Group of training its own engineers?

2 What are the benefits of having an airline and a tour operator under the same umbrella organisation?

3 Why does Dart Group have a food distribution business alongside its leisure and travel businesses?

4 Do some research to find out how the Dart Group is currently performing.

Technology in travel and tourism

As in any other industry, technology is of great importance in travel and tourism. If a business uses technology well, it can enhance the customer experience and make business operations easier to manage.

Technology for communication, booking and promotion

Ebrochures and websites

Many, if not all, travel and tourism businesses, from tour operators to hotels, use websites to provide information about their products and services, promote special offers and take customer bookings. Most tour operators still produce traditional printed brochures, but many also publish these brochures online as ebrochures. Because it is thought that customers are choosing to book holiday and travel online, it is also thought that ebrochures may replace printed brochures, and TUI says it hopes to get rid of print brochures by 2020. Research by *Travel Weekly* suggests that older people use the internet to research information about holidays just as much as, or even more than, young people.

> **Discussion**
>
> In small groups, discuss your opinions about replacing print brochures with ebrochures. Do you think that there are any customers who would miss out if print brochures were not available? How much money do you think organisations might save by not printing brochures? Do you think that they will lose customers?

Reviews, blogs and virtual tours

Tourists use online review sites such as TripAdvisor as research tools to choose destinations to visit and tourism businesses to use. Once a customer starts to use a review site, they are often repeatedly encouraged to post even more reviews. There are also many travel blogs on the internet, and the blogs with most followers can be good places to advertise tourism businesses. The number of such sites means that travel companies need to monitor review sites and blogs, and maintain a positive online presence.

Virtual reality technology and virtual tours have the capacity to totally change holiday bookings. It means that customers can 'visit' a destination before deciding to make a booking. Thomas Cook was one of the first tour operators to introduce virtual reality headsets for travel in 2015. Used with a mobile phone, the headsets gave users a 3D view of some of its holiday destinations.

> **Research**
>
> If you can, find a travel agency that uses virtual reality headsets in your local area and try it out. Report your findings back to the rest of your group.

Mailshots, pop-ups and adverts

Mailshots are promotional materials such as leaflets or brochures sent to a large number of people. Traditionally, these were sent by post but now more and more are sent by email. In order to send mailshots by email, a travel and tourism business needs people's email addresses. The business will gather these email addresses from customers making enquiries or bookings, subscribing to a newsletter or entering a competition. Once the business has the customer's email address, it can send information to them about its products and services.

An extension of contacting by email is to use pop-ups. These are advertisements that appear in a new browser window without being requested by the person browsing a site. There are different types of pop-ups.

▶ **Time-driven** – a pop-up appears to display an advert or an offer when a person has been browsing the site for a set time, such as 60 seconds.

▶ **Behaviour-driven** – a pop-up appears when certain criteria are met by the way that the person browsing the site behaves. For example, it might be triggered when you click on a certain part of the site.

▶ **Exit-driven** – a pop-up appears when the person leaves the site, usually to display a special offer to make them stay on the site.

Websites often carry banner adverts. These are graphics that stretch across the top or bottom of a website or along the side as a sidebar. Whenever you browse a website, the website will place a file known as a cookie on your computer, which remains there unless you remove it by clearing cookies in your browser settings. Cookies allow advertisers to recall your browsing history and direct relevant adverts to you. This may mean that if you had been browsing holidays with a tour operator you may later be targeted by adverts from that business or other similar businesses. This is useful for travel and tourism organisations as they can direct adverts directly to people who have demonstrated interest in their products.

Making and confirming bookings

The internet has grown rapidly as a means of booking holidays and flights. With increased customer confidence and easy access to information on the internet, 41 per cent of leisure travel is booked on the internet (Online Travel Marketing). However, these bookings still tend to be made on desktop and laptop computers rather than smartphones and other mobile devices, probably because it is easier to complete and view the booking on a larger screen.

It is difficult to assess how many holidays are booked online overall. Individual organisations can process their own data for bookings but overall information varies widely, depending on the source of the information. Kayak produces an annual Mobile Travel Report and claims that three-quarters of people prefer to book their holiday online. However, ABTA reports that some travel agents are opening new stores in response to an increasing demand for personal, tailored and expert travel advice.

Emailing tickets and vouchers

Many travel and tourism businesses now email tickets and vouchers to customers as standard, so that they can be printed at home or displayed on a smartphone. This includes airline tickets and boarding passes, theatre and concert tickets, train tickets and vouchers for visitor attractions. This has been a great advantage to customers and businesses because:

▶ tickets and vouchers cannot get lost in the post
▶ the system is cheaper to administer than posting tickets
▶ it enables and encourages last-minute booking, as customers do not have to wait for tickets to arrive in the post.

Apps for mobile and digital devices

Apps are applications installed on mobile devices such as smartphones. There are lots of travel and tourism apps, many of which are free, though not all of them are useful. Examples include journey planners, weather forecasts, translation apps and travel guides. Some apps are produced by a particular company and are used to provide customers with easy access to travel information, itineraries and documents. Other apps allow the customer to contact the tour operator directly. Some apps even allow you to book tickets. For example, the National Rail app allows you to access live train information and buy mobile tickets that do not need to be printed.

PAUSE POINT

Give four examples of how an organisation might use technology to communicate with customers.

Hint

Think about your own experience of looking at travel and tourism organisations or making bookings on the internet.

Extend

Can you think of an example where you would prefer to speak face-to-face or over the telephone rather than doing the task online?

Technology specific to different organisations

Visitor attractions

Visitor attractions often use interactive technology. Multimedia presentations can be used to tell stories and educate visitors in an immersive way that makes them feel part of the action. For example, at the Imperial War Museum North in Manchester, a multimedia trench action station exhibit allowed children to explore the terrible conditions for soldiers in First World War trenches through their own senses of smell, hearing and touch. Other visitor attractions use **animatronics**, such as in the Natural History Museum's dinosaur exhibit, and some use webcams to show potential visitors what they can expect to see when they visit.

Fast-track tickets are another recent development and are particularly popular at theme parks. For a higher entrance price, fast-track visitors get to skip the queues for some specific (or all) rides. Legoland Windsor uses a fast-track device called Q-Bot,

Theory into practice

Using the internet, create your own imaginary package holiday to Majorca for yourself and a friend for one week. Decide whether to use a site that will allow you to book everything in one place or to use separate websites for each element. Find a flight, a suitable hotel and car hire, and select the most suitable products for you. Do not use any resources other than the internet. Make notes on the products available, the web addresses and the costs (though stop before you get to the final booking page!).

Compare your findings with the rest of the group.

Key term

Animatronics – the use of lifelike robots, usually for entertainment.

which is carried by fast-track visitors. It displays a QR code that the visitor shows to skip the queue for a ride or attraction.

Case study

A virtual reality experience

The Lost Palace is an **augmented reality** exhibition in Whitehall, London. It is a collaborative project between the charity Historic Royal Palaces, theatre makers, interaction designers and creative technologists. It uses technology to build an experience of Whitehall Palace, a heritage site that burned down over 300 years ago and no longer exists.

Using handheld devices, **binaural** 3D sound and **haptic** technology, visitors are immersed in the experience of hearing, touching and feeling the past. Because The Lost Palace is mapped over present-day Whitehall, visitors are aware that they are experiencing history in the exact locations where it really happened.

Visitors wear headphones attached to a wooden object, which they hold in their hands. As they wander around Whitehall, they hear the sounds and stories of The Lost Palace. Thanks to digital technology, the handheld object 'becomes' a wand for listening to conversations, the beating heart of a king and the torch that burns down the palace.

Check your knowledge

1 Find another example of virtual reality used at a visitor attraction. Make a wall display about this use of virtual reality, including a photograph, an explanation of how the technology is used and how it has been received by tourists.

2 Try to find out how many visitors attend your chosen attraction and whether numbers have increased because of the use of technology.

Transport hubs and gateways

Many transport hubs provide self-service check-in machines. Passengers use the machines to check in and print their boarding passes, rather than checking in with a person at the check-in desk. Security scanners are also used at airports to scan baggage for dangerous items. The scanners are constantly updated to be more efficient at locating threats. Full body scanners to scan passengers have also been introduced in the UK alongside metal detectors. However, full body scanners are not used at every airport and not for every passenger.

Other new technologies used in transport hubs include electronic beacons that sense your smartphone entering an airport. These beacons can then send you information about the airport's facilities, such as the locations of restaurants and your departure gate.

Accommodation

Some accommodation providers also use self check-in technology, often in budget hotels that do not always have a manned reception desk. Guests can check-in online at home and then go straight to their room on arrival. While this has the advantage of being quick and convenient, it means that guests do not receive a personal welcome.

Theory into practice

Research or visit your nearest airport. Trace the passenger journey through the airport, giving a detailed description of the technology that a person meets at each stage of their journey. Explain how each of the technologies used benefits the passenger and the airport. Present your findings as a large poster with illustrations.

Key term

Global distribution system (GDS) – an IT system that enables travel and tourism businesses to interact with other businesses, such as airlines and hotels, to compare different options and book travel arrangements for customers.

It also means that the room will have been automatically allocated to those guests, so there is little opportunity to discuss what room guests might prefer, such as close to or away from the lifts. Thistle Hotels have overcome this drawback by sending guests an online hotel plan so that they can choose their room.

Other technologies used in hospitality include payment security measures and mobile technology. Village Hotels have combined mobile check-in with a mobile key, meaning that guests can access their rooms with their smartphones rather than picking up a key card from reception. They claim that this is highly secure as guests pre-pay for their rooms and they have a lot of information about the guest from the check-in process.

Guests usually expect to have Wi-Fi access to the internet in hotels and may have several devices with them. This means that hotels have to make sure they have a good Wi-Fi signal throughout the building and sufficient bandwidth to support all guests' devices. Other forms of technology used for entertainment purposes in hotels include interactive walls. The Renaissance New York Midtown Hotel already has interactive digital displays, and Butlins plans to introduce virtual holiday personal assistants, projected onto apartment walls, to help families plan their day.

Travel agents, tour operators and transport principals

Travel agents, tour operators and transport principals have had to embrace online and mobile technology to survive. Customers want to be able to access their services whenever and wherever they want, using a variety of devices, so these businesses need to provide this. This includes having reliable and easy-to-use websites, as well as good administrative systems that work with their websites to display the availability of flights and rooms, and enable customers to select their own seats.

Most systems used by travel agencies and tour operators combine everything that the agents need, such as contracts with individual tourism principals or access to **global distribution systems (GDSs)** to make reservations.

Technology can also influence businesses' strategies. In 2016, Google launched a 'travel dashboard'. It shares consumer search trends relating to travel and tourism. The data is based on Google search queries across 26 countries and is updated every quarter. Using it allows travel businesses to identify new trends and see the popularity of individual brands.

Eticketing and mticketing are methods of providing tickets by email or mobile app, to be printed off at home or displayed on a mobile device. One form of eticketing or mticketing is online check-in as an alternative to checking in at the airport. It is done before arriving at the airport and requires the passenger to print out their own boarding pass or use the airline's app to display the boarding pass. Some airlines now charge passengers to check-in with a member of staff at the airport.

PAUSE POINT   Explain the advantages and disadvantages of self check-in at a hotel.

Hint   Imagine you are travelling on business and are arriving late at night.

Extend   What specific facilities would a business customer expect in their hotel?

Assessment activity 1.2

Use the following information about Travel Green to help you answer the questions.

Travel Green offers holidays to long-haul destinations around the world, including South and Central America, Asia and Africa. They help their customers to explore new places and cultures, allowing them to experience local foods, lifestyles and traditions. They also aim to minimise the impact of their customers on the environments of their destinations.

For example, in Morocco, tourists can take a trek through the mountains in a group with a local guide. They stay in the homes of local people and eat with them or at small local restaurants. There are optional visits to the souk in Marrakesh and to a hammam spa, arranged using local transport.

1   One of the operating aims of Travel Green is to increase awareness of responsible tourism. Explain **one** other possible operating aim for Travel Green.   **(2 marks)**

2   Explain how **three** features of holidays offered by Travel Green meet the needs of leisure travellers interested in responsible tourism.   **(6 marks)**

3   Tour operators such as Travel Green interrelate with scheduled airlines. Discuss the potential advantages and disadvantages of an interrelationship between tour operators and scheduled airlines.   **(8 marks)**

4   Travel Green proposes to replace its printed brochures with ebrochures. Assess the potential effects of the proposed change to Travel Green and its customers.   **(10 marks)**

5   Evaluate the importance of the Association of Independent Tour Operators and the Association of British Travel Agents in supporting tour operators like Travel Green.   **(12 marks)**

Plan
- What is the question asking me to do? Do I need to give examples?
- What are the key words that I will need to include relating to each question?

Do
- I will write down the key terms that need to be included in each answer.
- I will ensure that I have given sufficient examples relating to the number of marks available.
- I will make sure I give more detail when answering higher mark questions.

Review
- I have given both advantages and disadvantages, rather than focusing on just one.
- I have assessed by giving positive effects and negative effects.
- I have evaluated by judging how important the given topic is and giving specific reasons for my judgement.

 C   # The scale of the travel and tourism industry

The travel and tourism industry is an important part of the British economy, contributing by providing jobs and income. This is also true of many countries around the world. In 2017, tourism represented over 10 per cent of the world's exports. In many developing countries, tourism is the most important export.

The scale and impact of travel and tourism on the economy can be measured locally, nationally and internationally. This is done by gathering and analysing statistical data on tourism and the types of employment supported by the industry.

The importance of the UK as a global destination

There are two main ways of measuring how important the UK is as a destination for inbound tourists:
- by looking at tourist numbers
- by analysing economic importance.

Tourist numbers

The number of inbound tourists to the UK in comparison with other nations gives a good indication of how important the UK is as a global destination. The best source for this kind of information is UNWTO, which produces international tourist statistics, such as how many tourists visit each country in the world. They gather and produce a lot of data, but they also publish an annual summary, *Tourism Highlights*, which can be downloaded free from their website.

Table 1.8 shows the number of international tourists arriving in the top ten global tourist destinations. This shows that, in 2017, almost 38 million tourists visited the UK. It also shows that the UK ranked seventh in the world for **tourist arrivals**, and how that compares with other popular tourist destinations. For example, France was ranked first, with more than 86 million arrivals.

▶ **Table 1.8:** International tourist arrivals (2017) (UNWTO Tourism Highlights, 2018 Edition)

Rank	Country	International tourist arrivals (millions)	Change from 2016 (%)
1.	France	86.9	5.1
2.	Spain	81.8	8.6
3.	USA	76.9	0.7
4.	China	60.7	2.5
5.	Italy	58.3	11.2
6.	Mexico	39.3	12.0
7.	United Kingdom	37.7	5.1
8.	Turkey	37.6	24.1
9.	Germany	37.5	5.2
10.	Thailand	35.4	8.6

Travel and tourism businesses also need to know the nations from which their inbound tourists come. These nations are known as **tourist generators**. Knowing this information helps businesses and organisations to provide the facilities that these tourists want and to advertise products and services to them. The best source for this information is the International Passenger Survey (IPS), carried out on behalf of the Office for National Statistics (ONS). The IPS has been run since 1961 and it gathers information about travellers entering and leaving the UK. It conducts 700,000–800,000 interviews every year. Of these interviews, over 250,000 are used to estimate overseas travel and tourism.

Table 1.9 shows the UK's most important tourist generators (or source markets) in 2016.

▶ **Table 1.9:** Data from the International Passenger Survey 2017 (Office for National Statistics)

Rank	Source market	Spend (£million)
1.	USA	3643
2.	Germany	1581
3.	France	1425
4.	Australia	1194
5.	Spain	1061
6.	Irish Republic	941
7.	Saudi Arabia	862
8.	Italy	841
9.	Netherlands	747
10.	China	694

Key terms

Tourist arrivals – the number of visitors to a destination.

Tourist generators – countries that produce outbound tourists.

Discussion

Are the figures in Tables 1.8 and 1.9 what you expected? Are you surprised by any of the data in these tables?

Economic importance

The economic importance of the UK's travel and tourism industry within the global industry is calculated by analysing how much tourists actually spend in each country. This information is also gathered by UNWTO and is shown in Table 1.10.

Although Table 1.8 shows that the UK was seventh in the world in terms of tourist arrivals in 2017, it was fifth in terms of **tourism receipts**, earning over $51 billion from its inbound tourists, just a few billion less than France but with less than half the number of tourists.

▶ **Table 1.10:** International tourism receipts (2017) (UNWTO Tourism Highlights, 2018 Edition)

Rank	Country	International tourist receipts (US$ billions)	Change from 2016 (%)
1.	USA	210.7	1.9
2.	Spain	68.0	10.1
3.	France	60.7	9.0
4.	Thailand	57.5	13.1
5.	United Kingdom	51.2	12.1
6.	Italy	44.2	7.7
7.	Australia	41.7	9.3
8.	Germany	39.8	4.2
9.	Macao (China)	35.6	17.6
10.	Japan	34.1	14.4

The economic importance of tourism to the British economy can be assessed by looking at how much the industry contributes to the **balance of payments** and to the **gross domestic product (GDP)**.

Tourism contributes to the GDP of a country because visitors spend money on goods and services, and also on transport to reach their destination in the first place. In 2019, the value of inbound tourists to the UK economy was expected to reach £25 billion.

In terms of the balance of payments, each sector of the economy is measured in terms of its exports and imports. The UK makes a large contribution to the global economy through its spending on tourism, accounting for 3.6 per cent of international tourism receipts.

Discussion

Why do you think France receives the largest number of tourists in the world? Why do you think the USA receives the most in terms of tourism receipts? Discuss whether it is better to receive lots of tourists, like France, or receive fewer tourists while making almost the same amount of money from them?

 **PAUSE POINT** Find the current figures for the value of tourism to the UK economy, UK world ranking for arrivals and receipts, and the current value of UK arrivals and receipts. Now write a short paragraph explaining what these figures mean.

 Hint Find the UNWTO latest *Tourism Highlights* publication.

Extend Draw graphs showing how the UK's tourist arrivals and tourism receipts have changed over the last five years, then work out the percentage change between last year and this year.

Employment in travel and tourism

Employment is an important factor in growing the economy, and there are two kinds of employment in the travel and tourism industry.

▶ **Direct employment** is any job at any level in a travel and tourism business or organisation such as an airline or hotel, even if it is a business support role such as human resources.

▶ **Indirect employment** is any job in an industry that supports the travel and tourism industry, such as in industries like hospitality and retailing.

Most tourism employment is in the food and beverage services industry and the accommodation sector. One in eight jobs in the UK depends on tourism. The majority of these travel and tourism jobs are permanent, although they include part-time hours. Almost 50 per cent of these jobs, however, are worked at weekends.

Roles in travel and tourism can be grouped into the categories shown in Table 1.11.

▶ **Table 1.11:** Types of role available in the travel and tourism industry

Type of role	Description
Customer-facing	Deal directly with customers face-to-face, over the telephone and over the internet, such as an agent in a tour operator's call centre
Support or administration	Enable the business or organisation to function and complete its aims, such as a human resources advisor working for a chain of travel agencies
Graduate programmes or trainees	People in these roles are recruited for and trained in a particular specialism, such as air traffic control
Managerial and supervisory	Manage or supervise the work of other employees, such as a call centre manager or the manager of a travel agent retail store

There are several different ways in which you can enter a travel and tourism career, depending on your qualifications and experience. These include:

▶ internships (a short period of experience with some pay and expenses)

▶ apprenticeships (combining further training with work)

▶ management trainee schemes (usually for graduates but sometimes for students who have completed a BTEC National)

▶ starting at a low level and working up to supervisory or management roles.

Direct employment

Transport principals

Different types of travel principal offer many different roles. Airlines employ personnel such as air crew, for example pilots; customer-facing cabin crew, for example flight attendants; and a supporting maintenance crew, for example engineers. Cruise ships offer an even wider range of jobs, some of which may not be directly related to tourism even though they are still forms of direct employment. These include beauticians, doctors, chefs and fitness instructors. Cruise companies also employ staff in more traditional customer-facing jobs such as port presenters, who arrange excursions at the different ports visited by a cruise ship.

Transport hubs and gateways

Airports are a good example, providing several different employment opportunities and roles, such as:

- check-in
- customer service, for example dealing with customers' problems and queries
- baggage handling
- security screening.

Some of these require few qualifications. For example, some support jobs such as baggage handling are unskilled and relatively poorly paid. Other jobs are highly skilled and may be open only to graduates. These include jobs such as operations management and air traffic control based in air traffic control centres such as Swanwick and Prestwick.

Tour operators

Jobs with tour operators are based either at head office or at a resort, often overseas. Each operator has its own career structure, and jobs may be available at head office in any of the following departments.

- **Reservations and sales** – part of the sales team works with travel agents and online agencies to ensure that the tour operator's products are sold well by the agents. This means training agents so that they have good product knowledge and offering agents incentives to sell more products. Another part of the team usually works in a call centre to sell holidays directly to the public.
- **Marketing** – the marketing team is a support team and is responsible for developing the business's marketing strategy, looking after the creation of marketing materials and advertising the business's products and services.
- **Customer relations** – large tour operators may have different customer care teams for the different methods of customer contact, such as phone, email or social media. It is important that customers receive the same high-quality service through each contact method. Most tour operators also divide customer care into pre-departure and in-resort.
  - **Pre-departure** – these staff members look after customers before they go on holiday, answering queries and making any amendments to bookings. There is usually a separate customer services team for customers who make contact on returning from their holiday. These queries may be more difficult to deal with, especially if they are complaints.
  - **In-resort** – the in-resort customer service team is based at the destination or resort and is responsible for looking after customers while they are on holiday. They meet and greet people at the airport, provide representative (rep) services and deal with any problems that occur in the resort.
- **Operations** – these support employees are responsible for finding accommodation in resorts, administering contracts with suppliers and allocation of accommodation. They liaise closely with the overseas team.

Link

You learned about key sectors such as transport principals and transport hubs and gateways in Section B.

Research

Many travel and tourism learners say that they would like to be an in-resort rep. Is this a job that interests you? What do you think are the advantages and disadvantages?

Travel agents

Travel agencies mostly employ customer-facing staff, though they will also recruit for support and management roles. For customer-facing roles, travel agencies often recruit people who have just left college. These recruits have acquired good background knowledge of the travel and tourism sector from their studies, as well as usually being enthusiastic and willing to learn essential retail skills.

Visitor attractions

As in every other sector of the travel and tourism industry, visitor attractions require customer-facing staff as well as support staff in teams such as marketing, human resources and accounting. These support roles are vital parts of any business. Other roles available at a visitor attraction will vary according to the type of attraction. For example, a theme park requires a support team of engineers to design, build and maintain its rides, whereas a stately home requires customer-facing guides with a detailed knowledge of the history of the house and grounds.

Accommodation

Most jobs in the accommodation sector require people who can work in a team, who are happy to work unsocial hours and who have initiative. The accommodation sector offers a number of potential roles. It also offers the opportunity to work either in your local area or further afield, even overseas. Some jobs can be taken by college leavers, whereas others might need specialist qualifications, such as in catering or accountancy.

Most accommodation businesses reward people who are hard-working. You might start out as a receptionist, but could quickly move into reservations, managing housekeeping, managing events or other business activities.

Trade associations and regulatory bodies

Jobs with trade associations and regulatory bodies are likely to be office-based administrative roles, though some customer-facing staff may deal directly with members or businesses. Staff working for a regulatory body may need to have knowledge of specialist legal and regulatory requirements. For example, if you worked at the CAA, you might become an expert in aviation security or become a compliance officer who ensures that Air Travel Organiser's Licence (ATOL) members comply with the regulations.

Information and promotional services

One example of a job in information services is working in a tourist information centre. This is a customer-facing role, dealing directly with tourists and customers. Because these centres are locally based, a knowledge of the local area is important and employees may also need specialist knowledge. For example, in the Lake District you would be expected to know the area and the facilities, but also the wildlife and flora, which are important tourist attractions in that area.

Promotional services include marketing agencies like the national tourist boards in the UK. Many of these roles are likely to be office-based support roles, though some, such as jobs in business development, involve going out and finding new partners to work with.

Indirect employment

Indirect employment in industries that support travel and tourism includes:

▶ **travel journalism** – writing for a newspaper, magazine or blog
▶ **insurance** – selling products used by tourism businesses, such as third-party liability insurance or buildings insurance
▶ **retailing** – selling souvenirs in local shops
▶ **manufacturing** – producing souvenirs and other products sold to tourists
▶ **IT support** – maintaining IT systems or websites used by travel and tourism businesses and organisations
▶ **publishing** – researching, producing and printing brochures and promotional materials
▶ **engineering maintenance** – maintaining vehicles such as trains, aircraft and ferries.

⏸ PAUSE POINT   Give an example of one job in each of the following sectors: airline, airport, cruise ship, travel agency, tour operator, insurance, travel journalism.

Hint   Use the careers sections of business websites in these sectors to help you find examples.

Extend   Choose three of the listed sectors and find a real job vacancy for each. Explain what the job involves and why it appeals to you, then present your findings to the rest of the group as a table or diagram.

Visitor numbers

You have already considered the number of inbound tourists arriving in the UK. However, this is not the only useful number when thinking about visitor numbers. For example, you may need to look at numbers of specific types of tourist to be able to compare different types of tourism and assess which areas are growing or declining.

Visitor numbers by type of tourism

You can split the total number of visitors into the following categories and find information on the websites listed.

▶ **Inbound** – look at the most recent edition of *Tourism Highlights* to find the number of tourist arrivals into the UK.
▶ **Outbound** – look at the *Overseas Travel and Tourism Bulletin*, found on the ONS website.
▶ **Domestic** – look at the number of overnight trips away in the *Great Britain Tourism Survey*, found on the VisitBritain website.
▶ **Business and VFR** – look at the annual *Travel Trends* report, found on the ONS website, which should contain the number of business and VFR visits (overseas residents' visits by purpose)
▶ **Day trips** – find the number of day visits in the *Great Britain Day Visits Survey*, found on the VisitBritain website.

Visitor numbers by other factors

Visitor numbers and spending can also be split by other factors, such as:

▶ type of transport
▶ country of origin or destination
▶ accommodation type
▶ region or city visited
▶ types of activities carried out.

Research

You have been asked to research the most recent numbers of visitors in the listed categories. Make sure that you look at the same year, then check whether the trend is up or down on previous years.

Make five key points about your findings, for example, 'there are three times as many day visitors as there are inbound tourists'.

Research

Choose one of the five listed categories and find the most recent figures for that category. Most of the information you will need can be found on the VisitBritain website, which has an A to Z of reports to help you find what you are looking for.

VisitBritain VisitEngland

Search   🔍

Latest news & media centre | Who we are & what we do | Campaigns & opportunities | Developing England's tourism | International marketing advice | England research & insights | Inbound research & insights | Inbound markets & segments

England Research & Insights

Understanding the English tourism landscape

Need the latest information about the size and the value of the English tourism market? Need the latest business performance trends or to find out who your visitors are and what they think?

Explore domestic overnight and day visitor data or take a look at our Research A-Z, which lists our research alphabetically by research topic. You can also take a look at our research timetable to find out when the next set of results will be released.

Great Britain Tourism Survey (GBTS)

This national consumer survey measures the volume, value and characteristics of domestic overnight tourism trips.

View our latest reports

From continuous surveys and research findings to recent conference presentations, take a look at our latest reports and summaries.

Volume & value	Tourism business research	Consumer behaviour
• The value of tourism in England • GB Tourism Survey (domestic overnight tourism): Latest results • GB Tourism Survey: 2015 overview • GB Tourism Survey: archive • GB Day Visits Survey: Latest results	• Business Confidence and Performance Monitor • Annual Survey of Visits to Visitor Attractions: Latest results • Annual Survey of Visits to Visitor Attractions: Archive	• The decision-making process and booking behaviour • England visitor segmentation • England visitor satisfaction research • Future Trends: Domestic leisure trends for the next decade

▶ **Figure 1.5:** VisitBritain/VisitEngland is the national tourism agency responsible for promoting Britain worldwide and developing English tourism. Their website contains plenty of reports and fact sheets about domestic tourism to England and inbound tourism to Britain.

The *Great Britain Tourism Survey* provides detailed information about domestic overnight tourism. The following are examples of visitor numbers split by some of these other factors.

▶ **Type of transport used** – most domestic tourists travel in their own car. This is different from inbound travellers, who are unlikely to come to the UK by car unless they are from neighbouring countries such as France or Ireland.

▶ **Purpose of visit** – the fewest domestic trips are made for business reasons. Almost half of all trips are for holidays, closely followed by VFR trips.

▶ **Region or city visited** – large cities or towns are most popular. However, the south-west is the most popular region to visit, despite the fact that it contains few large cities. The north-west and London are usually the next most popular regions to visit.

▶ **Accommodation type** – around a third of visitors stay in hotels but more stay in homes of friends and relatives.

⏸ **PAUSE POINT**   Do the trips that you and your friends and family have taken this year have the same characteristics as discussed above? Write down the similarities and differences.

Hint   You may need more details before deciding. Look for the latest domestic tourism statistics on the VisitBritain website.

Extend   Why do so many people choose the south-west for holidays? What other regions might you expect inbound tourists to visit and why?

Some questions in the International Passenger Survey are designed to find out what activities tourists undertake. This information is useful as it helps businesses plan for the future and market the right products and services to the right customers.

An example of the findings is shown in Table 1.12. Visitors were asked about activities in different categories. Our example concerns city life.

▶ **Table 1.12** Visitors experiences of city life in 2017 (from International Passenger Survey 2017)

Activity	Number of visits involving activity (000)	% of all visits	Amount spent in UK (£m)
Dining in restaurants	19,399	61%	£11,550
Shopping	20,985	54%	£15,850
Going to the pub	16,355	42%	£11,180
Socialising with locals	12,368	32%	£9,120
Visiting parks or gardens	11,873	32%	£8,880
Visiting museums or art galleries	10,438	28%	£8,130
Going to bars or nightclubs	4,894	12%	£4,430
Visiting a spa/ health centre	913	2%	£1,440

Visitor trends

Research data does not just tell businesses and organisations about what has already happened; it can also be used to identify trends that are likely to continue to grow or decline in the future. Some of the travel and tourism trends that research data may be used to identify include:

▶ growth areas of origin and destination

▶ changing purpose of visit

▶ transport type used

▶ length of stay

▶ increase and decline in popularity of destinations and tourism types.

VisitScotland produces many reports about visitors to Scotland. Our infographic example in Figure 1.6 shows information about previous visitors as well as the expected trends for the following year.

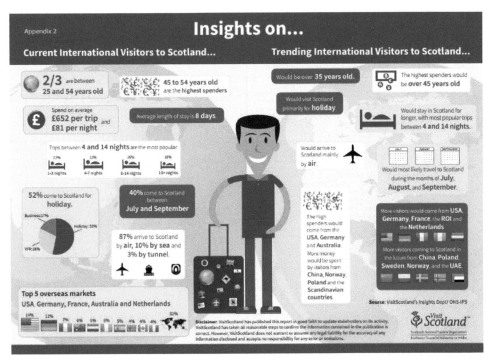

▶ **Figure 1.6:** This VisitScotland infographic shows the visitor profile of previous visitors and the expected trends for the following year

Theory into practice

Answer the following questions using the data or predictions in the image and additional data that you have researched for yourself into the most recent report on visits to Scotland.

1   Which areas of origin were expected to grow?

2   Was the most common purpose of visit expected to change?

3   Why do you think VisitScotland expected most tourists to arrive by air?

4   Comment on the most recent data on visitors to Scotland, comparing it with the expected trends.

Case study

Travel and tourism trends

The *ABTA Travel Trends Report* is an annual report on trends in travel and tourism. In 2019, they found that:

*   more than 60 per cent of people holidayed abroad in 2018
*   overseas holiday bookings were up 12 per cent from the previous year
*   beach and city breaks were the top holiday choices for the forthcoming year
*   Turkey and Egypt returned to popularity with an increase in bookings in 2018

*   key growth destinations were those where the pound might go further, such as Bulgaria and Greece.

Check your knowledge

1   Find the current edition of the *ABTA Travel Trends Report* on the ABTA website.

2   Read through the market outlooks and key trends, then write up to ten summary or highlight statements, like those given in the case study.

3   In pairs, identify anything that has changed since 2017 and discuss the potential reasons for these changes.

Income and spending

Travel and tourism contributes to a country's GDP – that is, the value of its economy. Every pound that is spent by a tourist on tourism-related purchases contributes to the UK's GDP. However, direct tourism expenditure has a wider impact on the economy. This is because of the **multiplier effect**. For example, if a tourist pays to stay in a hotel, the hotel spends money on local services, supplies and employees to run the business, and provide food and facilities for guests. The staff working at the hotel receive wages, which they then use to buy goods and services for themselves. This means that the impact of the initial amount of money spent by the tourist is 'multiplied' throughout the economy.

The economic benefits of tourism can be lost if products and services sold or used in the tourism industry are imported rather than locally produced. For example, hotels may import food and drink, or construction businesses may import the materials for a construction project. These are examples of **leakage**, where the cost of these products or services 'leaks' out of the economy by being paid into another economy.

In 2016, TfL introduced Night Tube services on some London Underground lines on Friday and Saturday nights. Research carried out for TfL suggested that, for each £1 that TfL spends on delivering the new Night Tube services, it would provide between £2.70 and £3.90 of benefits to the night-time economy (businesses such as bars, restaurants and cinemas).

Income from tourism is not just received by the country as a whole. Instead, it is earned by individual travel and tourism organisations and businesses. The greater their income and the greater their profit margin or level of commission earned, the more profit they will make. Increased profits allow businesses to invest more in their business activities or to spend on other businesses' products and services. Both of these benefit the wider economy. In addition, increased profit increases the amount of tax paid by businesses, which also benefits the economy and the nation.

Statistics about the level of tourist spending and what tourists spend their money on are also a good indicator of the value of tourism to the economy. The amount spent by tourists is more important than the number of tourists. The best situation for a destination is to attract lower numbers of high-spending tourists.

The list below shows what tourists in the UK spend their money on in in order of priority. After the general category of 'other consumption products', for example shopping, you can see that food and beverages account for the greatest spend, followed by air travel and accommodation.

1 Other consumption products
2 Food and beverage serving services
3 Air passenger transport services
4 Accommodation services for visitors
5 Cultural activities
6 Railway passenger transport services
7 Travel agencies and other reservation services
8 Sport and recreation activities
9 Road passenger transport services
10 Water passenger transport services
11 Transport equipment rental services
12 Exhibitions and conferences

Key terms

Multiplier effect – the additional revenue, income or employment created in an area as a result of tourism expenditure.

Leakage – the amount of money that leaves an economy for products and services purchased from other countries (this money therefore does not benefit the first nation's economy).

Visitor spending in York

Every year the destination management organisation for the city of York, Make it York, publishes research data on York's tourism economy. The latest data shows that:

- visitor spending in the city has reached £564 million
- visitor numbers are 6.7 million
- the number of jobs supported by tourism is 19,000
- the average day visitor spend by day visitors is £44.86
- the amount of money spent on conferences and events in York has reached £137 million
- food and drink was responsible for most visitor spending, followed by shopping

- of the overseas visitors, the top three generating countries are the US with 16 per cent, 9 per cent from China and 9 per cent from Australia.

Check your knowledge

1 What sorts of things do you think the visitor spending figures might include?

2 What do you think day visitors are likely to spend their money on?

3 Why do you think shopping attracted so much of visitor spending?

4 See if you can find similar figures for your own town, city or area.

PAUSE POINT   Explain the following terms: leakage, multiplier effect, gross domestic product.

Hint   Look back at the pages you have just read if you need to.

Extend   Can you give an example of each of these terms in your own local area?

Assessment activity 1.3   AO3 AO4

1 Complete Table 1.13 by filling in the **three** blank boxes.   **(3 marks)**

▶ **Table 1.13:** Terminal passengers at UK airports

	Q1 2016		Q1 2015		
	Passengers (millions)	**% of total**	**Passengers (millions)**	**% of total**	**% of change**
London airports	34.3	63	32.1	64	
Scheduled	33.6	62	31.3	63	7.3
Charter	0.7	1		2	−17.8
Regional airports	19.8	37	18.0	36	9.9
Scheduled	18.5	34	16.6	33	11.6
Charter	1.3	2	1.5	3	−9
All airports	54.1	100	50.2	100	7.8
Scheduled		96	47.9	95	8.8
Charter	2.0	4	2.3	5	−12.2

The data in Table 1.13 is produced by the Civil Aviation Authority to provide information for the aviation sector.

2 Discuss the ways in which the airline sector could use this data.   **(6 marks)**

3 Analyse the possible reasons for variations in data presented in Table 1.13.   **(8 marks)**

Plan
- What is the question asking me to do? Do I know how to do the calculations?
- Do I understand what the data means?

Do
- I will write down the key terms that need to be included in each answer.
- I will ensure that I have given sufficient examples relating to the number of marks available.

Review
- I have found at least three ways in which the data could be used.
- I have explained why there might be variations in the data.

D Factors affecting the travel and tourism industry

Product development and innovation

The travel and tourism industry changed dramatically in the 20th century and continues to change today. In the 1950s, only wealthy people had regular holidays. Today many people can afford the cost of foreign travel. This is mostly due to the developments and innovation in travel and tourism products and services, making it possible for many people to travel to more destinations than ever before.

Development and innovation

Developments in transportation and improvements in on-board facilities

Developments in transportation have had a huge impact on the travel and tourism industry. This is because improvements to modes of transport such as aircraft, ships and trains have made them more efficient and therefore cheaper to run. For example, the introduction of the Boeing 747 jet liner in 1970 had a great impact on package holidays. This was because the 747 seated more passengers and could fly faster and further than previous aircraft, making long-haul destinations more accessible. Now 747s are being replaced by more efficient airliners that are quieter and burn less fuel while flying long distances, such as the Bombardier CS100 and the Airbus A320neo.

Another improvement to modes of transportation is the fact that vehicles are capable of carrying more passengers. For example, the Airbus A380 usually seats 555 passengers but actually has a maximum capacity of 800. Similarly, super-sized cruise ships such as Harmony of the Seas™ operated by Royal Caribbean International can carry more people than ever before.

Case study

Go large

Large airliners are now popular with many airlines. The Airbus A380 was launched in 2005 and usually seats 555 passengers. It is flown by a number of airlines, including Singapore Airlines, British Airways and Air France. The Boeing 787 'Dreamliner' was introduced in 2010 and seats between 210 and 330 passengers.

Check your knowledge

1 What happened to the A380 in 2019?

2 Find out which airlines operate the Boeing 787 and the Airbus A380. Do some airlines operate both? Why do you think this might be?

3 What impact do you think developments in the size of ships and aircraft might have on transport hubs?

▶ Airbus A380

There have been significant developments in rail transport. In the 1960s, many rail services and railway stations were closed. This was done because increasing numbers of people were buying cars, which meant that they mostly preferred to travel by car on the road network than by train. However, governments are now investing more money in rail networks and new rail technology.

Research

What are the most recent developments in the HS2 project?

- Who promotes HS2 and why?
- Who opposes it and why?
- How much is the project going to cost?

For example, Virgin Trains started running a new high-speed Azuma train in 2018. This train travels at a speed of 125 miles per hour, cutting journey times between London and Edinburgh by more than 20 minutes and reducing journeys between London and Leeds to just two hours. If improvements are made to the tracks, the train would be able to run at 140 miles per hour.

High-speed rail such as the French TGV service has been used in Europe for many years. In 2019, the only purpose-built high-speed line in the UK is HS1 between London and the Channel Tunnel at Dover, which is used by Eurostar. However, in 2000, a project was launched to build a second high-speed line – HS2 – between London and the cities of Birmingham, Manchester, Sheffield and Leeds. The project has suffered many delays and the expected cost of the line has risen. Some people argue that the money should be spent on improving congested commuter networks.

Case study

The Channel Tunnel

For many years, a tunnel under the sea between France and England was just an idea. However, in 1986, the French and British foreign ministers signed the Franco-British Treaty, enabling the Channel Tunnel to become a reality. The tunnel would provide an alternative to ferries and airlines and was intended to encourage more travel between Britain and continental Europe. Work began in the UK in 1987, and the Channel Tunnel opened in 1994. The original budget of £4.8 billion was hugely exceeded, and the project actually cost more than £10 billion.

The construction work was completed by ten major British and French construction companies. The Channel Tunnel had a huge impact on the number of passengers taking ferries across the Channel. Since its opening in 1994, numbers travelling by the tunnel have steadily increased while those travelling by sea have decreased.

Statistics show that passenger numbers on sea or through the tunnel are now comparable, with a record high of 21 million taking the Channel Tunnel in 2014.

Check your knowledge

1 What are the advantages and disadvantages of the different methods of travelling between Britain and Europe?

2 What are the different methods of travelling through the Channel Tunnel? Where is the UK departure point? Where would you arrive in Europe?

3 Find out what the French call the English Channel.

4 Plan and cost out an itinerary for someone taking the Eurostar from London to Paris for a long weekend in a month's time.

Another significant development in transport is the improvement in the facilities available on aircraft, ships, trains and coaches. Many coach and rail businesses now offer wireless internet connections, better seats and a range of refreshments, while airlines and cruise companies continue to improve their on-board services to meet customer expectations.

Introduction and growth of low-cost airlines

Low-cost airlines came into being in the 1990s after the deregulation of air travel in Europe started to allow the sale of discount fares. Deregulation meant that airlines could establish themselves in any European Union (EU) member state and obtain an operating licence. All routes within the EU are available to all EU carriers, meaning that an airline such as Ryanair can have a base in Frankfurt Hahn and fly into and out of countries all over the EU.

In 1995, easyJet launched as a low-cost airline offering two routes: Luton to Glasgow and Luton to Edinburgh. Now low-cost airlines carry more passengers than other airlines.

Airport growth and improved facilities

Regional airports in the UK have expanded in recent years. They are popular with passengers, who like the convenience of travelling from an airport that is closer to home than larger airports such as London Heathrow Airport. They are also popular with low-cost airlines, which often use regional airports because the fees that they charge are cheaper than those charged by larger airports. This means that the growth of low-cost airlines has contributed to the growth of regional airports.

Many people believe that airport capacity in the south-east of England needs to be increased. However, it is less clear how this should be achieved. For example, both London Heathrow Airport and London Gatwick Airport campaigned to be allowed to build another runway. In 2018, the government agreed that the additional runway could be built at Heathrow. In the same year, the smaller London City Airport gained permission to expand its existing terminal with a planned budget of £344 million.

Improved facilities in terminals, hubs and gateways

Investment in transport hubs and gateways improves the customer experience, as you saw in the case study about Glasgow Airport. At London City Airport new investment will extend the existing terminal to provide more space for passengers and a wider range of facilities, as well as improving passenger transport links. Many airports now provide a huge range of facilities, including a choice of eating and drinking establishments, shopping and personal services. As cruises departing from the UK become more popular, many of the UK's ports are also improving their facilities to cater for cruise passengers. For example, the Port of Southampton now has four cruise terminals and acts as the gateway for cruises to almost anywhere in the world.

Increased range of choice of accommodation

There are many more types of accommodation available now than ever before. Modern tourists expect to be able to choose between different types of accommodation, including villas, hotels and camping. They also expect to choose different **board** packages, such as bed and breakfast or all-inclusive. These different options allow businesses to offer **differentiated** products to customers, ensuring that they can cater for all types of tourist.

A recent entrant to the market is the American business Airbnb, which is a marketplace for rooms around the world that are available to visitors. Almost anyone can join Airbnb to rent out a spare room or an entire house. Airbnb launched in 2008 and by 2019 was operating in 191 countries with over 150 million guests staying in properties found through Airbnb.

Holiday camps are popular holiday destinations in the UK. Holiday camps were at their most popular between 1945 and 1960, and examples included Warners, Butlins and Pontins. They declined as holiday destinations during the 1970s as demand grew for package holidays abroad. However, holiday parks such as Center Parcs are becoming more popular. Center Parcs's first village in the UK opened in 1987 at Sherwood Forest. It offers short-break holidays, with mid-week or weekend breaks all year round, and also accommodates longer stays.

Increased variety of visitor attractions

Visitor attractions are a key sector in travel and tourism, and the different types of visitor attraction have increased. VisitEngland reports annually on the number of visits to attractions in its survey of visits to visitor attractions. Attractions work hard to be more appealing to visitors, such as investing in new technology and by diversifying into different markets such as hiring out their premises for conferences or weddings.

Developments in reservations and bookings

The way in which bookings are made is one of the areas of travel and tourism that has seen the greatest impact from technological developments. As demand for travel

Research

The London Cruise Terminal at Tilbury is a Grade II listed 1930s building; it played an important part in the history of immigration into the UK. The port has excellent transport links and is close to the M25.

Research the facilities available inside the London Cruise Terminal, then find out which cruise lines operate from Tilbury and their destinations.

Key terms

Board – the meals provided with a tourist's chosen accommodation.

Differentiation – elements of a product or service that make it different from others on the market and therefore attractive to customers.

Research

Find out what is meant by each of the following terms relating to board and write a definition for each:
- full board
- half board
- bed and breakfast
- accommodation only
- all-inclusive.

Link

You have already learned about the ways in which visitor attractions use technology in Section B.

grew in the 20th century, travel and tourism businesses introduced reservations departments to manage bookings. Later, tour operators and airlines developed computerised systems to manage bookings. Eventually these computer systems were linked up to travel agencies so that travel agents could make airline and package holiday bookings on behalf of their customers. These original computer reservation systems (CRSs) seem unsophisticated by today's standards, but they revolutionised the way in which travel businesses operated.

Now travel businesses use internet-based IT systems called global distribution systems (GDSs). These are a development of CRSs and allow agents to view services in real time and across many suppliers. The early systems only linked to one supplier, meaning that separate systems were needed to access different suppliers. The latest GDSs allow travel and tourism businesses to interact with other businesses, such as airlines and hotels, to compare different options and book travel arrangements for customers. There are many specialist IT companies producing systems for travel agencies. These systems usually cover back-office administration tasks as well as sales, and normally include:

▶ reservation management tools
▶ multiple sales channels such as web booking and telephone
▶ inventory management tools to manage the products and services that are for sale
▶ report generation tools to allow businesses to analyse booking data and trends.

The best known global GDSs are Amadeus, Galileo, Sabre and Worldspan.

Because many customers book their own holidays online, it is important that booking systems and the websites supported by those booking systems are compatible with the technology that customers want to use. For example, customers may want to browse for or book their holidays on a laptop or a mobile device. If a website or system cannot support their device, they will not be able to complete their booking and may go to a rival business instead.

Similarly, price comparison websites have had an impact on the way in which travel businesses operate. Sites such as Trivago, TravelSupermarket and Skyscanner allow customers to compare available products and services for themselves, rather than relying on the services of a travel agent. Most large travel businesses also operate call centres to handle customer enquiries, bookings and complaints.

Developments in cyber security
Businesses and organisations must protect their data, particularly when they hold customer data such as names, addresses, email addresses and credit card details. Data protection regulations require businesses to protect customer data and, if they do not, they will be fined. However, there have been many examples in recent years where hackers have managed to breach businesses' security systems and steal customer data. For example, in 2018, hackers managed to gain access to Marriott's systems and stole the records of over 327 million customers.

Travel and tourism businesses and organisations need to put in place a number of security systems to protect their data. This includes training their staff to handle and manage data safely, such as not using their own laptops or devices for business purposes. This will help them to avoid causing security breaches.

Media factors

Television coverage, film locations and advertising
Many travel and tourism businesses and organisations advertise on television. TUI is one of the biggest spenders, with European-wide campaigns incorporating television, digital and print advertising. Online travel agents are also increasing their advertising, and Trivago is another business that spends a lot on television advertising.

Free publicity can also have a great impact on travel and tourism, and the settings for television programmes and films often become popular destinations. For example, the television series *Poldark*, which is set in Cornwall, led to more tourists visiting Cornwall. The television series *Wolf Hall* benefited the National Trust, which encouraged tourists to visit the six locations shown in the series by providing a map featuring all of the historic settings used for the filming. Similarly, Tourism New Zealand worked closely with the filmmakers behind *The Lord of the Rings* and *The Hobbit* films, which were shot in New Zealand. The tourist board promoted tourism to the 'Middle Earth' locations and produced DVDs showing locations with cast endorsements.

Social media use and influence
Social networks such as Facebook and Twitter are used by millions or even billions of people every day and can be used to reach a global audience. Many international travellers use social media such as review sites, blogs and social networks to research their trips. This means that travel and tourism organisations need to manage their presence and reputation on social media as far as possible.

Businesses can use social media well by:
▶ building a Facebook page that is up to date, is interesting to follow and invites people to 'like' it and post positive comments

- providing useful up-to-date information for customers, such as real-time travel updates on Twitter
- measuring numbers of visitors to identify the content that interests users and providing more of it
- keeping in contact with former customers and encouraging them to come back to the business.

▶ Many businesses use social media platforms to interact with customers

Media coverage of events and management of public relations

News coverage of events and issues such as terrorist attacks and outbreaks of illnesses can have a significant impact on the operations of travel and tourism businesses. Managing this requires expertise in **public relations (PR)**, and many travel and tourism organisations employ specialist travel PR companies to do this for them. These PR businesses liaise with media publications such as newspapers and online reviewers to secure interviews and endorsements for new products, arrange publicity events and manage businesses' social media presence.

Larger operators may employ their own PR staff. For example, TUI uses its Media Centre to publish news about its products and services as well as to issue statements about topical events that may have an impact on their customers. For example, in September 2016, they issued the following statement on behalf of their then Thomson, First Choice and Thomson Cruises brands.

> The Foreign and Commonwealth Office has updated its travel advice to recommend that pregnant women postpone non-essential travel to countries affected by the mosquito-borne Zika virus. The Foreign Office also continues to advise people, particularly if they're pregnant or planning to become pregnant, to refer to the advice of the National Travel Health Network and Centre.

The speed of communication is such that news reporting can influence the outcome of negotiations being held or new services being released to the public. In September 2016, there was a lot of speculation that Monarch might fail as it was raising investment to renew its ATOL licence. To allay public fears, Monarch issued a press release emphasising that the organisation was operating normally and anticipated healthy profits. Unfortunately, Monarch still went into administration in 2017.

It is good practice to have plans in place to handle any potential bad publicity.

> **Key term**
>
> **Public relations (PR)** – the maintenance of a positive public opinion of something, such as a business or a destination.

Other factors affecting the travel and tourism industry

Factors that affect travel and tourism organisations can be:

▶ **external** – arising from issues outside the organisation's control

▶ **internal** – within the control of the organisation.

Generally, external factors have the biggest impact on businesses and organisations, and these cannot be controlled. However, the business can control how it reacts to these external factors.

Economic factors

The strength of the economy

The state of the economy is important to travel and tourism as it impacts heavily on how much money people can spend on travel and holidays. The economy also affects how much money businesses and organisations can borrow and how much they can invest back into their businesses. A country's economy can be either in recession or growing.

▶ **Recession** – the economy is in recession when there is a significant decline in the production of goods and services, employment and income for longer than two **financial quarters** in a row.

▶ **Growth** – the economy is growing when there is a positive change in the production of goods and services over time. In a period of growth, customers are likely to spend more money.

Disposable income

In a recession, people have less **disposable income** and may be more likely to lose their jobs. This means that they are more likely to take cheaper holidays or no holidays at all. Disposable income can also be affected if the interest charged on mortgages goes up or down, as this influences the amount of money people have to spend on their mortgage repayments.

Currency exchange rates

Exchange rates are linked to recession or growth. If an economy is growing, the currency becomes stronger (is worth more) compared to currencies in other economies. If an economy is in recession, the currency becomes weaker (is worth less). For example, when the pound (£) is strong against the euro (€), UK outbound travellers will get more euros for their pounds and will have a cheaper holiday in Europe. However, a strong pound might also make potential inbound tourists from Eurozone countries less likely to visit the UK, because their holiday in the UK would be more expensive for them. Businesses and organisations monitor exchange rates closely as they affect the prices that they pay for accommodation and services in overseas resorts.

Oil prices

The price of oil has an effect on transport principals such as airlines. Air fares are particularly dependent on the price of oil and tour operators are indirectly affected by this as they have to buy flights for their customers. World prices for oil fluctuate depending on the supply of oil and also any political situations that may affect access to oil reserves.

> **Key terms**
>
> **Financial quarter** – a quarter of a year or three months.
>
> **Disposable income** – the amount of money left over from a person's wages after they have paid tax and necessary expenses, such as rent and food bills.
>
> **Exchange rate** – the amount of money that one currency is worth in another currency.

> **Discussion**
>
> Before the 1970s, tourists were only allowed to take £50 out of the UK. What effect do you think this had on outbound tourism? What do you think was the impact of changing these currency restrictions?

 **PAUSE POINT**   Check the exchange rate of the pound (GBP) against the euro and the US dollar. Write a short paragraph to explain the current trend for each rate.

Hint   Try to get into the habit of checking exchange rates at regular intervals, as this will help you to identify trends.

Extend   Work out the value of the following amounts of money in euros at the current exchange rate: £10, £35, £150, £200.

Responses to economic factors

During recessions, travel and tourism businesses may try to bring prices down to attract more customers. They will look at competitors' prices for similar products or services and try to undercut them, known as competitive pricing. However, this strategy can lead competitors to continue to undercut each other until prices get so low that they are unsustainable and cause businesses to fail because they cannot make a profit.

In response to changing fuel prices, airlines may buy fuel when the price is low and engage in **fuel hedging**. This means they fix the price that they pay suppliers for fuel at the current price for a period of time. It is a gamble because if the price of oil falls, the airline will still have to pay the agreed price. Alternatively, if the price goes up and the business has not allowed sufficient funds for the cost of fuel in the price of a flight or holiday, they may pass the fuel charge onto the customer, which is an unpopular strategy.

Social and lifestyle factors

Travel and tourism businesses need to understand the lifestyles of their customers to know their market. Useful **demographic** data includes age, gender, income and employment.

Rise of the grey market

The **baby boomers** are the generation of people born shortly after the Second World War between 1946 and 1964, and they have been an important market for travel and tourism throughout their lives. This is because they are a large social group, making up a significant proportion of the UK population. It is also because they had more disposable income than previous generations and therefore control most of the UK's wealth.

Most of these baby boomers have now retired and have become known as the **grey market**: older retired people with time and available funds, who want to travel. Many have contributed to private pension schemes during their working lives, meaning that they now have a good income during their retirement and time to spend on pastimes such as travelling. Also, improvements in health care have led to increased life expectancy, meaning that this generation is expected to travel into old age. Saga is the most prominent tour operator catering for older people, but many organisations recognise this as an important market.

Millennials (or Generation Y)

The millennials are people born between 1980 and 1999, and as they get older they are becoming just as important as the baby boomers. They are the children of the baby boomers and have grown up in the internet age. They have good technology skills and generally want to try new experiences, go on adventures and experience different cultures. They are more likely to research their own trips and book them online, and they are also the most likely group to post reviews online.

Education has also been a major social factor in increasing travel. More people go to university and more of the population achieve at least a level 2 qualification (such as a GCSE). Better education leads to a population that is more aware of the outside world, curious about different cultures and languages, and keen to experience them. As the UK has a multicultural society, British people are more familiar with different religions, foods and cultures, and so they are less anxious about the unfamiliarity involved in travelling to new places. Students often opt for a gap year before starting at university and this opens up a whole market in travel and tourism.

Key terms

Fuel hedging – an agreement to purchase fuel at a predetermined price for a specified future time period.

Demographics - statistical data relating to the population, such as average age and average income.

Baby boomers – the generation of people born between 1946 and 1964.

Grey market – older people with substantial disposable income.

Research

You can find out about the UK population by visiting the website of the Office for National Statistics. What is the current UK population? What are the distributions of different demographic measures such as age, gender and income?

Changing family structures

According to the ONS, there are nearly 2 million single parents with dependent children in the UK. This is a big increase from 1.6 million in 1996. This has led to holiday companies offering specialist products for single parent families.

Despite this increase in single parent families, families are actually bigger than they were previously because life expectancy has increased, meaning that families are often **multi-generational**. They are also more geographically dispersed as people are more likely to move to different areas of the country. Despite living a long way from close family, the internet has made it easy to stay in touch with free or cheap forms of communication such as Skype, WhatsApp and Instagram.

Changing working patterns

In 2003, the Flexible Working Regulations came into force in the UK. These regulations give employees who are looking after young or disabled children the right to request flexible working arrangements from their employer. In 2007, this was extended to people with other dependents. More flexible working patterns became normal, and this means that people now often have more flexibility about when they can go on holiday.

For example, many people choose to work reduced working hours to allow them to carry out other responsibilities or have a better work–life balance. Some parents opt to work term-time only so that they can care for their children during the school holidays. An employee wanting to earn an extra day off to take a long weekend break might be allowed to work extra hours each day on 'flexitime' to create the extra day off. Technology has also improved work flexibility, as lots of people are now able to work at home using mobile phones, email and video conferencing.

Holiday allowance and pay

In 1938, the Holidays with Pay Act entitled workers in the UK to take a certain amount of paid holiday. The current legal entitlement to holiday in the UK is 5.6 weeks for an employee working five days a week. Part-time workers get the same proportion of holiday, but it is calculated **pro rata** for the number of days they actually work. Some employers include bank holidays in their employees' allowance, whereas others are more generous and allow bank holidays in addition to the legal entitlement. Of course, employers can choose to give their employees more holiday. If holiday entitlement increases in the future, employees will have even more opportunity to travel.

People's salaries also have an impact on travel and tourism. For example, BA research suggested that people with a salary of £15,000 would take an average of three breaks in 2016, whereas people who earn £55,000 were expected to take seven holidays.

Current fashions and trends

Trends in destinations have moved back towards traditional western Mediterranean resorts that holidaymakers consider to be safe, such as Spain. However, popular long-haul locations include a variety of countries such as Thailand, Kenya and Cuba.

ABTA, in its annual Travel Trends report, says there is an increase in take-up of long-haul holidays, in particular to Mexico and Cape Verde. Cruises are also increasing in popularity, as are city breaks and so-called **'hipster holidays'**.

Other trends include the use of smart technology, such as the Apple Watch, which give people on holiday push notifications about things that might be of interest to them, such as restaurants and visitor attractions in the area.

Responses to social and lifestyle factors

Organisations need to know the demographics of the travel market and plan ahead for changes in the population. This may mean commissioning external research or using research carried out by others, such as VisitBritain, ABTA and BA. They also need to analyse internal data so that they know who is buying their products or services and identify their own customer trends. For example, they should monitor which products are in decline and which are growing in popularity.

Based on this, businesses could introduce products or services that meet the needs of their market. This might mean specialising in a newly growing market segment such as the millennials. To do this, they could extend their product portfolio to include new destinations, like Iran, or start offering adventure holidays. They could also identify personalised products or services that they can offer based on analysis of their customer data. Research can also affect business operations. For example, knowing that millennials are heavy users of technology will lead businesses to provide mobile-optimised versions of their websites so that this important target market will want to use their business.

Relation vacations are also becoming a key product. These holidays are marketed to meet the needs of multi-generation families who are taking a trip together. These are most popular in the domestic market and family members may take them in addition to their separate holidays. Butlins offers several options for multi-generational family groups, including banquet-style dining tables large enough to seat large family groups and holiday assistants to help plan itineraries.

Case study

The Night Tube

London is known as a 24-hour city. However, until 2016, the London Underground did not run services throughout the night. Recently, Transport for London (TfL) has seen demand for night services rise. Its research showed that passenger numbers on Friday and Saturday nights have increased by about 70 per cent since 2000, with over half a million people using the tube after 10 p.m. on Fridays and Saturdays.

In 2016, TfL introduced the Night Tube on certain lines on Friday and Saturday nights. This allows passengers to travel between central London and the outskirts of the city, helping London's night economy and complementing existing Night Bus services. Research has suggested that Night Tube services will boost jobs in the night economy.

Check your knowledge

1 How do you think the extended service could boost the number of jobs in London?

2 What is meant by the night economy? Give some examples.

3 How might the extended tube service benefit travel and tourism businesses such as theatres, restaurants, museums and sporting venues? Try to find some real examples of how these businesses have changed their offering.

PAUSE POINT   Name three different markets for holidays.

Hint   Think about particular age groups and the names of those groups.

Extend   Why do travel and tourism businesses need to know about these different groups? How does this knowledge help them to plan their products and services?

Government legislation and legal factors

Legislation is the written law of a country. The UK government has always recognised the importance of tourism to the economy and has introduced new policies and laws over the years to encourage tourism.

Link

You learned about VisitBritain towards the end of Section B.

Key terms

Legislation – set of laws made official by Parliament.

Deregulation – the process of removing legal restrictions on the operation of an industry to allow greater competition, with the intention of ensuring greater efficiency and reduced prices for customers.

Duty of care – moral or legal responsibility for the safety of a person or group of people.

Development of Tourism Act 1969

This Act established a British Tourist Authority and tourist boards for England, Scotland and Wales. The British Tourist Authority and the English Tourism Council were eventually merged to form VisitBritain. The Act's aim was to co-ordinate all the organisations that make up the tourism sector and provide the industry with a single voice. Since 1969, the responsibility for tourism funding and development in Scotland and Wales has been devolved to the Scottish Parliament and the Welsh Assembly.

Transport Acts 1980 and 1985

The Transport Act 1980 ended licensing regulations affecting express coach routes and tours of over 30 miles. It led to competition between National Bus (then a public company) and private companies. The Transport Act 1985 brought about complete **deregulation**, meaning that private companies could operate on any route.

The Package Travel and Linked Travel Arrangements Regulations 2018

The regulations set out tour operators' responsibilities to their customers and what customers can do if the regulations are breached.

Tourism Action Plan

The Tourism Action Plan sets out the government's tourism strategy. The current plan published in 2016, and updated in 2017, includes the following main areas.

- **Providing an overarching industrial strategy** – co-ordinating the policies and actions of the multiple government departments that affect tourism so that they work together.
- **Co-ordinating action on events** – an Events Industry Board advises the government on the implementation of the UK's Business Visits and Events Strategy.
- **Clarifying the roles of VisitEngland and VisitBritain** – being clearer about the responsibilities of these boards.
- **Offering a £40 million Discover England fund** – an incentive fund for projects that encourage tourism or improve tourists' experiences.

Health and safety legislation in travel and tourism

Travel and tourism employers in the UK must comply with the Health and Safety at Work Act, just like any other employer. Tour operators in particular have a **duty of care** to people who take their holidays and need to have safety management policies in place. This extends to taking care of tourists in resorts abroad as well as in the UK. The aviation sector is particularly heavily regulated to ensure passenger safety when flying, and this is managed by the CAA.

Other pieces of legislation are also relevant to tourism. Understanding legal requirements can be difficult for small businesses, so trade associations offer support. For example, ABTA offers seminars about legislation for travel agents and tour operators. Similarly, the British Hospitality Association offers a chart listing the legal considerations for accommodation providers, covering 73 different acts ranging from manual handling to licensing laws (examples are given in Table 1.14).

▶ **Table 1.14:** Examples of legal considerations for accommodation providers from the British Hospitality Association chart

Legal consideration	Legislation	Explanation of legislation	Reason	Notes
Smoking in public places	**Health Act 2006** Smoking is banned in enclosed spaces and places of work	Smoke-free (Signs) Regulations 2012 (England only) require the display of at least one legible no-smoking sign. There is no requirement on the location or size of the sign, provided that it is able to be seen by customers and staff	Public health	Designated bedrooms, self-contained short-term rental accommodations and private areas of bed and breakfasts and guest houses
Signs for your premises	**The Town and Country Planning (Control of Advertisements) Regulations 2007** and **Consumer Protection Regulations 2008** Applies if you display any outdoor signs and/or advertisements	Consent depends on whether signs are fully, partially or non-illuminated and where they are situated. Signs must not be misleading, as this could constitute a breach of unfair trading and misleading marketing legislation	Community protection	
Gyms, swimming safety and outdoor safety	**Health and Safety at Work Act 1974** and **Management of Health and Safety at Work Regulations 1999** Applies where a gym, pool or particular outdoor activity is offered	Safety in swimming pools requires a thorough risk assessment and an assessment of the need for constant supervision	Guest protection	
Outdoor activities	**Adventure Activities Licensing Regulations 2004** Anyone who sells adventure activities intended for young people under 18	Providers must have a safety management system in place that involves a systematic approach to recognising risks and making sure something is done to control them. Covers 26 activities	Child health and safety protection	

Air passenger duty and airport taxes

Air passenger duty (APD) is a tax paid by passengers who use airports. It was introduced in the UK in 1994 and is collected by airlines on behalf of the UK government. APD is not a fixed amount and varies according to the length of flight, as shown in Table 1.15. It is paid on flights departing from UK airports. However, other countries also often charge APD, meaning that passengers departing from that country will pay APD to that country's government.

Key term

Air passenger duty (APD) – a tax paid by airline passengers to the government, collected when the passenger purchases their ticket from the airline.

▶ **Table 1.15:** Air passenger duty rates from 1 April 2017

Destination bands and flight distance from London (miles)	Reduced rate (for travel in the lowest class of travel available on the aircraft)	Standard rate (for travel in any other class of travel)	Higher rate (for travel in aircraft of 20 tonnes or more equipped to carry fewer than 19 passengers)
Band A (0 to 2000)	£13	£26	£78
Band B (over 2000)	£75	£150	£450

Airports also charge airlines for using their facilities, such as the runway, passenger handling, ramp handling, emergency services and security. The airlines include these charges in their ticket prices.

Passport and visa requirements

All UK residents must have a passport to travel abroad. As a member of the EU, the UK's tourists also had the right of free movement throughout the EU. It is not yet known how the decision to leave the EU will affect this.

To travel elsewhere in the world, it is important to check whether a visa is needed. For example, a tourist taking a holiday to Egypt will need a visa. Similarly, many inbound tourists to the UK from outside Europe require a visa, depending on their home country. Usually, visas must be bought in advance, though some countries allow visitors to buy visas on arrival. Following the UK's decision to leave the EU, there was much discussion about whether visas would be needed to travel from the UK to EU countries and vice versa.

Data protection requirements

The Data Protection Act of 2018 requires businesses that hold customer information to protect that data. This includes travel and tourism businesses such as airlines, tour operators and hotels. Customers must be allowed to access information about them if requested, as well as being able to have the information corrected or deleted. They must also give consent for their data to be collected and processed. Personal data must be kept up to date and held securely, and must not be kept for longer than necessary.

Responses to legal factors

Travel and tourism businesses must make sure that they comply with legislation both in the UK and in their destination countries. Larger businesses have their own legal departments, and businesses that do not can join the relevant trade associations to get legal advice and support.

Many passengers and organisations are unhappy about APD. Over 30 travel organisations have formed 'A Fair Tax on Flying' campaign, which lobbies the UK government to reduce the tax because they think it has a negative impact on the economy. When the Norwegian government introduced a new airline seat tax in 2016, Rygge airport closed down. This was because the only airline serving the airport was Ryanair, who said they needed to severely cut or halt flights due to the tax. The airport board of directors then decided to close the airport.

The UK government is making the visa process simpler to encourage more inbound tourists to visit the UK. For example, it has already opened new visa application centres in China, bringing the number of centres in China to 15. For UK outbound tourists, travel agents and tour operators advise on visa requirements and often apply for visas on behalf of customers.

 PAUSE POINT

How would a travel and tourism organisation find out about all of their legal obligations?

 Hint

Think about organisations that might offer advice and support to businesses.

Extend

Identify some of the different types of important legislation that affect restaurants and travel agencies.

Safety and security

Terrorist attacks and security measures

The devastating terrorist attacks of 11 September 2001 (9/11) in the USA had a significant and lasting impact on the worldwide tourism industry. Immediately afterwards people were afraid to fly, resulting in a short-term decline in visitors to the UK and a decline in worldwide travel for leisure and business. Although tourism recovered, terrorist attacks have occurred since 9/11 with devastating effects for the families affected and also for travel and tourism businesses.

One impact of terrorist attacks is increased security at transport hubs such as airports and cruise terminals, as well as at tourist destinations and large events. These security processes have prevented attacks and have also developed to meet new risks. For example, after plots involving liquid explosives were prevented in 2006, international travellers were prevented from taking liquids on aircraft, and these restrictions are still in place in 2019. Similarly, after a man attempted to set off an explosion on a flight to Detroit in 2009, the US government put even stricter security screening measures in place.

In the last few years, there have been devastating attacks on tourists in Tunisia, as well as terrorist incidents in Pakistan, Turkey, Brussels, Paris, Nice and the Ivory Coast. When such attacks occur, there is a significant short-term impact on the local economy because visitor numbers drop. Sometimes this effect continues for quite a long time. However, the travel and tourism industry as a whole usually recovers and continues to grow. This shows that people do not stop travelling after terrorist attacks, but that they may avoid destinations that they perceive to be unsafe.

Case study

Bastille Day, Nice

On 14 July 2016, a lorry was deliberately driven into a crowd in Nice, France. The crowd included families and children who were watching a fireworks display to mark the French national holiday, Bastille Day. In total 86 people were killed, including 10 children and teenagers, and 303 people were treated for injuries.

At the time, France was already in a state of emergency following terrorist attacks throughout 2015. Afterwards, the French president, François Hollande, announced that the state of emergency would be extended.

Check your knowledge

1 Research the current Foreign and Commonwealth Office travel advice regarding France.

2 Find out the current figures for visitor arrivals to France and the countries that generate these tourists.

3 What other factors currently affect tourism to France?

4 What do you think the French government could do to encourage tourists?

War and civil unrest

Political problems can rapidly turn into civil unrest or even lead to war, posing significant risks to tourists in those countries. If a country is known to be politically unstable, the Foreign and Commonwealth Office (FCO) will advise against travelling to that country. You can find out which countries are restricted by looking at the FCO website. It also becomes difficult to reach countries that are experiencing war or civil unrest, as airlines usually limit or stop their services for staff and passenger safety. Civil unrest can even affect services that simply fly through a country's airspace. For example, in July 2014, a Malaysia Airlines flight (MH17) travelling from Amsterdam to Kuala Lumpur flew through Ukrainian airspace, where it was shot down, killing all people on board.

Transport disasters

Any disruption to a transport system has a severe impact on travel and tourism as it affects the mobility of the population and tourists. Thanks to increased safety measures, air and train disasters with loss of life are unusual. However, examples still occur. In March 2014, Malaysia Airlines lost a flight (MH370) over the Indian Ocean. This had the potential to damage both the business and Malaysian tourism as a whole, as people may have become more cautious about the safety of flying with Malaysia Airlines, especially when combined with the loss of MH17 in Ukraine.

Health

People are discouraged from travelling to areas where there are significant health problems such as **epidemics** of contagious diseases. This is because modern travel allows people to travel so far and so easily, meaning that it would be almost impossible to contain a disease if tourists are still flying in and out of a country. Epidemics can give rise to **pandemics**, such as 'swine flu' in 2009.

In 2016, travel and tourism was affected by the Zika virus. This illness is carried by mosquitoes and can damage unborn babies. It appeared first in South America and spread to Miami and Thailand. Pregnant women, or women who were planning to become pregnant in the near future, were advised to avoid any areas affected by Zika.

E-safety

The safety of electronic and digital systems is becoming increasingly important, especially as payment systems rely more on mobile devices and applications such as Apple Pay. Travel and tourism businesses and organisations are directing a lot of IT investment into security systems that prevent intrusion and hacking.

Responses to safety and security factors

The success of a travel and tourism business or destination depends on its ability to provide a safe and secure environment for its customers. When there is a security threat, the first thing that businesses must do is improve security measures. Visible security on transport and at airports in particular can help to reassure the public, as can passenger screening procedures.

Businesses and organisations take safety security advice from trade associations. For example, the International Association of Amusement Parks and Attractions runs seminars on security. Another source of advice in the UK is the National Counter Terrorism Security Office, which provides security advice for businesses that operate in crowded places.

Recommended safety and security measures include:
- undertaking risk assessments
- employing specialist security staff for crowd management, access control, car parks and boundary security
- providing uniforms for employees
- briefing staff thoroughly
- searching visitors at events
- creating evacuation plans and major incident plans in case of emergencies
- investing in technology such as CCTV cameras.

Crises can take many forms, such as accidents or a terrorist attack. They are almost always unexpected, which makes them difficult to plan for, so businesses need to have created major incident plans in advance. A major incident plan will:
- assign different crisis management roles to senior managers
- outline who speaks to the media and when they do this
- who prepares statements for the media.

During an ongoing crisis, the immediate priority for travel and tourism businesses is to ensure that all tourists are safe and to manage media coverage to avoid reputational damage. Repatriation may be a significant element of a crisis affecting travel and tourism. Any business selling package holidays is responsible for the safety of their customers on holiday. If something happens, such as an act of terrorism or an accident, the tour operator will repatriate the holidaymakers. However, travellers who have not bought a package holiday may be stranded, although travel insurance should provide travellers with repatriation. In extreme cases, tourists may even have to be repatriated by the FCO.

Because businesses and organisations are highly dependent on the use of IT and databases containing customer information, they also have to respond to the threat of hacking. Hackers constantly develop new techniques, which means that security systems have to be constantly updated to ensure that they remain secure. Keeping IT security systems and staff training up to date should help to protect businesses against the threat of hacking or system failures.

⏸ **PAUSE POINT**   What is a major incident plan and when might it be used?

         Hint   Think about relevant news reports and use them to help you find examples when major incident plans might be used.

         Extend   What are the different elements of a major incident plan?

Environmental and climatic factors

Climate change

Climate change can affect travel and tourism in many ways, including:

▶ changing weather patterns, which affect tourists' destination choices and the length of holiday seasons

▶ unreliability of snow, which shortens the ski season

▶ higher temperatures, which lead to longer summer seasons in some areas

▶ alterations to the chemical make-up of seawater, which affects marine life and coral.

Sustainability

Sustainability is the avoidance of using up natural resources. Tourists' awareness of environmental issues has grown steadily in recent years, which has led to increased demand for sustainable tourism and customer expectations that companies will adopt environmentally friendly policies. The government also puts pressure on businesses to reduce the environmental impact of travel and tourism, particularly of air travel. Airlines in the UK have responded by investing in more fuel-efficient and quieter aircraft.

Responsible or sustainable tourism seeks to uphold the following basic principles.

▶ Minimise any negative economic, environmental and cultural impacts on the tourist destination.

▶ Create economic benefits for local people and improve their quality of life.

▶ Promote the conservation of the natural landscape and local cultural heritage.

▶ Promote respect between tourists and local people.

Extreme weather events and natural disasters

Extreme weather such as hurricanes, and natural disasters such as earthquakes can have a devastating impact on destinations and their tourist industry. For example, in 2009, flooding affected an area of the Lake District popular with tourists. The floods devastated the area's infrastructure and affected its tourist industry.

Extreme weather and natural disasters can even have an effect on far-away businesses and countries. For example, in 2010, a volcano in Iceland called Eyjafjallajökull erupted. The resulting ash cloud and concerns about flight safety caused aviation authorities to shut down most European and transatlantic flights for almost a week.

Besides the immediate effect on tourism, extreme weather and natural disasters can also damage the natural environment that tourists travel to see. For example, it takes years for destinations to recover following a tsunami.

Responses to environmental and climatic factors

Governments and, in some cases, international aid agencies support areas hit by natural disasters and extreme weather. Following the floods in the Lake District, the Cumbria local enterprise partnership provided funding for a Cumbria tourism marketing campaign to encourage tourists to return to flood-hit areas, to minimise the impact of the flooding on the tourist trade. If a disaster occurs while tourists are in the area, travel and tourism businesses will implement their major incident plans, just as in response to a political crisis or terrorist attack, and will repatriate holidaymakers.

In response to sustainability issues, businesses can take steps to ensure that they are acting responsibly. For example, tour operators can join the Global Sustainable Tourism Council, which aims to encourage sustainable tourism development and to promote responsible tourism practices.

Assessment activity 1.4   A05

The travel and tourism industry has grown rapidly over the last decade.

1 Analyse how the development of low-cost airlines has contributed to the growth of the travel and tourism industry as a whole. **(6 marks)**

2 Discuss how the growth of low-cost airlines has created direct employment in **two other** sectors of the travel and tourism industry. **(8 marks)**

3 Assess the potential effects of safety and security considerations on the operations of an airport. **(10 marks)**

Plan
- What is the question asking me to do? Do I need to give examples?
- What are the key words that I will need to include relating to each question?

Do
- I will write down the key terms that need to be included in each answer.
- I will ensure that I have given sufficient examples relating to the number of marks available.

Review
- Have I spent most of my time on the question with most marks?
- Have I given a balanced assessment by considering potential negative effects and potential positive effects?

Further reading and resources

VisitBritain: **www.visitbritain.org**
Britain's national tourism agency.

Marketing Manchester: **www.marketingmanchester.com**
The agency promoting Manchester as a destination.

Visit York: **www.visityork.org**
York's official information service.

Visit East Anglia: **www.visiteastofengland.com**
The visitor website for the east of England.

The Department for Culture, Media and Sport: **www.gov.uk/government/ organisations/department-for-culture-media-sport**
Information about the DCMS.

Association of British Travel Agents: **www.abta.com**
Advice and research for the travel trade.

Take Off in Travel: **www.takeoffintravel.com**
Careers information from Travel Weekly.

Dart Group PLC: **www.dartgroup.co.uk**
Information on Jet2 holidays and JET2.com

THINK ▶FUTURE

Hollie-Rae Brader

Deputy news editor,
Travel Weekly

Hollie-Rae sources and writes news stories relevant to the UK travel trade. She might report on the launch of a new product, interview a senior industry leader or write reviews of hotels, cruise ships and destinations. The work she does is incredibly varied, which means that work is never dull.

Once Hollie-Rae has carried out her research or interviews, she has to put all her information together and collate it into a lively attractive feature that will engage the reader. She also has to consider her word limit, as articles can only take up a certain amount of space in the publication. The articles she writes may appear in the print version of the publication or on the publication's website to ensure that they meet as wide an audience as possible.

As deputy news editor, Hollie-Rae is also responsible for checking and editing the work filed by other reporters in her team. She always has an eye on deadlines to ensure that *Travel Weekly* breaks industry news first, before any rival publications. She also works closely with the production team who design the layout of the magazine's pages in order to plan future content.

To get to where she is today, Hollie-Rae studied journalism at the University of the Arts London. After completing her degree, she worked with Archant on two daily newspapers in Suffolk – *East Anglian Daily Times* and *The Ipswich Star*. This involved covering all aspects of local news, including human interest stories and court reporting. After three years at Archant she moved to *Travel Weekly*, starting as a reporter and eventually being promoted to deputy news editor.

Focusing on skills

If you want to become a travel journalist, what do you need to do?

- You need to be a great communicator. It is crucial for you to be able to get your messages across accurately and easily when talking to interviewees and writing articles. Building relationships and communicating with your key contacts is also the best way to get good news stories.

- You have to be prepared to research everything that you are told before writing it down. This will ensure that you report accurate facts, which is a key skill in journalism.

- Practise writing. Build up a portfolio of written work to develop your skills and show what you can do. You could write articles about destinations that you have visited, or you could write a blog about the travel and tourism industry.

- Improve your command of the English language. Use English language textbooks or attend a writing course to help you build your writing skills.

- Build up a network of contacts through your current research and assignment work. It is important that your contacts and sources trust you, and this takes time to develop.

Getting ready for assessment

This section has been written to help you to do your best when you take the examination. Read through it carefully and ask your tutor if there is anything you are still not sure about.

About the examination

The examination will last 1 hour and 30 minutes and there is a maximum of 75 marks available. The examination is in three sections with a series of short and longer answer questions. Short answer questions are worth 1–3 marks. Longer answer questions are worth up to 12 marks. Remember that all the questions are compulsory and you should attempt to answer each one.

Preparing for the examination

To improve your chances on the examination you will need to make sure you have revised all the key assessment outcomes that are likely to appear. The assessment outcomes were introduced to you at the start of this unit.

Sitting the examination

- Listen to and read carefully any instructions that you are given. People often lose marks by not reading questions properly and misunderstanding what the question is asking them to do.
- Most questions contain command words. Understanding what these words mean will help you understand what the question is asking you to do.
- Organise your time in the examination based on the marks available for each question. Set yourself a timetable for working through the examination and then stick to it – don't spend ages on a short 1–3-mark question and then find you only have a few minutes for a longer answer question.
- If you are writing a longer answer, try and plan before you start writing. Have a clear idea of the point your answer is making, and make sure this comes across in everything you write, so it is all focused on answering the question.

Arrive in good time so you are not in a panic.

Remember: you cannot lose marks for a wrong answer, but you cannot be given any marks for a blank space.

Try answering all the simpler questions first, then come back to the more complex questions. This should give you more time to focus on the complex questions.

Sample answers

For some questions you will be given some background information on which the questions are based. Look at the sample questions which follow and our tips on how to answer them well.

Answering short answer questions
- Read the question carefully.
- Highlight or underline key words.

- Note the number of marks available.
- Make sure you make the same number of statements as there are marks available. For example, a 2-mark question needs two statements.

Worked example

Give a definition of the term 'inbound tourist' and give an example. [2]

An inbound tourist is someone coming into a country for tourism reasons. An example is a tourist from Italy staying in the Lake District for a week-long hiking holiday.

Look carefully at how the question is set out to see how many points need to be included in your answer.

This answer gives a brief definition (a description of what the term means) and a simple example of the term.

Answering extended answer questions

Worked example

Evaluate the impact of increased use of social media on the travel and tourism industry. [12]

Social media has impacted greatly on the travel and tourism industry. It impacts on customers because they are able to post reviews about destinations and experiences, read other people's reviews to help them plan trips, put pictures of their holiday on Instagram or Facebook immediately and use apps to find out information about hotels and destinations.

For a question that uses the command word 'evaluate', you must consider all the relevant knowledge you have about the topic and make a judgement on it (for example, on the success, importance or impact of the topic). Your judgement should be clearly supported by your knowledge of the impact of social media on the travel and tourism industry.

This answer gives several examples of how both customers and travel and tourism businesses can use social media. For a higher mark, the answer should mention the disadvantages of social media such as the problem of customers posting bad reviews that cause harm to a company's reputation.

Travel and tourism organisations can use social media to make contact with their customers by using Twitter to engage or having their own Facebook page. They can hold competitions via Facebook to encourage customers to look at their pages.
They can respond to complaints or questions over social media.

This answer could be improved by mentioning that false reviews can be posted on social media.

They can announce new products over social media.
Organisations can also measure how many people visit their pages or follow them on Twitter.
Social media can be used to keep in contact with customers who have been on holiday or used their service.

For full marks, the answer should come to a judgement about whether the advantages of using social media outweigh the disadvantages within the context of the travel and tourism industry.

Global Destinations

2

Getting to know your unit

Assessment

You will be assessed using an externally set written task set and marked by Pearson.

In this unit you will develop the skills to use maps and atlases to locate and research different global destinations and their geographical features. You will also start to research the transport options for travelling to a range of destinations, and the reasons why destinations can appeal to visitors. You will research information on travel routes and itineraries for customers using a variety of sources and evaluate the suitability for different types of customers. You will investigate current consumer trends and reasons for the changing popularity and appeal of global destinations.

How you will be assessed

This unit will be assessed externally using a supervised assessment set by Pearson. The supervised assessment will contain two parts.

Part A is a travel and tourism scenario and it will be supplied a set period of time before the supervised assessment. This allows you to carry out independent research to prepare yourself to produce a travel report under examination conditions.

Part B is the supervised assessment, like a written examination. It will require you to use your research notes in order to complete a set task. You will be assessed on your ability to:

▶ locate and understand features and appeal of global destinations

▶ explain how features of destinations contribute to their appeal and support different types of tourism

▶ evaluate information to determine how travel plans, routes and itineraries best meet different customer needs

▶ evaluate consumer trends influencing the changing popularity of global destinations.

As the guidelines for assessment can change, you should refer to the official assessment guidance on the Pearson Qualifications website for the latest definitive guidance.

Throughout this unit, you will find assessment activities to help you prepare for the supervised assessment. Completing these activities will give you an insight into the types of questions you will be asked and how to answer them.

Unit 2 has four assessment outcomes (AOs) which will be included in the supervised assessment. Certain 'command' words are associated with each assessment outcome. Table 2.1 on page 67 explains what these command words are asking you to do.

Here are the assessment outcomes for the unit.

▶ **AO1** Demonstrate knowledge and understanding of the location, features and appeal of global destinations.

▶ **AO2** Apply knowledge and understanding of the features that contribute to the appeal of global destinations and the types of tourism and activities they support.

▶ **AO3** Evaluate information to make informed decisions about the suitability of travel plans, routes and itineraries to meet the needs of specified customers.

▶ **AO4** Be able to evaluate factors and consumer trends that influence the changing popularity and appeal of global destinations, synthesising ideas and evidence to support recommendations.

▶ **Table 2.1:** Command words or terms used in this unit

Command word or term	Definition – what it is asking you to do or what it is
Analyse	Present the outcome of methodical and detailed examination either by breaking down: • a theme, topic or situation in order to interpret and study the relationships between the parts • information or data to interpret and study key trends and interrelationships
Article	A piece of writing about a particular subject suitable for a magazine or newspaper
Email	A communication that gives information and is written using appropriate technology
Evaluate	Draw on varied information, themes or concepts to consider aspects such as: • strengths or weaknesses • advantages or disadvantages • alternative actions • relevance or significance Leads to a supported judgement
Explain	Provide detail and/or reasons to support an opinion, view or argument
Illustrate	Include examples and diagrams to show what is meant in a specific context
Justification	Give reasons or evidence to: • support an opinion or decision • prove something right or reasonable
Presentation	Use software to prepare materials for an audience
Report	A formal document that is clearly structured and written in appropriate sector language
Travel plan	A structured document giving a range of details and information with dates, times and places

Getting started

The range of global destinations available to UK outbound travellers has increased dramatically in the last 20 years, and even distant countries like Vietnam, Cambodia and China are now accessible. Different destinations will appeal to different tourists. For example, travellers can visit well-known cities such as New York and Sydney to experience their unique culture, while holiday destinations like Florida offer beaches and exciting visitor attractions to suit all family members. In groups, discuss all the places where you, your family and your friends have been on holiday. If you haven't travelled much yet, make a wish list of three destinations that you would like to visit. Locate all of the destinations on a wall map.

A Geographical awareness, locations and features giving appeal to global destinations

Geographical awareness

In order to recommend appropriate destinations to meet the needs of your customers, you need an extensive knowledge of geographical locations. It will be useful to have a good atlas, designed for the travel industry, to help you learn the locations of different destinations and features.

Geographical scale

Geographical scale helps us understand the relationship between distances on a map and distances in real life by stating the ratio between them.

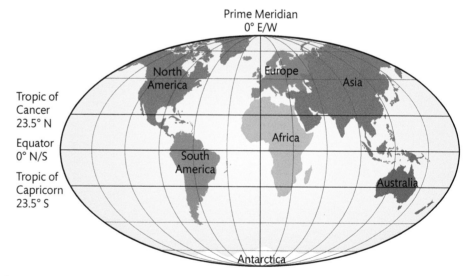

▶ **Figure 2.1:** A world map showing the continents and lines of latitude and longitude

The Earth is divided into halves or **hemispheres**. The **Equator** is an imaginary line around the middle of the Earth, where the planet is widest, and it divides the hemispheres. The Northern Hemisphere is north of the Equator, and the Southern Hemisphere is south of the Equator. The Earth is also divided into an Eastern Hemisphere and a Western Hemisphere by a second imaginary line called the **Prime Meridian**. The Eastern Hemisphere lies to the east of the Prime Meridian and the Western Hemisphere to its west.

The Earth is further divided into large areas of land known as **continents**. These are Asia, Africa, North America, South America, Antarctica, Europe and Australia. The continents are then divided into regions, such as Northern Europe, and these regions are subdivided into countries, such as the UK and Denmark.

Location

Locations on a map are pinpointed using lines of **latitude** and **longitude**, which are imaginary gridlines. The Equator is a line of latitude, and the Prime Meridian is a line of longitude. This allows you to locate a place using numbers in **degrees (°)**. Latitude is measured north and south from the Equator, located at 0°, all the way to 90° north and south at the poles. For example, London is located at 51.5° north. Longitude is measured east and west to 180° from the Prime Meridian, which runs through London, also at 0°. For example, New York is located at 74° west. You can then use a location's latitude and longitude to pinpoint its position on a map. If you are struggling to remember which is latitude and which is longitude, think about the fact that the lines of latitude are flat.

Two other significant lines of latitude are the **Tropic of Cancer** and the **Tropic of Capricorn**. The Tropic of Cancer marks the imaginary division between the tropics and the subtropics at 23.5° north. The Tropic of Capricorn marks an equivalent division at 23.5° south. All lines of longitude meet at the North and South **Poles**.

Theory into practice

For this activity you will need an outline world map, showing gridlines and the outlines of the continents and/or countries.

1 Locate and label the following on the map:
- the Equator
- the Northern Hemisphere
- the Southern Hemisphere
- tropics of Cancer and Capricorn
- the continents of Asia, North America, South America, Africa, Australia, Antarctica and Europe
- the Atlantic, Pacific and Indian oceans.

2 Use an atlas to help you complete your first map. Keep practising until you can locate and label all the features without checking the atlas.

Features and appeal of destinations

Different destinations will have different features that attract tourists. These include:
▶ natural attractions, such as the landscape and other natural **phenomena**
▶ the weather or climate, such as snow for skiing or sun for beach holidays
▶ man-made or built attractions, such as historical buildings or theme parks
▶ tourist facilities, such as accommodation and entertainment.

Natural attractions

Different types of natural attraction and landscape features attract tourists as they allow them to admire natural beauty or support activities they may want to take part in.

Landscape and topography

The landscape and **topography** of an area is a big draw to tourists.
▶ **Beaches** – beaches are very appealing and are usually a natural attraction although some are man-made such as South Beach, Miami and beaches in Tenerife where the natural beach is volcanic sand. A 2016 survey by *The Guardian* found that Source

Key terms

Continent – the Earth is divided into seven major landmasses known as continents.

Latitude – imaginary lines that run horizontally around the Earth, about 110 km apart.

Longitude – imaginary lines running vertically around the Earth.

Degrees (°) – latitude and longitude is measured in mathematical degrees.

Tropic of Cancer – a line of latitude located at 23.5° north of the Equator, marking the most northern point of the tropics.

Tropic of Capricorn – a line of latitude located at 23.5° south of the Equator, marking the most southern part of the tropics.

Poles – these are the points on which the Earth turns, known as the North Pole (located at 90° north) and the South Pole (located at 90° south).

Phenomena – remarkable things (plural of 'phenomenon').

Topography – the arrangement or relative positions of the physical features in a landscape, such as mountains, rivers, beaches, roads and **conurbations**.

Conurbation – a densely populated urban area, usually made up of several towns connected together to form the suburbs of a major city.

d'Argent beach in the Seychelles was the 'best in the world'. However, in 2019, Trip Advisor users opted for Baio da Sancha in Brazil, showing that there are beautiful beaches all over the world. Another beach in *The Guardian's* top five was Shoal Beach in Antigua, a 3 km long beach with white sand, an offshore coral reef where visitors can dive or snorkel and clear blue seas. Table 2.2 contains some examples of popular beach areas in Europe.

▶ **Table 2.2:** Examples of popular beach areas in Europe

Country	Beach resorts
Italy	The Adriatic resorts of Rimini, Sirmione and Cavtat. Sirmione was once a Roman spa and has a fifteenth-century castle, which is an important attraction. Cavtat has beautiful beaches and luxurious hotels
Turkey	The Mediterranean Sea, but also the Aegean Sea in the south and west and the Black Sea in the north. Bodrum is a popular and pretty Turkish resort on the Aegean coast with a busy nightlife. Other resorts along this part of the Turkish coast include Cesme and Altinkum. This part of the coast is known as the Turquoise Coast, because the sea is very blue
Greece	The Aegean Sea lies between Turkey and Greece; many popular Greek resorts and islands can be found there – examples include Chios and Samos
Bulgaria	Bulgaria's Black Sea coast stretches from the Romanian border south to the Turkish border. Golden Sands is a famous resort on this coast. Varna was the first important resort on this coast, and it has spa centres with mud treatments, a lively nightlife and casinos

▶ **Waterfalls and rivers** – waterfalls and rivers can be popular attractions in their own right, attracting tourists from all over the world. The most famous waterfall is probably Niagara Falls, located on the border between Canada and the USA. One of the most visited rivers is the Nile, which flows through 11 countries but is most associated with Egypt. Other famous waterfalls and rivers include:

- Jog Falls – located in India and at its best during the monsoon season
- Victoria Falls – located in Zambia
- Amazon River – located in South America
- Colorado River – located in Southwestern United States.

▶ **Mountains** – mountains are high **altitude** destinations that provide dramatic landscapes with high peaks and deep valleys, and they are popular for activity holidays. Mountainous areas popular for holidays include the Atlas Mountains in Morocco, the Pindos Mountains in Greece, or more difficult terrain such as the Karakoram range in Pakistan. Ski resorts are the most obvious example of tourist destinations in mountainous areas. The UK has some ski resorts in Scotland, such as Cairngorm and Glencoe. For outbound UK tourists, France is the most popular ski destination, with resorts including Courchevel, Meribel and Belle Plagne. St Moritz in Switzerland is another famous ski resort in the Alps. Outside Europe, popular skiing and snowboarding destinations include Whistler and Banff in Canada.

▶ **Flora and fauna** – some tourists travel specifically to see a destination's plants and animals, or its flora and fauna. For example, tourists to New Zealand may visit nature reserves to see some of the unique wildlife found only in New Zealand, while tourists to Kenya might go on safari to see the local wildlife. Similarly, visitors to California in the USA may choose to visit Sequoia National Park to see the famous giant redwood trees.

Bhutan flora and fauna

Bhutan is a tiny landlocked kingdom, nestled between India and China. Its profile in the UK was raised in 2016 when the Duke and Duchess of Cambridge paid a royal visit.

It is the ideal destination for horticultualists. More than 60 per cent of the common plant species found in the Eastern Himalayas are here. The Royal Botanical Park in Lamperi hosts a collection of 46 species of rhododendrons and many types of medicinal plants. The national flower is the blue poppy, but along with this, visitors might be lucky enough to find magnolias, orchids, edelweiss, gentian, daphne, giant rhubarb, and even pine and oak trees.

Bhutan is also home to a wide variety of animals. These include snow leopards, black bears, blue sheep, red pandas, takin, marmots and musk deer. Many more inhabit tropical forests in the south of the country. Here you might find clouded leopards, elephants, one-horned rhinoceros, water buffalos and golden langurs.

Many tours are on offer for visitors to see the flora and fauna and allow access to the beautiful crystal clear rivers, forests and Himalayan mountains.

Check your knowledge

1 Look up definitions for and explain the terms:
   - flora
   - fauna
   - horticulturist.

2 Locate Bhutan on a map.

3 Find out five more facts about Bhutan.

4 Find out how to get to Bhutan from the UK by air. How much would it cost?

Natural phenomena

Natural phenomena can be very attractive to tourists. Examples include volcanoes, geysers and auroras.

A volcano is an opening on the Earth's surface which allows magma or molten rock from within the Earth to escape, sometimes in violent eruptions. They are popular with tourists, but can be very dangerous if they erupt. Famous examples include Mount Fuji in Japan, Mount St. Helens in the USA and Mount Etna in Italy.

A geyser is a vent in the Earth's surface that periodically ejects a column of hot water and steam. Large geysers can be spectacular, ejecting water hundreds of feet into the air. There are many geysers in Yellowstone National Park in the USA as well as in Iceland.

Auroras are light displays in the sky seen around the magnetic poles of the Northern and Southern Hemispheres. In the Northern Hemisphere, they are known as the aurora borealis or Northern Lights. In the Southern Hemisphere, they are called the aurora australis or Southern Lights. They are caused when electrically charged particles released from the Sun enter the Earth's magnetic field and collide with gases such as oxygen and nitrogen, producing coloured lights that dance in the sky.

Climate and weather

The climate of a destination is the normal weather conditions for that area. Tourists from northern European countries with cool climates, such as the UK and Germany, tend to travel south to the Mediterranean to enjoy a warmer climate and sunnier weather while on holiday. During the summer, it is possible to enjoy good weather within Europe, so summer sun holidays do not have to be long haul. However, because European countries share fairly similar climates, winter sun holidays have to be taken further afield. The Spanish Canary Islands are particularly popular because they enjoy a warm sunny climate all year round. This is because they are located off the west coast of Africa, even though they are part of Spain. The Caribbean is another popular choice for winter sun as it has a hot climate all year round, and **hurricane** season ends before the British winter.

Key term

Hurricane – a storm characterised by very strong winds, particularly in the Caribbean.

Weather can affect tourists' choice of holiday destination. Poor summer weather in a destination will negatively influence sales for the next season. For example, Brittany in France offers lush countryside and gorgeous beaches. However, it has a rainy climate, and a rainy summer one year may put visitors off booking for the following year. Similarly, a hot British summer one year usually encourages people to book domestic holidays for the following summer. Ski resorts are heavily dependent on the weather, as they require snow in order to operate. If the snowfall is poor, bookings will be seriously affected. For this reason, some outbound UK tourists choose to go on long-haul skiing holidays in Canada and the USA where destinations are much more likely to enjoy plenty of snow. Planning long-haul trips in particular means thinking about time and seasonal differences. For example, if you visit the Southern Hemisphere at Christmas it will be the height of summer. Tourists need to be aware of which hemisphere their destination is located in.

Working in the travel and tourism industry, you will need to be able to advise your customers about the climate and average weather conditions in different destinations. In order to do this, you will need to find information about average temperatures, average **precipitation**, hours of sun and seasonal variations in the weather, such as the rainy season or **monsoon** and the hurricane season. It is also useful to be aware of the hours of sunshine in different locations, as this will vary depending on where in the world they are.

Case study

Bali, Indonesia

Figure 2.2 shows the climate of the Indonesian island of Bali.

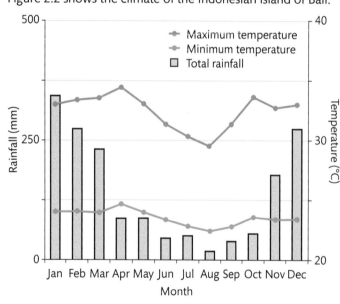

▶ **Figure 2.2:** The climate in Bali

Check your knowledge

1   Write a short blog for a travel agency's website that advises customers on the best time of year to visit Bali, and explain why this is the case.

2   Are there any times of year that you would recommend avoiding travel to Bali? Why is this?

Built attractions

Built attractions may be ancient, historical or religious parts of a country's cultural heritage. Others are newly built, such as theme parks, museums, galleries, clubs and theatres.

Cultural heritage and religious sites

Heritage sites are popular with many tourists, particularly those who want to find out more about the culture of their chosen destination. European destinations are particularly rich in heritage sites, and examples in the UK include Stonehenge in Wiltshire and Hadrian's Wall in the north of England. Other examples in Europe include the Eiffel Tower in Paris, the Colosseum in Rome and the Brandenburg Gate in Berlin.

Theme parks

Some theme parks attract people from all over the world, such as Disneyland Paris and Walt Disney World Florida. Theme parks mostly appeal to the teenage market or the domestic market, rather than attracting whole families from overseas. However, the Walt Disney Parks and Resorts have been designed to appeal to families, with on-site accommodation and rides and entertainment that whole families can enjoy together.

Museums and galleries

Museums and galleries are often found in city destinations and they are important attractions to visitors. Famous examples that are popular tourist attractions include:

▶ the Uffizi in Florence, where visitors can see paintings by Botticelli, Da Vinci and Michelangelo

▶ the Louvre in Paris, where visitors can see the Mona Lisa

▶ the Prado in Madrid

▶ the Smithsonian Institute in Washington DC.

Research

Havana is the capital city of Cuba, an island in the Caribbean. The city is a UNESCO World Heritage Site and contains plenty of museums, including the famous Museum of the Revolution. The climate is hot all year round but it is subject to hurricanes in the late summer. There is little public transport but taxis are widely available. A range of accommodation is available, catering for all budgets, from basic to five star luxury. The city is renowned for its salsa music and this can be heard in many bars and on the streets.

Use brochures to find an example of a holiday to Havana. Note the features of Havana in detail, including natural and built attractions, the weather, the facilities, the transport options and the culture, and specify the attraction of each feature for potential tourists. Draw up a short A4 fact sheet of your findings.

Ⅱ PAUSE POINT　　Give two examples of built attractions and two examples of natural attractions found in Europe.

　　　　　　　　Hint　　Looking at an atlas or a tourist website will help you to identify examples.

　　　　　　　　Extend　　Explain what is meant by a 'heritage attraction'.

Tourist facilities and amenities their availability and standards

A travel destination needs to offer a range of facilities and amenities to meet the needs of its visitors. If a destination has a limited range of amenities, it is less likely to attract tourists unless travellers are specifically looking for a destination that is undeveloped or 'off the beaten track'. A new or emerging destination may not have many facilities but, initially, this can be part of the appeal for tourists who want to visit somewhere that few other tourists have discovered.

Transport and communication links

This refers to the transport and communication links within the destination, rather than the transport routes to and from the destination.

Developing transport **infrastructure** is crucial if a destination is going to develop its tourism industry. Without adequate transport links, tourism is limited to the area that tourists can reach from the arrival airport or port. This means that other areas of the destination city or country fail to benefit economically from tourism. In addition, as tourists are unable to travel around easily to experience local culture and see local attractions, they are unlikely to return for a second visit, as they may feel that they have 'done' it all.

One example of this is the islands of Cape Verde, located 300 miles off the coast of Senegal in the Atlantic Ocean. There are ten islands, but only four have international airports: Sal, Boa Vista, Santiago and Sao Vicente. However, there are poor links from these islands, so it is difficult for tourists to visit the other islands. This means that tourists tend to stay in the hotels near the international airports, having a sun and sand holiday rather than experiencing local culture and benefiting the other islands. Local air links and rapid ferry routes would open up the other islands to tourism, and this could improve the tourist experience and benefit the economies of the other islands.

Types of accommodation

Different tourists have different budgets and preferences when it comes to their choice of accommodation, which means that destinations should offer a range of accommodation types to suit their target customers. The range can vary from **serviced accommodation** to self-catering, and might include:

- hotels of different grades
- guest houses
- bed and breakfast
- Airbnb
- holiday centres
- campsites
- self-catering villas.

The types of accommodation on offer should be carefully planned as part of a tourism strategy, so that they attract the types of tourist that bring the biggest benefits to the destination. Destinations that allow people to build cheap low-grade accommodation may find that they only attract tourists who want to have a cheap holiday and have no interest in appreciating or interacting with local culture. This will have a negative impact on the wider economy of the destination and will also make the destination less appealing to other tourists who may be likely to spend more money in the local economy.

Events and entertainment

Most tourists enjoy some form of entertainment or nightlife on holiday. This may be music and dancing events, such as jazz or salsa festivals, or a show in a hotel bar. Sometimes, the entertainment can be the main attraction to tourists. For example, many cities or resorts appeal to younger tourists because of the nightlife they offer, such as San Antonio in Ibiza and Magaluf in Majorca, which are Spanish destinations where clubbing is a prime feature. Casinos are another form of entertainment, usually directed at older tourists. The glamorous destinations along the French Riviera, such as the city-state of Monte Carlo, are famous for their casinos. Similarly, the USA has many casinos, most famously in the city of Las Vegas.

Local culture

Experiencing local culture is about trying the local food and drink, and observing and appreciating local traditions and customs. For example, tourists who wish to experience the local culture may choose hotels that offer local food, rather than full English breakfasts or tea with milk, and understand that shops may close from lunchtime until 4 p.m. in many countries where the temperature is too hot at that time of day.

Some tourists love to experience a different culture and lifestyle when on holiday. Some do not, preferring to visit resorts with hotels, bars and restaurants that serve familiar food and offer British daily newspapers. In destinations where tourists are encouraged to interact with the local culture, local people and communities can benefit enormously. Examples include projects such as **village home-stays** and the sale of traditional food and local crafts to tourists. In Kerala, India, tourists can take a two week holiday spending two nights at a time in a series of local people's homes with local cuisine provided.

> **Key term**
>
> **Village home-stay** – a scheme that allows tourists to live with a local family while on holiday.

Case study

STA Travel

STA Travel is a travel company that specialises in student travel. The following information is their advice on the costs of travelling in the Philippines.

PHILIPPINES TRAVEL COSTS

BEERS
A bottle of local beer (which happens to be San Miguel) can cost you as little as 50p, whereas imported drinks go up in price considerably.

MEALS
A meal from a cheap restaurant or café will normally set you back £2. Something a bit fancier, for example in a sit-down restaurant will cost around £5 per head.

TAXIS
A half-hour taxi ride will cost you around £5. Always make sure your driver has the meter on!

TRANSPORT
Short bus or jeepney journeys cost pennies, longer ones are a few pounds, and an overnight sleeper bus will set you back £5-10. Boat tickets are cheap too, but for longer ferry journeys, we recommend going with the bigger companies to be safe.

HOSTELS
A dorm bed in a hostel can cost anything between £4 and £15 depending on the level of luxury, or size. A single room will set you back about £15, and a double, about £25.

HOTELS
You can often find rooms in midrange hotels for the same price as upscale hostels. Expect to pay around £20-30 a night.

Check your knowledge

1   Why do you think STA Travel provides this information for travellers?
2   List prices of similar goods at home.
3   Choose another two destinations, one in Europe and one elsewhere, and compare the prices of local goods and services with those in the Philippines and at home. Which destination provides the best value for money?

Facilities for business and leisure activities

Even in a beach resort, tourists may want to look for additional leisure activities, perhaps to do some activity or to have fun when the weather is poor. For example, destinations can offer sporting activities, such as water sports, or guided excursions around the local area.

Business tourists also need specialist facilities, such as:

▶ good Wi-Fi connections
▶ business services, for example, teleconferencing and photocopying
▶ early breakfast
▶ meeting rooms
▶ desks and good lighting in rooms.

Case study

Aarhus, Denmark

Every year, two cities in Europe are designated 'European Capital of Culture'. In 2017, it was the turn of Aarhus, Denmark's second-largest city, known as the 'city of smiles'. The theme for the year was 'Let's Rethink' and encompassed four major events, 12 'full moon' happenings and more than 300 activities lined up for visitors.

The Art Museum introduced an international art project THE GARDEN – End of Times, Beginning of Times. The International Institute of Gastronomy, Culture, Arts and Tourism awarded Aarhus and the surrounding area the title of European Region of Gastronomy for 2017, with many gourmet food events on offer.

A brand new hotel, the Wake Up, located with gorgeous views over the city, showcased furniture from top Danish designers. To encourage cycling around the city, a 450 km cycle route was developed.

Check your knowledge

1 Which of the features mentioned in the case study have been developed specifically for Aarhus's year as a 'Capital of Culture'?

2 What are the short-term and long-term advantages to Denmark of having a European Capital of Culture?

3 Find out which cities are the current European Capitals of Culture. Identify the following factors and describe how they may contribute to the destinations' appeal:
   • location of the city
   • access for UK tourists
   • special activities planned for the year.

Key terms

Tourist Area Life Cycle (TALC) – the series of changes in the life of a tourist destination.

Finite – limited in its size or lifespan.

Stages of development as a tourist destination

In 1980, R.W. Butler developed a model known as the **Tourist Area Life Cycle (TALC)**. This can be used to help us understand how tourist destinations develop and evolve. It cannot be strictly applied to all destinations, but it is a useful planning guide and shows how destinations can be viewed as **finite** resources. Some communities can become heavily dependent on tourism, which means that if the local tourist destination begins to decline, their livelihood is at risk, as are the businesses, resources and infrastructure that are also dependent on tourism.

Stage 1: Exploration

A destination with tourism potential will be located at this stage, at the very start of the destination life cycle.

At this stage, there are few tourists visiting the destination, and awareness of the destination is limited. In fact, the few tourists who do visit are more likely to be termed 'travellers', as they are the type of people who are looking for adventure and new experiences. They will have booked their own independent transport to the destination as the area will have poor access. There are few facilities and basic infrastructure. Nothing has been put in place for tourism and, because there are so few tourists, their impact is not significant. The local culture remains intact and the natural attractions remain undisturbed, which make the destination even more attractive to independent travellers. As more people become aware of the destination and it attracts more tourists, it is known as a recently emerging destination.

People can be very snobbish about being a traveller rather than a tourist. Often, travellers do not like to think of themselves as tourists but as explorers or adventurers who immerse themselves in new cultures and new destinations, talk to local people, eat local food and then move on to the next emerging destination. They want to learn everything they can about the destination and try and speak the native language.

Stage 2: Involvement

The destination begins to develop, travel companies start to organise transport links to it, and there is an increase in tourist numbers. Local people may start to take advantage of the new opportunities by building tourist facilities such as restaurants and starting to offer accommodation in their homes. The local government starts to investigate how tourism can be developed and to invest in facilities and infrastructure, and the destination may start to be advertised as a tourist destination.

Stage 3: Development

The early explorers or travellers will no longer visit this destination. Instead, tourists are more likely to arrive as part of organised tours. There is a rapid growth in the number of tourists. Typically, the local people start to lose control of tourism development as private companies move in and take control of the tourist market. The infrastructure will be noticeably different, and there will be changes in the appearance of the destination. For example, there may be large building projects to provide accommodation, facilities and attractions. The role of the local government is very important at this stage if they are going to protect the interests of the local people and to ensure that the tourism will be **sustainable**. A tourist season will have emerged and there is heavy advertising to market the destination to potential tourists.

Stage 4: Consolidation

Tourist numbers are still growing, but not so rapidly as at Stage 3. The local population may have become resentful of the tourists rather than expressing an interest in the visitors. There is extensive marketing to try to extend the tourist season and attract yet more visitors.

Stage 5: Stagnation

This is the stage of mass tourism. Peak tourist numbers have been reached and the tourists are likely to look for the same experience as they would have at home but possibly with a better climate. Mass tourism, at its worst, attracts UK outbound tourists who want to go to all-inclusive resorts,

ignore the local culture and eat British food. They expect the local people to speak English and, if they do go out into the local area, they go on organised excursions with other holidaymakers and will not take local transport.

In destinations that have reached this stage, the natural environment may have been spoilt or hidden by the man-made attractions and infrastructure that are in place to cater for tourists. The problems and negative impacts of tourism are now evident. The destination is over-commercialised and overcrowded, and it cannot attract more tourists or even sustain its current number of tourists. It is said to be a **mature destination**.

Stage 6: Decline

At this stage, some of the tourist facilities start to close or fall into disrepair as tourist numbers decline and visitors go elsewhere. Figure 2.3 shows some of the signs of decline. The destination's tourism industry may even fail altogether.

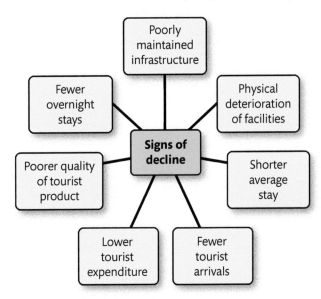

▶ **Figure 2.3:** Some of the signs of decline in a tourist destination

Stage 7: Rejuvenation

If action is taken, destination managers can avoid a complete decline and the resort can be **rejuvenated**. Sometimes this can require drastic action, such as a large amount of investment and total redevelopment, which may include sustainable tourism strategies.

Key terms

Sustainable – something that can be maintained at a certain rate.

Mature destination – has reached the stage where it attracts the maximum number of tourists and the peak of development.

Rejuvenated – brought back to life through reinvestment and redevelopment.

PAUSE POINT   Explain what happens at the stagnation stage of the tourist life cycle.

Hint   This is the stage of mass tourism.

Extend   What are the possibilities for the destination following stagnation?

Appeal and types of tourism

The different features of global destinations support different types of tourism and tourist activities. Tourists are looking for different things on their holidays according to their needs at that time. Some people may always be looking for the same thing on holiday, for example, always wanting to enjoy relaxation and sunshine. Very active people may choose always to look for sports or adventure on holiday. Many others choose to have different kinds of trips throughout the year; for example, a city break for sightseeing, a relaxing week in the sun, reading and sunbathing, and maybe a special interest holiday such as learning to dance. In this section, you will explore the different types of tourism and where they can be found.

Cultural tourism

Cultural tourism includes attending events, ceremonies and festivals. Events and ceremonies are usually relevant to the culture of the region visited. For example, tourists on holiday in Brittany often attend local 'fetes' where they can see people in local costume and join in traditional dancing. In Rio de Janeiro, the carnival is internationally famous and attracts lots of tourists. Festivals such as Exit, a summer music festival, held annually at the Petrovaradin Fortress in Serbia, and Benicassim held in Spain, attract lots of young people.

Some cultural events can also be dangerous. In Pamplona, Spain, there is an annual 'bull run', in which people choose to run through the city's streets while chased by bulls.

Staying in someone's home is a practical way of participating in responsible tourism as it ensures that the money spent goes straight into the local economy and uses local resources, maximising the positive economic impact of a visit. Traditional crafts can be revived, as tourists are interested in seeing them and buying souvenirs

Dark tourism

The term '**dark tourism**' is used to describe the appeal of places like:
▶ Ground Zero in New York
▶ Auschwitz in Poland
▶ Anne Frank's house in Amsterdam
▶ Chernobyl in Ukraine
▶ the Cu Chi tunnels near Ho Chi Minh City.

There are contrasting opinions about whether such places should be commercialised for tourism. Some people could argue that allowing tourists to visit is disrespectful and even gory. Others say that such experiences are educational and help people learn about history.

Key term

Dark tourism – visiting places historically associated with death or tragedy.

Discussion

Choose one of the examples of dark tourism locations above or another of your choice. Research it and present the arguments for and against tourism in that location. Discuss with your group.

Some heritage sites were originally built as religious sites. In Mexico, tourists flock to see Chichen Itza, which is a temple built by the ancient Mayan people almost 1000 years ago. Other religious sites still have significance as **pilgrimage sites** for people today, including:

▶ Lourdes in France, which attracts Roman Catholic pilgrims

▶ Mecca in Saudi Arabia, which receives millions of Muslim pilgrims every year as part of the **Hajj**.

Key terms

Pilgrimage site – a site that people travel to as an act of religious devotion.

Hajj – the Muslim pilgrimage to Mecca, which all Muslims are expected to undertake if possible.

UNESCO – the United Nations Educational, Scientific and Cultural Organization, which is an agency of the United Nations responsible for which sites are deserving of special protection.

World Heritage Site – a site that is thought to be of outstanding importance to the world and future generations and therefore deserves special protection.

▶ Chichen Itza is a popular heritage site for tourists travelling to Mexico

Sometimes the history and culture of a region are so interesting that a large part of its tourist industry is based on it. For example, in Peru, the Inca Trail is a popular hiking trail through dramatic mountain landscapes to the ancient city of Machu Picchu.

Case study

Cultural tourism

Machu Picchu is an Inca city located in the rainforest-covered mountains of Peru. Before it was rediscovered in 1911, it was hidden by the dense tree cover. The city was built of stone on a narrow mountaintop, bordered by a 400 m drop to the Urubamba River below. The site's extraordinary architecture led it to be designated a **UNESCO World Heritage Site** in 1983 and it is now one of South America's major travel destinations.

Many adventure holiday companies offer tours to Machu Picchu and local operators sell day tours from the nearest city, Cusco. The only available transport is a train from Cusco to Aguas Calientes, which is the nearest town to Machu Picchu. After that, tourists can take a 20 minute bus journey up the mountain to the ruins.

Unfortunately the popularity of the site has led to

problems, and parts of this culturally significant site are in danger of being destroyed because of the large number of visitors. The Peruvian government has already limited the number of tourists who can visit the city, but it is likely that further restrictions will be needed.

Check your knowledge

1 Using the internet and other resources, find out more about Machu Picchu and write a short report on your findings.

2 Research the arguments for and against restricting visitor numbers to sites like Machu Picchu. You could use your findings for a debate in your group.

3 Find out about another global destination that is based on a historical or cultural attraction. Produce a brief fact sheet about the attraction and its importance to the appeal of the researched destination.

Leisure tourism

Beaches are popular for leisure tourism as they allow tourists to relax and sunbathe. Many entrepreneurs have taken commercial advantage of this desire for beach tourism by providing sunbeds, umbrellas, snacks and drinks on beaches.

Cities are perfect places for leisure activities such as shopping and sightseeing tours on foot, bus or riverboat, alone or guided. In fact, city trips rose by 82 per cent between 2007 and 2017 to reach a 22 per cent share of all holidays across the world, according to World Travel Monitor. In 2017, 46 per cent of people surveyed by ABTA planned to take a city break.

Many tourists look for holidays where they can indulge their hobby or start a new one. Holidays are wide ranging, for example, where people learn to dance, learn languages, practise cooking and painting.

Cruises are a good example of leisure holidays that combine many of the leisure features mentioned. Different ports offer different attractions whether natural or urban and the cruise itself can be tailored to a special interest such as playing bridge.

Weddings and honeymoons are big business for tour operators and travel agents. Such important occasions require expert help and are not often booked online or without much consideration. A wedding abroad can be cheaper than planning one in the UK and has the advantage of being combined with the honeymoon. ABTA reports that a wedding abroad may cost up to £8,000 rather than about £20,000.

The natural attractions of a destination are usually what appeals for a wedding or honeymoon. Many weddings abroad take place in beach resorts. Couples planning to marry abroad have to consider residency requirements, that is how long you have to be there before you are allowed to marry. In some countries the requirement is only between 1 and 7 days so these are popular choices. Examples include Italy, Greece, Cyprus, Mauritius, Seychelles, Sri Lanka, Bali, Thailand and the Caribbean.

Tour operators offer specialist wedding and honeymoon departments with specialist brochures detailing destinations and wedding planning services.

Nature tourism

Natural areas often allow tourists to engage in particular activities such as trekking, whale watching, bird watching or participating in conservation activities. Most of these activities can be defined as ecotourism, which means engaging in tourism or travel that is environmentally responsible in relatively undisturbed natural areas to enjoy and appreciate nature.

Trekking offers adventure but can be tailored to the ability of different groups of people. Families can trek together in mountain ranges such as the Himalayas. Experienced climbers might try the sheer-sided Mount Roraima in Venezuela.

Safaris offer a great way of seeing animals in their natural habitat and contributing to their conservation; a trek to the gorilla sanctuary in the Parc du Volcan rainforest in Rwanda helps ensure the survival of the gorillas. Safaris are popular in Tanzania, South Africa and Kenya.

Birdwatching holidays are available across the world for enthusiasts and are usually guided as tourists may not know where to find the various species.

Conservation holidays can apply to historical sites, the natural environment or to animal species such as the gorillas discussed earlier. These are often working holidays where tourists are prepared to participate in conservation work while there, perhaps in return for board and food.

Case study

Trekking

There are millions of trails around the globe, including:
- Milford Track, New Zealand (four days)
- Annapurna Circuit, Nepal (three weeks)
- Inca Trail, Peru (four days)
- Jhomolhari trek, Bhutan (nine days)
- Mount Kilimanjaro, Tanzania (five days)
- Camino de Santiago, Spain (six weeks)
- Toubkal & M'goun, Morocco (two weeks)
- Torres del Paine Circuit, Chile (eight days)
- GR20, Corsica (10 to 16 days)
- Mt Roraima, Venezuela (six days).

Check your knowledge

1 Locate all the trekking destinations on a map.

2 Choose a trek that would be suitable for a family of one parent in her forties with two teenage children. Research the trek and justify your choice.

3 Say what other activities are available on the route, for example, birdwatching.

Sports tourism

Sports tourism can include active sports or spectator sports. Beach areas are appealing for many sports, for example beach volleyball. The sea itself can provide a variety of activities of interest to tourists such as sailing, scuba diving, waterskiing, windsurfing, surfing or deep-sea fishing.

Case study

Scuba diving

There are several specialist diving tour operators catering for divers. Some divers take at least two diving holidays a year.

Examples of diving sites include:
- Philippines
- Northern Oman
- Maldives
- British Virgin Islands
- Raja Ampat, Indonesia.

Check your knowledge

1 Locate and label these diving destinations and four more of your choice on a map.
2 Research the destinations you labelled via specialist tour operators and choose one diving holiday that would be suitable for your client, a newly qualified diver. Describe the features of the holiday.
3 Evaluate its suitability for your client.

Land-based sports include cycling, walking and skiing in the mountainous areas as discussed earlier. Serious cyclists can take their bikes by plane and carry their kit with them. At the other end of the spectrum Cycling for Softies provide a range of tours, some of which are very gentle, with good accommodation and luggage carried by courier to each stop.

Spectator sports events

Major sporting events for spectators are great tourist attractions. For example, in 2014 and 2016, Brazil received huge numbers of tourists travelling to see the FIFA World Cup and the Olympic Games. Russia's hosting of the FIFA World Cup in 2018 similarly attracted many tourists. Most of these events are in different destinations each year but some are always in the same place, for example, the Grand Prix takes place in Monte Carlo every year and tennis happens at Melbourne, Australia every year.

▶ **Table 2.3:** Examples of spectator sports events

Sport	Example event	Example destination
Golf	The Masters	Georgia, USA
Tennis	Grand Slam – Australian Open	Melbourne 2017
Cycling	Tour de France	France
Rugby	Six Nations	England, France, Ireland, Italy, Scotland and Wales
	Rugby World Cup	Japan 2019
Football	FIFA World Cup	Russia 2018
Motor	Grand Prix	Monte Carlo

Adventure tourism

Natural areas are also popular destinations for adventure sports, such as rock climbing, abseiling, mountaineering and white water rafting. Adventure can mean discovering a more far-flung destination or undertaking an activity like safaris or sports.

The growing importance of adventure tourism is evident as there are many specialist operators and also an annual Adventure Travel Conference in the UK.

Theory into practice

Choose one of the examples opposite. Find an example of a similar holiday suitable for a family of two adults and three children aged 11 to 15 seeking an adventure holiday. Explain the location and features of the holiday and why it might suit them.

Key term

Wellness – the state of physical or spiritual health.

Most visitors tend to be in the 25–44 age group. Recognising that this is the age group when people have their families, many companies offer family adventure holidays so that people can still get their thrills and include the children. Here are some examples presented in an article in the travel pages of *The Telegraph*.

▸ Camping in the Wild West – family camping under the stars, visiting four national parks and landscapes, water sports, horse rides and trail hiking.
▸ Iceland – exploring thermal hot springs, boiling mud pools and geysers along with hikes to waterfalls and over glaciers.
▸ Vietnam – exploring national parks, villages, temples and caves by bicycle, travelling from Hanoi to Hoi An.
▸ Morocco – hiking through the snow-capped peaks of the High Atlas and also exploring the Medina in Marrakesh.
▸ Costa Rica – cruising the canals of Tortuguero, trekking the rainforest of Corcovado, zip lining and river rafting.

Wellness tourism

Wellness tourism means taking holidays or trips in order to engage in activities that make us feel better either physically or spiritually. This type of tourism capitalises on the trend to take better care of health and fitness.

The holiday might be based around a health and fitness activity such as yoga or tai chi, or may be spent in a hotel that has spa facilities. Often, guests in hotels are hoping to detox, that is to eat healthily and probably less than usual and to allow their bodies to recover from a lifestyle of overeating and drinking. Day spa trips are also very popular. Sometimes the holidays may be a retreat, which means retreating from the rush of normal life into peace and quiet and possibly religious meditation.

Suitable destinations may be natural areas of calm and quiet or hotels with luxurious facilities.

Digital-free tourism

A new type of wellness tourism that has recently emerged is digital-free tourism. Digital-free destinations are designed to appeal to people who have become heavily reliant on technology, such as addictively checking their smartphones, and who feel that they need to escape the stress this causes. Such resorts will deliberately offer no Wi-Fi connections, no mobile phone signal and no television. This digital 'detox' is usually combined with holistic therapies and meditation so that tourists return home feeling rested and restored.

Business tourism

Business tourism can take many forms. Individuals may be travelling for meetings, incentives, conferences or events (MICE). Groups of people may meet or travel together to take part in a conference or corporate event.

Destinations that support conferences and events must be easily accessible by different types of transport, for example, air, car and rail. As well as a major conference centre, they will have sufficient hotels to cater for attendees at the event or conference.

Meetings can be held in hotels and most global chains cater for business needs with business services, fast Wi-Fi, conference and small meeting rooms. Organisations can hire the rooms for the day or longer according to their needs. All major cities have a wide range of business and conference centres. Paris, for example, has many fashion events held centrally in the city, perhaps at the Louvre or in one of the exhibition centres on the outskirts like Paris expo Porte de Versailles, accessible by metro and from airports.

Incentive tourism may be supported by leisure destinations as the people attending are supposed to be relaxing and having some time off. A group of employees might be invited to a luxury resort in the sun or to an event where sport is happening such as the Grand Prix.

Education tourism

Many tourists visit other countries in order to take language courses, often in major cities. Language schools abound in cities like Seville and Barcelona in Spain, for example, allowing tourists to learn the language but also to do some sightseeing and immerse themselves in local culture.

Students often participate in exchange visits arranged by their schools so that they get to stay in someone's home and experience life in another country. These might be in any destination but the students involved would expect to be taken on visits and see what attractions the destination has to offer.

Schools and colleges also arrange study visits to support the subjects their students are taking. As a travel and tourism student, you might visit a destination and visit its attractions and hotels to understand it better. University or postgraduate students often go abroad to carry out research.

Case study

Spas for mind and body

The Mandarin Oriental, Bodrum, Turkey
At the Mandarin Oriental Bodrum, coffee coloured beds perch around a sleek, slate pool with uninterrupted sea views. It is a great destination for indulgence, but there is also the opportunity to get serious too: the spa has partnered with a New York-based medical clinic to offer everything from one-off health assessments to intensive five-day retreats.

The Ranch at Live Oak, Malibu
The Ranch offers a body and digital detox. As a Wi-Fi-free zone, you're encouraged to hand over gadgets on arrival. Swap Instagram for compulsory 10-mile hikes through the Santa Monica Mountains and make the most of back-to-back workouts to occupy your time. The regimented seven-day programme encourages physical endurance, sheds unwanted pounds, tones up the body, detoxifies the mind, and most importantly, gets you back in tune with nature.

Sha Wellness Clinic, Alicante, Spain
At the Sha Wellness Clinic you can change your eating habits with a macrobiotic diet and be pampered. When you arrive, a medical team of therapists and consultants draw up a personalised programme according to your needs. The futuristic complex is made up of infinity pooled-rooftop terraces, suites as large as City apartments, two floors full of hydrotherapy, treatment, relaxation and Zen zones and beautiful tropical gardens.

Check your knowledge

1   Choose one of the spas mentioned above. Find the website and research the main features of the holiday.

2   Draw up a profile of the type of tourist the spa would appeal to and explain why. Display your information as a slide presentation on behalf of the spa.

PAUSE POINT   Give four examples of types of tourism supported by natural attractions.

Hint   Natural attractions include the type of landscape, flora and fauna and natural phenomena.

Extend   Give examples of specific destinations for your four examples of types of tourism.

Potential advantages and disadvantages of travel options to access global destinations

Different types of gateways and transport hubs and their facilities

Ease of travel is a major factor in the ability of global destinations to attract tourists. International **gateways** and travel **hubs** such as airports and seaports enable tourists to access a variety of different travel routes to their destination. Some destinations are more difficult to get to than others but, for some visitors, this may be part of their appeal as they are less likely to be mass tourism destinations.

Major and emerging gateways and transport hubs and their facilities

Airports

Airports measure the number of international passengers that they receive, and these numbers can be used to identify which airports are the most important gateways and hubs. These airports may receive passengers on the way to their destination. Alternatively, they may also receive passengers who are transferring from one flight to another in order to reach their destination, and these passengers may expect extensive facilities to pass the time while they await their connecting flight. In addition, some of these gateways and their host cities or countries may choose to develop themselves as a stopover destination to encourage passengers to visit the area.

▶ **Table 2.4:** Total numbers of all passengers in 2018 (total passengers enplaned and deplaned, passengers in transit counted once)

Rank (2018)	Rank (2017)	Airport (Country)	Enplaning and deplaning 2018	Percentage of change from 2017
1.	1.	Atlanta International (USA)	107,394,029	3.3
2.	2.	Beijing International (China)	100,983,290	5.4
3.	3.	Dubai International (Dubai)	89,149,387	1.0
4.	5.	Los Angeles International (USA)	87,534,384	3.5
5.	4.	Tokyo Haneda Airport (Japan)	87,131,973	2.0
6.	6.	Chicago O'Hare International (USA)	83,339,186	4.4
7.	7.	London Heathrow (UK)	80,126,320	2.7
8.	8.	Hong Kong International (Hong Kong)	74,517,402	2.6
9.	9.	Shanghai Pudong International (China)	74,006,331	5.7
10.	10.	Paris-Charles de Gaulle Airport (France)	72,229,723	3.7

Table 2.4 shows that Dubai Airport is the world's third busiest airport in terms of passengers. This is because Dubai is the hub that connects long-haul international flights from east and west, and also from north and south. It also shows that London Heathrow Airport is one of the busiest in the world, which may help to explain why a new runway is needed at Heathrow to develop its capacity.

Each airport has a three-letter code known as its **IATA code**. This code is unique so there can be no confusion about which airport is which, even if they share the same name. For example, Manchester Airport in the UK has the IATA code MAN, whereas Manchester Airport at Boston in New Hampshire, USA is known as MHT.

Key terms

Gateway – a place where travellers enter or leave a country or destination, including airports, seaports, railway stations and coach and bus stations.

Hub – a central transport facility, such as an airport, from which other transport facilities operate, such as buses, coaches, trains and taxis.

IATA code – a unique three-letter code issued to every airport in the world by the International Air Transport Association (IATA).

Theory into practice

1 Locate all the airports in Table 2.4 on a world map, and then identify their three-letter codes.

2 Identify the airports from the following codes: AMS, MAD, TOJ, LBG, CDG, ORY, IBZ, PMI, LMZ and AGP.

Case study

Changi Airport

▶ Changi Airport, Singapore

In the 2019 World Airport Awards, Changi Airport in Singapore was voted the world's best airport for the seventh consecutive year. The awards are based on more than 13 million passengers who were surveyed about customer satisfaction. The airport has been developed to such an extent that it is almost a destination itself, containing a cactus garden, an entertainment centre with cinema and Xbox Kinect room, and even a hot tub. There is also a swimming pool on the roof. Currently, there are further plans to improve the airport, including building the world's tallest indoor waterfall.

Check your knowledge

1 Imagine that you have a six-hour connection time between flights. What facilities do you think you might want in the airport while you wait?

2 How do you think the array of facilities at Changi Airport might encourage passengers to use the airport?

3 Where is Changi Airport listed in Table 2.4? Check this ranking against the latest figures. Has the airport moved up or down the rankings?

4 Where might you be going if you were travelling from the UK via Singapore? Give at least three examples of potential destinations.

Train terminals

Passengers choosing to travel by train also expect easily accessible connections and facilities. One example is the Eurostar service between the UK and mainland Europe, which has important terminals at London St Pancras, Paris Gare du Nord and Brussels Midi, as well as intermediate stations in Ashford and Ebbsfleet in Kent, and Lille in France. Eurostar also offers its passengers connecting tickets to more than 100 additional destinations in France, Germany and the Netherlands. This service makes travel by rail much easier for passengers travelling from the UK, as it means that they can book the whole trip through Eurostar and get all the information they need without having to book with individual rail networks in each of the different countries.

Other major railway terminals in Europe offer their passengers the ability to connect to other transport hubs and destinations. For example, the Roma Termini railway station in Rome provides rail connections to Leonardo Da Vinci Airport every 15 minutes, as well as to other Rome stations, other stations in Italy and internationally to Paris and Zurich.

Services that passengers may find in a railway terminal include:
▶ left luggage
▶ toilets
▶ restaurants and cafés
▶ shops
▶ currency exchange.

Sea ports

Sea ports are the hubs that allow travellers to join ferry and cruise services. The world's busiest cruise ports are in the USA, with Miami and Port Everglades in Florida ranking highest. Port Everglades serves 11 different cruise lines. For travellers originating in the UK, these ports cater for fly-cruise passengers who take a long-haul flight from the UK to the USA and then join their ship at these American ports, especially if they are joining a Caribbean cruise.

Research

Liverpool Cruise Terminal was awarded 'Best UK Port of Call' by Cruise Critic in 2016, but was overtaken by Guernsey in 2017 and 2018. Research some examples of cruises that originate from and stop at Guernsey and find out what sort of facilities are offered. Find out which UK port currently holds the award.

Link

In Unit 1: The World of Travel and Tourism, Section B you investigated the Port of Dover and in Section D, the London Cruise Terminal at Tilbury.

However, many cruise operators now offer more cruises that originate in the UK, meaning that passengers do not have to take a flight before they can join their cruise. This means that cruise ports have had to develop their facilities in order to accommodate these passengers, who are likely to have higher expectations of port facilities than ferry passengers.

Ferry ports are not as well equipped as cruise ports but still provide a range of facilities for passengers. Their locations are due to their ease of access to other countries. For example, the Port of Dover is located at Dover because the shortest point across the English Channel is between Dover and Calais. Some ports were historic naval bases, such as Portsmouth, and have historical attractions about their naval history for tourists to visit.

Ferries and cruise ships often use the same ports, as long as they are big enough to accommodate cruise ships. However, ferry and cruise passengers will use different terminals. Cruise holidays are usually marketed as luxury holidays, and this is reflected in the more comfortable and lavish facilities provided in cruise terminals, whereas passengers travelling by ferry are using the ferry as a means of transport to reach a destination, which means that they expect less luxury in their terminal. Ferry terminals usually only contain basic services such as toilets, cafés and small shops.

Transport hubs – integrated transport systems and services

A transport hub is a place where passengers can move from one mode of transportation to another. For example, many airports now provide options to take a rail, bus or light rail link to the nearest city centre and other transport hubs such as central railway stations and coach stations. For example, passengers arriving at Schiphol airport in Amsterdam have access to a train network across the Netherlands and beyond, transit links to air travel to other countries and local transport into Amsterdam. Where these local links have not been developed, passengers might have to find a shuttle bus or taxi for themselves, meaning that their journey is less convenient, and this may put off some travellers. This may also cause the airport to become more congested with traffic as passengers cannot access it easily by public transport and so choose to access it by car or taxi instead.

PAUSE POINT

Give three examples of facilities at an airport or rail station that cater for a large number of passengers.

Hint   Imagine you are spending some time at the terminal waiting for a connection.

Extend   Can you think of any disadvantages of waiting at a port?

Potential advantages and disadvantages of travel routes and transport providers

Travel routes include air, road, rail and sea. The type of route chosen will depend on its suitability, both in terms of meeting the needs of the customer and providing the best access to the destination. Travel routes link **tourism receivers** and **tourism generators**.

Modes of transport and providers

Travelling by air

Air travel is the main form of long-distance travel and it is the most rapidly expanding transport sector. To cope with increased demand for air travel, many gateway airports have had to expand capacity. In 2019, London Heathrow Airport has five terminals and two runways, with approval for a new third runway opening. There are more than 50 regional airports in the UK, but distances are not so great as to make air travel a preferred option within the UK, unlike in larger countries such as the USA.

Table 2.5 on page 87 shows some examples of air travel providers.

Key terms

Tourism receiver – a destination that attracts or receives tourists.

Tourism generator – a country from which tourists originate.

▶ **Table 2.5:** Examples of air travel providers

Type of airline	Examples
National flag carriers – airlines that used to be or are owned by the national government	Qatar Airways, Alitalia, Air India
Scheduled flight airlines – flights sold on a seat-only basis and run to a timetable, revised for winter and summer schedules	British Airways, Virgin Atlantic
Charter flight airlines – flights that operate to holiday destinations and according to holiday demand; they do not operate every day to the same destination	TUI Airways, Thomas Cook Airlines
Budget airlines – airlines that offer fewer services included in the price, such as catering or free baggage, but sell seats on their flights for very low fares	Ryanair, easyJet
Luxury – scheduled airlines offer first class travel with higher class dining and luxuries such as branded toiletries, seats that convert to beds and free drinks	British Airways, Virgin Atlantic, Emirates
Private – private jet is considered to be a luxury option	Many small businesses, usually booked through independent websites However, some adventurous travellers use flight-sharing websites such as Skyüber to travel on a private plane

The main advantages of air travel are the short journey times, even over long distances, and the ability to travel long distances with ease, especially as the number of direct flights increases. However, one disadvantage is the time that it takes to check in and go through thorough security procedures. Another disadvantage is that there are many restrictions on what passengers can take as luggage, especially if they travel with hand luggage and are subject to liquid restrictions.

Most long-haul flights from the UK fly from London Gatwick and London Heathrow, but major airports such as Manchester also offer long-haul flights. This is good news for people who previously had to travel from the regions to a London airport to catch their long-haul flight.

One disadvantage of travelling with airlines is that seats often need to be booked weeks or months in advance to get the best prices, and booking at the last minute often means paying much more, especially when flying with budget airlines. However, budget airlines have advantages too: the growth of these carriers has opened up routes to many destinations that were previously only served by expensive scheduled flights. For example, Ryanair offers flights to many Eastern European destinations.

Travelling by road

Road travel relates to vehicles using major and minor roads including motorways and road tunnels. It is most suitable for domestic tourism and shorter trips, but can also be used to make longer and international journeys.

Thanks to the Channel Tunnel and the Channel ports, it is very easy for tourists travelling between the UK and the rest of Europe to make their journey by road. From northern France, there are excellent motorways connected to the rest of Europe. These motorways are less congested than those in the UK, so journeys are often quicker and less stressful. Traditionally, for example, tourists planning to go camping in France and Spain will travel by road, and if they have booked a holiday package the ferry or Tunnel costs may even be included.

▶ **Table 2.6:** Different types of road travel

Mode of travel	Examples	Advantages	Disadvantages
Car	• Personally owned car • Hire car, for example Hertz or Europcar	• There are extensive road networks in developed countries • It is easy to find petrol stations, motorway services and rest areas • Roads are usually well signposted • Passengers can carry as much baggage as they like • It is easy and comfortable, especially for families with children • Travellers can choose their own route and travel whenever they like	• Roads can become congested in holiday periods, causing traffic jams • Fuel is expensive in most countries • Distances may be too long for convenience • Traffic in busy cities can be off-putting
Coach operators	• Eurolines is a well-known international coach operator that runs scheduled services. It brings together 29 different coach companies, including National Express, Transdev and Deutsche Touring	• There are national coach services in most countries • It is usually cheaper than other forms of road transport	• They take longer than other modes of transport, such as travelling by air and by rail • The route and stops are fixed
Bus companies	• In cities that are popular with tourists, bus companies run sightseeing bus tours	• UK services – reputable companies with regular services • Sightseeing bus tours – allow tourists to see the attractions in a convenient way • Services in other countries – most common and usually the cheapest means of travelling long distances	• UK services – services are based on demand so outlying villages with few residents get infrequent services • Sightseeing bus tours – these tours can be expensive • Services in other countries – buses can be old and poorly maintained. Passengers also have to take care not to leave their luggage unattended
Local transport services	• Local transport includes local buses, taxis and trams in cities such as Lisbon and Dublin. Underground rail networks are useful local services in cities such as London, New York and Paris	• Underground services and trams are not affected by road traffic • Local transport is usually reasonably priced, offering day or weekly tickets for tourists or commuters	• Underground services do not allow tourists to see the sights of a city • Heavy traffic can affect local buses and taxis
Taxi	• Taxis are also known as hackney cabs (like the black cabs in London) and can be hailed in the street. Private hire cars or minicabs are also called taxis but cannot be hailed: instead, they must be pre-booked. An alternative is the system of Uber cabs, which are privately owned vehicles hired through the Uber app. All forms of taxi and minicab must be licensed by the local authority	• Good value for short journeys	• Costly if used to travel long distances
Safari and expeditions	• Safaris and other road vehicle expeditions are types of special interest holidays, and the travelling is part of the holiday experience	• Exciting holiday experience often with like-minded travellers	• Take a long time if the whole expedition is overland from the UK

Research

Find out the cost of travelling from London to Morocco on Eurolines. What services can you expect on board the coach? How long does the journey take? How many stops does the service make en route?

Travelling by rail

Travelling by rail can be a holiday experience in its own right. Rail can be a convenient alternative to air travel for a long journey, especially with the increasing availability of high-speed rail networks. It is faster than travelling by road and is not affected by traffic, and railway stations are often more conveniently located than airports, which are often well outside their host cities. However, rail travel is often more expensive than coach travel, and it is not as fast as travelling by air.

▶ **Table 2.7:** Different types of rail service

Type of rail service	Examples	Advantages	Disadvantages
Long distance	• Long-distance rail services are common in large countries like the USA and Russia. For example, in the USA long-distance rail passengers have comfortable seats and the opportunity to eat in a restaurant car. If the service runs through the night, passengers are provided with 'roomettes' with seats that convert into beds, as well as shared showers. For a supplement, passengers can also purchase bedrooms with their own en suite shower	• Cheaper than flying and relatively comfortable, depending on the class of accommodation booked	• The rail journey will take longer than flying, but can often be done overnight
Scheduled train services	• Scheduled rail services run to a fixed timetable, usually between a number of towns and cities. Conventional railway travel can sometimes be a bit slow over long distances, especially on a service that makes a lot of stops, but high-speed rail is becoming more popular, especially over longer distances. For example, tourists in Japan may choose to travel by high-speed rail on the bullet train or 'Shinkansen', which links major cities and runs on a frequent schedule at up to 200 miles per hour	• There is a fixed timetable, making it easy to plan a journey. In developed countries like Japan, these services are very reliable	• This is not always the case in some developing countries
Heritage	• Heritage rail services are usually tourist attractions rather than modes of transport. For example, the Bluebell Railway in Sussex is a heritage railway that runs steam locomotives, allowing tourists to experience travelling by steam train	• Offer visitors a good day out, making them a popular tourist attraction	• They are not useful for actual travel
Luxury	• The Orient Express is probably the most famous luxury rail service in the world. It first ran in 1883 between Paris and Istanbul. The original train has been withdrawn but the name continues with a train of restored carriages dating from the 1920s, 30s and 50s. A similar service, the 'Palace on Wheels', is a venture that runs luxury trains through India, allowing passengers to visit famous cities and landmarks along the way	• Tourists receive excellent service while on board and they will have an experience to remember	• Tickets are very expensive

---

Research

1 Find out who operates scheduled rail services in the following countries.
   - Australia
   - India
   - Thailand
   - Netherlands
   - France
   - England
2 For each country say whether the rail companies are owned by the state or by private businesses.
3 What are the advantages and disadvantages of private ownership?
4 Find out more about the 'Palace on Wheels' venture and investigate their other routes.

Travelling by sea

Travelling by sea can be a convenient option, especially if the distance to be travelled is very short. However, seasickness can be a problem for some travellers, and some boats or ships cannot operate in bad weather.

▶ **Table 2.8:** Different types of sea travel

Mode of travel	Examples	Advantages	Disadvantages
Ferry	• A common way of travelling to or between destinations, such as in Greece, where ferries are used to travel from the mainland to the islands, or between islands • P&O offer a range of products and services to encourage people to travel by sea, such as ferry-based 'mini-cruises' to tourist destinations like Bruges in Belgium • The British mainland is linked by ferry to Ireland and also to France, the Netherlands, Belgium, Spain and Scandinavia	• Reasonably cheap • Stringent safety regulations in developed countries	• Limited facilities for passengers on short crossings • Some people suffer from travel sickness • In developing countries passengers should always check the ferry company's compliance and safety record before sailing with them
Cruise	• Cruises can range from international cruises that cross oceans in order to visit several different countries, all the way to regional river cruises taken as day trips • 'Fly cruises' involve either flying to the port of departure or flying home from the port of arrival. This means that the prices quoted usually include the flight and all travel arrangements are made for the passengers	• New ships are longer, wider and taller to accommodate more people and generate more revenue for cruise lines by achieving economies of scale, some ships carrying as many as 6000 passengers • Cruise companies are also introducing a greater variety of cruises, including smaller ships, carrying just 700 or 800 passengers. One advantage of these ships is that they can reach smaller ports and destinations that are inaccessible to the bigger ships. Another advantage is that they provide a more intimate atmosphere while still being luxurious	• Some people suffer from travel sickness • Long international cruises and round-the-world cruises can be very expensive and time-consuming • Larger ships have impact on the choice of ports of call, which have to be able to accommodate them and the large numbers of passengers and baggage that they carry. **Berths** have to be wider and gangways and terminals have to be higher to meet the passenger disembarkation point

> **Key term**
>
> **Berth** – a designated place for a ship to moor in a port.

> **Link**
>
> In Unit 1: The World of Travel and Tourism, Section B you learned about the ferry connections between the UK and the rest of Europe.

> **Research**
>
> Find out more about the main cruise operators – Carnival Corporation, Royal Caribbean Cruises and Norwegian Cruise Line Holdings. What brands do they own? How many ships do they have? How many destinations do they offer?
>
> Norwegian Cruise Line Holdings introduced a more informal style of cruising known as 'Freestyle Cruising'. Find out what this style of cruising offers the customer.
>
> Research Cruise Lines International Association (CLIA). Who are they and what do they do?

Most cruise companies operate international routes, with ships travelling between two or more countries. However, some companies offer national cruises, such as sailing around the coast of a country.

River cruises are another way of exploring a country or region. This type of cruising is growing in popularity; passenger numbers from the UK grew by 21 per cent in 2017. European river cruises account for 90 per cent of bookings. The river cruise is a popular way of exploring Egypt, with sightseeing cruises taking tourists up and down the Nile in order to visit famous historical sites such as the temples of Karnak and the Luxor and magnificent Valley of the Kings. Political unrest in recent years has meant that the Nile cruise bookings have declined, while cruises on the Rhine and the Danube are most popular.

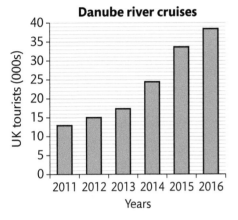
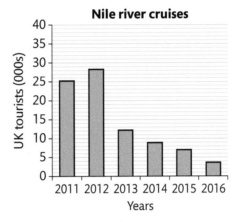

▶ **Figure 2.4:** Numbers of outbound UK tourists taking river cruises (000s)

Another form of cruise is the local cruise, which is often used as a way of providing tourists with an unusual or exciting way of seeing attractions. For example, in Vietnam, lots of local companies offer day or overnight tours to visit Ha Long Bay, which is a UNESCO World Heritage Site. All food, accommodation and smaller boat tours can be included in the price. The companies collect their passengers from their hotels and start the tour with a guided drive to Ha Long Bay from Hanoi. Local cruises can also double as a form of transport from one destination to another, as crossing the border from Vietnam to Cambodia is made easier by travelling on an organised cruise along the Mekong Delta.

PAUSE POINT   Compare the advantages and disadvantages of travelling from Paris to Rome by road and rail.

Hint   Remember that there are high-speed rail services in mainland Europe.

Extend   How does flying between Paris and Rome compare with the options by rail and road?

You work for a travel agency called Sensational Travel. The agency has an in-house travel magazine that is used to inform and educate staff across the country. Your manager has asked you to prepare an article for the magazine explaining how Rhodes' appeal has changed as it has progressed through the stages of the tourist area life cycle.

1 Carry out research into the following features of Rhodes:
   - geographical features and location
   - changes in visitor numbers
   - examples of different types of holidays available
   - visitor types and purpose of travel
   - transport gateways
   - tourist facilities, amenities and any new developments on the island

2 Write the article making reference to:
   - the stages of the tourist area life cycle
   - the key factors affecting change in Rhodes over time.

Plan
- What information do I need?
- Where will I find my information?
- I need to plan the sections of the article.
- I must plan my time.

Do
- I have sections of information in my file on each of the key factors affecting change in Rhodes.
- I have decided on the layout of the article.

Review
- My article is well presented and suitable for the audience.
- I have explained clearly how Rhodes has progressed through the life cycle stages to its current position and the factors affecting change at each stage.

Travel planning, itineraries, costs and suitability matched to customer needs

Planning travel for yourself or for a client involves weighing up the advantages and disadvantages of different modes of transport. It is also important to ensure that the chosen modes of transport suit the customer's needs.

Sources of information for travel planning

Both trade professionals and tourists use a range of sources of information to help them plan trips and holidays. Table 2.9 lists some examples that will help you determine the suitability of different travel options.

▶ **Table 2.9:** Potential sources of information that can be used when planning travel

Maps	Maps provide the geographical location of the destination and its features as well as details of routes such as roads and railway lines
Atlases	Atlases provide a series of detailed maps and information about different countries
Brochures	Tour operator brochures are distributed through travel agents and contain information about their destinations and holiday packages. Remember that some tour operators now produce electronic brochures which you can download from their websites
Travel guides	Travel guides usually contain factual information about countries, including transport links, accommodation, visa requirements, health information and a social profile of the population. The best-known is *The World Travel Guide* (www.worldtravelguide.net), but other examples include Fodor's (www.fodors.com), Lonely Planet (www.lonelyplanet.com) and Rough Guides (www.roughguides.com). Most are available online and in print
Websites	A variety of websites can provide a vast range of information. They can be very useful when researching destinations, for example, www.geographia.com. Tour operator websites provide information about their own products and services. Websites like www.seatguru.com can even tell you about the best seats on any aircraft
Timetables	Timetables are published by all transport carriers and are readily available in published form and on the internet. Airports amalgamate the timetables of their carriers and post them on their websites. Other businesses, such as the aviation intelligence organisation, OAG, may produce schedule guides for different forms of transport. The travel trade commonly uses the schedules produced by OAG, although some of them can be quite complex and demand a good knowledge of time zones and airline codes

▶ **Table 2.9:** *Continued...*

Travel agents	Travel agents provide a range of brochures and travel advice, though some are linked to specific tour operators. Examples of travel agents include Trailfinders, Premier Travel, STA Travel and Thomas Cook
Visitor centres	Most destinations have tourist information centres. Alternatively, you may find visitor centres linked to specific tourist attractions as a welcome and interpretation centre, such as the official visitor centre at Niagara Falls
Tourist boards	Most countries have tourist board websites, such as www.discovertunisia.com and www.tourismthailand.org
Government advice	The British government website (www.gov.uk/foreign-travel-advice) gives information and advice about safety and security in destinations

Potential advantages and disadvantages of transport options

Different types of tourists have different travel needs and preferences that influence their choice of route. For example, a business traveller will expect to arrive at a destination in the shortest time possible and will want to travel in relative comfort. In comparison, a family may have a smaller budget but may have the time to take a longer journey.

Figure 2.5 shows the factors that you should consider for your customers when planning.

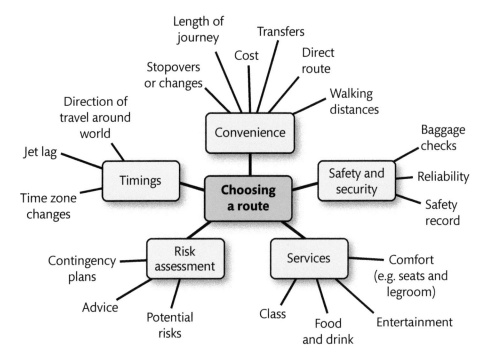

▶ **Figure 2.5:** Factors to consider when planning travel arrangements for customers

Convenience

Most people will want to plan their journey to ensure that it is as easy and as convenient as possible. Travellers need to consider:

▶ the length and total cost of the journey
▶ whether the transport service is direct or if changes are required
▶ the number of changes or stopovers necessary
▶ the waiting times
▶ any required onward transfers, connections and the transit time involved.

Convenience often comes at a cost. For example, flights that seem cheap may not be convenient, as they may involve a change of flight halfway through the journey with a long transit time at an airport.

The time of travel is an important consideration. A very early flight may be cheaper than flights later in the morning, but it might not be convenient if there is a long journey to the airport. Transfers and connections may be organised as part of a package holiday, but independent travellers will have to research and plan these for themselves. Travellers also need to consider how far they still have to travel once they have arrived at the gateway airport or port. Without planning, travellers could get stranded, especially if they arrive late at night when other transport services might have stopped running. Therefore, tourists require accurate departure times and reliable connections.

Timings

The 24-hour clock is used internationally to express time from midnight to midnight, which is given as 00:00. This system does not use a.m. and p.m., so 1 p.m. is expressed as 13.00 hours. This can cause confusion when dealing with midnight as, for example, 00:00 on 1 January could refer to the beginning or end of that day, so it is best to use 00.01 or 23.59 for clarity.

It is very important to ensure that changes in **time zone** are included in any time calculations when planning travel, as failing to do so could mean that travellers are late for connecting transport services or have a very long wait between two services.

Greenwich Mean Time (GMT) is the standard time in Great Britain. The time in the rest of the world is calculated in relation to GMT. For example, the time zones to the west of GMT are 'behind' GMT and this is represented as –1 hour, –2 hours and so on away from GMT. In comparison, the time zones to the east of GMT are 'ahead' of GMT and this is represented as +1 hour, +2 hours and so on.

Daylight Saving Time (DST) or summer time is adopted in most regions of the world during the summer months. In the UK, it is known as British Summer Time (BST) and the change is made on the last Sunday in March every year, when the clocks are put forward by one hour. The change is then reversed every October, when the clocks are put

back one hour. However, other countries may make these changes on different dates, so you will need to check carefully. The purpose of this change is to match the hours when people are working or studying with the period of available daylight.

The International Date Line is the imaginary line of longitude on the Earth that separates two consecutive calendar days. Travelling east across the line takes the traveller back one calendar day, while travelling west takes the traveller forward one calendar day. Cruise passengers crossing the Pacific Ocean will be most affected by the date line. On a map, it is drawn on the opposite side of the world (180° away) from the Prime Meridian, which goes through Greenwich in London.

Crossing time zones can cause extreme tiredness known as jet lag. The reason for this is that moving to a new time zone means that a passenger's mind and body has to adapt to the new hours of daylight, and this can take a few days. For example, New Zealand has one time zone, which is 12 hours ahead of GMT. A traveller from the UK arriving in New Zealand will have to cope with the fact that their body thinks that it is 12 hours earlier than the time in New Zealand. This means that, at midnight in New Zealand, their body will think that it is midday, because that is the time in the UK. It can take several days to adjust, and in the meantime travellers can find that they fall asleep during the day in their new time zone and cannot sleep at night.

The impact of jet lag depends on whether you are going west through different time zones or east. Usually, going east has a more disturbing impact on travellers than going west. People who regularly travel between time zones know that it is possible to minimise the effects of jet lag.

Remember that time zones extend longitudinally – that is, along the lines of longitude. This means that some journeys may cause little jet lag, even though the journey itself is very long. For example, if an outbound UK tourist travels to Cape Town in South Africa, they will find that the time difference between South Africa and the UK is only one or two hours, depending on whether the UK is on GMT or BST.

It is 14.00 GMT. Using a time zone map or the internet, work out what time it is in the following cities:

- Houston, Texas, USA
- Moscow, Russia
- Kuala Lumpur, Malaysia
- Lagos, Nigeria.

Services and level of comfort

Another important consideration for travellers is the level of service and comfort provided by the transport operator. For example, when a tourist decides to travel by air, they will have to decide which class to travel in. Those who can afford to pay higher fares will be able to have a more comfortable or luxurious journey. Scheduled flights offer economy, business and first-class options, although different airlines use different names for these services. Charter flights may also offer premium class for passengers who are willing to pay a higher fare. Depending on the length of the flight and the class that the traveller has chosen to fly, airlines may offer free food or snacks during the flight. However, on short flights, it is unusual to have any food or drink offered for free. This is because selling refreshments and other goods is a valuable method of making more money, especially for low-cost airlines, which sell their fares at cheap prices and make up the revenue in other ways.

A key feature of premium class travel is a more comfortable seat and extra legroom. This is true of most modes of transport, including air, rail and even coach. When travelling by air, passengers may also have the option to purchase priority boarding and extra legroom seats.

Rail companies also operate a first-class service, usually offered in separate carriages. Seats in first class can be a bargain when travelling at off peak times, as passengers can upgrade to first class for a small **supplement**. First-class service on trains usually provides passengers with free drinks and food, as well as free Wi-Fi and a more comfortable seat. Usually, rail services and some coach services have Wi-Fi, but they may charge extra for it. Some airlines now offer Wi-Fi on board their aircraft and allow passengers to make calls, although this is not yet widespread.

Discussion

Ryanair offers priority boarding for customers who buy premium seats or who upgrade a regular seat. The cost of an upgrade is at least €/£5.00 per person per flight. Passengers with priority boarding will not be asked to put their cabin bags in the aircraft hold. Discuss the advantages of paying for priority on a Ryanair flight of 2 hours 30 minutes. What types of passenger do you think would benefit from priority boarding?

Key term

Supplement – an amount of money paid for an additional service.

Case study

Business or premium class

Many airlines offer different classes of cabin on flights. The more expensive services are often labelled as premium, business or first class. Before passengers even board the plane they can take advantage of special treatment in the airport, including fast-track through security, VIP lounge access and priority boarding. Once on board seats have greater seat pitches and more of a recline or even a seat that transforms into a bed so passengers experience greater comfort.

Premium passengers usually receive better food with more choice and proper cutlery! Many types of drinks are included too.

Check your knowledge

1 Choose a flight to a destination of your choice, with an airline of your choice, then find out how much it would cost to upgrade to premium or first class.

2 Decide whether you think it is worth it and justify your decision.

3 Find out what is offered in first class on a long-haul British Airways flight, then compare the price and the benefits with those of Thomson Premium Club.

Safety and security

The safety and security measures on most transport options are stricter in the developed world. Air travel and rail travel on services like Eurostar involve extensive checks on baggage and passengers by trained security personnel, and there are regular police patrols and CCTV coverage at rail stations and airports. These measures are designed to prevent terrorist attacks as well as to reassure travellers.

Passengers will also consider the safety record and reliability of transport options and travel providers when they choose them. A previous incident such as a crash might dissuade passengers from travelling with a particular provider or by a particular mode of transport, even if there is no real increase in risk. Transport operators reassure passengers by making sure that their staff undergo regular training in safety procedures such as evacuation.

Link

You learned about the impact of transport disasters in Unit 1: The World of Travel and Tourism, Section D.

Research

Airlineratings.com carries out safety ratings for more than 435 airlines. The website awards stars for a range of safety factors. In any year as many as 150 airlines receive the top rating of seven stars, including British Airways and Virgin Atlantic. However, some airlines get three stars or fewer. Go to airlineratings.com and find out:
- how the stars are awarded
- which airlines are in the top 20
- which airlines are considered least safe.

Risk assessments

Risk assessment is the process of identifying potential dangers or risks. Performing a risk assessment is an important way of helping to prevent accidents and injuries. The process of carrying out a risk assessment involves:
1 identifying things which may cause harm to people (called hazards)
2 deciding who might be harmed and how
3 evaluating the risks and deciding how they can be reduced
4 recording significant findings
5 reviewing and updating the risk assessment.

Customers may carry out their own informal risk assessments about the destination and mode of transport and make their choices accordingly, but they will also rely on the tour operator, transport provider and travel agent to have done thorough risk assessments on their behalf. For example, tour operators are held responsible for the safety of the hotels that they use and so they carry out extensive checks and risk assessments on the safety of the buildings.

Travel restrictions are put in place by the Foreign and Commonwealth Office (FCO) when it is dangerous for tourists to visit a particular destination. These restrictions are usually enforced if there is a dangerous political situation or an outbreak of disease in that country. You can find out about any current restrictions on outbound travel from the UK on the FCO website. If tourists have already booked a holiday when restrictions are put in place, then tour operators should offer an alternative holiday or a refund.

Tour operators also have **contingency plans** in place to **repatriate** their customers if a dangerous situation occurs in one of their destinations. However, for independent travellers who have booked their own holiday arrangements, the situation can be more serious. This is because, even if a tourist has purchased travel insurance, the insurance may not provide cover in the event of terrorist activity or an outbreak of war.

Health restrictions usually relate to vaccinations. For example, some countries will not permit tourists to enter unless they have had vaccinations for typhoid and yellow fever, and tourists have to carry a certificate to prove they have received these vaccinations. Occasionally, outbreaks of disease may prevent people travelling. For example, the outbreak of the Zika virus in 2016 affected travel to several countries.

Link

You learned about FCO travel advice and the impact of health restrictions in Unit 1: The World of Travel and Tourism, Section D.

Key terms

Contingency plan – a plan that takes account of or is designed to cope with possible future events.

Repatriate – send someone back to their home country.

 **PAUSE POINT**   List the factors that are important when choosing travel options.

     Hint   Think about a journey you made and the factors that influenced your choice of transport.

     Extend   What are the risks that you would consider when travelling to London by train and underground?

Understanding of travel itineraries

An itinerary is a detailed plan for a journey or holiday. A travel itinerary should be so well planned that the trip happens seamlessly with very little effort on the part of the customer.

The format for an itinerary will be determined by the organisation that produces it, as they will have a preferred layout that must be used. However, all itineraries should be laid out with clear headings so that customers can find the information they need very easily. Many companies now use e-itineraries, which customers access online using a password. The customer will find different links to essential information about their trip, such as health information, visa requirements and information about their destination.

Case study

Travel itinerary

The following is an example of a travel itinerary published by a tour company. This itinerary has not been personalised for a client as it is included in a brochure and on the tour operator's website.

Highlights of St. Petersburg

- Day 1 – Fly from London Heathrow Airport to St. Petersburg. Transfer to your chosen hotel for four nights. Breakfast is provided at your hotel everyday.
- Day 2 – A morning city tour viewing St. Isaac's Cathedral, the Admiralty and the Church of the Saviour on Spilled Blood. Afternoon visit to the Hermitage.

- Day 3 – Optional excursion to Catherine and Pavlovsk palaces (£85). Afternoon visit to the Peter & Paul Fortress.
- Day 4 – Free day to explore the city.

Check your knowledge

1 How is this itinerary being used by the tour operator?

2 Think of three questions that a potential customer might ask before booking this tour.

3 Why do you think this itinerary only includes breakfast?

General information included in an itinerary

Once a booking has been confirmed, you can start to put together the itinerary for the customer. Some of the more general information that needs to be listed in the itinerary includes:

▶ the number of people travelling
▶ the dates and duration of the trip
▶ the outward and return transport provider(s)
▶ the travel dates and times, including any adjustment for time zones
▶ total costs with a cost breakdown, detailing any extras or supplements
▶ currency requirements
▶ insurance if added
▶ entry and visa requirements
▶ health requirements, including any required vaccinations or medications
▶ contact details of the travel organiser, including emergency contact details.

Travel details and onward arrangements

A travel itinerary needs to include all details of travel for the outward and return journeys. It should also include more detailed information about the outward and return journeys, such as the departure dates and times and the means of travelling to the departure point, including the method of travel, the duration of the journey and the transport providers used.

Theory into practice

Produce a basic journey itinerary for Amélie Besson and Maureen Robson who will be travelling from Gatwick to Brussels for a business meeting. They are travelling on Monday morning next week and returning on Wednesday morning. Find suitable flights from Gatwick and a hotel in Brussels city centre for two nights, and write out an itinerary for the pair.

Customers will also find it useful to know:

▸ details of the service that has been booked, as well as IATA airport codes and relevant terminal numbers for all airports visited
▸ **embarkation** details, security requirements and passport check information
▸ seating arrangements, catering and assistance available once on board
▸ travel time to the destination gateway, including the method of travel, duration and provider of transport
▸ any details about changes in time zones, if relevant
▸ onward travel arrangements, including the location of accommodation, the expected time of arrival at accommodation, duration, method of travel, room bookings, board arrangements and activities (planned excursions, tours, day trips, optional extras and leisure time)
▸ return travel details including departure date, time, travel to departure point, method of travel, duration of journey and transport provider.

You may have to create a more complex itinerary if the customer has booked transfers to and from airports or other terminals, tours, activities or excursions, and any special assistance. For cruises and complex tours, information about all these arrangements will be presented as a folder of information. This extended itinerary will also include:

▸ the type of trip – **one centre/two centre**, guided tour or independent
▸ transfer from arrival gateway to destination – times and mode of travel
▸ any free leisure time, usually if the customer has booked a tour
▸ any optional extras that the customer may want to purchase while on holiday
▸ special assistance provided and how to access this assistance.

Bookings may be made in different currencies, especially when booking accommodation. A customer will not expect to see an itinerary that costs out bookings in the original currency used when booking, so the agent must convert all prices into the customer's preferred currency.

Figure 2.6 is an example of an itinerary.

> **Key terms**
>
> **Embarkation** – the process of getting on board an aeroplane or ship.
>
> **One centre/two centre** – a term used to describe the number of destinations over the whole holiday.

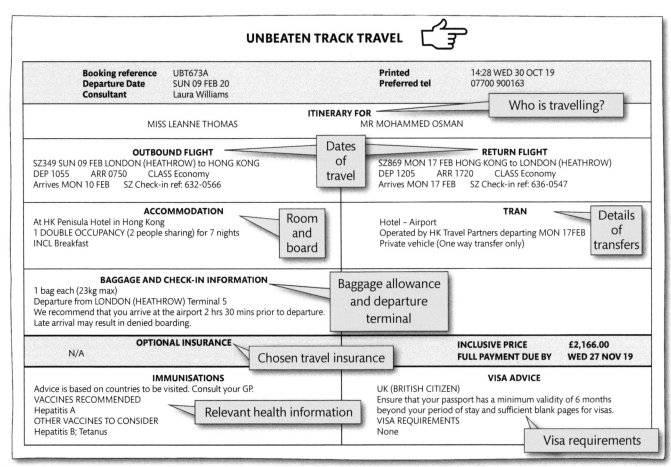

▸ **Figure 2.6:** An example of an itinerary

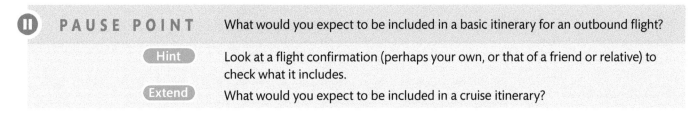

What would you expect to be included in a basic itinerary for an outbound flight?

Hint   Look at a flight confirmation (perhaps your own, or that of a friend or relative) to check what it includes.

Extend   What would you expect to be included in a cruise itinerary?

Cost factors

The cost of a holiday and transport is often the most important factor in determining the suitability of different options. This does not necessarily mean that the cheapest holiday is the most appealing, but that tourists need to know what level of service they will receive for their money and what is included in the price. For example, an all-inclusive holiday might appear to be more expensive than other holidays, but once you consider the cost of meals and drinks outside of those included in half board or bed and breakfast, the all-inclusive price might turn out to provide better value for money.

Total cost

Costs may be presented per person, per room or per night. All variations or potential variations to costs will be shown in the booking terms and conditions and, although the terms and conditions are usually long, it is important to read them.

Discounts

Discounts may be offered in conjunction with a promotion such as a sale. They may be a fixed amount off or a percentage off the total cost of the holiday. Types of discount include:
▶   advance booking
▶   last-minute offers
▶   free places
▶   reward schemes, such as hotel loyalty programmes
▶   **integrated travel**.

Supplements

A supplement is an amount of money paid for an additional service. Examples include:
▶   under-occupancy of rooms, such as a double room being occupied by one person
▶   rooms or cabins on cruises which have particularly attractive views
▶   luggage charges, such as extra baggage on a flight
▶   pre-allocated seats on a flight or rail journey
▶   class of service, such as first class or business class
▶   fuel surcharges designed to cover increases in the cost of oil
▶   a dedicated private transfer service for an individual or a group of travellers
▶   excursions into the local area
▶   booking fees
▶   travel insurance.

Supplements will be explained in detail in the booking conditions, so it is important that you read the booking conditions.

Exchange rates

The exchange rate may have an impact on a tourist's choice of destination. For example, tourists have to consider the price of visiting local attractions and entertainment, car hire and eating out when they choose a destination, and if the exchange rate is unfavourable then these purchases will cost more. Tour operators often provide useful comparisons with the UK to help tourists work this out, but

Key term

Integrated travel – booking all travel arrangements with one operator. This should result in a cheaper price rather than booking a separate transfer to the hotel or to the airport.

Link

You learned about currency exchange rates and strong and weak exchange rates in Unit 1: The World of Travel and Tourism, Section D.

Key term

Rupee – unit of currency in Sri Lanka, India and other neighbouring countries.

these comparisons are made at one particular rate of exchange, so they may not be completely accurate because the exchange rate goes up and down. Tour operators and tourists try to manage fluctuations in exchange rates by buying foreign currency when the exchange rate is favourable.

Some countries restrict the amount of currency that a tourist can bring with them. However, these restrictions usually apply only to very large amounts, so are unlikely to affect regular tourists.

Research

The Sri Lankan High Commission states: 'Visitors to Sri Lanka bringing in more than US$10,000 should declare the amount to the Customs on arrival. All unspent **rupees** converted from foreign currencies can be re-converted to the original currency on departure as long as encashment receipts can be produced.'

Find three more examples of countries that have currency restrictions. Why do you think these restrictions are in place?

⏸ PAUSE POINT Explain why the exchange rate affects the price of travel and accommodation for a UK family visiting Spain.

Hint Find out what the sterling/euro exchange rate is.

Extend How would the current exchange rate affect a Spanish family visiting the UK? Would they find it cheap or expensive in comparison with holidaying at home in Spain?

Type of customers and their needs

There are many different types of customer, and they are likely to have different needs. Some travel and tourism organisations identify the types of customer they carry and their purpose of travel by extracting it from booking data. For example, Eurostar can use its passenger data to see how many people travel on Eurostar for business and for leisure. In general, about two-thirds of the service's passengers travel for leisure and one third travelled for business.

This sort of general information is quite useful, but businesses need to have more detailed information about their customers in order to cater for their specific needs.

Different types of customers and their needs

All customers will consider the factors that you have just learned about, i.e. the:
- length of their journey
- timing of their journey
- cost
- convenience, for example the speed of travel.

Link

You learned about the different purposes of travel in Unit 1: The World of Travel and Tourism, Section A.

Customers' choices will also be affected by their purpose of travel, such as leisure, visiting friends and relatives (VFR) or business. In addition to these factors, different groups of people have specific needs that must be met by their transport provider. These needs depend on their age, life stage and other personal situations, as shown in Table 2.10.

▶ **Table 2.10:** Different types of customers and their needs

Customer type	Needs to consider
Families	Families will need enough space for their children and luggage, possibly including buggies and other equipment. They are likely to want convenient timings and are likely to want seats together, and they may be prepared to pay extra for these things. Their needs will change depending on the ages of the children, and families with babies will require additional facilities such as bottle-warming and baby-changing facilities

▶ **Table 2.10:** *Continued...*

Customer type	Needs to consider
Senior citizens	Senior citizens (usually people of 65 or over) may be retired, which will mean that they are likely to have plenty of time to travel. Many also have enough money to choose more luxurious modes of transport. In addition, they are also able to choose when to travel and avoid costly school holiday periods. However, some may have poor mobility or health problems, which may mean that they have additional needs
Couples	Couples without children may want to holiday in places where there are no children in order to have peace and quiet. They may also have more money to spend on their holidays than families. There is a growing trend for older people to take a **sabbatical** later in life. These people are sometimes known as 'SKIs' (spending the kids' inheritance)! An older, wealthier couple might fly to travel within their destination country or take private taxis. They might choose a four- or five-star hotel with a pool and fine dining Another sub-group of couples are in their late twenties, who take a year out before settling down and having families. These are known as 'QLCs' (quarter life crisis)
Young people	Young people are often students or **gap-year** travellers. These tourists usually travel on a budget and are prepared to use cheap accommodation and transport. For example, a group of students visiting Thailand might take long but cheap bus rides to travel around the country, or use bicycles or **tuk-tuks** for local travel. They may also choose to stay in a very basic hut right on the beach and go to beach parties known as full moon parties for entertainment
Customers with special interests	Some tourists go on holiday in order to meet new people. This is especially true of single people. Others go on activity holidays, such as hillwalking or scuba diving. Some people combine activity holidays with meeting new people by joining a walking or cycling tour. Special interest cruises are also very popular, such as cookery or wine-tasting cruises
Corporate travellers	Corporate travellers are particularly concerned about the accessibility of their travel options, as well as their convenience and the facilities available in the destination, such as easy transport connections
Groups	Large groups travelling together usually want to be able to sit together, in order to enjoy each other's company en route
Customers with specific needs	People with mobility needs will need assistance or wheelchair access onto transport. Transport providers should have assistance plans for a wide range of specific needs, including hearing or visual impairments. Providing for medical and health needs may include the provision of special diets, such as gluten free, well-signposted medical facilities or the provision of equipment such as defibrillators Facilities for people with specific needs can be very limited due to lack of space on modes of transport. However, communication assistance should always be possible by providing: • crew members who speak more than one language • safety instructions in Braille or audio formats • induction loops for people with hearing impairments
Children and babies	Some airlines will provide a service to look after unaccompanied **minors**, usually between the ages of 5 and 12. Etihad, American Airlines and Air New Zealand offer this service. It can be expensive and is only provided by airlines, rather than other forms of transport. On other forms of transport, parents have to find someone to travel with their child, such as a paid companion
Travellers with phobias	A phobia is a powerful and irrational fear of something, such as flying or being on water. Travellers with **aviophobia** may need additional support when attempting to take a flight. For example, British Airways offers a Flying with Confidence course to help people overcome their fear
Travellers with equipment and oversized baggage	Most trains allow passengers to carry equipment such as bikes, although Eurostar only carries folding bicycles in a protective case. Alternatively, passengers can use luggage services such as Eurostar's Eurodespatch service to transport conventional bicycles to passengers' destinations. On airlines, most large items of equipment or baggage can be taken in the hold on planes as long as the passenger pays an extra charge for the service. Airlines are quite generous with items of luggage for babies and children, and most will carry booster seats, car seats, buggies, pushchairs and travel cots for free. Travellers with sports equipment such as skis or snowboards or large musical instruments may have to pay an additional charge for these items

> **Key terms**
>
> **Sabbatical** – a break from work, paid or unpaid.
>
> **Gap year** – a period of time, usually a year, taken as a break between school and university.
>
> **Tuk-tuk** – a motorised rickshaw, usually three-wheeled, popular throughout many Asian countries.
>
> **Minor** – someone who is under the legal age of responsibility.
>
> **Aviophobia (or aerophobia)** – fear of flying or of being in an aeroplane.

Theory into practice

Imagine that you are taking an eight hour long-haul flight with a six-month-old baby and a three-year-old child. Make a list of all the facilities that you might need in order to make the journey easier or safer.

Go to the Emirates website and find out what they would offer for you and the two children. Think about the entertainment, seating and food that you will need. Compare their offering with your list. Has Emirates met or exceeded your expectations?

PAUSE POINT

Why do transport providers need to know who their customer types are?
Give examples of four different types of customer.

Hint Think about what you have read and the types of customers you see when you travel.

Extend What should be provided for a wheelchair user travelling by coach?

Assessment activity 2.2

At your travel agency, Sensational Travel, you have been visited by Mrs MacAskill who wants to arrange a trip at Christmas for her family. The people travelling will be two adults and two teenage children, all of whom hold UK passports. They are going to stay with a family in Tangier. As it is Christmas, they will be taking lots of gifts with them, although they don't need a lot of other luggage. The MacAskills live in London and can reach London airports quite easily by public transport. They have a comfortable family car so they could make the travel by road.

Mrs MacAskill says that her main considerations are comfort, convenience, adventure and cost. Time is the least important consideration for her.

1 Research three possible travel options and present the options to Mrs MacAskill. You must make sure that your advice meets the needs of the customer and covers all the potential advantages and disadvantages of the options. You should also include information about the routes and the terminals or stops en route.

2 Create a short slide presentation with supporting notes, explaining your chosen routes and justifying your recommendation of one of them.

Plan
- I need to make a list of the client's needs.
- Where will I get the information?
- I need to make a list of other questions that I need to ask, such as dates, length of trip and budget.

Do
- I have chosen three different options.
- I have decided which one to recommend to the MacAskills and why.
- I have prepared my presentation.

Review
- Was the cost of my recommended route realistic?
- I know how to improve my presentation skills.

D Consumer trends, motivating and enabling factors and their potential effect on the popularity and appeal of global destinations

Key term

Motivate – give someone a reason to do something.

The needs and expectations of customers change over time, and this means that what they want from a destination will also change over time. If destinations fail to adapt to meet customers' changing expectations, they will become less appealing to tourists. Businesses must constantly research current and emerging trends and markets in order to understand their customers and meet their expectations. In this section you will consider some consumer trends and the different factors that **motivate** people to travel.

Consumer trends affecting the appeal of global destinations

Changing demographics

Organisations must be familiar with the demographics of their customers. Demographic groups include the baby boomers, the grey market, **adrenaline seekers** and the millennials. The grey market is particularly important to travel and tourism organisations.

The grey market is important because the proportion of older people in the global population is growing rapidly. In the UK, the money spent by this demographic group (the 'grey pound') accounts for £320 billion of consumer spending and it is estimated that the over 50s hold over 75 per cent of the UK's wealth. The increase in the number of **silver surfers** and **grey gappers** means that organisations must keep up with the demographic's demand for internet bookings, interesting holidays and exciting activities.

Table 2.11 shows the countries whose outbound tourists spend the most. You can see that China is the country whose citizens spend the most on tourism. This makes China an important market to attract and, in the UK, VisitBritain has specific campaigns aimed at Chinese tourists. There are many senior citizens in these countries with a high disposable income.

▶ **Table 2.11:** Outbound tourist expenditure categorised by country in 2017

Rank	Top six outbound markets by spending
1	China
2	USA
3	Germany
4	UK
5	France
6	Australia

However, marketing to the grey market can be difficult, because advertising that focuses on age or patronises older people will alienate them. In addition, there is a huge variety in the needs of this demographic group; for example, a 55 year old will have very different needs to an 85 year old. Destinations which focus only on providing quiet relaxation holidays will miss out on the sections of this demographic group who are still looking for adventure and interesting experiences, which is why the travel company Saga Holidays has added a 'Go For It' range of adventure holidays to its offering.

Changes to family structures

As you considered in Unit 1: The World of Travel and Tourism, families come in very different shapes and sizes. More people divorce and remarry, creating new families with stepchildren. Older people with healthier lifestyles can go on intergenerational holidays with their children and grandchildren. Cruise holidays are rising in popularity with various demographic groups, not just older people, and the newer ships cater for different generations holidaying together, offering supervised kids clubs, activities for toddlers, teenage clubs and lots of fun facilities. Safaris are also suitable for families and some provide educational talks for children.

Villas are a popular accommodation option for families, especially for **intergenerational holidays**. This style of accommodation can provide the number of bedrooms that they need and allows them to do their own shopping and cooking, giving parents the opportunity to go out for a meal together while other family members look after the children.

Link

You considered some trends in Unit 1: The World of Travel and Tourism, Section C. You will also learn about the types of market research used to identify customer needs and trends in Unit 5: Travel and Tourism Enterprises, Section A.

Link

Revisit what you learned about these demographic groups in Unit 1: The World of Travel and Tourism, Section D.

Key terms

Adrenaline seekers – people looking for adventure and exciting experiences.

Silver surfers – older people who are comfortable using the internet and mobile devices.

Grey gappers – older people who have left their jobs in order to take a gap year later in life.

Intergenerational holidays – holidays with features to suit different generations of a family from grandparents to young children.

Research

Talk to some older people, preferably over 60 years old – perhaps grandparents or family friends. Ask them:

- how many holidays they take each year
- where they go
- what they are looking for from their holiday
- how they book.

Collate your results with the rest of your group and present the group's findings with graphs or charts and your conclusions.

According to ABTA, key destinations for growth in the family market in 2018 included the Canary Islands, the Caribbean, Cyprus and Cape Verde. Some companies have embraced the intergenerational family market with specific brochures and packages aimed at multigenerational travel. For example, the travel company, Tauck, offers a fun family river cruise in France, with activities such as a scavenger hunt at the Louvre, cycling around Versailles and tours of the D-Day beaches and war cemeteries in Normandy.

Changing lifestyles and tastes

There is a growing trend for outdoor lifestyle holidays, which may be linked to nostalgia for simpler times or because of adventure television programmes such as those by Bear Grylls. These holidays can be described as 'back to basics' holidays or microadventures and are popular with 16–24 year olds. Taking an activity holiday can be combined with spending a few days at a beach resort, and popular destinations for this type of holiday are Cuba, Mexico and Sri Lanka.

Case study

Aspirational family fun

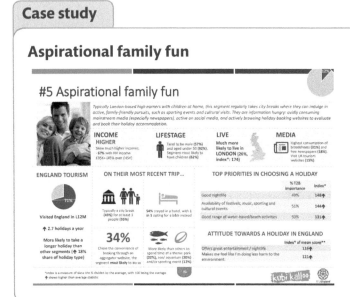

VisitEngland commissioned research into different market profiles of domestic and outbound tourists. One market profile that they identified was 'aspirational family fun'.

Check your knowledge

1 What aspirations does this group have for their holidays?

2 Suggest a city break abroad that would suit a family in the aspirational family fun profile and justify your recommendation.

3 Typically, this type of customer is aware of the environmental impact of their activities. How might choosing a holiday in Holland support this lifestyle choice?

Other tourists seek authentic experiences while on holiday by staying with local people and immersing themselves in the culture of their destination (see Section A). Some tourists do this by volunteering while on holiday. Volunteering allows these people to enjoy a break while the environmentally aware can also contribute to a community project in their destination, such as clearing footpaths, building walls and working in animal conservation. In Italy, 2000 bed and breakfasts take part in a yearly 'bartering' week, where tourists can trade their skills in exchange for a week's accommodation. The bed and breakfast owners look for skills that they would like to benefit from, such as translation, English lessons or treatments such as the Alexander Technique.

Other people are influenced by celebrities when choosing their holiday destinations. In 2016, Holiday Hypermarket carried out a survey to find out whether tourists were influenced by celebrities when choosing a holiday. Overall, 25 per cent of people surveyed claimed not to be influenced, but 15 per cent of people under the age of 35 said that they were. Hotels and destinations can exploit this interest by advertising the names of celebrities who have visited, and others even provide celebrities with free holidays in return for celebrity promotion of their resort.

As you have already seen in Section A, some tourists choose holidays and destinations that will help them to get away from their digital devices. These digital detox or silence retreats advertise their lack of connections to the outside world, such as their location or the fact that they have no Wi-Fi and no mobile signal. Other tourists choose spa or activity holidays such as yoga or meditation to feel healthier, or special interest holidays to experience new things or learn new skills, such as dancing, cookery or another language. Some, like the adrenaline seekers mentioned earlier, may seek adventure on their holidays.

Changes to holiday patterns

According to World Travel Monitor, the main trend in world outbound travel is strong growth in the popularity of city breaks, cruises and long-haul travel. Most city breaks are short breaks – around 2 or 3 days. Short breaks may also be to spas, the countryside or special interest breaks.

Alongside this growth in city breaks, there has been an increase in off-season travel. This is because people are more willing to take short breaks that are cheaper out of season because they are not priced for high demand times during the school summer holiday. This trend has also been driven by the availability of cheap flights and cheaper, more flexible forms of accommodation such as Airbnb.

The increased popularity of short city breaks can also have a positive impact on the area around the city. These are known as **metropolitan destinations**, including not just the city but the surrounding area as well. Popular examples include Hong Kong, New York and Paris, although Paris's popularity declined following the terrorist attacks in 2015.

Increased concern over sustainability

Many people are concerned about the sustainability and the **ethics** of their day-to-day activities, and this includes going on holiday. Tourists may choose destinations based on judgements about whether or not their holiday will damage the destination's environment or exploit the host community or the destination's natural resources. For example, tourists may avoid particular destinations because they feel that there are too many tourists, or they may choose a destination that is well-managed to protect its environment. One example is Venice in Italy, which is visited by huge cruise ships that are thought to be damaging the city, and their passengers all try to visit the city's historic sites at the same time. Concern about this may cause a tourist to choose a different type of cruise that carries a smaller number of passengers and visits quieter ports.

Link

Sustainability and ethical considerations are discussed in greater detail in Unit 3: Principles of Marketing in Travel and Tourism, Section B.

Key terms

Metropolitan destination – a city and the immediate surrounding area that attracts tourists. For example, as a destination, Paris includes Versailles and Disneyland, which are outside the city itself.

Ethics – the moral guidelines or principles that guide the actions of a person or organisation.

Motivating and enabling factors affecting the appeal of global destinations

It is important to consider consumer trends, such as changes in demographics and behaviours, alongside tourists' motivations for travel.

Motivating factors

It is important to target the right products and services at the right people. This means that different types of holidays are aimed at groups of people who have similar motivations for travel.

Traditionally, tour operators separate markets by destination. For example, they will produce one brochure for the USA as a destination, another for Spain, another for European beach areas and so on. However, as tourists become more sophisticated and well-travelled, they are less likely to choose their holiday by destination but also by considering what they want to do when they are on holiday. These are their motivating factors.

This means that tourists are motivated to choose a destination by the leisure experience that they want to have, such as:

▶ relaxing on a beach in the sun, motivated by a desire to unwind and sunbathe

▶ sporting activities such as skiing or cycling or adventurous activities such as diving or trekking, motivated by the desire to learn a new skill, indulge in a hobby or have some excitement

▶ exploring a city and its culture, motivated by a desire to learn and see different sights, or to shop and eat out in restaurants.

However, different tourists on holiday at the same resort do not necessarily have the same motivations for being there. It is also worth remembering that a trip or holiday may be chosen as a result of a range of motivating factors behind it. For example, football fans who visited Rio de Janeiro for the Olympic Games in 2016 might have been motivated by a desire to see their favourite sports, a wish to see a new country and also to experience its culture.

Visitor motivations include the following.

▶ **Wanderlust** – the desire to travel and see other cultures and experience how other people live. Gap-year students often express a wish 'to travel' and what they usually mean is that they want to meet new people, see places and enjoy new experiences.

▶ **Sunlust** – the desire to go somewhere warm and escape from their home climate for a while.

▶ **Rest and relaxation** – many tourists want a holiday as a break from work, which may motivate them to choose a simple beach holiday for relaxation in the sun or a spa holiday that focuses on health, rest and well-being.

▶ **Escape** – tourists may want to escape temporarily from their job, family or home life, climate and everyday experiences.

▶ **Socialisation with friends** – groups may choose to go on holiday as a means of meeting up with friends or spectating at a particular event such as the football World Cup, or they may do so for special events such as hen or stag parties.

▶ **Prestige** – some people enjoy spending time at a luxury resort or visiting a newly emerging destination because of the prestige associated with these activities.

▶ **Special occasions** – some people choose to get married abroad, often in places that are naturally beautiful or that have a good climate. Many special occasion holidays take place in beach resorts, as they can provide the necessary facilities such as catering and accommodation, especially if there are guests who all want to stay in the same hotel.

▶ **Culture and history** – many tourists are motivated to visit a destination in order to see historic architecture or experience the arts and music. More widely, many tourists want to experience the language, lifestyle and food and drink offered by another culture.

Another motivating factor that may be considered is the tourist's purpose of travel. For example, the desire to see friends and family leads to VFR tourism, the need to attend a conference leads to business tourism and the desire to learn a new language leads to educational tourism.

❚❚ PAUSE POINT Explain why the grey market is so important to travel and tourism organisations.

Hint Think about what age group this is, how many people there are in this age group and what they like to do.

Extend Describe another demographic group and evaluate their importance to the travel and tourism industry.

Case study

UK outbound tourists

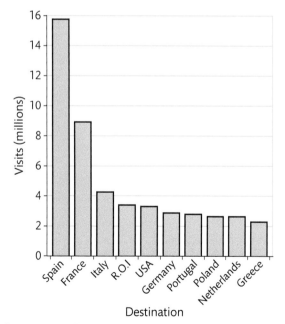

▶ **Figure 2.7:** Outbound visits from the UK listed by destination in 2017

Figure 2.7 shows outbound visits from the UK by the country of destination.

Check your knowledge

1 Why do you think most UK outbound travellers choose to visit European destinations?
2 What could be the motivations for tourists to visit Spain?
3 Why do you think Poland is in the top ten destinations for UK outbound tourists?
4 What do you think is the main purpose of travel for a UK tourist to Poland?

* R.O.I – Republic of Ireland

Enabling factors

Enabling factors are the things that allow tourists to follow their motivations and visit a destination.

▶ **Having enough time and money** – tourists can only visit a destination if they can afford it. For most people, this means having a job, which also means having little time for holidays – most people have four or five weeks holiday a year, often plus bank holidays. Sometimes this is described as being 'money rich and time poor', because these people have the money to travel but not the time. In comparison, students are often 'time rich' but also 'money poor', which has an impact on their travel arrangements. This is known as the 'leisure paradox'.

▶ **Availability of travel** – how easy is it to get to the destination? What transport and communication links exist at the destination? Destinations will invest in their infrastructure in order to attract tourists.

▶ **Availability of suitable product or holiday type** – if a tourist wants to go on a package holiday they will only go to destinations targeted by package holidays. They are unlikely to go to newly emerging destinations as it is unlikely that a package holiday will exist for that destination.

▶ **Influence of destination marketing** – potential tourists are targeted by advertisements, special offers and articles in the press, which are all designed to entice customers to a particular destination.

▶ **Consumer confidence** – if customers have a lot of confidence in a destination, they are more likely to visit it. This may be affected by positive and negative customer reviews, as well as by incidents reported in the media.

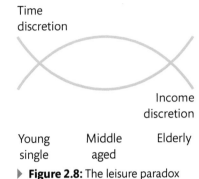

▶ **Figure 2.8:** The leisure paradox

 PAUSE POINT   Explain your own motivations for travelling on your last trip.

> Hint   Use the list of motivating factors to help you. Consider what you were thinking or feeling when you arranged your trip.

> Extend   Now consider the enabling factors that allowed you to make that trip. Explain each of the factors.

E   Factors affecting the changing popularity and appeal of destinations

Destination managers try to be aware of and react to changing consumer trends, but they cannot control these trends. Many other factors affect the appeal of destinations and, while some of these factors can be controlled by **stakeholders** in those destinations, some factors cannot. In Unit 1: The World of Travel and Tourism, you saw how many factors affect travel and tourism organisations. Here, you will consider how similar factors affect destinations.

> **Key term**
>
> **Stakeholder** – someone with an interest in the operations of a business or industry.

Political factors

A country that hopes to attract tourists must try to arrange its tourism policies and relevant legislation in order to make the destination seem appealing and welcoming to inbound tourists.

Legislation

Legislation is often needed to support tourism and protect the local communities. For example, a country may need to amend existing legislation about land ownership in order to ensure that the land and assets in a destination cannot all be bought by foreign investors, as this will help to protect the interests of the local community.

Trinidad and Tobago in the Caribbean introduced the Tourism Development Act, which brought in tax benefits designed to encourage tourism and measures to protect national ownership of development projects.

Tourism policy

All countries wishing to promote tourism have a tourism policy. The policy is interpreted and implemented by tourist boards like VisitBritain. These tourist boards determine which markets to target and organise promotions for these markets. They also co-ordinate destination management.

For example, the New Zealand tourism board, Tourism New Zealand, has determined the policy for growing international tourism by 2025. The five main themes of the policy are:
- **air connectivity** – improving air travel as around 99 per cent of international visitors arrive by air
- **targeting for value** – identifying opportunities that deliver the biggest economic benefit
- **visitor experience** – improving visitors' experience so that visitors stay longer, travel more widely and spend more
- **productivity** – improving tourism productivity for existing investments and attracting new investments
- **insights** – driving strategic and operational decision-making for tourism businesses.

Target markets and promotion

Governments sometimes target specific markets and offer their tourists special promotions or relax entry requirements. They may choose these markets because they have fast-growing economies, meaning that they could be a lucrative source of tourism income. Alternatively, these markets may be chosen because travel restrictions from the generating country have been relaxed, allowing their tourists to visit the destination that is marketing itself. You can find examples of such promotions at the VisitBritain website. For example, at the end of 2016 India launched a promotion at the World Travel Market in London, termed 'India – the Land of Eternal Heritage', highlighting the variety of experiences to be enjoyed in India. The government was also expanding its e-visa scheme to make it easier for tourists to enter the country.

Destination management affects the way in which a country promotes tourism and who it targets in its marketing activities. The government of a country usually controls destination management, but works with partner organisations. For example, in Mexico the Mexican Tourism Board is in charge of promoting the destinations and activities on offer in Mexico.

Visa requirements or travel permits

Countries may require incoming tourists to have a visa, usually to help control their borders or raise revenue from incoming tourists. However, visas and travel permits can form a barrier to travel because of the expense and the difficulty of acquiring one. Destinations can make it easier for particular groups or nationalities of tourists to travel by lowering the cost of visas or allowing them to buy electronic visas online.

Compatible travel arrangements

Governments have to ensure that the way in which visitors are allowed into countries is compatible with legislation. For example, within the European Union (EU), there is a policy of free travel, meaning that anyone with a European passport has the right to enter any other European country. This means that UK citizens may enter other EU nations without having to purchase a visa. However, these arrangements can change. For example, after the UK leaves the EU, UK citizens may not have freedom of movement in Europe, and this would have an impact on travel and tourism.

Research

A series of terrorist attacks in Paris in 2015 had a heavy impact on the city's tourist industry. As a result, a €23 million investment was announced, backing a series of measures to entice tourists back. For example, the plan intended to recruit English-speaking volunteers to provide information at strategic points around the city, offer English lessons to taxi drivers and launch a new tourist website and app called 'Welcome to Paris'.

Investigate the reasons for the decline in tourists to Paris. Find out the statistics for decline in the number of tourists.

Safety and security

Political problems in a country may cause war, civil unrest, violent demonstrations or other dangers that may make it less appealing as a tourist destination. This decline in appeal may be short term, or it may have a longer-term impact. If a country is known to be politically unstable, the UK government will advise against travelling to the area. You can find out which countries are restricted by looking at the FCO website. It is more difficult to reach countries that are suffering political unrest because airlines will limit or stop their services in order to protect their passengers and staff. For example, flights to Sharm el Sheik in Egypt were suspended in 2015 following a suspected terrorist incident. It is useful to note that travel insurance policies are invalid if the travel is against FCO advice.

 **PAUSE POINT**   Give examples of two political factors that affect the popularity of a destination. Explain how they do so.

> Hint   Political factors are usually to do with legislation, regulations or government policy.
> Extend   Does the FCO advise against travelling to Columbia, Egypt and Somalia? If so, why?

Economic climate

Strong economic growth in a country leads to a growth in travel from that country. This is because people have more disposable income, which they can choose to spend on leisure travel. In addition, when there are strong global economic conditions companies may start to operate in new countries, which causes their employees to travel more on business.

In comparison, during recessions people have less money to spend on holidays and so they may choose cheaper destinations or destinations that are closer to home to save on transport costs. A recession can affect a number of countries worldwide, particularly through its impact on tourism.

Exchange rates

The UK economy is one of the strongest in Europe, and when the UK economy is doing well, the pound is strong against other currencies. This means that outbound tourists from the UK can buy more euros, dollars or other currency and get more of it for their pounds sterling, resulting in more spending money whilst they are away. When the pound is weak against other currencies, outbound tourists can buy less foreign currency and so travelling abroad becomes more expensive.

When the economic situation is good, the number of outbound trips made by UK residents and other Europeans increases. However, if tourists are worried about security, they may choose destinations that they perceive to be safer or take a **staycation**, even if they could get better value for money elsewhere.

The introduction of the euro had a great impact on tourism within Eurozone countries. This is because tourists can travel between Eurozone countries without having to change currency and can expect less variation in prices as they travel. There are even advantages for UK outbound tourists because it means that, if they are visiting a number of Eurozone countries, they only need to change their pounds into euros rather than into a number of different currencies.

Currency fluctuations

Many of the costs paid for by tour operators are in foreign currencies, usually euros or dollars. Examples of these costs include accommodation, airport charges and

> **Key term**
>
> **Staycation** – domestic tourists taking a holiday or day trips in the UK rather than holidaying abroad.

> **Link**
>
> You learned about exchange rates and the impact of exchange rates on travel and tourism in Unit 1: The World of Travel and Tourism, Section D.

transport. When the exchange rate varies, tour operators may have to pay more or less than they had originally calculated. The price of oil also varies, and this can have a significant impact on the price of air travel.

Case study

Greek recession

Greece has been through a great deal of political and economic turmoil over recent years. The country's gross domestic product (GDP) reduced by 26 per cent during the world recession between 2008 and 2014, and Greek employment dropped in the same period by 23 per cent. However, international tourist arrivals increased by 38 per cent and tourist receipts by 12 per cent at the same time.

There were various reasons for this growth in tourism. Political problems in North Africa made destinations in Tunisia, Morocco and Egypt less appealing. In addition,

the Greek government understood the importance of tourism to the economy and eased visa requirements, particularly for Russian visitors. Aegean Airlines, a Greek airline, invested in new planes and routes to link different cities to destinations in Greece and new hotels were built.

Check your knowledge

1   Explain some of the problems that affected Greece during the recession of 2008–2014.
2   Explain why tourism to Greece was strong despite the recession.
3   What other political issues have affected tourism in Greece?

PAUSE POINT

Write your own definitions for the terms 'recession', 'disposable income' and 'exchange rate'.

Hint

Try to write your definitions without looking back at the previous pages but, if you get stuck, you will find definitions in the text.

Extend

What happens to tourism when a country's economy is doing well?

Cost of visiting

The price of a holiday is very important when choosing a destination. The cost is determined by the chosen method of transport, the cost of living in the destination and the standard of accommodation required. Some countries have a higher cost of living than others, which makes a significant difference to the overall amount spent on a holiday in that destination. For example, food and drink in Thailand usually seems very cheap to tourists whereas visitors to Norway may find its food and drink expensive.

Accessibility and availability

Accessibility refers to the ease with which tourists can access gateways to the destination, and the travel and transport routes to those gateways. Destinations with a good transport infrastructure are more accessible and so they are more popular with tourists than destinations with poor connections.

Accessibility is not just about a gateway airport or seaport being close to the destination. It also considers the degree of access that someone from the tourist-generating region has to the destination. For example, New York has regular flights from London, but someone living in Newcastle would either have to travel to London to take a flight to New York or may have to fly with a change at an airport like Dublin. The UK remains one of the best-connected countries for international tourism, with hundreds of air routes, sea routes and the Channel Tunnel. The accessibility of long-haul destinations is also increasing due to the wider availability of new aircraft that are cheaper to run.

Once a tourist reaches a destination, the least that they require is basic facilities such as local transport, accommodation and things to do or attractions to see. The destination has to develop these amenities, as well as transport and utilities such as running water, waste management and electricity. These utilities are considered to be basic in the western world but are not always available in developing countries, and this means that hotel operators have to work with destination management organisations to determine how these utilities will be provided.

Sometimes, tourists have to accept that facilities will not be as luxurious as they are used to. For example, in Greece it is still usual to put toilet paper in a waste bin as it cannot be flushed away efficiently. Water scarcity is another problem that affects many countries around the world and may have an impact on tourists' experiences. Tourism often consumes a lot of water, especially if facilities like golf courses are provided as they need watering.

Case study

St Helena

▶ St Helena

St Helena is a remote island in the South Atlantic and a British Overseas Territory. Tourists visit the island for its natural attractions, especially Diana's Peak National Park, which is home to 50 species of plants and 217 invertebrate species unique to the island.

St Helena is the island where Napoleon was exiled in the 19th century, so there are several properties connected with him for people who are interested in history. There is a handful of hotels and guest houses with only 150

rooms. Most tourists used to arrive by mailboat from South Africa, which takes five days, or by yacht at the harbour in James Bay.

When plans to build an airport were announced, the island community had hopes of attracting many more tourists, mainly from South Africa, as flying would reduce the journey time from South Africa to five hours. As a result of the plans, the tour operator TUI planned to start packages from London in 2017. The airport was built by 2016 and opened in May 2016. However, the first aircraft to land experienced severe turbulence problems which delayed the start of weekly flights until December 2018.

Check your knowledge

1 What are the motivating factors for tourists who visit St Helena?

2 How has accessibility affected the development of tourism in St Helena?

3 Find out what has happened to the airport at St Helena.

PAUSE POINT Explain why the UK is very well-connected in a way that allows access to international tourism.

> Hint Think about ports, airports and air routes.

> Extend What amenities, other than transport, would a destination need to develop in order to attract tourists?

Image and promotion

Publicity

The way in which a destination is promoted has a major impact on its popularity and appeal. National tourist boards spend a great deal on marketing to attract tourists, targeting specific countries that they think are lucrative markets. These promotions give the message of what is available in terms of accommodation, attractions and facilities. For example, Tourism Australia has offices in London and Frankfurt and focuses its efforts on campaigns in the UK, Germany, France and Italy. Promotional campaigns use a large range of media including press, digital or online and television.

Other media

Destinations can also be promoted through other types of media presence, such as in films and television programmes. Films and documentaries increase interest in a destination and can be exploited to appeal to potential tourists. For example, lots of tourists in Bruges want to see where Colin Farrell stayed when he was making the film 'In Bruges' and look for the settings from the film. In Palermo, Sicily, tourists take photos on the steps of the Teatro Massimo, recreating a famous scene from The Godfather. Conferences are often held discussing film tourism, for example in Barcelona and Croatia, as it is recognised that millions of tourists make their choice of destination after seeing a film or documentary shot or set in that destination.

International events, conferences and exhibitions appeal to business travellers and are an important contribution to global economies. These are usually about specialist subjects, such as the International Conference on Sustainable Development held in New York. The best known travel and tourism event in the UK is the World Travel Market (WTM) held annually in November in London. It attracts thousands of visitors from around the world and is an opportunity to find out about new developments in the industry and network with colleagues.

Link

You learned about the significance of film and television in promoting destinations in Unit 1: The World of Travel and Tourism, Section D.

PAUSE POINT

Think about films that you have seen in which the locations have made you want to travel to that destination. What is appealing about the destination and how would you be able to access it?

Hint For inspiration, discuss with your group some of the films that you have seen recently and list their locations.

Extend How could television programmes make destinations seem more appealing to potential tourists?

Changing markets

Emerging markets and emerging tourist-generating regions

New destinations emerge as countries realise the economic importance of tourism and start to develop their tourism industry. In the previous section, you learned about St Helena's efforts to encourage tourists to visit. Once potential tourists realise that new destinations are accessible, many people are keen to try visiting a new destination.

Emerging destinations

▶ Gabon

- Gabon is an African nation with jungle landscapes and a range of wildlife such as gorillas and elephants.

Gabon hosted the 2017 African Nations Cup, which promoted the country to potential tourists.

- Japan is becoming more popular as a tourist destination, with further developments to its transport infrastructure and additional flights from Europe. Its unique culture is particularly attractive to tourists.
- Alaska currently attracts few tourists, despite its national parks, stunning scenery and wildlife. Glacier Bay is part of a UNESCO World Heritage Site and can be accessed by small ship.

Check your knowledge

Choose one of the destinations described above. Produce a fact sheet on what the destination has to offer an outbound UK tourist and explain how they would reach the destination. Share your findings with your group.

The major tourist-generating countries are Germany, the USA and the UK. Emerging tourist-generating regions are countries and areas whose economies are growing enough that the population can spend its money on outbound travel and where people have international freedom of movement. For example, in China the government has eased its restrictions, allowing Chinese people to travel outside their own country at a time when their economy is growing at a phenomenal rate.

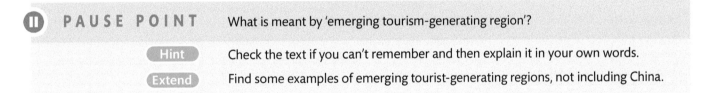

PAUSE POINT   What is meant by 'emerging tourism-generating region'?

Hint   Check the text if you can't remember and then explain it in your own words.

Extend   Find some examples of emerging tourist-generating regions, not including China.

Natural disasters

A natural disaster is a natural event that causes damage to buildings and loss of life, such as:

▶ volcanic eruptions, where molten rock is violently expelled from volcanoes
▶ earthquakes, where the ground shakes due to the movement of rock masses deep in the Earth's crust
▶ tsunamis, which are huge sea waves caused by earthquakes or other disruptions
▶ landslides, where a mass of earth or rock falls down a steep slope
▶ avalanches, where a mass of snow and ice falls rapidly down a steep slope or mountainside.

After a natural disaster has occurred, tourists immediately avoid that destination because:

▶ the infrastructure is so damaged that usual transport is unavailable
▶ they are worried that it might happen again
▶ accommodation and other facilities are damaged and unavailable
▶ they feel ethically uncomfortable about visiting a destination where people are suffering.

However, the long-term impact of these natural disasters depends upon a variety of factors such as whether tourists perceive they are at risk and the speed with which the destination can rebuild its facilities.

> **Research**
>
> In November 2016, New Zealand's South Island was hit by a 7.8 magnitude earthquake. Kaikoura is a popular tourist resort about 100 miles from Christchurch, and it was very close to the centre of the quake. The town was cut off by landslides and its utilities were damaged. No airports were affected. Because of this, only tourists who were travelling to Kaikoura or the surrounding area needed to cancel or change their plans. As the airports were open, accessibility to New Zealand's major cities was unaffected.
>
> Use newspaper or news websites and find your own example of a natural disaster that has had an impact on travel and tourism. Explain:
> - the nature of the disaster
> - its impact on tourism
> - the likely recovery period.

 **PAUSE POINT**   What is the difference between an avalanche and a landslide? In which types of destination do these natural disasters occur?

 Hint   Think about places where you have heard about these disasters happening.

Extend   Find out and explain how a tsunami can be caused by an earthquake.

Climate and its influence on travel

Travellers need to find out about or be made aware of relevant climate zones and seasonal variations when they are arranging trips. For example, many tourists arrive in Thailand and find that it is the monsoon season, which they did not check when they were organising their travel arrangements. This problem – encountering unexpected poor weather – has increased as tourists have become more adventurous in their choice of destinations.

▶ **Table 2.12:** Examples of different climate zones

Climate zone	Climate
Equatorial	The area between roughly 10° north and 10° south of the Equator has an equatorial or tropical climate. The hours of daylight are the same every day without any variation throughout the year. Temperatures are consistent at about 26–29°C on average, though they may rise to 35°C and fall to 18°C at night with no seasonal variation. **Humidity** is high. The amount of rainfall is high and rain is heavy, but it tends to fall in predictable short downpours. Tropical rainforest is often found in equatorial areas and monsoons may occur
Arid	This climate is found in desert areas. Most deserts are found around 30° north and south of the Equator. Arid climates may also exist in the centre of continents or in the **rain shadow** of large mountain ranges. There is very little rainfall – often less than 25 cm per year. Temperatures are very high during the day and very cold during the night. The climate is uncomfortable and not appealing for most tourists unless they are on a desert safari. Large parts of Australia and California are in the arid climate zone
Mediterranean	The Mediterranean climate consists of hot, dry summers and mild winters. Winter temperatures rarely reach freezing and snow is unusual. In the summer, temperatures may reach 40°C. Southern Mediterranean areas are hotter than northern ones. Tourists tend to visit in the summer to take advantage of the high temperatures, and many resorts close down completely in the winter. In the summer, the lack of rain combined with the heat can lead to forest fires in many areas, including the south of France and the French island of Corsica
Temperate	A temperate climate zone can be found in a range of areas. Some temperate climates are maritime, which means that they are influenced by the oceans, like in the UK. Summers are warmer and drier than the rest of the year and there is no rainy season, meaning that rain falls throughout the year. However, this climate has four distinct seasons. Most of Europe and the USA have a temperate climate

▶ **Table 2.12:** *Continued...*

Climate zone	Climate
Snow	In snow climate regions, temperatures are below freezing throughout the year. Examples are Antarctica and Greenland
Polar	Polar climates are found in the Arctic and surrounding areas in the north and in Antarctica in the south. These are the coldest places on Earth, with typical winter temperatures of –30°C. In the Arctic, the summers are short, but they can be warm enough for some plants to grow. The Antarctic is even colder: 98 per cent of it is covered with snow and ice, although very little snow falls and the interior of the continent is almost empty of animal and plant life

Influence on travel

Seasonal variations in climate affect travel plans. Tourists avoid potential climactic disruptions to their travel and holiday plans if they can. Some weather patterns can be predicted as meteorologists recognise the warning signs and seasonal patterns. These include:

▶ hurricanes – powerful stroms common in the Caribbean region during our autumn period. For example, Hurricane Matthew devastated Haiti and the Bahamas in 2016
▶ tornadoes – strong winds that form themselves into funnel-shaped clouds and are common in certain parts of the USA
▶ snow and ice – welcome in ski resorts and when they are lacking tourists stay away
▶ monsoons – heavy rainfall in the summer in Asian countries
▶ typhoons – powerful and destructive storms similar to hurricanes but in the western Pacific.

Flooding and bush fires are other climatic extremes that deter tourists although these are not so predictable and therefore not easy to plan to avoid.

The effect of such extreme climatic conditions is that the economy of the affected region suffers because tourists are not able to visit until the danger has passed and any repairs are carried out. Table 2.12 gives examples of the six different climate zones.

Key term

Piste – a ski run made of compacted snow.

Case study

Alpine ski resorts

In November 2016, Alpine ski resorts including Verbier, Courchevel and Alpe d'Huez had their best November snow since 1996. Workers at the resorts had already covered the slopes with artificial snow, but 40 cm of real snow fell on top. When the local skiers heard that the **pistes** were open, they caused traffic jams up to Courchevel. Local hotel owners and resort mangers had only realised about 24 hours in advance that the snow was coming early and had opened the lifts, as well as a few restaurants and cafés. Tea parties and concerts were arranged to welcome the early skiers. The clientele was mainly local people, rather than the tourists who usually frequent the slopes.

Traditionally, European ski resorts open on the second Saturday of December, but lack of snow in recent years has caused delays in opening. Some low-lying resorts have even had to delay opening until after Christmas, meaning that they lose a lot of revenue. In 2016, though, travel agents and resort managers anticipated a rush for last-minute holidays from keen skiers wanting to get to the slopes before Christmas.

Check your knowledge

1 Explain why the early snow is so important to the tourist industry in the Alps.
2 Why are the locals skiing in November rather than inbound tourists?
3 What do ski resorts do to try and ensure conditions are good for skiing?

 **PAUSE POINT**   What are the six climatic zones? Which climate or climates are most appealing to tourists?

Hint   Consider what tourists like to do on holidays. What climate is most suitable for this?

Extend   What kind of tourism is offered in the Arctic?

Assessment activity 2.3

Your employer, Sensational Travel, has been asked to contribute to a trade conference where travel professionals will discuss the consumer trends affecting the appeal of global destinations.

Prepare notes for a presentation which evaluates how consumer trends are affecting the popularity and appeal of city breaks to New York and Krakow. Include your ideas on who these destinations are likely to appeal to and why.

Recommend one of these destinations as a must-have to be included in tour operators' new programmes and justify your choice.

Plan
- Where will I find my information on consumer trends?
- What can I find out about city breaks to New York and Krakow?
- How can I find out who goes to these cities?
- What is it that appeals to these groups of tourists?

Do
- I have gathered my information and divided it into different areas of consumer trends (such as the age of population).
- I have looked at each area and thought about how if affects people going to New York and Krakow.
- I have decided how to do my presentation.

Review
- I have thought about the feedback I received for next time.
- I have considered alternative ways of presenting my work.

Further reading and resources

Gray, H. P. (1970) *International Travel – International Trade*, Lexington Heath: Lexington Books.

World Travel Atlas: www.worldatlas.com
Maps.

World Travel Guide: www.worldtravelguide.net
Country information.

Foreign and Commonwealth Office: www.fco.gov.uk
Government travel advice.

VisitBritian: www.visitbritain.org
Tourist board for Britain.

Government research briefings: http://researchbriefings.parliament.uk/
Select topic 'Culture, Media and Sport' and sub-topic 'Tourism'

THINK ▶FUTURE

Nick García

Tour guide

Nick would sum up his job as: sunshine, travel, beaches, bars and very hard work. He has been working as a tour guide in Greece all season. He works for a company that sells tours all over the world, mainly to young people.

His tour starts in Athens. From there, it takes in Mykonos, Santorini, Paros and Ios over nine days. He meets his group at a hotel in Athens and gives them a welcome talk the night before the tour starts. He must ensure that he knows exactly who is coming and any special needs that they have. He also has to liaise with the hotel, arrange welcome drinks and organise all the ferry tickets ready for distribution. Some members of the group are likely to have organised their own accommodation, but some book through his company and so he has to allocate rooms to these tourists and direct them to their hostels or hotels.

The next morning he meets the group at the ferry port and they set off together for Mykonos. However hot it may be – and it is often very hot – Nick has to be ready to give a guided tour of the island's main town on foot. He has to know all of its history, the available facilities, the best beaches and the bars and restaurants. He also has to know this information about the other island stops as well. After a couple of nights on Mykonos, the group moves on by ferry to the next island and so on until they have visited all four, and then return to Athens at the end of nine days. The group of tourists goes home and Nick has two days off before starting all over again with a new group.

It can be very tiring, and during the tour Nick will try to get a couple of hours' sleep during the day if he can, as he might have to be out late if the group chooses to go clubbing. He often has to stay up all night to look after tourists who are sick or cannot find their accommodation. If this happens, he still has to work his normal hours the next day.

Focusing your skills

If you want to work as a tour guide, what do you need to do?

- Be independent and self-sufficient – you might be with a group of holidaymakers, but you are in charge all by yourself.

- Stay calm at all times because you never know what is going to happen – ferries can be delayed, people can forget to book accommodation and sometimes tourists can even end up in hospital. It is crucial to stay calm and think about potential solutions before rushing in.

- Be organised – don't underestimate how much administration there is to do when managing a group of tourists, and you will have to do it on the move on a laptop.

- It is important to moderate your own drinking and partying and to sleep when you can, because being a tour guide is not like being on holiday.

- Having a second language will serve you well. One of Nick's colleagues speaks Croatian so she gets to run the company's Balkan tour.

Getting ready for assessment

This section has been written to help you to do your best when you take the assessment. Read through it carefully and ask your tutor if there is anything you are still not sure about.

About the assessment

There are two parts to the assessment. Part A is your preparation stage. A set period of time before the assessment, you will be given a research brief on specific global destinations. You are expected to carry out research on this brief. Part B is the assessment itself, which will contain tasks which you must complete in controlled conditions.

As the guidelines for assessment can change, you should refer to the official assessment guidance on the Pearson Qualifications website for the latest definitive guidance.

Preparing for the assessment

To improve your chances of success, you need to revise all the key assessment outcomes likely to appear.

Once you receive the research brief for Part A, you should spend a set period of time conducting some independent research and making careful notes about your research. You will be allowed to take some notes into the supervised assessment. Your tutor will tell you how many notes you can take and in what format. Make sure that you are very familiar with your research findings and your notes by the time you sit the supervised assessment.

Sitting the assessment

- On the day of the assessment, read Part B carefully, paying attention to any instructions and the activities that you need to complete. Make sure that you refer to your prepared notes.

- Most questions contain command words. Understanding what these words mean will help you understand what the question is asking you to do. The relevant command words were introduced at the start of this unit, so look again at their definitions and make sure that you understand them.

- You must plan your time well. Work out what you need to do and then organise your time so that you have enough time to do it. If you are writing an answer to a longer question, plan your answer before you start writing. Have a clear idea of the point that your answer is making, and then make sure that everything you write is focused on communicating this point and answering the question you have been set.

If you finish early, use the time to reread your answers and make any corrections. This could help make your answers even better and could make a big difference to your final mark.

Sample answer

Worked example

Chris and Pavlina are about to go skiing. They have approached you, an independent travel agent, to advise them on a suitable destination that will meet their needs in terms of budget, travel requirements and purpose of travel.

Chris has a UK passport, Pavlina has a Czech passport. They have a total budget of £5,000 for the holiday. Their requirements include:

- depart – Manchester
- duration – two weeks
- timing – January
- accommodation – luxury hotel
- half board
- Pavlina is a fairly competent skier but will not attempt black routes
- Pavlina has her own boots and skis to take
- Chris wants ski lessons
- both want activities outside skiing.

You need to consider the suitability of three options to meet their needs. Choose three potential ski destinations and research their suitability for the clients. **Create an email to the clients explaining how each option meets their needs. Make a recommendation for the most suitable option with justification.**

Dear Chris and Pavlina,

Re: your enquiry on ski destinations. Please see information below.

Whistler

Flight direct to Vancouver from Manchester.

Transfer to resort included.

Has a vast range of ski slopes so suitable for all levels of competence, Chris and Pavlina can ski at their own level.

Ski school available for Chris (extra cost).

There are other activities such as zip lining and a peak-to-peak cable car, ice-skating amongst others.

Shuttle bus from Vancouver airport to Whistler.

Chosen hotel is the Fairmont Chateau five star as requested – can ski in and out from the hotel.

Includes:
- half board
- free shuttle bus to Whistler village
- hot tubs
- health club with indoor and outdoor pool
- Wi-Fi
- spa treatments (extra charge)
- choice of restaurants for dinner.

£2,600 per person.

Courchevel

Flight direct to Geneva from Manchester.

Transfer to resort included.

Has skiing suitable for all levels.

Ski school available (£153 for four half days) for Chris.

Ski and boot hire about £200 for Chris.

Lots of activities outside skiing.

Six minute walk to the resort centre from chosen hotel and next to Aiguille du Midi cable-car.

Chosen hotel Belle Epoque four star includes:
- *half board*
- *Wi-Fi*
- *spa treatments (extra)*
- *outdoor heated pool*
- *double room with mountain view.*

£2,028 per person

My recommendation is Whistler as flights are direct from Manchester, the hotel is of superior quality to match your requirement for a luxury hotel. There are a range of slopes so you will be able to ski at your own ability but together when you wish to. Plenty of other activities are available such as skiing and zip lining and there is a health club in your hotel for those days when you don't feel like skiing. The hotel is right on the slopes so you can ski in and out for convenience.

Please give me a call when you are ready to discuss further.

Regards

These findings generally meet the clients' requirements but do not give sufficient detail. Transfers to resorts are included, but there is no information on mode of transport or duration of journey. Although exact timings are not needed at this stage, the approximate time of day of the flights is important, as is the duration of the flights, as this information will help the clients to choose their destination.

There is insufficient information about the non-skiing activities in Courchevel. While the prices of ski lessons and ski hire are given for Courchevel, prices are not given for lift passes.

The cost of Whistler is high and outside the clients' budget but it does offer some points that meet the requirements very well so is worth including. The email does not give enough detail about how the options meet requirements and the agent should not leave it open ended but should say when they are going to call the client to discuss further.

Only two options have been offered where three were required.

Principles of Marketing in Travel and Tourism

3

Getting to know your unit

Assessment
You will be assessed by a
series of assignments set
by your tutor.

Successful travel and tourism organisations constantly change their products and services to meet changing customer expectations. They must also have a strategy to market their offer to different groups of customers in a profitable way. In this unit, you will learn about different marketing activities and their role in influencing customer decisions and meeting their needs. You will learn how marketing impacts on organisational success. You will carry out market research for a new travel and tourism product or service and produce a promotional campaign for that product or service. You will draw on your learning about the industry from other units to develop your campaign.

How you will be assessed

This unit will be assessed by a series of internally assessed assignments set by your tutor. Throughout this unit you will find assessment activities that will help you work towards your assignments. Completing these activities will not mean that you have achieved a particular grade, but that you will have carried out useful research or preparation that will be relevant when it comes to your assignments.

In order for you to achieve the tasks in your assignment, it is important to check that you have met all of the Pass grading criteria. You can do this as you work your way through the assignment.

If you are hoping to gain a Merit or Distinction, you should also make sure that you present the information in your assignment in the style that is required by the relevant assessment criterion. For example, Merit criteria require you to analyse, and Distinction criteria require you to evaluate.

The assignment set by your tutor will consist of a number of tasks designed to meet the criteria in the table. These may include the following:
▶ producing a report evaluating how the interrelationships of marketing and customer service influence customer decisions and meet customer needs
▶ collecting and analysing research data to help identify a new product or service
▶ producing a promotional campaign for a new product or service
▶ evaluating how well the campaign meets its objectives.

Assessment criteria

This table shows what you must do in order to achieve a **Pass**, **Merit** or **Distinction** grade, and where you can find activities to help you.

Pass	Merit	Distinction
Learning aim A Explore the role of marketing activities in influencing customer decisions and meeting customer needs in travel and tourism		
A.P1 Explain how effective marketing and customer service in travel and tourism organisations work together to influence customer decisions and meet customer needs. Assessment activity 3.1	**A.M1** Analyse the potential impacts of the marketing mix and the ways in which effective marketing and customer service work together to influence customer decisions and meet customer needs. Assessment activity 3.1	**A.D1** Evaluate the potential impacts of the marketing mix and the ways in which effective marketing and customer service work together to influence customer decisions and meet customer needs. Assessment activity 3.1
A.P2 Explain the potential impacts of the marketing mix on travel and tourism organisations and customers. Assessment activity 3.1		
Learning aim B Examine the impact that marketing activities have on the success of different travel and tourism organisations		
B.P3 Explain how marketing activity is conducted differently by two travel and tourism organisations to achieve organisational objectives, taking into account internal and external factors. Assessment activity 3.2	**B.M2** Analyse the different approaches to marketing activities used by two travel and tourism organisations to achieve organisational objectives, taking into account internal and external factors. Assessment activity 3.2	**B.D2** Evaluate the potential impacts of the different approaches to marketing activities used by two travel and tourism organisations to achieving organisational success, taking into account internal and external factors and justifying recommendations for improvement. Assessment activity 3.2
B.P4 Explain how marketing activities contribute to the growth and customer relationships of two travel and tourism organisations. Assessment activity 3.2		
Learning aim C Carry out market research in order to identify a new travel and tourism product or service		
C.P5 Identify a new travel and tourism product or service through the use of data obtained from primary and secondary market research. Assessment activity 3.3	**C.M3** Identify a new travel and tourism product or service through the analysis of data obtained from primary and secondary market research. Assessment activity 3.3	**C.D3** Identify a new travel and tourism product or service, justifying the data obtained from primary and secondary research. Assessment activity 3.3
Learning aim D Produce a promotional campaign for a new travel and tourism product or service, to meet stated objectives		
D.P6 Produce a promotional campaign for a new travel and tourism product or service, including promotional material or activity, explaining how campaign objectives can be achieved. Assessment activity 3.4	**D.M4** Produce a detailed promotional campaign for a new travel and tourism product or service, including promotional material or activity, analysing how campaign objectives can be achieved. Assessment activity 3.4	**D.D4** Produce a comprehensive promotional campaign for a new travel and tourism product or service, including promotional material or activity, evaluating the extent to which campaign objectives can be achieved. Assessment activity 3.4

Getting started

In small groups, discuss what you think the term 'marketing' means. Write down your group's definition and then compare it with the other groups and try to come to an agreement on a definition. How much emphasis have you put on the needs of customers in your definition?

A Explore the role of marketing activities in influencing customer decisions and meeting customer needs in travel and tourism

Interrelationships between marketing and customer service in travel and tourism organisations

Successful marketing attracts customers to a travel and tourism organisation and its **products** and services. The marketing department must work closely with customer service teams as without effective customer service, the efforts of the marketing department will be in vain. In this section we introduce the concept of marketing and explore how it interrelates with customer service.

Definition of marketing

The Chartered Institute of Marketing (CIM) defines marketing as 'The management process responsible for identifying, anticipating and satisfying customer requirements profitably'.

This definition illustrates that successful marketing depends upon meeting customer needs. All products and services must be designed based on a knowledge and understanding of customer needs or preferences. All business activities, interactions with customers and brand promotions must be carefully monitored and managed to keep customers satisfied and to ensure commercial success.

Principles of marketing

The key principles of marketing are to:
▶ research the market to establish customer needs
▶ produce products or services that meet those needs
▶ know what is currently happening in the market, especially competitor activity
▶ ensure the whole organisation is customer focused – not just the customer service department
▶ build great customer relationships.

All marketing activities should follow these key principles. These key principles form part of a marketing strategy and plan following a structured marketing process. We will look at the marketing process in more detail in section B.

Marketing activities to attract and retain customers

Marketing activities are all about attracting and retaining customers. Most organisations have separate departments for marketing and customer service.

However, the organisations are most effective and most successful when their marketing and customer service teams work closely together to:

▸ deliver superior service
▸ exceed customer expectations
▸ build great customer relationships to boost retention and repeat business
▸ resolve problems and complaints and use them to improve service.

Marketing and customer service teams work together in a number of ways on marketing activities as shown in Table 3.1.

▸ **Table 3.1:** Interrelationships between marketing and customer service

Activity	Marketing	Customer service
Identifying appropriate target markets **(market segmentation)**	Use market segmentation techniques and develop profiles and personas of customers	Inform customer profiles through direct customer knowledge and observation of customer behaviour
Researching customer needs and preferences	Determine research to be carried out into trends and behaviour	Give feedback from customers to the marketing team Say how products and services are used in practice
Establishing a demand for a product or service	Test demand for new products and services through research	Promote new products and services to customers Feed back to the marketing team
Creating promotional activities to influence customer perceptions	Determine methods and content of promotion and ensure customer service teams are informed about current promotions Ensure image, brand, products and services promote positive impressions of the organisation, including the values of trustworthiness and reliability	Keep aware of all promotional activity and uphold messages to customers Feed back examples of successful promotions to marketing Ensure positive first impressions with the customer, further enhancing the organisation's good reputation Provide a message that emphasises quality and value for money of the product or service
Communicating with customers to stimulate demand and persuade them to buy	Determine content and channel of promotional campaigns Update customer service teams on all communication plans Design loyalty programmes in conjunction with customer service teams	Use direct sales techniques that align with the marketing communications plan
Obtaining and interpreting feedback from customers	Carry out research to obtain feedback	Obtain direct feedback from customers and pass it onto marketing to inform future strategy
Consistency of product or service	Consistent communication with customer service teams	Consistent communication with marketing teams

Key term

Market segmentation – dividing up the whole market for a product or service into different groups of customers with similar characteristics.

Link

You can learn more about customer service in travel and tourism in Unit 4: Managing the Customer Experience in Travel and Tourism, pages 186–204.

Link

You will find out more about market segmentation on page 128.

Obtaining, interpreting and acting on feedback from customers

Obtaining customer and employee feedback leads to improvements in customer service, as long as the feedback is acted upon. For example, customers will discuss their experiences of good and bad service on social media sites and review sites, and businesses should monitor such feedback and analyse any trends that might lead to improvements in their service. Negative feedback and complaints provide an opportunity to find out what is going wrong and make changes to prevent reoccurrence.

Key term

Subjective – based only on someone's personal judgement or taste.

Social media

▸ **Review sites** – sites like TripAdvisor and other social media sites are very popular as they allow people to read and post reviews about travel and tourism businesses. One downside is that these reviews may not be completely reliable as people's opinions are often **subjective**. Sometimes, customers give very poor ratings even if only one small thing went wrong. This can seriously impact a business, as even one bad review can affect customer choice. However, if a customer finds that there are numerous reviews all saying similar things, they are more likely to trust these reviewers' judgements. Careful management of reviews is important for the reputation of travel and tourism organisations. A prompt response, for example a thank you, and appreciation of a positive review, shows that the organisation is listening to and engaging with customers. Equally, a quick reply to negative feedback shows that the organisation cares about complaints and is prepared to act upon them. If a complaint is drawn out, the organisation will invite the customer to DM (direct message) to deal with the complaint privately.

▸ **Community forums** – these provide businesses with a way of inviting customers to share their experience with the business. This makes customers feel privileged and enables them to give feedback. For example, Hilton used a forum to gather customer feedback on their new room selection feature. This feedback suggested that customers also wanted information about the locations of facilities outside the hotel, such as attractions and restaurants, as well as facilities provided in the hotel. This led Hilton to change the feature to include the information that customers wanted.

▸ **Instant feedback** – some organisations give customers instant incentives in order to collect feedback from them while they are still interacting with the organisation. For example, a restaurant could give customers a free cocktail or dessert in exchange for answering some on-the-spot questions.

Trade articles

Travel and tourism publications publish news and articles about different organisations. These may cover aspects of marketing and customer service and give positive or negative reviews. See page 166 for examples of publications. Reporters from the publications may pose as 'mystery shoppers'.

Link

You can learn more about mystery shoppers in Unit 5: Travel and Tourism Enterprises, Section A.

Questionnaires and satisfaction ratings

Travel and tourism organisations carry out surveys to gain feedback from customers. They may also ask for a quick satisfaction rating following a purchase or use of a product or following a visit to a website.

Identifying improvements from customer communications and feedback

As mentioned, organisations use feedback to identify and make improvements so they can provide excellent service. They use tools to help analyse feedback:

▸ **Service-quality gaps** – A service-quality gap analysis compares how the business is currently operating with where it ideally wants to be. Carrying out this analysis helps highlight what an organisation needs to change or improve to achieve the aim set out in its mission statement. Service-quality gap analysis can also be used to analyse what competitors are doing and whether their service or quality is better and has some aspects worth copying.

▸ **Model of excellence** – Whether a business is reviewing its customer service delivery or just starting up, it may need support in setting up and reviewing its customer service standards. Some businesses use a model of excellence to help them get started. For example, The Institute of Customer Service offers a system of accreditation called ServiceMark for organisations meeting excellent standards of customer service. Organisations seeking ServiceMark accreditation undergo an:

Key term

Model of excellence – a tool or set of standards that measures areas of customer service that are most important for customers.

- internal assessment of their customer service strategy and how employees engage with it
- analysis of customer feedback
- onsite assessment visit.

With support from the Institute, they produce an action plan for improvement and are accredited when they reach the required standards. Edinburgh Trams is an example of a travel organisation that has achieved ServiceMark.

▶ **Case studies** – Case studies of other organisations can also help businesses to make improvements. They allow organisations to see what has worked well in another company and make improvements to their own customer service. The Institute of Customer Service provides many case studies about service excellence to demonstrate how companies, such as the rail company First Trans-Pennine Express, use customer feedback to influence major long-term decisions, meet corporate targets and achieve high staff retention rates.

> **Theory into practice**
>
> If a customer made a complaint on holiday that could not be resolved in resort, it would be logged in resort and entered onto the organisation's Customer Relationship Management (CRM) system. The customer service team at head office would then note the complaint and, if needed, follow up with the customer whilst they're still on holiday to resolve the complaint, rather than waiting until the customer returns and makes a complaint.
>
> How would the marketing team use this information?

Influencing customer decisions and meeting needs

Identifying different types of customer

Customers have different reasons for buying products. Marketing teams must understand the different types of customers and decide which ones they want to target with their organisation's products and services. Organisations usually have a range of products or services catering for different types of customer or target markets.

The practice of dividing up a market into different types of customers is known as market segmentation.

The different types of customer a travel and tourism organisation serves are:
- families
- individuals
- groups
- leisure tourists
- business tourists.

Market segmentation allows the marketing team to analyse these basic groups more specifically to provide detail on who is purchasing products and services and why. They can then use this information to tailor the **marketing mix** to best meet the needs of these different customers.

Table 3.2 shows ways of carrying out market segmentation:

> **Key term**
>
> **Marketing mix** – the combination of the four main elements of marketing: product, price, promotion and place.

► **Table 3.2:** Ways of segmenting the market

Demographic segmentation	• Demographics is the study of the make-up of the population • Demographic trends show how the population is changing (e.g. people are living longer or having fewer children) • Customers are grouped according to age, gender, marital status, family size, income, religion, occupation and nationality

Socio-economic segmentation	• The population is divided according to socio-economic groupings
	• In the UK, these groupings are usually based on those used by the National Readership Survey:
	
	    A Higher managerial, administrative or professional
	    B Intermediate managerial, administrative or professional
	    C1 Supervisory or clerical, and junior managerial, administrative or professional
	    C2 Skilled manual workers
	    D Semi-skilled and unskilled manual workers
	    E State pensioners, casual or lowest-grade workers
	
	• The classifications above are widely used in advertising and are useful in marketing to target different groups
	• A more detailed classification has been developed (National Statistics Socio-Economic Classification) which groups occupations by employment (e.g. professional, clerical or manual roles) and the degree of responsibility (e.g. number of people managed)

Geographic segmentation	• People are segmented according to the geographic region in which they live (e.g. the Isle of Wight ferry services offer special services and prices on their ships for Isle of Wight residents)
Psychographic/ lifestyle segmentation	• Consumers are categorised according to personality types, lifestyle and motivations • When it is done well, it is very effective in determining targets, but it is difficult to do accurately • Successful research produces profiles of customers and their motivations

The most successful organisations use a combination of these segmentation methods to produce profiles of customers. Here is an example from Visit Britain.

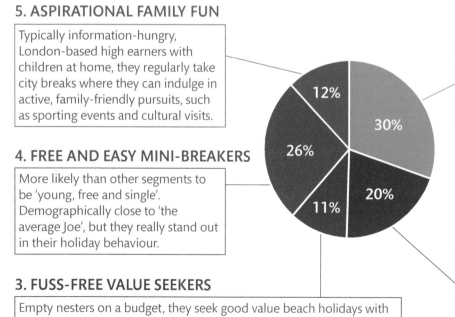

5. ASPIRATIONAL FAMILY FUN

Typically information-hungry, London-based high earners with children at home, they regularly take city breaks where they can indulge in active, family-friendly pursuits, such as sporting events and cultural visits.

4. FREE AND EASY MINI-BREAKERS

More likely than other segments to be 'young, free and single'. Demographically close to 'the average Joe', but they really stand out in their holiday behaviour.

3. FUSS-FREE VALUE SEEKERS

Empty nesters on a budget, they seek good value beach holidays with convenient transport links. Tend to be less digitally active than other segments – less likely to engage in social media or book holiday online.

1. COUNTRY-LOVING TRADITIONALISTS

Empty nesters with traditional values, they are likely to have recently taken a countryside break in England. Good quality, secure accommodation is a priority when booking a holiday.

2. FUN IN THE SUN

Typically parents looking for family-orientated summer holidays where beaches play a starring role. Tend to seek cheaper, more 'social' alternatives to hotel accommodation, such as caravans or holiday camps.

► **Figure 3.1:** VisitBritain market segmentation

Specific customer needs

Customers may have special needs regardless of market segment, such as:

▶ cultural needs – special diets or religious needs
▶ medical or mobility needs.

These needs must be considered when carrying out marketing activities, for example:

▶ ensuring that marketing content is unlikely to cause offence to different cultural groups
▶ considering whether leaflets should be available in different languages
▶ promoting mobility/accessibility measures in hotels or tourist attractions.

You should also consider that customers do not always state their needs. This could be because they are not sure what they want or do not want to tell you. These needs are known as **unstated needs** and customer service teams are often skilled in uncovering them through skilful questioning.

Influence over purchasing decisions

It is important to distinguish between the user of a product or service and the purchaser. A holiday may be bought by a mother in a family but the decision on where to go and when is influenced by discussion with the whole family.

The decision to buy is influenced by many factors, such as desire or need for the product, customer service, reputation of the organisation and perceived quality of the product.

> **Link**
>
> You can find out more about specific customer needs in Unit 4.

> **Key term**
>
> **Unstated needs** – those needs which the customer does not mention outright but are implied from other things they say or do.

Theory into practice

Think about the last holiday you or your family and friends went on.

How did you all decide on where to go, when to go and how to go? Which organisation(s) did you use to take the trip?

Complete Table 3.3 reflecting on those decisions and share your ideas with your group.

▶ **Table 3.3:** Factors influencing customer decisions

Influence on your decision	Comments
What you were looking for, your desires or specific needs	
The features and quality of the product or service (e.g. hotel, transport, destination)	
The way the product/service was promoted	
Your confidence in the organisations you chose	
The reputation and image of the organisation(s)	
Value for money	
Customer service	
Whether your trip met your expectations	

Balancing customer satisfaction with organisational objectives

Customer satisfaction is of the utmost importance to the reputation and commercial success of a business. However, there may be times when customer expectations are unrealistic, unsafe or too costly to meet. The case study on Stonehenge gives an example of managing visitor expectations.

Case study

Stonehenge

The construction of Stonehenge took place about 2500 BC and is one of the most impressive structures of its time. Each of the larger stones weighs around 25 tons, while the smaller stones weigh 2–4 tons. The Neolithic people who built it had little technology to help them move the stones from the quarry sites many miles away. The purpose of Stonehenge remains a mystery despite extensive archaeological investigation.

Stonehenge is managed by English Heritage. Anybody wishing to access the stone circle must arrange this in advance with English Heritage, and these visits can only take place outside normal working hours. During normal operating hours, visitors must walk around the circle on a fixed path and are given free audio guides explaining different aspects of Stonehenge. There is also a visitor centre which is designed to house permanent and temporary exhibitions, and a spacious cafe.

Check your knowledge

1 What is the appeal of Stonehenge to tourists?
2 How does English Heritage balance access to the site for visitors with protecting the stones?
3 Explain whether you agree with restricting access to the stones and why.

 **PAUSE POINT** Give three examples of factors that influence customer decisions when buying a holiday.

 Hint Think about what you reflected on when choosing your own holiday.

Extend How might a tour operator manage these influences?

Link

You can find out more about marketing plans and strategy in Unit 5: Travel and Tourism Enterprises (page 259).

Link

You can learn about product features and benefits in Unit 5: Travel and Tourism Enterprises.

The marketing mix

The marketing mix refers to the 4 'P's: product, price, promotion and place. The Ps are interdependent; a product or service must have a price, be promoted in some way and available in a place. Creating a suitable marketing mix for a product is part of a marketing plan.

The marketing plan should document the following:
▶ a description of the market segment to be targeted
▶ an explanation of the benefits of targeting that segment or segments
▶ the aims and objectives of the marketing strategy
▶ details of strategies for the four elements of the marketing mix:
•• price •• product •• promotion •• place.

Product

To determine strategy for the product element of the marketing mix, organisations must consider:

▶ the lifetime of each product or service – the product life cycle

▶ the range of products to have in their **product portfolio**, sometimes decided through a **product portfolio analysis**

▶ the brand or brand names to be adopted for the products

▶ how tastes and trends change between geographic markets and different social groups – ensuring products continue to meet customer needs and expectations

▶ what is a product's **unique selling point (USP)**.

Case study

Beth Chatto Gardens

Beth Chatto Gardens are located near Colchester in Essex.

'Beth Chatto OBE was an award-winning plantswoman. Her work at the Gardens began in 1960. She took an overgrown wasteland of brambles, parched gravel and boggy ditches, transforming it using plants adapted by nature to thrive in different conditions. An inspirational, informal garden has developed. Beth oversaw the development of the Gardens into her 90s, and worked closely with her team which include Garden and Nursery Director, David Ward, and Head Gardener, Asa Gregers-Warg. The Gardens remain a family-run business, managed by Beth's granddaughter, Julia Boulton.'

What was once a car park is now a world-renowned Gravel Garden (which is never watered), and the dozens of plants Beth used to give to friends and family have morphed into one of the UK's leading plantsman's nurseries. A light and airy tearoom, built in 2006, allows visitors to relax and take in their surroundings over a homemade cake and is also available for special private events such as wedding receptions, christenings and wakes.'

Check your knowledge

1 What are the products and services at Beth Chatto Gardens that attract tourists?

2 What other facilities are offered for visitors?

3 Explain how to get to the gardens by private and public transport.

4 What type of visitor do you think visits the gardens?

Link

The product life cycle was specifically developed for tourism by Butler. You can find out about the Tourist Area Life Cycle (TALC) on page 76 of Unit 2: Global Destinations.

Key terms

Product portfolio – the range of products and services a business offers.

Product portfolio analysis – businesses look carefully at the product range and decide which products and services are worth keeping or developing and which should be discarded.

Unique selling point (USP) – a quality or feature that sets a product apart from its competitor is known as the USP.

Product life cycle

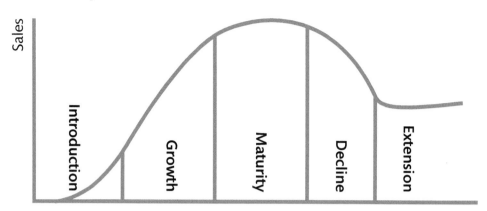

Sales

Introduction | Growth | Maturity | Decline | Extension

Time

▶ **Figure 3.2:** The product life cycle

The product life cycle (see Figure 3.2) shows how a product moves through different stages in its life, until it becomes obsolete. It is a useful concept in marketing as the stage a product is at impacts on the marketing activity.

▶ **Introduction:** The launch of a new product is a very exciting, but tense, period. A lot of the marketing budget is assigned to advertising and letting customers know it exists. The people most likely to buy the new product or to try out a new service are known as 'innovators', people who like to try something new. The new product may be targeted at a **niche market** to start with.

▶ **Growth:** This is the most profitable stage in the product's life cycle and companies are eager to gain these profits while they can. Word-of-mouth promotion is important at this stage, as consumers hear about the new product or destination and want to try it. Competitors will rapidly enter the market, bringing out their own versions of the new idea. Because of this increased competition, it is important for companies to try to build up some brand loyalty, especially as more people are buying the product or service. The promotional budget is usually devoted to **differentiation**.

▶ **Maturity:** Competition is at its most intense at this stage. Marketing efforts focus on being competitive, often by promoting low prices. Maturity is the longest stage of the life cycle. Products and services at this stage are appealing to the **mass market**.

▶ **Decline:** Sales and profits start to fall at this point. Marketers must recognise when products are likely to move into this stage, as they must decide whether it is worth staying in the market. An organisation should be diversifying into other markets or products at the beginning of the decline stage (at the latest) to ensure survival.

▶ **Extension:** The life cycle is extended. For example, a company might manage to make good profits from being the only player in a market that everyone else has abandoned – appealing to a niche market.

Key terms

Differentiation – stressing the product's benefits over competitive products.

Mass market – appealing to large numbers of customers.

Niche market – appealing to a small market segment.

Theory into practice

1 Study the list of destinations below and discuss with your group where the destinations are geographically and what they have to offer. Then decide where you think they are in terms of the product life cycle.

- Majorca
- Bali
- Prague
- Barbados
- Tunisia
- Kenya
- Paris

2 Repeat the exercise, this time with these travel products and services:

- free meals on flights
- Channel ferries
- London Underground Oyster cards
- spa holidays.

Case study

Kuoni

Kuoni is a travel company that specialises in luxury holidays. The following extract is information about its all-inclusive holidays.

'For complete relaxation and peace of mind, opt for a Kuoni all-inclusive holiday and let the sunshine and sea breeze wash over you, content in the knowledge that your meals and drinks are catered for. You might find little extras included, too.

We've hand-picked the best options for all-inclusive escapes, from family favourites – complete with kids' clubs, pint-sized pools and babysitters – to luxury resorts with exquisite accommodation and superb dining.

As well as convenience, travelling on an all-inclusive holiday package can often add significant extra value to your travel plans when compared to paying locally. Paying up front for most of your holiday meals and refreshments can also significantly lessen the impact of those dreaded post-holiday credit card bills and reduce the amount of holiday currency that you need to purchase and carry.'

Check your knowledge

1 Summarise the product features and benefits of an all-inclusive holiday according to Kuoni.

2 Where are all-inclusive holidays positioned in the product life cycle? Give reasons for your answer.

3 Find out what other types of holidays are in Kuoni's product portfolio.

⏸ PAUSE POINT   List the stages of the product life cycle.

> Hint   Remember it starts with a new product in the introduction stage.

> Extend   Which stages appeal to mass market tourism?

Price

A product or service is made at a cost but sold at a price. The difference between the two is profit. Travel and tourism organisations usually aim to make money so getting the price right helps them achieve this objective. There are a number of different pricing strategies that organisations can use (Table 3.4).

Link

Pricing strategies are covered in detail in Unit 5: Travel and Tourism Enterprises, page 261.

▶ **Table 3.4:** Pricing strategies

Strategy	Description, advantages and disadvantages
Cost plus	Calculates the cost of producing the product and then adds a percentage to give the return the business wants as profit. This is an easy-to-calculate strategy that gives a clear profit; however, it does not take into account what the customer is prepared to pay
Economy	Very similar to cost plus pricing, but costs are kept low to keep prices very low. The customer perceives that they are getting a good deal but quality may be sacrificed
Penetration	Starts off with a low price to get customers interested. As the number of customers grows, the price increases. This can build a lot of initial interest in the product, and lead to an early large market share but can lead to customer dissatisfaction with potential later price rises. Low prices can also lead to a customer perception that goods are low quality, or if the product or service does not provide a good customer experience, they may not keep customer loyalty with later price rises
Skimming	A new product is introduced at a high price, aimed at 'innovators'; people who want to be first to try something or somewhere new and are prepared to pay for the privilege. This provides a high profit margin and often leads to a reputation for high quality. However, it can also limit sales and lead to competitors challenging with lower-priced alternatives. Early adopters can also be annoyed by later price drops
Premium	A high price is charged to suggest to the customer that the product or service is high quality
Competitor based	The organisation keeps a close eye on competitor prices and matches them when necessary. While it is easy to calculate and maintain, it can lead to low prices and the risk of unprofitability
Dynamic	Prices fluctuate at different times or vary for different groups of people. It is commonly used in transport, for example airlines, where prices are linked to demand
Seasonal (dynamic pricing based on time of year)	The price of the product changes according to time of year, particularly school holidays when demand is high. The seasons for holiday products are commonly: • **peak** – the most popular season for a particular type of holiday, when prices are highest • **shoulder** – the seasons either side of peak season • **off-peak** – the least popular season for that type of holiday, when prices are lowest. This can lead to larger profits at busier times of the year, but can also alienate customers who see products cheaper at other times of the year
Promotional	Links the price of the product to a special promotion for a limited time. This draws attention, quickly builds market share and gains publicity. However, lower prices affect profits and don't always mean that customer loyalty is maintained when prices rise again
Discounting	Discounts are offered to specific groups of people; for example, students or seniors on trains. This can attract new business and customers quickly. However, it also affects profit margins, could lead to other competitors making similar discounts and lead some customers to believe your product is lower quality

When deciding on their pricing strategy, businesses must consider:

▶ what customers will be prepared to pay, especially in different countries or regions of the UK
▶ at what stage of the product life cycle the product or service is
▶ what competitors are charging, especially if competitors run a promotion or discount which the business might consider matching
▶ the costs required to deliver the product or service
▶ the **break-even point**.

Pricing in global markets

Pricing in a global market is more complex as there are more factors to consider. Besides the factors mentioned above, companies must also consider:

▶ how they wish to position their product in the specific country
▶ any tariffs that have to be paid, for example, import duties
▶ prices already offered in the target country
▶ local taxes, for example, value added tax or a tourist tax
▶ the exchange rate
▶ where taxes from profits will fall due
▶ extra transport costs.

Key term

Break-even point – the point at which a business's revenue from sales is exactly the same as its costs. This is the point at which the business is about to start making a profit.

Research

You are booking a Mercure hotel in Norwich for two nights. The booking is for two people and is for next Friday and Saturday night. Check prices on the internet using:

· Accor hotels (the Mercure brand belongs to Accor)
· a consolidator site, such as Trivago
· booking.com.

1 Make a note of the prices available and any variations in price.
2 How else could you book this hotel room?
3 Why are there variations in price between the booking methods?

Case study

Premier Inn

Premier Inn is a budget hotel chain owned by Whitbread. The brand dominates the budget hotel sector, with over 800 hotels providing over 70,000 rooms in the UK. The chain is expanding. They had plans for a further 13,000 rooms in 2020.

There are seven Premier Inn hotels in the Middle East and the business has a significant expansion programme in Germany.

How Premier Inn succeeds

· Dynamic pricing – prices are not fixed and change according to demand, so prices are very cheap during periods of low demand.
· Product and service consistency – the chain provides a 'Good Night Guarantee', guaranteeing that they will give a refund if customers' sleep is disturbed.
· Investment in maintenance, repairs and refurbishment – the company invests heavily in maintaining its hotels so that they are up to standard.
· Use of social media – particularly used to direct people to the website in order to make direct bookings.
· Brand extension (hub by Premier Inn) – launched to capitalise on the hotel trend for contemporary, small rooms in city centres.

Check your knowledge

1 Why might tourists end up paying different prices, even on the same night?
2 Check the price of rooms at your nearest Premier Inn. Compare a week night with a bank holiday weekend. What is the difference in price?
3 Now, check the prices at a Premier Inn in the Middle East compared to the one nearest you. Use the internet to get both prices in GBP. What is the difference in price? What reasons do you think there are for any difference?

Link

For further information about brand extensions, see pages 144–146.

Link

You can learn about the promotional mix in detail on page 263 in Unit 5: Travel and Tourism Enterprises.

Promotion

To achieve their marketing objectives, travel and tourism businesses must make sure that their customers are aware of their products and services. The tools they use to do this are collectively known as promotion and form part of the marketing mix.

Promotional activity will include all or some of:

▶ advertising
▶ direct marketing (including printed media)
▶ **digital marketing**
▶ sales promotion
▶ public relations
▶ mobile apps.

Advertising

The advantages and disadvantages of the different forms of advertising are shown in Table 3.5.

▶ **Table 3.5:** Advantages and disadvantages of different forms of advertising

Medium	Advantages	Disadvantages
Newspapers	• Can be print or online • Can target precise audience or readership • Can include detailed information in advertisements • Short lead time, so last-minute travel advertisements can be included at short notice	• Do not use much colour • Newspapers are soon thrown away • Advertising space can be cluttered
Magazines	• Can be print or online • Can contain colourful, glossy advertisements • Can target precise audience • Can include inserts (leaflets inside the magazine)	• Colour advertising is expensive • Most magazines are national so cannot target regional audiences • Long lead time so not suitable for last-minute travel offers
Radio	• Listeners are often loyal to a channel and will hear the advertisements • Cheaper than television • Can have an immediate impact, especially when promoting offers and events	• Advertisements cost more than print advertisements • Listeners may be doing something else at the same time so they may not be engaged by the advertisement
Television	• Reaches a large number of people • Can target audiences by time and programme • Can have a high impact due to colour, moving images and audio	• Expensive to produce and place advertisements • Potential audience may be dispersed over several channels • People can avoid advertisements by channel-hopping or fast forwarding on catch up
Online (websites and social media pop-ups)	• Can have a high impact due to moving images and video embedded into websites/social media • Are paid on a pay-per-click system so the organisation only pays if people express an interest in the product by clicking on it	• Require regular maintenance to keep up to date • Can take time to find the most suitable host websites/social media platforms • Advertising space can be limited

▶ **Table 3.5:** *Continued…*

Cinema	• Can have high impact due to use of big screen • Has a captive audience	• Expensive to produce advertisements
Billboards	• Can allow regional targeting • Can be very eye-catching in public places • Low cost	• Usually static • Prime locations are expensive • People have short exposure to the message

Direct marketing

Advertising and promotions are directed by mail, email or social media to a particular individual and contain messages specifically targeted to that customer based on previous purchase history or internet searches.

Sales promotion

A sales promotion is designed to bring about a speedy sale of a product or service and offers an incentive to make the purchase, such as free entry to an attraction or a discounted price. Promotions are often run with partners who share similar marketing objectives. For example, train companies often partner with attractions and offer special deals.

Digital marketing

Travel and tourism businesses cannot ignore travel forums and social media networks. For example, if customers do not review a hotel, the hotel will not appear on review sites and forums, and it will lose business. The strategies that businesses use to manage customer-generated content about their products and services include:

▸ motivating customer-facing staff to encourage tourists to place reviews
▸ giving customers cards asking them to complete a review
▸ responding quickly and positively to comments on forums, review sites and social media sites
▸ employing a digital marketing manager
▸ developing a content marketing strategy to engage customers and publish their own original content.

Sponsorship

Organisations pay for or contribute to the cost of running an event, such as a sporting fixture, or television programme in return for promotion of their brand. Travel programmes on television are often sponsored by travel and tourism organisations.

Public relations (PR)

PR is about maintaining a good public image. PR activities are an important part of an organisation's marketing strategy and are sometimes arranged by a separate PR team or even a specialist company. PR activities include:

▸ producing press releases
▸ dealing with media enquiries and producing press packs
▸ organising events
▸ publishing newsletters.

Link

You can find out about digital marketing and public relations on pages 266 and 267 in Unit 5: Travel and Tourism Enterprises.

Research

Take a look at the 'Inbound Markets' list on the VisitBritain website and choose a country from the list. Using the information provided by VisitBritain, find out how much people use social media in that country and the popular sites that are used.

Using your findings, make recommendations to a UK-based inbound tour operator about the ways in which they should manage their social media and review site presence in that country.

Virgin competition

As part of its promotional activity, Virgin launched a new competition. This competition was directed at travel agents, not at the general public and so it was only advertised in the trade press.

'10 weeks, 10 prizes,
10 chances to win.

Simply book Virgin Atlantic and Delta Air Lines flights, through Virgin Atlantic Flightstore, from 8 January until 17 March.

Each qualifying booking will earn an entry into the prize draw to win one of 10 prizes at the end of the incentive period.

All prizes above will be awarded at RANDOM at the end of the incentive period.'

Check your knowledge

1 What is the aim of this promotion?

2 How effective do you think it is and why?

Link

You can learn more about distribution channels in Unit 1: The World of Travel and Tourism and on page 267 in Unit 5: Travel and Tourism Enterprises.

Selecting an appropriate promotional mix

When deciding on its promotional mix a business must consider which promotional channels to use based on:

▸ the best way to reach its chosen target market; for example, mobile apps or adverts on social media might not be appropriate for an older target market, whereas a printed newspaper advert may not be appropriate for a younger group

▸ the brand image it wishes to portray; for example, it may not be suitable to advertise a fast-paced, exciting adventure holiday on a radio station popular with older listeners

▸ how promotion should differ locally, regionally, nationally or internationally; for example, a global celebrity endorsement may be a useful promotional tool for a global market, whereas an organisation may choose to use direct marketing through flyers for a local market

▸ the stage of the product life cycle; for example, a product in the maturity phase can be advertised to the current market through known means, whereas a product in the introduction phase may need a different form of promotion to reach more customers.

Place

Place is the element of the marketing mix that considers how to get the product or service to the customer, or in the case of visitor attractions and destinations, how to sell the product to the customer and get the customer to the attraction or to the destination. The means of getting the product to the customer is known as the distribution channel, supply chain or marketing channel.

Distribution channel/supply chain

Figure 3.3 shows an example of a traditional distribution channel for a tour operator for a package holiday, including accommodation, transport and transfer.

▸ **Figure 3.3:** Traditional supply chain or chain of distribution

However, there are now many variations to this traditional supply chain in travel and tourism as customers can choose to buy without using travel agents by purchasing full package holidays on the internet. Customers can also choose to bypass tour operators when purchasing more tailor-made holidays by researching and purchasing each individual element of their holiday online.

Traditional travel agencies still exist on our high streets but focus much more on giving face-to-face information and sales advice to remain competitive with online distribution. Some travel agents, such as On the Beach, operate solely online. The internet has considerably reduced distribution costs for airlines and tour operators. Bookings for low-cost airlines are almost exclusively made on the internet.

Customers have grown accustomed to this convenience too. Tour operators also sell over the internet and often through call centres. Ebrochures are now easily accessible on the internet. They are a huge cost-saving for tour operators compared to paper versions and are more efficient as they can be readily updated.

When deciding on place within the marketing mix, a business must consider which distribution channels to use based on:
▶ reaching its chosen target market; for example, understanding which websites or agents people prefer
▶ the cost of distribution
▶ whether to use more than one channel; this is called a multi-channel approach.

Case study

Emirates

Emirates is expanding its UK distribution through a deal with On the Beach, an online travel agent. New technology integration will see the online travel agent sell Emirates flights to Dubai from eight UK airports.

The online travel agent will introduce medium- to long-haul holidays, with a focus on Dubai and Gulf beach resorts such as Ras Al Khaimah, having fine-tuned its core business which has historically focused on short-haul holidays.

This has been enabled by On the Beach becoming the UK's first online travel agent to launch a direct integration with Emirates through online B2B (business to business) to allow On the Beach to connect directly to Emirate's reservation system.

On the Beach has optimised its offerings in the destinations and is now directly contracting its hotels in the region, focusing on four- and five-star properties

in Dubai with a mix of board basis options, and all-inclusive properties in Ras Al Khaimah.

Its online platform has also been optimised to handle scheduled flights, along with its current offering of low-cost and charter services.

The launch of the Emirates integration will be supported by 'significant marketing investment' by On the Beach, with contract staff also joining the business to focus on the new offering.

Check your knowledge
1   What are the advantages to On the Beach of being an online travel agent?
2   Why do you think Emirates chose to partner with On the Beach?
3   What do you think is meant by 'significant marketing investment'?

PAUSE POINT   List at least three ways in which a business can influence a tourist's decision about where to go on holiday through promotion.

Hint   Review the possible advertising and promotion ideas discussed in this section.

Extend   How can a travel and tourism business influence what happens on social media?

Link

We will look at the potential impacts of marketing and success of travel and tourism organisations in more detail in section B on page 146.

Potential impacts of the marketing mix and customer service

Getting the marketing mix right (with an excellent product at the right price, reaching the target market through appropriate channels and supported by excellent customer service) has positive impacts for both the customer and the organisation. Of course, the opposite is true, a poor marketing mix and poor services will adversely impact the customer and the organisation.

▶ **Table 3.6:** Potential positive and negative impacts of the marketing mix and customer service

Positive impacts	Negative impacts
Customers are happy and post good reviews and tell their friends	Unhappy customers tell their friends, post poor reviews and harm the reputation of the organisation
Customers stay with the organisation and buy more products and services – they are loyal and are likely to spend more money	Customers go elsewhere to buy products or book their holidays – the organisation loses this income
Partner organisations want to work with other organisations who have high standards and a good reputation	Adverse publicity harms the reputation even more
With more revenue the organisation can invest in new products and services and beat the competition	There are complaints due to poor service – which cost money to resolve and result in lost customers Revenue decreases
Happy customers make for happy employees who want to stay with a successful company	Employees are unhappy and leave if they can

Assessment activity 3.1 A.P1 A.P2 A.M1 A.D1

You work for a travel marketing publication, *Getting Ahead in Travel*, which is a trade publication aimed at travel and tourism industry professionals. Your editor has asked you to produce an article showing how marketing and customer service can work together effectively in travel and tourism organisations to both persuade customers to make a purchase and to ensure that customers' needs are met. Your editor has suggested that in your article you:

- use appropriate industry examples to show your understanding
- come to conclusions and make evaluative judgements about the relationship between effective marketing and customer service in terms of influencing customer decisions and meeting customer needs.

The article should also evaluate the impacts of the use of effective and ineffective marketing mix strategies on both customers and organisations. Using examples from travel and tourism organisations, it should consider, analyse and evaluate the positive impacts of an effective marketing mix and the negative impacts of an ineffective marketing mix.

Make sure you include:

- each of the 4 Ps
- judgements about positive and negative impacts on customers and organisations
- industry examples.

Plan

- What specific information should I include in my article?
- What publications could I research to find industry examples?
- How should I present my article? Should I include visuals?

Do

- I have chosen my examples and they are from different organisations within travel and tourism.
- I have decided to structure my article in two parts, one to cover marketing and customer service together with examples and the other to evaluate different marketing mixes and their impacts.
- I have planned my time between carrying out research and putting my material together.

Review

- I can evaluate the impacts of different marketing strategies used by organisations and say why they are effective or not.
- I have presented my article so that it appeals to industry professionals.
- I have checked that I have covered all the tasks thoroughly.

B Examine the impact that marketing activities have on the success of different travel and tourism organisations

The role of marketing in different travel and tourism organisations

Remember that the definition of marketing is 'The management process responsible for identifying, anticipating and satisfying customer requirements profitably'. The marketing process allows us to develop the key elements of this definition and implement the tools that will influence customers to buy products and services and build positive customer relationships.

The marketing process

The marketing process is cyclical:

▶ It begins with reviewing the organisation's current position in the market, in relation to competition, and understanding all the other external factors that may affect the business in the short and long term. It requires knowledge and understanding of the target market and how that may change or develop.

▶ Once this review is complete, the marketing plan is devised to support the business strategy and meet the needs and expectations of the organisation's customers.

▶ The plan is constantly monitored and amended to ensure it is successful and, at the end of the business period, the whole process is repeated.

Figure 3.4 outlines the marketing process.

▶ **Figure 3.4:** The marketing process

Marketing aims and objectives

In order to achieve its goals and purpose, a business identifies specific aims and objectives. The aims of different businesses vary, often depending on whether the business is a private business, a public organisation or a not-for-profit organisation. The aims and objectives of a business will also depend on its mission, vision and values.

Private businesses

A private business must make enough money to stay in business and to satisfy its shareholders, who will expect dividends in return for their investment in the business.

A private business may have aims such as to:

▶ increase **market share**

▶ make as much profit as possible (also known as profit maximisation) – the **profitability** of a business will affect its short-term and long-term future

Key terms

Market leader – the business that controls most of the market for a particular product or service.

Market share – the portion of the overall customer sales market that a business's products or services makes.

Profitability – the extent to which a business's products or services produce a financial profit.

Sustainable tourism – the practice of developing tourism products and services that consider current and future economic, social and environmental impacts but that also meet the needs of visitors, conserve the environment and benefit local communities.

141

- be the **market leader**
- practise **sustainable tourism**
- be competitive
- diversify into new markets or new products.

The marketing objectives are set to support these overarching business aims and objectives and help determine the kind of marketing activity. They set the goals of the marketing plan.

If a business's aim is to 'be the market leader', the marketing objectives to achieve this aim might be to increase:
- brand awareness by 25 per cent within 18 months
- customer satisfaction scores from 75 per cent to 85 per cent in 12 months.

Whereas, to achieve the aim of 'profit maximisation', the marketing objectives might include:
- increasing sales by 15 per cent within 12 months
- reviewing the pricing strategy to increase sales while maintaining profits within one month.

Case study

Tour operators

The aim of tour operators like TUI is to sell holidays and related travel products. These businesses express their aims through their vision, mission statement and values. For example, the vision might be 'to be the world's best holiday company'.

The values express the behaviours staff should demonstrate when talking with customers.

Tour operators have to remember that marketing to customers begins as soon as customers search for holidays or notice advertising or websites. It continues throughout the booking process, in an agency or online, and is just as important after the holiday is finished.

Check your knowledge

1 Decide on a name and vision for your own tour operator.
2 Decide on the marketing objectives.
3 Draw a typical customer journey from researching a holiday to coming home. How does tracking the customer journey help achieve the marketing objectives?
4 Choose a set of values for your tour operator and say why you chose them.

Public organisations

Public organisations may share some of the same aims as private businesses but some of their aims will be different because they need to:
- provide a good service for taxpayers
- meet standards set by the government
- keep a control on costs.

VisitBritain

VisitBritain is a non-departmental public body funded by the Department for Digital, Culture, Media & Sport (DCMS). Its purpose is to raise Britain's profile worldwide, increasing the volume and value of tourism exports and developing Britain's visitor economy. Its scope is international, as it has offices in the UK and overseas, and it is a large organisation, employing around 250 staff.

The organisation's mission is 'to grow the volume and value of inbound tourism across the nations and regions of Britain and to develop world-class English tourism product to support our growth aspirations'.

Its aims are to:
- market the nations and regions of Britain overseas to drive growth in international leisure and business tourism
- maintain distinct activities to develop and market British tourism.

These aims are broken down into priorities, which are then broken down further into objectives or targets, and details about how these targets will be achieved through specified outcomes.

For example:
- **Objective** – establish a clear strategy and role in the business visits and events sector
- **Details** – working alongside strategic partners (including key cities), UK industry, UK Trade and Investment (UKTI) and the Great Britain and Northern Ireland promotional campaign (GREAT), playing an active role on the cross-government Events Industry Board
- **Outcome** – an increase in demand to host business events in Britain, and an increase in revenue from events held in the UK.

Check your knowledge

1 Why is it important for VisitBritain to set very clear aims with specified outcomes?

2 VisitBritain is a marketing organisation. Discuss how the business and marketing objectives in the case study overlap.

3 Investigate VisitBritain's success in attracting more people to hold business events in the UK. If it has had any successes, what marketing activities did it employ to achieve these?

Not-for-profit or voluntary organisations

Not-for-profit or voluntary organisations may also share some of the same aims as private businesses, but any profits that they make will be reinvested into the organisation to continue fulfilling their aims. The aims of a voluntary organisation could include:
- supporting a community
- protecting the environment
- educating people
- conserving historic or natural sites.

All businesses aim to build and maintain customer loyalty. Many customers, if they feel a bond or connection with a product or service, will continue to use it for a long time. Businesses need to keep this positive feeling alive through excellent customer service and high-quality products. A single negative experience of an organisation can shatter years of positive feelings and significantly reduce the possibility of a customer choosing that business's projects or services again.

National Air Traffic Services (NATS)

National Air Traffic Services (NATS) is a public–private partnership between the government and a number of partners, including Airline Group, NATS staff and the airport operator LHR Airports Limited. Its purpose is to provide air traffic navigation services to aircraft flying through UK-controlled airspace and at numerous UK and international airports. Its scope is national and international, providing air traffic control for the UK and operating internationally for engineering contracts and consultancy. The company is large, employing 4,500 people around the world.

NATS makes profits, but providing a safe service is its main priority, and it must do this to standards set by the air regulator – the Civil Aviation Authority (CAA). Its vision is 'advancing aviation, keeping the skies safe'. Its priorities for 2019–2020 included the following:

- Provide safe and resilient air traffic services from our airports and centres.

- Drive airspace modernisation, include the delivery of the network airspace designs needed to support the London Airspace Modernisation Project (LAMP).
- Provide a digital air traffic service to London City Airport from Swanwick Terminal Control
- Invest in our people by launching a new digital workplace and intranet to improve how we collaborate, communicate and stay connected.

These priorities are broken down into SMART objectives in the organisation's strategic plan.

Check your knowledge

1 NATS is the only organisation providing air traffic control in the UK. What do you think are the reasons for its success?
2 Why do organisations like NATS use SMART objectives to break down their priorities?
3 Discuss the reasons why an organisation like NATS might be set up as a public–private partnership.

Setting SMART objectives

Whenever objectives are set, for marketing purposes or even for yourself, they should always be SMART.

- ▶ **Specific** – the objective is explained clearly and contains specific details that will be achieved.
- ▶ **Measurable** – it will be easy to see when the objective has been achieved.
- ▶ **Achievable** – the objective is realistic.
- ▶ **Relevant** – the objective will help you to achieve what you set out to achieve.
- ▶ **Time-bound** – the objective has a specified end point.

 **PAUSE POINT**   What does SMART stand for?

 Hint   It is an acronym, so each letter stands for a word.

Extend   Give an example of a SMART objective relating to travel and tourism marketing.

Development of a brand and brand extensions

A brand is the means by which the customer recognises a business and by which a business differentiates itself from the competition. It influences customers' perception of a business.

A brand represents the business's values and is how customers identify with the business, so it is vital for reputation. An organisation builds its brand awareness through its name, logo, website, social media presence and, most of all, through its customer experience. Many businesses have more than one brand under their main company name; building up brand extensions or a family of brands. Accor Hotels group, for example, has more than 20 brands. This allows it to target different markets, from budget to luxury, with different brands.

Marketing activities should try to achieve the following brand values:
▶ differentiation – showing something that is unique about the brand
▶ knowledge – enhancing the customer's knowledge about the brand and how they perceive it
▶ esteem – demonstrating the extent to which the customer perceives the brand to be of good quality and popular
▶ relevance – showing how appropriate the brand is for a customer.

> **Research**
>
> Expedia is one of the largest online travel companies in the world. It owns several other brands. Find out which brands it owns.

Implications of organisation size for marketing activity

Large organisations often have departments with different functions and specialist staff to provide expertise in a certain area and serve the whole organisation. For example:
▶ human resources (HR)
▶ research and development
▶ sales
▶ marketing
▶ purchasing
▶ product development
▶ finance and accounting
▶ IT
▶ customer services.

Dividing an organisation into functional areas can be useful as it allows employees within each department to become highly specialised and expert in their area. However, employees may think that they have no responsibility for functions outside their own team. For example, employees working in IT might think that they have no responsibility for customer service.

Smaller organisations, particularly start-ups, cannot afford to have all these departments and may have to manage different areas with few staff. For example, founders of start-ups may fulfil a number of roles and usually handle their own recruitment process so that they concentrate on filling key roles with suitable people who fit the ethos of their company.

Marketing roles ideally require specialist expertise, but the number and status of roles depends on the budget available.

Mass and niche markets

Mass market products and services appeal to large numbers of people and are related to the 'maturity' stage of the product life cycle, where a product or destination has reached a stage of such high popularity that everyone wants to try it.

A product or service appeals to a niche market when it is a specialist product or service that appeals to a small target market with very similar interests. For example, diving holidays generally only appeal to divers. Some tourism businesses choose to specialise in a niche market and can be very successful if there are few competitors and they can easily achieve the main market share. When a new product or destination is introduced, it might be targeted at a niche market of innovators who want to try something new and are willing to pay a higher price for it.

Companies which specialise in each type of market are likely to be very different in size. A mass-market tour operator, such as TUI, is likely to have a large marketing department, whereas a tour operator operating in a niche market may have a much smaller department, potentially just one marketing person.

Marketing activities for mass and niche markets will also inevitably vary in the style and form of the marketing activity and the amount of budget they have to spend on the activity:

▶ For a mass-market holiday, such as a cruise, a company may advertise on TV, using an expensively produced advert in a prime-time TV slot. Adverts by mass-market operators may be rarer, as they are already so well known. However, even mass-market operators need to ensure that they are remembered by their current customers to keep ahead of the competition.

▶ For a niche-market holiday, such as a walking tour of the Highlands, the company is more likely to advertise in a specialist walking magazine through a low-cost print advert.

 **PAUSE POINT** Describe the stages of the marketing process.

 Hint Look back at Figure 3.4 to help you.

Extend Explain why the marketing process is cyclical.

How marketing contributes to the success of travel and tourism organisations

Growth strategies

An organisation may choose growth as its objective and develop marketing strategies to achieve this. There are different ways of achieving growth and these are illustrated in the Ansoff Matrix (Figure 3.5).

Products

	Existing	New
Existing (Markets)	Market Penetration	Product Development
New (Markets)	Market Development	Diversification

▶ **Figure 3.5:** the Ansoff Matrix

Market penetration

Existing products or services are unchanged and are marketed to existing customers. The organisation tries to increase market share through more promotions and advertising.

Market development

A new market is found for existing products or services. This could be a new target market domestically or internationally.

Principles of Marketing in Travel and Tourism

Product development

Products or services are improved or amended. Modified products are marketed to the same customers who have purchased them previously, but with the new features included.

Diversification

The organisation goes into new areas; for example, by offering new destinations or offering brand-new products.

Acquisition

An organisation may achieve some of the Ansoff growth strategies through **acquisition**. For example, in 2020, the UK tour operator, Shearings, went into administration. Leger Holidays then bought the brand, website and customer database. This allowed Leger to increase its market share by offering UK-based products alongside its more European-focussed offering.

> **Key term**
>
> **Acquisition** – the purchase of one company by another.

> **Theory into practice**
>
> Caribbean Dreams sells package holidays to different Caribbean islands to UK tourists. They are attempting various marketing activities to increase their market share. Match each statement to the correct box in the Ansoff Matrix.
> - We are going to keep the same product portfolio but market to people in France.
> - We are going to increase our advertising budget in the UK and have more advertising aimed at our existing target market.
> - We will design a new brochure and send it out to everyone on our customer database.
> - We will introduce a different island destination, St Lucia, to our portfolio.
> - We will invest in a hotel in Barbados and market it in the UK.
> - We will run an online competition for our existing customers.
> - We will introduce a new campaign targeting millennials, a group that is new to us.

Links between marketing and an organisation's aims and objectives

All marketing activity must link back to the organisation's aims and objectives to ensure that it is helping the organisation achieve its goals and is meeting customers' needs. It can take some time for marketing activities to be successful, particularly where objectives are difficult to achieve. For example, the objective of building a brand and gaining recognition in a crowded market may be longer-term goals.

If any element of the marketing plan or marketing mix is wrong the organisation will not meet its aims and objectives and will have to audit its marketing plan to determine where the problem lies. For example, they may need to address the following questions:
- Have we identified the right target market?
- Do we have sufficient understanding of the customer and their behaviour?
- What is the customer's perception of the product and brand? Is it as anticipated?
- Does the customer understand the product features and benefits?
- Are we promoting the products appropriately across all channels?
- Is the price right?
- Are we using the right marketing channels to reach the customer?
- Is our social media message appropriate?
- Are we allowing sufficient customer interaction through social media?
- Has our marketing team got the skills needed to deliver the plan?
- Are we spending our marketing budget in the right way?
- Is the marketing plan aligned to our business objectives?

Continuous monitoring of marketing activity and regular evaluations of the plan should ensure that, where necessary, recommendations are made and implemented to improve the plan.

Case study

Ryanair

In 2018 Ryanair made further changes to its five-year marketing strategy. Following cancellations due to disputes with staff and the subsequent reputational damage, Ryanair decided to focus on customer improvements rather than the low price of its flights. According to YouGov, Ryanair's brand impression score, the measure of whether the brand has a good impression of the brand, had dropped substantially. However, Ryanair's own internal satisfaction surveys showed that more than 86 per cent of customers were satisfied.

Ryanair continued its marketing programme: 'Always getting better' and rolled out some new initiatives over the following year:

- **Price promise** – If customers find a cheaper fare, they can apply for a refund for the difference in cost and receive some credit to their RyanAir account.
- **Punctuality pledge** – 90 per cent of flights would be on time.
- **Easy bag policy** – Customers are allowed to take two free cabin bags and checked bags at €25 for 20 kg.
- **Dedicated claims team** – All valid EU261 claims will be processed within ten days.
- **Being green** – They are working towards being plastic-free, and are offering customers a carbon offset scheme, to be the greenest airline.
- **Savings when booking Ryanair rooms** – Discounts are available on flights when booking hotels.
- **Transfers** – Offering customers a wider choice of ground transport by working with a partner, Car Trawler.
- **Connecting flights** – Offering connections both in Europe and long-haul.
- **Travel info service** – Providing destination information on Ryanair.com with content in seven different languages.

Check your knowledge

1 Carry out some research and assess the success of the latest initiatives in Ryanair's marketing plan in terms of:
    - customer satisfaction with the airline
    - current profits
    - extent to which the above policies are still current or have been changed
    - progress on targets defined above.
2 Make recommendations for improving Ryanair's marketing plan in light of your research.

 **PAUSE POINT** Explain why it's necessary to monitor and evaluate the marketing mix and plan.

 Hint Think about how the marketing plan should support business objectives.

Extend Give examples of measures that can be used to assess a marketing plan's success.

Different approaches to planning marketing

Push and pull approaches

Pushing a product or service is letting a customer know about a product directly by showing it to them and offering incentives to buy. Examples include:

▶ sending targeted emails direct to particular inboxes, reminding customers to purchase after they have left a company's website
▶ showing products at exhibitions, such as travel shows.

Pulling customers takes longer but is when customers demand the product and ask for it. The 'pull' is created by building up interest and desire perhaps through influencers on social media or **guerrilla marketing** to create lots of excitement and interest. Pull can also be created by more traditional advertising campaigns.

▶ An example of guerrilla marketing

Customer relationship management

Customer relationship management (CRM) is a strategy for managing a company's interaction with its customers. Every time a travel and tourism organisation takes a booking, it receives information about the customer, such as their personal details and their preferences. By collecting and analysing customer information, an organisation can use this information to understand customer trends, provide excellent customer service and retain existing customers. One of the keys to successful marketing is knowing and understanding your customers' needs.

B2B and B2C marketing

Travel and tourism marketing may be business to business (B2B), for example, a travel app developer would market its services to tour operators, or business to consumer (B2C), for example, a travel agent selling direct to customers. Some organisations may run two different marketing strategies, one aimed at businesses – such as a tour operator marketing its products to travel agencies (B2B) – and another strategy marketing directly to customers (B2C).

Potential impact of marketing on customers

Successful marketing supports an organisation as it can:

▶ attract new customers, by appealing to a different target market, entering a different geographic market or gaining customers from a competitor
▶ retain customers by building strong brand relationships and by providing good customer service
▶ increase customer spend by introducing premium products such as first-class air cabins or upmarket hotel rooms

- generate customer loyalty by:
  - operating customer loyal schemes, such as loyalty points schemes for a free holiday or hotel nights
  - managing promotional activity and social media to generate positive images and strengthen the organisation's brand
  - making it easy for customers to do business by offering different channels and mobile apps.

Potential impact of marketing on the organisation

Marketing also has positive impacts for the organisation itself:

- It can strengthen and support the organisational objectives, such as entering a new market, increasing market share or making greater profits. For example, budget hotel chains Travelodge and Premier Inn both launched premium brands to appeal to a new market – corporate customers. In 2017, Travelodge marketed and launched Travelodge PLUS hotels and SuperRooms™. Premier Inn followed in 2019 with Premier Plus rooms. For an extra £15 to £20 per night, customers can expect better broadband, a rainfall shower, luxury toiletries, more space and a luxury coffee-making machine amongst other comforts. Premier Inn found that the product attracted a lot of interest from leisure customers as well as the business target market.

- It can also develop the brand through promotion to new or niche markets by trying to extend the life cycle of the product. Once a product goes into decline, it can either be replaced by something entirely new or rejuvenated by adding an improvement or starting the cycle again in a new market. In the 19th and early 20th centuries, seaside towns in the UK were popular tourist destinations. However, as a result of the growing trend for overseas holidays from the 1970s, these towns gradually declined. There are many projects across the UK aimed at regenerating seaside towns. Margate, in particular, has had some success in attracting tourists and extending the destination's life cycle. Dreamland, the UK's oldest pleasure park, reopened after millions of pounds of investment and the Turner Contemporary gallery, which opened in 2011, has attracted more than 2.9 million visitors.

- Successful marketing should result in an increase in profits, where that is the objective. The resulting profits can be reinvested into the business allowing a bigger budget for further marketing activity or given as a dividend to shareholders. Of course, if there is a decrease in profits, the opposite is true – there will be less money to spend on marketing and the business may have to adopt different strategies to encourage sales, such as a pricing strategy of loss leading. In 2018, Grupo Pinero, the Spanish holding company of the Bahia Principe hotel chain made a profit of over $900 million. It was able to reinvest and plan product differentiation and improvements and also invest in digital technology for 2019. Success in 2018 can be attributed not only to a varied marketing campaign but also to the innovative approach of segmenting customers by the kind of experience they desired. For customers wanting to connect with local nature and culture, Bahia offers hotels with the 'Treasure' experience with opportunities to connect with nature, to attend local art workshops and to listen to local live music.

PAUSE POINT   Give three examples of how customer loyalty can be encouraged.

> **Hint**   Think about the sort of things a company does that encourage you to use that company's services again.

> **Extend**   How does a CRM system support customer service?

Influences on marketing activity

External factors

External factors are those outside of the organisation and which the organisation cannot necessarily control. The organisation must monitor and review external factors continually. This section will look at the external factors that may influence how a company organises its marketing activity.

PESTLE analysis is an analytical tool that a business can use to evaluate the external environment in which it operates. It is too easy for a business to overlook the impact of external factors and become too focused on the internal factors affecting its day-to-day operations. Failing to analyse the trading environment is very dangerous as the business may be taken by surprise by changes in the external environment. Businesses can also miss opportunities to expand or to break into new markets if they do not analyse the external environment.

Political factors

▶ **Unrest:** Civil unrest often arises from difficult economic and political situations and can result in protests which may become very violent. Local and national government may lose control resulting in dangerous situations and violence and crime. Although tourists might not be the target of any unrest, they can easily get caught up in it when it occurs. Any destination in a situation of unrest is best avoided.

The British Foreign and Commonwealth Office (FCO) provides up-to-date information on safety across the world. Any political unrest, potential for conflict or terrorist activity in an area may make it too dangerous to visit. Even if the immediate risk is low, customers may still have a negative perception of certain destinations based on previous conflict, which will affect their willingness to visit.

Travel and tourism organisations have to be aware of the political situation in the destinations that they offer to customers and of that country's relations with the UK.

Case study

Hong Kong

Throughout 2019 and 2020, pro-democracy protests took place in Hong Kong. The protesters took part in anti-government rallies and there was significant disruption throughout the region. The airport was occupied by protestors resulting in hundreds of flights being cancelled. Hong Kong is one of the world's most visited cities by tourists, but by August 2019 visitor numbers were down 40 per cent on the previous year. Many potential tourists were worried about travelling to Hong Kong and governments around the world issued safety warnings.

Check your knowledge

1 Find out the background and reasons for the Hong Kong protests.
2 What impact has the unrest had on marketing Hong Kong as a destination?
3 Research the current situation and decide whether you think it is safe to travel to Hong Kong.
4 What is the appeal of Hong Kong as a city destination?

- **Terrorism:** The immediate impact of a terrorist attack on tourism in a destination is devastating. Following a terrorist attack, tour operators need to get tourists out of the destination, which may require special charter flights. They may also need to cancel contracts with suppliers in that destination and replace the destination with another. This has a significant impact on their revenue. The impact on the destination is just as bad; there is likely to be an immediate steep decline in the number of visitors from all countries, affecting the revenue of local tourism businesses and some may even cease to operate.

Figure 3.6 shows the various factors that influence the length of decline in tourism following a terrorist attack.

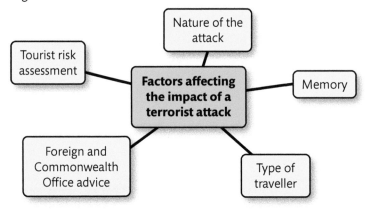

▶ **Figure 3.6:** The factors that affect the impact of terrorism on a destination

If an attack is a one-off event and can be blamed on a lone terrorist, visitor numbers are likely to recover quite quickly as customers forget what happened. If a number of attacks occur or the attack is severe and widely reported, customers are more likely to have negative associations with that destination for a long time.

Case study

Sri Lanka

Following the terrorist attacks of 2019, tourism stopped in Sri Lanka. In May and June, the low season in Sri Lanka, there were not many bookings. Tourists who had already booked cancelled because they were scared or because their government had issued advice not to travel. Even after governments lifted their restrictions on travel, visitor numbers were still 57 per cent down from the previous year. Some hotels had to close temporarily, keeping staff where they could, but paying them less than their usual wages. Others with small businesses, such as tuk-tuk drivers, guides and souvenir sellers, were devastated and many couldn't work. Some drivers had to sell their tuk-tuks as they could no longer afford to repay the loans with which they had bought them. In response to these issues, the

Sri Lankan Tourism Alliance, which represents over 160 hotel owners and tour operators, launched a campaign to bring tourists back to the country.

Check your knowledge

1   Research tourist numbers in Sri Lanka and assess how far visitor numbers have recovered since this incident.

2   Find out more about the Sri Lankan Tourism Alliance. Why and when was it formed? What are its achievements?

3   Why do you think visitors are returning to Sri Lanka following the terrorist attacks?

Look at tradingeconomics.com/sri-lanka/tourist-arrivals for statistics.

▶ **International political relations:** Governments have policies and make decisions that not only affect their own tourist industry but also the tourist industries of other countries. For example, in 2020 following the COVID-19 pandemic, countries across the world negotiated quarantine arrangements and travel 'bridges' between one country and another to protect the safety of their citizens and yet promote tourism.

Changes in visa requirements can also have a huge impact on the number of tourists who travel to a particular destination. The UK's decision in 2016 to leave the European Union (EU) may have implications on travel between the UK and EU.

Economic factors

▶ **Recession:** A recession occurs when a country's economy is in decline and there is little economic activity, as occurred following the COVID-19 pandemic in 2020. A recession impacts on disposable income so that customers have less money to spend, particularly on non-essential products like holidays.

▶ **Taxes:** Increased taxes in general and on package holidays raise costs for businesses. Passengers on airlines have become used to paying air passenger duty, but when other taxes are introduced or existing taxes raised this can cause customer anxiety about rising costs and result in less travel, at least in the short term.

▶ **Interest rates:** Interest rate rises can affect a business's ability to repay its loans. Not repaying loans causes financial difficulty and may be one reason a business fails. When interest rates are low, businesses can borrow more money for investment. Interest rate rises may also affect customers if they have borrowed money, such as for loans or mortgages, as their repayments will increase meaning they have less disposable income.

▶ **Exchange rate:** Changes in the exchange rate can also dramatically affect a business's costs and impact on businesses' pricing strategies. For example, a UK tour operator with contracted accommodation in Spain pays the accommodation providers in euros. A weak British pound will buy fewer euros, meaning that the cost of accommodation to the tour operator increases.

Social factors

▶ **Demographic changes:** Demographic changes can affect the market for a product or service. As people live longer and healthier lives in many parts of the world, this creates a market for travel and holidays for older people. If people have fewer children, the market for family holidays will decrease. A current trend is for multi-generational holidays, where grandparents, parents and children go away together.

▶ **Consumer trends:**
  • **New experiences:** As people travel more and enjoy experiencing different cultures, they want new experiences and remote destinations 'off the beaten track'. Central American countries such as Guatemala, Panama and Nicaragua are increasing in popularity, especially group tours, as tourists feel more confident about being safe there. Technology allows travellers to these places to book accommodation ahead, check safe routes and keep in contact with friends and family making it easier to stay safe. Central Asia is also becoming more accessible with countries such as Uzbekistan and its Silk Road tours becoming highly popular. These countries offer different cultural experiences and climates to explore so appeal to young people who love to experience other cultures and explore history.
  • **Domestic holidays (or 'staycations'):** These are becoming increasingly popular as people are more concerned about the value of the pound and their safety while on holiday overseas. Following the COVID-19 pandemic in 2020, many UK residents preferred to take holidays in the UK even when overseas travel opportunities opened up.

- **Responsible travel:** People are becoming more aware of their social responsibility and are therefore choosing to spend their money with businesses that share their values and ethics. When planning holidays, they may look at companies who support the local economy and people by using local tour guides and operators or who offer homestays in local people's houses.
- **Wellness:** People are increasingly looking to escape the stress of everyday life, relax and improve their well-being. As a result, there is a growing interest in the 'wellness' tourism market, such as fitness holidays or well-being retreats. In addition, people who lead a healthy life want to continue this on holiday with healthy food and exercise, such as cycling, yoga or swimming. Marketing activity for wellness tourism can emphasise the provision of facilities such as gyms, pools and spa facilities and promote menus catering for different tastes and diets (e.g. vegetarian and vegan).

Technological factors

▶ **Social media:** Businesses that only use traditional media (such as mailshots, television advertising and billboards) for promotion are in danger of not reaching large groups of people who only watch TV through streaming services and who only make contact with friends and businesses through social media. Most companies now have a presence on Facebook, Instagram and Twitter etc., but not all are using social media to its full advantage to fully engage with customers.

▶ **Apps:** Smartphone apps have been developed for a wide range of uses within the travel and tourism industry, such as for booking travel tickets or checking in online (Figure 3.7). These apps are used often and allow customers to do their own travel research and booking. Tourists can even download walking tours for cities and attractions so that they don't need to use a guide. Tourist information centres must consider what they can offer to tourists to be able to compete with this online travel information and continue to provide services that attract customers.

Travel and tourism apps are some of the most popular apps to download. Travel and tourism businesses therefore need to provide apps to keep up with customer demand and to compete with their rivals. Apps can help businesses to increase revenue and achieve a personalised relationship with customers. Depending on users' privacy settings, apps can also allow organisations to find out specific information about their customers and their behaviours, which they can use to market to different demographics.

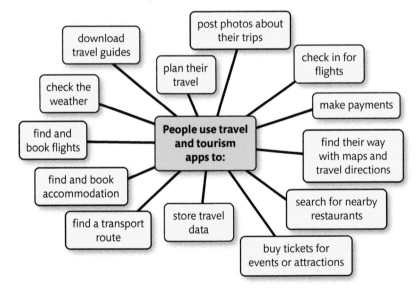

▶ **Figure 3.7:** Different uses of travel and tourism apps

Many businesses offer a **bespoke** app to make customers' experience with their business easy and straightforward, and to encourage customer loyalty. For example:

- the InterContinental Hotels Group app – gives customers access to hotel reservations for all the hotels in the hotel group, as well as directions and other information
- the Emirates airline app – allows customers to search for flights, book tickets, manage bookings and display boarding passes
- the Tour Radar trip assistant – allows customers to access trip notes and vouchers and manage bookings on the go.

▶ **Transport development:** The primary trend in the transport sector is for faster and more environmentally friendly transport due to increased environmental awareness and customer desire to make sustainable transport choices. Airlines that can afford to invest in new planes are taking advantage of advances in technology, meaning that new aircraft are lighter and more fuel efficient. Jets are now built of carbon plastic fibres and other composite materials and weigh up to a fifth less than they used to. Lightweight seats are also available. Improvements to aircraft manufacture mean that they are able to fly further without stopping. In March 2018, Qantas introduced a non-stop route from London to Perth in Australia, using 787 Dreamliner planes. Advances in rail technology, such as automatic train operation and high-speed trains that can travel at speeds of 267 mph, mean that train travel is faster and more efficient.

Companies can emphasise these product features and benefits in their marketing.

Legal and ethical considerations

▶ **Consumer protection:** It is important for travel and tourism businesses to keep up to date with relevant legislation, such as the Consumer Rights Act, 2015. Failure to do so could result in heavy fines. This Act has implications for the accuracy of marketing literature and digital content.

▶ **Advertising standards:** Advertising in the UK must also adhere to standards set by the Advertising Standards Authority.

▶ **Codes of practice:** Trade bodies, such as ABTA, issue sector codes of practice which provide useful guidance for members on legal and ethical issues.

▶ **Other legislation:** The airline industry is very heavily regulated for safety and must also consider environmental legislation and consumer rights. All businesses will adhere to general health and safety, consumer rights, employment rights and data protection legislation.

An organisation should consider the ethics of any partners or suppliers it is considering using and make sure they align with the highest of standards. Any lapses in legal and ethical considerations can result in bad publicity.

Environmental factors

▶ **Extreme weather and natural disasters:** The weather plays an important role in determining where tourists choose to go on holiday. A poor summer in the UK always leads to increased bookings for holidays abroad the year afterwards, as the domestic tourists who opted for a staycation during a poor summer choose to go abroad next time. Conversely, the excellent weather of summer 2018 encouraged domestic tourism in 2019.

The reporting of severe weather conditions and natural disasters, such as the Sulawesi earthquake and tsunami in Indonesia in 2018, the 2019/2020 bushfires in Australia and even too much snow in winter ski seasons affects holiday bookings. Marketing activity could seek to reassure customers about safety and suggest alternative destinations.

Key term

Bespoke – created specifically for a particular individual or business.

Research

Write some survey questions about the use of travel and tourism apps. Use these questions to carry out a small survey of at least ten people (from different age groups and backgrounds if possible). Compare your survey results with others in your group and present the whole group's findings using charts and graphs that can be displayed.

Extreme weather is likely to continue to influence tourism due to climate change. For example:

- rising sea levels are threatening environments and communities that are popular tourist destinations, such as Venice in Italy
- longer periods of intense heat may cause discomfort and illness to tourists
- decreasing cloud cover could increase tourists' exposure to dangerous levels of sunlight radiation
- less snowfall and shorter skiing seasons could lead to a decrease in ski destinations
- the bushfires in Australia in 2019 affected air quality.

Case study

Australian Bushfires

Australia experienced some of the worst bushfires in its history. The fires started in the northern areas of New South Wales and spread quickly across the region. In Queensland, 49,000 acres of land and six homes were destroyed on one day in November. By December, more than 700 homes had been destroyed. In January 2020, New South Wales declared a week-long state of emergency as high temperatures and strong winds threatened further devastation. On 17 December 2019, Australia experienced its hottest day on record with the national average temperature reaching 40.9°C. The extreme temperatures can be linked to a pattern of changing climate. By mid-January, torrential rain fell, which put out the fires but caused flash floods. To help the tourism industry recover, the Australian government promised a recovery package of AUS $76 million. AUS $25 million was used by Tourism Australia to carry out an international marketing campaign to get tourists back to Australia. AUS $20 million was devoted to a domestic marketing campaign to encourage Australians to holiday in Australia and support the affected regions. AUS $9.5 million was given to the International Media Hosting Programme, to invite TV, newspapers and magazines to come and see that Australia is open for business.

Check your knowledge

1 What was the impact of the fires on tourism in Australia?
   Tip: look for reports on visitor numbers.

2 How successful was the recovery package in persuading tourists to visit Australia in 2020?

▶ **Sustainable tourism:** Concerns about climate change and global warming have meant that people are increasingly considering the effect of travelling on the environment. Customers are choosing to spend their money with travel businesses that are environmentally and ethically responsible and offer sustainable tourism. People are more aware and concerned about their own environmental impact when they travel, and the impact on host communities. The trend for sustainable tourism and environmental awareness is influenced by media coverage of the issues and climate change campaigns, such as those led by Greta Thunberg, which have made people more aware of the issues.

Most holidaymakers want to be responsible travellers but may not know how to go about this themselves. It is therefore the responsibility of the various sectors within the travel and tourism industry, such as airlines, airports, cruise ships and tour operators, to practise sustainable tourism on behalf of their customers. Organisations can use their marketing activities to promote their sustainable tourism practices. For example, Virgin Atlantic runs a sustainability programme called 'Change is in the Air', and one of its commitments is to protect the environment. Virgin aims to make its aircraft more efficient, and by 2021 all aircraft in the fleet will be 30 per cent more efficient than the aircraft used previously.

A business with sustainable principles can have a positive effect on its reputation and is likely to attract customers who are responsible tourists. Sustainability determines the type of products and services that an organisation can offer to its customers.

Theory into practice

Work with a partner to complete the following tasks.

1   Choose a tourist facility in your area. Describe the facility and its location and think about its target market.

2   Identify all the external factors that will influence its business strategy. You may need to do some research to find out what is going on in your local area; consider national events and issues as well.

3   Present your findings to the rest of the group. Discuss any differences between the factors that you have identified and those identified by other pairs. Do the external factors present opportunities or threats to your chosen business?

PAUSE POINT   Give examples of two political and two technological factors that influence marketing activity.

> Hint   Look back at examples in the text if you are unsure.
>
> Extend   Give an industry example that illustrates each aspect of your factors.

Internal factors

Internal factors are those that the organisation can control, but which they must still monitor and review continually.

Size of the organisation

As we have seen on page 145 the size of an organisation can impact on the type of products that it offers and therefore marketing activity that is carried out. Larger organisations are more likely than smaller organisations to have a dedicated marketing department. The organisation's aims and objectives (e.g. to increase market share or practise sustainable tourism) will also affect marketing activity.

Culture of the organisation

The overall aims and objectives of an organisation and its organisational culture can also have a significant impact on marketing activity. The culture of an organisation expresses the kind of company it is or aspires to be. Where the culture is one of openness and transparency with clear internal (within the organisation) and external (to customers) communication, then this positive culture is reflected in its marketing activity. As a result, the company is well respected with a positive customer perception in terms of ethos and social responsibility.

Effective leaders within an organisation communicate the organisation's vision and values to all employees so that they understand and commit to the same vision and values. Employees feel trusted and empowered to do their job to the best of their abilities and ultimately create satisfied customers.

The Lake District National Park's vision is to be 'an inspirational example of sustainable development in action'. The vision was developed by the Lake District National Park Partnership and has four elements encompassing the local economy, the local community, the visitor experience and the landscape. To achieve its vision, it needs to carry out any actions in line with its organisational values, which you can find at www.lakedistrict.gov.uk/aboutus/nationalparkvision.

Read through the values and then find examples of the partners that the Lake District National Park has chosen to work with.

Choose two partners it works with. Write some bullet points about how the Lake District's values might affect how they work with these partners and how they might help to achieve the Lake District National Park's vision.

A positive cultural ethos within an organisation is evident through:
▶ engaged and motivated employees who strive to meet the needs of customers
▶ employees who feel valued
▶ good working practices and fair salaries
▶ good social responsibility – the organisation supports local community projects and charities.

An organisation must also consider its cultural ethos and responsibilities within the destinations it operates in by:
▶ employing local people where possible and training them for management posts and beyond
▶ encouraging tourists to respect and experience local culture
▶ not offering activities that cause harm to local natural habitats or animals, such as elephant rides, photos with chimps, boat trips that impact on coral reefs
▶ supporting initiatives in the destination that protect the environment and culture
▶ equipping hotels and their restaurants through local suppliers and sourcing local produce
▶ encouraging sustainable use of local resources – for example, managing the use of water especially for golf courses and pools.

Budget

The overall financial position of an organisation has a direct impact on its marketing activity. A healthy financial position means a larger marketing budget. The marketing team is accountable for the marketing budget and is expected to keep all spending/costs within the budget whilst also generating good returns in terms of sales and customer reputation. The marketing team regularly assesses marketing performance against targets, to ensure that marketing activity is providing value for money and driving sales performance. Increases in profit can be reinvested in the business (as we saw on page 150). Greater profits allow an organisation to reinvest in:
▶ more marketing activity, for example a television or digital billboard advertising campaign in addition to a more traditional campaign
▶ expertise in a particular marketing activity, such as hiring an agency specialising in digital advertising.

Large, successful companies are more likely to have a large marketing budget and therefore be able to engage in more high-profile (and expensive) promotional campaigns. Smaller organisations, with a smaller budget, may be more reliant on creative public relations campaigns and cheaper editorial coverage to create market awareness.

Resources

The marketing department not only needs finance, but it also needs resources both in the form of technology and people.

All organisations, both big and small, need to invest in technology to keep their websites and apps up to date and ensure that they run properly.

Technology updates can be quite capital intensive and consume large amounts of the budget, if unchecked.

Marketing staff should be specialists in their field in order to provide expertise and the best service to their organisations and customers. Motivated, productive and well-trained staff will provide outstanding customer service and give the organisation a competitive advantage.

Case study

Visit Belfast

Visit Belfast is a public/private sector partnership that is funded and supported by Belfast City Council, Tourism Northern Ireland and other private sector partners with the aim of promoting Belfast as a world-class destination for short breaks, conferences and cruises. It provides platforms for tourism businesses to promote their products and services to potential customers and businesses and partner with them in marketing campaigns.

Visit Belfast's approach to marketing campaign activity is to target:
- cities with direct access to Belfast via sea, air or road
- segments and regions with potentially high visitor numbers and revenue growth in the short term.

Its partners have the opportunity to buy into marketing campaign activity from as little as £5,000.

In 2019-20, it planned to spend over £1 million on a range of marketing campaigns in conjunction with Tourism Ireland, air and sea carriers and industry partners. The aims of the campaigns were to increase:
- market share of short city breaks
- repeat visits
- spend from Great Britain and other key European city markets.

In addition, through targeted promotional activity, Visit Belfast will continue to promote day trips and overnight visits from the rest of Northern Ireland and the Republic of Ireland, but with the additional aim of encouraging visitors to stay longer so they can explore Belfast further.

Visit Belfast works with industry partners through bespoke promotions, offers, deals, packages and competitions to promote Belfast and welcomes opportunities to work with industry partners on campaign activity.

Campaigns 2019-2020

Northern Ireland/Republic of Ireland market
- Maritime Festival – ROI, May 2019
- Make It Belfast – NI, June–August 2019
- Make It Belfast – ROI, Summer 2019
- Christmas campaign– NI/ROI Nov–Dec 2019

Campaigns with industry partners, Great Britain market
- Aer Lingus – September 2019
- Expedia – spring and autumn 2019

Campaigns, European market
- Paris, September 2019

Check your knowledge

1 Why are Aer Lingus and Expedia partners in Visit Belfast's campaigns?

2 Explain the external and internal factors currently influencing the marketing of Belfast as a tourist destination. You might consider:
- external factors:
  - political e.g. Brexit
  - economic e.g. the impact of the COVID-19 pandemic, funding from external partners
  - social e.g. trends in tourism, relevant target markets
  - technological e.g. social media presence
  - legal and ethical e.g. current legislation, government guidance following COVID-19 pandemic
  - Environmental e.g. focus on sustainable tourism
- internal factors:
  - size of the organisation (i.e. Visit Belfast)
  - culture of the organisation
  - available budget and potential cuts, sources of funding
  - available resources.

3 Write up your findings or present as an infographic to share with your group.

Globalisation

Globalisation is the process by which businesses operate on a global scale, leading to the interdependence of national economies and the creation of global markets. These globalised businesses are known as multinational corporations (MNCs) or transnational corporations. Table 3.7 highlights the advantages and disadvantages of globalisation.

Key term

Globalisation – process by which businesses operate on a global scale, leading to the interdependence of national economies and the creation of global markets.

▶ **Table 3.7:** Advantages and disadvantages of globalisation

Advantages	Disadvantages
Creates economic growth in countries where MNCs develop businesses	Developing economies can become more dependent on developed ones
Creates jobs in countries where MNCs function	Can cause unemployment where work is outsourced to cheaper economies
Increases competition	May cause small businesses to collapse
Gives consumers greater choice	May increase demand on public services
Creates new markets for organisations	May increase prices for local people
Can improve understanding of different cultures	Can displace indigenous people from areas developed for industry or tourism

Globalisation has occurred as a result of:
▶ reduced trade barriers between countries and the creation of trade agreements
▶ rising income in developed countries
▶ a more international outlook – travelling on holiday, to study or migration
▶ improved communication networks through new technology
▶ improved transportation.

Discussion

Choose a global tourism organisation. Find out what kind of businesses it contains, what countries it operates in and how it markets its operation in those countries.

Discuss the strengths and weaknesses of its marketing in different countries.

Case study

TUI Group

TUI is the world's leading tourism business. The broad portfolio gathered under the group umbrella consists of strong tour operators, 1,600 travel agencies and leading online portals, six airlines with more than 150 aircraft, over 380 hotels, 16 cruise liners and many incoming agencies in all major holiday destinations around the globe.

Check your knowledge

1 How do you think globalisation affects the TUI Group?
2 How do you think the TUI Group affects other businesses?

 **PAUSE POINT** Give three examples of globalisation in tourism.

 Hint Think about organisations that operate internationally.

Extend Give three advantages and three disadvantages of globalisation, preferably in the context of your chosen examples.

Changes in the competitive environment

Organisations must follow both their domestic and international competitors' activities constantly by:
▶ monitoring any press releases, reports in the media and advertising
▶ visiting their agencies if they are travel agents
▶ monitoring their website and social media activity
▶ attending trade exhibitions and industry events.

Adaptation of marketing activity for different markets

It is important to research new markets in detail and take account of local regulations, culture and any competitive activity. Of course, there may be language barriers that make it more difficult to find out what requirements are and to negotiate with suppliers. Table 3.8 lists some of these considerations.

▶ **Table 3.8:** Adaptations when entering a new market

Benefits	Changes to consider
Increased market share Increased market diversification	Gaining an understanding of international business contexts, such as the laws, the politics and the social norms in other countries and reflecting these in marketing activities
Increased competitiveness	Effect of exchange rate fluctuations on costs and prices to charge
Growth of business and improved returns Outsourcing work to a cheaper labour force	Service quality if outsourcing services, such as using overseas call centres. Customer service training and effective processes may need to be implemented
Access to new markets	Increased competition from other businesses, so may need to consider competitive pricing and promotional activity
Ability to offer 24-hour service by operating in different time zones, without having to pay overtime and shift work pay	Understanding cultural differences and upholding the values and reputation of the organisation and its culture

Case study

Secret Escapes

Secret Escapes is a travel website that offers luxury holidays and hotel deals to subscribers. However, it is free for customers to subscribe to.

The business is based in the UK and was rebranded in 2010. It now operates in 13 countries including the Netherlands, Italy, Belgium and Spain. In 2016, the company announced that it was entering the Asian market and was expanding its operations in the USA. In Asia, the business has launched websites in Singapore, Malaysia, Hong Kong and Indonesia.

The company chose these countries as they have an affluent population that speaks English, meaning that the websites could be in English. The company also chose well-developed countries where traditional media and social media can be used to reach customers. However, Indonesia does not quite fit that model, so it may be

that the business is treating its operations in Indonesia as an experiment. The company's growth will continue into Japan and possibly South Korea, with the aim of becoming a global business.

Check your knowledge

1   What are the potential risks of expanding into Indonesia?

2   How will it need to adapt its marketing activity in Singapore, Malaysia and Hong Kong compared to the UK? What different marketing activity might be needed?

3   How successful has the expansion into these new countries been for Secret Escapes?

4   What types of jobs are available at Secret Escapes? Where are its headquarters based?

PAUSE POINT   Give three benefits and three risks of international marketing.

Hint   Use your research from the case study about Secret Escapes to help you answer the question.

Extend   How do you think businesses can overcome the language barrier when expanding internationally?

Following the success of your article, your editor has given you another assignment. She wants you to select two travel and tourism organisations with very different approaches to marketing and prepare and deliver a presentation to her. This will allow her to assess your presentation techniques ahead of a meeting with her boss and the senior editorial team.

For each of your two chosen organisations you must:

a) identify the organisation's objectives

b) explain how the organisation carries out marketing activity to ensure that it achieves its stated objectives, taking into account internal and external factors

c) explain how each of the organisation's marketing activities positively contributes to growth and customer relationships

d) evaluate how each organisation's success is impacted by its different approach to marketing, taking into account the relevance of internal and external factors.

Provide justified recommendations for improvements to future marketing activities.

Plan
- Which organisations should I choose? I need to consider the availability of information; for example, access to their annual reports, websites and marketing information.
- How should I deliver my presentation? Should I include visuals? I must remember to prepare speaker notes.

Do
- I have chosen my organisations and checked they are from different sectors.
- I have identified all the sources of information.
- I have planned my time between carrying out research and putting my material together.
- I have produced speaker notes and visual aids.

Review
- I can explain the improvements in marketing activities I have suggested and why.
- I have practised my presentation with colleagues.
- I have checked that I have covered all the tasks thoroughly.

C Carry out market research in order to identify a new travel and tourism product or service

Market research is vital to the marketing process. It enables an organisation to find out about the market, the competition and what customers want. Many different research methods are used depending on the specific purpose of the research project. The research may be carried out on behalf of an organisation by a specialist company or it may be carried out in-house.

Organisations use market research to see whether a business idea is viable or to help identify a gap for a new product or service in a particular sector. The research can:
▶ identify or review the characteristics and behaviour of the target market
▶ establish customer needs
▶ identify a gap in the market
▶ identify competitors.

You will be carrying out market research to identify a new product or service for a real travel and tourism organisation or destination.

Collecting market research data

Prepare for a market research activity

A market research plan will identify:
▶ the objectives of the market research activity, aligning them with the organisation's aims and objectives as discussed in section B

▸ the research method(s) that are most suitable to achieve the objectives, using primary or secondary sources
▸ the target group on which to focus research.

▸ **Figure 3.8:** Planning market research

Sources of primary research

Primary research is research undertaken first hand. The advantage of new research is that researchers collect fresh data, tailored to their objectives, rather than depending on data collected from previous research. Methods of primary research include:

▸ surveys
▸ interviews
▸ observations
▸ trials
▸ questionnaires
▸ focus groups.

Surveys and questionnaires

A survey is a way of gathering information from people. A survey can be carried out in person through the post, online or over the telephone. It may only ask a few questions, or it may be more detailed, but each person taking part in the same survey must be asked the same questions so that the survey results are consistent.

Questionnaires are a type of survey and are often used at airports, for example the International Passenger Survey asks outgoing passengers or returning tourists about their travel destinations, spend and activities. Surveys are often used to get feedback from guests in hotels, to find out about visitors' experiences at visitor attractions or on holiday, and to complete research into potential products and services. SurveyMonkey® is a free online survey tool that you could use for your own research.

> **Key terms**
>
> **Primary research** – information or results that are being collected for the first time.
>
> **Secondary research** – studying information that has already been collected by another researcher. It may be an article in a publication, a report, or sets of statistics.

> **Link**
>
> Identifying gaps in the market for new products or services is discussed in Unit 5: Travel and Tourism Enterprises.

Interviews

An interview is a structured conversation between an interviewer and someone being interviewed (interviewee). Interviews may be formal or informal.

▶   **A formal interview** is structured and the interviewer (interviewee) asks the interviewee a list of prepared questions. It is similar to carrying out a survey one-to-one or with a small group.

▶   **An informal interview** allows more scope for the interviewee to influence the flow of the interview. The interviewer still needs a prepared list of topics to be covered, but they can be more flexible about the order in which the topics are covered. If the interviewee suggests an issue that they consider particularly relevant, it can also be included in the discussion.

You may find that an informal interview is an appropriate research method if you are speaking to a subject expert, such as the manager of a visitor attraction or a tour operator. This is because the expert will make points that you may not have previously considered. On the other hand, if you are interviewing consumers, you may want to use a formal interview approach on a one-to-one basis, as the interviewees are more likely to need you to direct the interview.

Observation

Observation simply means watching people and observing their behaviour. Its advantage is that it allows you to see what people actually do, rather than relying on people telling you what they do, which might not be accurate. However, it takes a lot of time to conduct an observation on a large sample of people.

Observation can be conducted by placing fixed cameras in a location. For example, some researchers have put them in an airport lounge to see what people do and which facilities they use while waiting for their flight.

Case study

Observation research

Two researchers at the University of Girona in Spain conducted a piece of observation research on over 500 tourists to the city. Their method involved following visitors at a distance and using a voice recorder to record the tourists' movements around the city over a period of time.

The researchers selected people randomly by observing every fifth visitor to pass a specific sampling point. The researchers recorded what the visitors were doing while walking along two streets and looking at tourist sites.

People did not know they were being observed. They were only informed at the end of the observation when the researchers asked them to complete a questionnaire, which captured the characteristics of the visitors, such as their gender and age.

Check your knowledge

1   Do you think it is ethical to observe tourists without their knowledge?

2   Summarise the advantages and disadvantages of direct observation.

3   What sort of research do you think you could use this method for? Explain how you would conduct the observation and what it would aim to find out.

Trials

A trial is used to test a new product or service. For example, if a business is launching a new travel app, they could either try it out on a small group of customers or launch a limited beta version to identify any missing features or glitches before full launch. For example, in July 2020, The World Tourism Organization introduced a pilot scheme in the Canary Islands for an electronic health passport and a track and trace app to identify and isolate any COVID-19 infections amongst visitors.

Focus groups

A focus group is a kind of informal group interview. The researcher invites a group of people with an interest in the research topic to a discussion. Participants might receive an incentive to attend, such as cash or a shopping voucher. The aim of the discussion is to find out people's attitudes to a product or service. The group leader guides the discussion with pre-prepared questions. However, the discussion flows freely with the questions used to bring the group back to the topic if they digress.

Sources of secondary research

Secondary research is studying information that has already been collected by another researcher. It may be an article in a publication, a report, or sets of statistics, for example. It is sensible to carry out secondary research before embarking on primary or new research. This may save time and money if the information you want has already been researched somewhere else. Secondary research can use either internal or external sources of information.

▶ **Internal sources** of information are a business or organisation's own publications or back data. They are only accessible to people who work for the organisation. For example, if you worked for a travel agency, you would have access to customer data and information about the revenue from different types of bookings. If you worked for an airline, you would have access to information on passenger numbers and revenue from sales of flights and add-ons such as priority boarding.

▶ **External sources** of information are available to everyone and are much easier to access. They cover the industry as a whole and are published by organisations such as the government, market research companies and trade journals.

Table 3.9 lists some sources for secondary research.

▶ **Table 3.9:** Potential sources for secondary research

Source	Useful for:	Description	Examples
Online websites and media	• industry research and insight reports • travel and tourism news • competitor news • consumer trends	You can subscribe to these websites at no cost. Subscription to news websites also gives you access to their **archives** and past features	• VisitBritain – www.visitbritain.com • VisitScotland – www.visitscotland.com • Visit Wales – www.visitwales.com • Discover Northern Ireland – www.dicovernorthernireland.com • www.tourismalliance.com – tourism statistics • www.travelmole.com – a news and resource centre for the travel industry • www.traveldailynews.com – a news portal for travel professionals • www.skift.com – an industry intelligence platform providing insights about key sectors of travel • www.tourism-review.com – a tourism industry news channel

---

Theory into practice

A tour operator wants to find out what kind of group adventure holidays young people between 18–24 years of age would like to try. They will use the information from their research to develop new holiday packages. You are to arrange a focus group of at least six people from the identified age group who are interested in adventure holidays. Prepare a plan for the focus group, including details of:

- aims
- target group
- when
- where
- questions or areas for discussion
- means of reporting.

Key term

Archive – a collection of documents or files from the past.

Trade journals and travel gazettes	• travel and tourism news • competitor news • consumer trends • new product launches	These websites and printed magazines contain a lot of news about the travel and tourism industry and are usually aimed at industry professionals You can access them online, and your library may stock some of them. You may have to register to access them online, but registration is usually free	• *Travel Trade Gazette* – www.ttgmedia.com • *Travel Weekly* – www.travelweekly.com • *Caterer & Hotelkeeper* – www.thecaterer.com • *Leisure Opportunities* – www.leisureopportunities.co.uk • *Attractions Management* – www.attractionsmanagement.com • *Leisure Management* – www.leisuremanagement.co.uk
Government statistics	• population data • employment data • travel trends data	The Office for National Statistics gathers and publishes government statistics An example relevant to travel and tourism is the International Passenger Survey	• Office for National Statistics – www.ons.gov.uk
Published reports	• specialist knowledge about specific topics • holiday trends	May be one-off publications or reports on a particular topic e.g. ABTA Annual Travel Trends report Annual reports for travel and tourism companies (e.g. TUI and Whitbread) They may be produced by businesses, tourist boards, trade associations or international organisations	• The World Travel and Tourism Council – www.wttc.org • The UN World Tourism Organization – www2.unwto.org • ABTA Travel Trends – www.abta.com • ITB World Travel Trends – www.itb.com
Newspapers	• general news affecting travel and tourism • specialist travel pages • competitors' advertising	Newspaper websites and print newspapers are good sources Most have a travel section or supplement Having an up-to-date knowledge of current affairs is also important because a wide range of national and international news stories can be relevant to travel and tourism, such as news stories about terrorism or natural disasters	• *The Times* – www.thetimes.co.uk (requires a subscription, though your library may have one) • *The Telegraph* – www.telegraph.co.uk • *The Guardian* – www.theguardian.com/uk • *The Daily Mail* – www.dailymail.co.uk/travel
Travel guides	• researching destinations and their attractions	Destination guides aimed at consumers but are often useful for people working in the industry as well Travel agents, in particular, often use travel guides to learn about destinations	• *World Travel Guide* – www.worldtravelguide.net • Rough Guides – www.roughguides.com
Social media	• checking and responding to feedback on own products and services • checking competitor's products and services • trend spotting	Websites and apps that gather feedback from tourists and visitors are useful to check regularly	• Trip advisor – www.tripadvisor.co.uk • Facebook • Instagram • Twitter

Using secondary sources regularly will improve your topical knowledge of current travel and tourism issues. You will also find that some news stories develop over days and weeks and can grow to have an even greater impact on the industry than you might have expected at first.

Other online sources of information that may help you to improve your knowledge include the following:

- Department for Digital, Culture, Media & Sport – www.culture.gov.uk
- English tourist board – www.visitengland.com
- British Association of Leisure Parks, Piers and Attractions – www.balppa.org
- FCO travel advice – www.gov.uk/government/organisations/foreign-commonwealth-office
- Association of British Travel Agents – www.abta.com
- Association of Independent Tour Operators – www.aito.com
- Civil Aviation Authority – www.caa.co.uk.

The importance of validity, reliability and currency of research methods

In order to produce useful information, research methods have to be:

- **valid** – the research method produces findings that actually represent what they are supposed to represent
- **reliable** – the research method could be repeated and would produce the same (or similar) results
- **current** – the research methods and information used are up to date and relevant to the context of your research.

These considerations also apply to sources of information used in secondary research. You need to make sure that your source of information is accurate, up to date and unbiased. It is important to do this with every source, but it is more difficult to assess internet websites because anyone can set up a website and they may not have used reliable research methods or data.

Table 3.10 shows some criteria that you could use when judging the reliability of a secondary source.

Research

Choose three of the news sources listed in Table 3.9 and find a news story that is relevant to travel and tourism that is being covered by all three sources. Describe the story and compare how the different sources have reported it. Comment on the similarities and differences and discuss your conclusions with your group.

Key term

Bias – prejudice for or against a subject, person or group.

▶ **Table 3.10:** Assessing a source

Who wrote it?	Are they qualified to write it? For example, a letter in a newspaper complaining about a package holiday may not be valid as it only represents one person's experience. Newspaper articles tend to be more trustworthy, but they can reflect the newspaper's own political opinions, so be careful to assess them for **bias**
What is the purpose of the information source?	Holiday brochures and sales literature are designed to sell products and services. This means that they are biased in favour of those products and services and will not tell you if there was an outbreak of food poisoning in a particular resort last season. A publication such as *World Travel Guide* is considered a more reliable source than brochures, as it is based on factual information and serves as an aid to the travel trade, rather than trying to sell a product or service
Is the information up to date and current?	When was the information written? If it is a web page, how often is it updated? If it is not up to date don't use it. However, sometimes older sources can still be useful if you are researching a topic that does not change, such as the development of tourism in the UK
Does the author give sources of facts and figures?	You need to quote your sources, and the authors of your sources of information should do the same. You may even be able to go back to the quoted source and check that it has been reported accurately
Does the author seem to be biased in their presentation of information?	You will find it easier to recognise bias as you gain more experience of using different sources of information. Initially, bias can be difficult to identify but you can practise this skill by reading several different newspaper accounts of the same event and seeing how they differ

Assess the validity of the following four pieces of information. Comment on the likely audience for each extract. Make notes on your findings and discuss them with your colleagues.

A: From *Jenni's Travel Blog* (16 June 2020)

Madrid doesn't have to cost a lot of money but you need to be careful. Here are a few tips to make your cash go further.
- Use Groupon for discounts – spas, entertainment and clubs feature – lots of 2 for 1 offers as well.
- Get *Time Out* – it has all the listings of everything going on – it also has some offers listed.
- Eat street food – fast, cheap and delicious – highly recommended and on every corner.

B: From the GB Day Visits Survey (October 2019)

▶ **Figure 3.9:** A VisitBritain graph comparing day visits in England in August 2019 with the previous year

C: From Tui's ebrochure *Faraway Shores* (May 2019–April 2020)

Platinum hotels are ones that score highly – both with us and you. We check that each hotel's TripAdvisor ratings are consistently reaching four or more before we add them to the collection. So, whether it's a family friendly resort in the Canaries or an adults' only retreat in the Caribbean, you can look forward to impressive cuisine, tranquil spas and standout rooms.

D: From UNESCO report World Heritage and Tourism in a Changing Climate (25 May 2016)

The report's goal is to provide up-to-date information and a basis for action on climate change, tourism and World Heritage in the follow-up to the adoption of the Paris Agreement by the Conference of the Parties to the United Nations Framework Convention on Climate Change (UNFCCC) in December 2015 and the 2030 Agenda for Sustainable Development, adopted by the United Nations General Assembly in October 2015.

Quantitative and qualitative data

Research data can be:
▶ **quantitative** – consisting of facts and figures which can be measured and illustrated through numbers (e.g. the number of people admitted to a museum in one day)
▶ **qualitative** – consisting of opinions and judgements that represent an individual person's view of something. Qualitative research is more difficult to conduct, and the data is more difficult to analyse, as it is about why people behave and think in the ways that they do. Sometimes, customers themselves find it difficult to explain why they choose to buy certain things.

Methods and purpose of collection

A business must decide whether to research quantitative or qualitative data for any marketing planning. Quantitative data is collected for the purpose of analysis. Statistics are analysed to identify trends, such as the number of visitors to a destination or the number of seats sold by an airline. If the researcher wants to find out what people think about a product or service or how they behave, such as why they chose to visit a certain attraction, they are more likely to choose qualitative methods of research.

Quantitative and qualitative research can also be used together. This can help increase the validity of the findings because one set of findings can be checked against another. For example, statistical information can be gathered and then that information can be tested by following it up with a survey.

Theory into practice

1 Say which of these is quantitative data and which is qualitative data:
  • number of day visitors to a theme park
  • attitudes of visitors regarding the cleanliness of the theme park
  • how long someone is willing to wait for a ride at the theme park
  • prices of entry to the theme park.
2 Describe which data collection method might be used for each of the above.

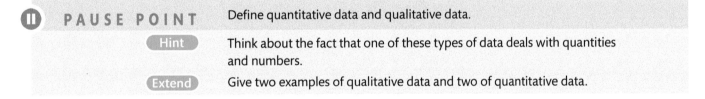

II   PAUSE POINT   Define quantitative data and qualitative data.

Hint   Think about the fact that one of these types of data deals with quantities and numbers.

Extend   Give two examples of qualitative data and two of quantitative data.

Analysing market research data

There is little point in carrying out research if the data does not lead to action or improvement in terms of marketing activity. This means that all data that has been collected should be analysed to derive meaning and inform change. The data may be analysed manually or by computer – for example, with coded surveys. The information and analysis should be presented in a clear, informative way with recommendations and conclusions so that any interested stakeholders can understand the results and implications.

Case study

VisitBritain research and analysis

In 2019, VisitBritain produced a report entitled 'Interest in Holiday Activities in Britain' based on the findings of an online survey it had carried out using a specialist market research organisation – IPSOS. The survey asked one question, 'If you went on a holiday/vacation to Britain, which of the following activities would you be most likely to do?'.

Respondents from over 15 countries were asked to choose as many activities as they liked from a list of 35. There were approximately 500 respondents from each country. The results were analysed by looking at the percentage choosing each activity. The most popular activities overall were:
- driving through the countryside
- a canal boat tour
- a food tour of a popular food market in London
- taking a traditional afternoon tea.

However, when the results are explored in more detail by country/market, there are big differences. While 85 per cent of Germans chose driving through the countryside, only 37 per cent of Brazilians chose this activity. 63 per cent of Japanese respondents wanted to shop for quirky goods in a seaside town but only 14 per cent of Dutch people wanted to do this.

You can see the full results of the survey at www.visitbritain.org/sites/default/files/vb-corporate/markets/foresight_168_-_dream_activities.pdf.

Check your knowledge

1 Why did VisitBritain use a specialist market research organisation for this research?
2 What type of research was this – primary or secondary research?
3 How did analysis of the results show differences between different countries/markets? Give further examples from the report.
4 How would the results of this survey help travel and tourism organisations in the UK? Give examples.

Competitor analysis

Competitor research can:
- ▶ inform an organisation about its competitors and what they are doing
- ▶ help an organisation determine its own objectives and define its business strategies, including marketing activity
- ▶ help identify an organisation's own strengths and weaknesses, and opportunities against its competitors.

Organisations analyse competitor research data to:

▶ **assess competitors' strengths and weaknesses:** by understanding more about their competitors, businesses can begin to identify any weak points in competitor organisations, or potential gaps in competitors' offerings that they can target with their own new products and services. The focus of the business is therefore on competing with its competitors based on their weaknesses, rather than focussing on and promoting its own strengths

▶ **determine strong and weak competitors:** to identify which of these competitors the business should focus on. The stronger the competitor, the larger its presence or reputation in the market. A business should follow the actions of a strong competitor and put in place plans to exploit any potential opportunities (and protect its own market share)

▶ **determine close and distant competitors:** to understand which competitors are far away from its market share or product offering, and which competitors have a very similar market share, or offer very similar products or services

▶ **estimate the reaction of competitors to any marketing activity that the organisation undertakes:** understanding how competitors react to what your business does, can help identify the competitors' aims and objectives so the business can plan to confront these.

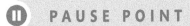

PAUSE POINT   Suggest three ways that an airline could find out about a competitor's activity.

    Hint   Think about where airlines publish their results and where they advertise.

    Extend   How would it help the airline if they found that a competitor airline was opening a new VIP lounge at an airport?

Using research results to help identify a new product or service

Once you have carried out your research, you will be able to use the data you have collected to present a business case for a new product or service.

You will need to use your data to:

▶ justify the target market you have chosen – showing that they want this product or service

▶ establish the essential purpose and features of the product so that it meets the needs of the target market

▶ start planning a promotional campaign that will explain the purpose and features of the product and that will reach the target audience

▶ plan a marketing mix with the right product at the right price and place to inspire the target market to buy.

We will examine a piece of research to see how this might work.

The National Coastal Tourism Academy (NCTA) research into activity holidays

Research was carried out by The National Coastal Tourism Academy (NCTA) into the market for activity holidays. The key findings are shown below.

- 49 per cent of those interviewed had been on an activity holiday in England – but 31 per cent didn't perceive it as such!
- Walking and cycling are the most popular activities but there is significant interest in water sports too.
- Activity holidays are popular with all generations – but there is some variation in their needs and preferences.
- The ideal activity holiday involves at least three different active experiences and a mix of other holiday activities.
- Successful holidays are not just about the activity – the local scenery, accommodation, food and drink and other attractions play an important part.
- 37 per cent would choose a coastal destination for an activity holiday.

The key recommendation for businesses interested in this market is to work together to connect activity products and services with other activity and accommodation products to make it easy for consumers to find and book active experiences.

Other important points were:

- Different age groups liked different activities. For example, although all age groups like cycling, it is most popular with 35–55-year olds and water sports are most popular with younger age groups.
- Although the activity is the main motive for the holiday, accommodation, food and transport are still important and there are not many packages where these are all put together and marketed.
- There is a desire for ethical tourism and to promote 'local' products and services, which support the community.

You can access the full report at coastaltourismacademy.co.uk.

How could this research by NCTA be used by a local tourism organisation developing and marketing an activity package focusing on cycling and hiking?

▶ The data shows that cycling is popular with 35–55-year olds in the main. They could target this age group or market a softer cycling trail to older people. They might have less competition with the older market.

- They know that holidaymakers like three activities so could offer cycling, hiking and an optional water activity such as paddle boarding. Other sources have shown that this is a popular trend.
- They could work with local partners to add accommodation, meal options and local transport to the package. Breakfast could be included with recommendations for local restaurants for other meals. These features meet the needs of the target market and appeal to the desire for responsible tourism by supporting the local economy and community.
- They need to think about how to reach their target market. An older target market may be less likely to access social media than more traditional media, such as press advertising. They are very likely to use the local tourist office.
- They need to do some more research into partners (for accommodation and activity suppliers etc.) and decide firmly on their target market. Once complete, they could put together the marketing mix in line with the following company objectives:
  - making a profit
  - growing market share
  - promoting responsible tourism
  - supporting the local community.

Assessment activity 3.3   C.P5 C.M3 C.D3

You work in the marketing department of a tour operator. You offer a wide range of products from cruises to adventure tours and from flight-only packages on your dedicated airline to fully inclusive packages. The product development team would like you to help research ideas for new products by looking at what other travel and tourism organisations are doing or could do. They would like you to put together your research and findings in a written report.

Within your research, you should perform the following activities:
- Choose either a real travel and tourism organisation or a tourist destination.
- Carry out primary and secondary market research and interpret and analyse any information and data from your research in order to identify a new travel and tourism product or service to add to an existing portfolio.
- Justify how your data from your research proves the demand for the new product for the chosen target market.

Summarise each aspect of your research and findings in a written report. You should present samples of the market research used and you must remember to reference all market research sources and produce a bibliography.

Plan
- Which travel and tourism organisation or destination should I choose to develop a new idea for?
- Where can I find out the kinds of new products and services that are being produced?
- What methods of data collection should I use?
- How will I analyse my research?

Do
- I have used primary and secondary research methods and sources.
- I have presented my research findings.
- I have produced a bibliography in my report.

Review
- I can explain why I chose my research methods.
- I have justified the demand for a new product from the data I collected.
- I have checked my report and have included samples of my research in appendices.

D Produce a promotional campaign for a new travel and tourism product or service, to meet stated objectives

Designing a promotional campaign to meet stated objectives

You will be producing a promotional campaign for your assessment for this unit and you will need to consider the following important factors when designing your campaign.

1 Determine the aims and objectives of the campaign

Figure 3.10 gives some examples of promotional campaign objectives.

▶ **Figure 3.10:** Examples of promotional campaign objectives

2 Support overall organisational objectives and brand values

Some of the campaign objectives in Figure 3.10, such as increasing sales, reflect possible organisational objectives. The promotional campaign also needs to support brand values by making potential customers aware of the brand and its core values.

Raising awareness of a brand and its values is of particular importance when a brand is at the introduction stage of the product life cycle – when it is new or entering a new market.

Norwegian Airlines

When Norwegian Airlines entered the UK market in 2015, they had a product, a low-cost airline, with a unique selling proposition (USP) of low-cost transatlantic flights. They had new planes, a selection of destinations and offered affordable fares but no one in the UK was aware of their brand in relation to long-haul flights. The aim of marketing was to heighten awareness of the brand. They based their marketing plans on low prices, high quality and using local insight.

To increase brand awareness, they created a virtual reality Norwegian Airlines flight experience in a 787 Dreamliner at Westfield Shopping Centre in London. Shoppers used VR headsets to experience the flight.

These shoppers were not able to buy a flight straight after the experience but would remember the experience when they were thinking of booking a flight. They may have been more likely to purchase a Norwegian Airlines flight in the future and would have been likely to tell their friends about their virtual reality experience. Norwegian Airlines would have assessed the success of this marketing activity, not in immediate sales, but in attendance at the virtual flight experience and by tracking its discussion on social media.

3 Identify the target market

You should have different promotions for different markets so be very clear about who your particular campaign is aimed at. Choose a promotional method or combination of methods that is appropriate for the target market. Decide how the promotional materials and message will be distributed to the target market, for example, social media, advertising or a press release.

4 Content of the campaign

Once you have identified the target market, you will be able to determine the content of the overall message of the promotional campaign using the elements of the marketing mix:

▶ product or service information, such as features of the product and the USP
▶ price details, especially if you are using a discount pricing strategy
▶ place – the customer needs to know how and where to buy the product
▶ promotion – what types of promotional activities will you use for your target market and how will you ensure that your promotion reaches them?

5 Timescale

Consider the timescale. The right time for a promotion to reach the customer is when they are planning to buy. When are your customers likely to book holidays? When might they book theatre tickets or events or choose experiences? Think about whether your campaign is seasonal, perhaps running in peak time or off peak. Decide how long the campaign will run for and why.

6 Budget

Consider the budget for the campaign. The budget will determine what promotional activities you can afford to carry out.

7 Key performance indicators (KPIs)

Determine the KPIs you will use to measure the success of the campaign. What data do you need to collect during the campaign? You should regularly monitor and evaluate the success of your promotional campaign in meeting its objectives.

> **Key term**
>
> **Key performance indicators** – measures for sales targets, profit, number of customers retained, new leads and market share or any other targets the business finds useful. They are set in terms of numbers to be achieved (e.g. percentage increases) and are always measurable. Businesses continually monitor and evaluate KPIs against objectives and in terms of meeting the business's objectives.

> **Theory into practice**
>
> The Cricket World Cup was held in England and Wales in 2019. The British Tourism Authority, Visit Britain, designed a six-month campaign targeting cricket loving fans in India. It included a competition to find India's biggest cricket fan with a prize of travelling to Britain and visiting the match destinations of Birmingham, Leeds and London.
>
> Why was this campaign suitable for India? Find an example of a campaign that promotes the UK to other countries. Explain why it is effective or not.

The following case study of a fictional destination, Seachester, illustrates the use and measurement of objectives in a promotional campaign.

Seachester

Each year the region of Seachester produces a tourism marketing plan to promote tourism in its region. The objectives align to Seachester's ambition to be a world-class destination.

The plan supports key organisational and marketing objectives, for example:

- to deliver and develop special events and festivals across the region
- to promote Seachester as a key destination for business tourism
- to develop and build a "Better than the Med" brand for marketing campaigns.

The objectives are further broken down to make them more 'SMART'. For example, the objective 'to develop the "Better than the Med" brand' includes:

- developing a brand awareness campaign to target new market segments (under 35s)
- creating campaigns and content to showcase to potential visitors that Seachester is a year-round resort.

The plan then illustrates the marketing mix, concentrating mostly on which marketing channels and types of promotion they will use. Magazine articles, adverts, the website and blogs are among the many channels they use. Seachester's marketing team plan specific promotional activities for the whole year; such as a series of blogs showing the hidden side to Seachester out of peak season. Having developed all the stages of planning, Seachester's marketing team must monitor the success of the plan as it is rolled out. They decide what **metrics** will tell them if their brand promotion is reaching the intended audience:

Brand awareness

They measure awareness using:

- visitor traffic – the number of views on its website or social media

- impressions – general feelings about its brand/the destination received from customer feedback, through surveys and focus groups
- advert recall – how well do customers remember the adverts they have seen and did they respond to them as hoped.

Engagement with the promotions

They measure customer engagement with promotions by looking at and analysing:

- how long someone spends looking at the website or an advertisement
- favourable perception – do people recommend the destination and its products and services to their friends? This can be collected anecdotally through customer feedback or through more formal research
- the interest customers show in the destination and its products and services, measured by the length of time they spend on the website or a particular web page.

Response to the promotions

The marketing team also measure and analyse the actions people take in response to the promotions through:

- click-throughs from a third-party website, for example from an advert placed on another website – if the advert points customers towards a particular page on Seachester's website, do they go on to explore any other pages?
- phone calls to customers – to find out more about their attitudes and feelings towards the destination
- sales – has there been a noticeable increase in bookings, sales and customer engagement since a particular promotion began?
- sign-ups, such as for further information emails – this shows that customers are keen to engage with what Seachester is doing and offering.

Key term

Metrics – the measures used to assess progress against targets.

Case study *(continued)*

Website traffic and customer engagement

Every year, the Seachester team measure visitor traffic to their website and last year they set a target of at least 700,000 website hits. Similarly, they planned to send out emails to 15,000 people, with a target response rate of 3 per cent (engagement). Their targets for the whole year's promotional campaign are shown in Table 3.11.

▶ **Table 3.11:** Evaluation of Seachester's promotional campaigns

Measurement	Sources of information/data	Targets	Reporting
Website visitor traffic/reach Email engagement Social media reach and engagement	Google Analytics New Mind CMS Granicus Email Platform, Mailchimp Facebook Instagram Twitter YouTube	Website traffic: 700,000 Email reach: 15,000 Email engagement: 3% Social media audience: 150,000 Social media reach: 13 million Social engagement: 1.5 million	Monthly quarterly trade update
Media coverage/ reach/value	Kantar Media Monitoring	Media coverage: 1,600 items* National newspaper volume: 160 items* Blog volume: 8 items* Total news value**: £5 million	Monthly quarterly trade update

items – articles, adverts, blog post, editorials, product placements, mentions
** the amount Seachester would have to spend if it actually paid for all this coverage*

Check your knowledge

1. Seachester decides to include printed magazine articles and adverts alongside their digital promotional methods. Suggest specific newspapers or magazines where adverts might be placed to reach the intended target market.
2. How would Seachester get an article placed in a magazine?
3. How would response to traditional advertising be measured?
4. What other traditional media would you suggest for Seachester and why?
5. Why would someone choose to discuss Seachester in their blog?

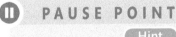

PAUSE POINT   What does KPI mean? How do they help organisations to achieve their objectives?

     Hint   Look at the examples of KPIs in this section.

     Extend   What kind of KPI would an organisation use to measure brand recognition?

Producing promotional materials and activities

Promotional materials need to be appealing, appropriate to the target market and appropriate for the chosen promotional methods, so you need to bear this in mind when designing your own promotional materials for your campaign. Depending on your chosen promotional methods, you might consider advertisements, a mailshot, content for social media, a leaflet or an endorsement of merchandise, for example.

If your promotional campaign is aimed at an international market, you need to be aware of your target audience and all materials must reflect culture and diversity. This might be as straightforward as having materials in different languages and that reflect diversity, but could also mean thinking about the cultural aspects, humour and trends of the target market.

Table 3.12 shows some examples of types of promotional materials and activities, but you can be as creative and imaginative as you like.

▶ **Table 3.12:** Examples of promotional materials and activities

Material/activity	Example of use	Advantages, disadvantages and usage
Leaflets/flyers	Advertising a tour	• Can be used for most products and services for a short-term promotion • Easy to distribute in public places or in hotels • Can be inserted into magazines • Contain detailed information • Can become out of date quickly
Brochures	Tour operators use to promote holiday packages	• Much more expensive than leaflets • Have to be reprinted when updated • Lots of detail and glossy
Door hangers	Often used in hotels by third parties e.g. pizza delivery	• Cheap and effective as customer can't miss the door hanger • Contain limited information
Posters/banners	Billboards for destinations or airlines Smaller scale posters in resorts on streets	• Can be targeted well geographically – location must be considered carefully • Information needs to be brief and targeted
Direct mail/email	Travel offers direct to existing customers	• Useful to build up/maintain customer relationships • Can send targeted offers
Endorsements	Sports kit Racing car Event	• A good way of promoting a brand as the name is prominent
Blogs/vlogs	Travel blogs by individuals, sometimes supported by advertising Many organisations now have their own blogs	• Cheap • Good use of social media • Can use influencers to promote products/services • Allow for customer engagement/interaction
Traditional advertising: – television, newspaper, magazines, websites	Advertisements for holidays e.g. post-Christmas	• Mostly used by larger travel and tourism organisations as most expensive type of promotion • Wider reach • Can target niche markets/specific demographics by choosing certain publications to advertise in
Demonstrations/presentations	Travel agents use headsets to show destinations Travel shows/fairs have presentations and talks about resorts	• Useful to give customers an insight into a destination or product • Opportunity for interaction with the target audience
Presence at trade fairs	Stands promoting products or destinations	• Travel trade fairs are very well attended • Good for B2B marketing • Expensive to exhibit at
Landing page	A single web page with a promotional message and a call to action arrived at from a click-through advert	• Differs from other web pages as does not carry lots of different information so very specific for promoting a simple message
Call to action (CTA)	Tour operator requests customers to engage with online content, for example upload their holiday photos to social media with an incentive of a prize for the best	• Promotes interaction and engagement with customers • Good for building customer relationships

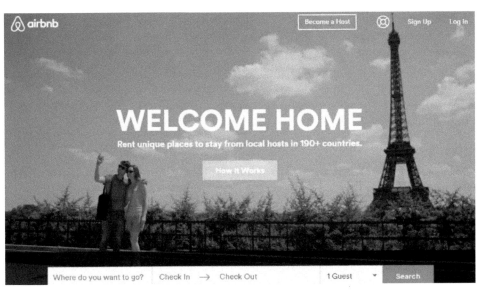

▶ **Figure 3.11:** An example of a landing page

Case study

Abu Dhabi

In the 2019 International Travel and Tourism Awards, the Department of Culture and Tourism in Abu Dhabi (DCT) won best digital influencer in the industry for one of its digital promotional campaigns. The aim of the campaign was to showcase the Emirate's unique combination of tourist hotspots and culturally important local heritage. DCT worked with content creators from their chosen target markets to increase awareness of Abu Dhabi as a destination via a multi-influencer campaign, especially on Facebook, Twitter and Instagram. Effort was focused on peak times such as student graduation and orientation weeks in various countries (when students are more likely to engage with social media). The team took care to listen to the latest trends and topics on social media and engage. The results were a reach of 250 million people and over 10 million engagements across the world.

Check your knowledge

1   Why do you think the DCT chose a social media campaign? What groups of people were they hoping to reach?

2   What is meant by the terms:
   - 'social influencer'   • reach
   - content creator   • engagement?

3   How could social media influencers and content creators be used to introduce a brand-new product or service from Abu Dhabi?

4   Check social media for examples of this campaign and comment on your findings.

Theory into practice

1   Evaluate a promotional campaign. Choose a current promotional campaign for a travel and tourism company. Collect materials from the campaign or make detailed notes on the materials and media events.

   Evaluate the campaign by trying to decide what the original objectives were and whether you think it meets them. Use AIDA and KISS to help you.

2   Write possible KPIs for the campaign and assess the campaign against them. Report on your findings, suggesting recommendations for improvement.

AIDA and KISS

There are a couple of acronyms that will help you decide if your promotional materials and activities are likely to be effective:

▶   AIDA: According to AIDA, the aim of a promotional activity is to take the customer through four key stages that will lead to a purchase:

A – Attention: the promotion attracts the attention of the customer

I – Interest: having spotted the promotion, the customer is intrigued and wants to know more

D – Desire: the customer decides they want the product

A – Action: the final stage where the customer takes action and buys the product.

▶ KISS: **K**eep **i**t **s**hort and **s**imple – This is an easy message to follow. Over complicated promotions confuse the customer and lose their interest quickly.

Assessment activity 3.4   D.P6   D.M4   D.D4

The product development team and marketing team would like you to produce a promotional campaign for the new product or service you identified in Assessment activity 3.3.

1 They have asked you to produce a full written promotional campaign that includes:

- the aims and objectives of the campaign
- a description of the target market
- a description and explanation of the product features, and price and place elements of the marketing mix
- details of all the planned promotional activities and materials for the new product or service, including timescales and distribution methods, and reasons for choices
- an evaluation of how the campaign objectives can be achieved through effective marketing strategies and activities, including the use of key performance indicators (KPIs) to determine its success.

2 As part of your work, the marketing team would like you to produce to a professional standard one of the planned promotional activities or pieces of promotional material.

Plan

- What should my written promotional campaign look like?
- What kind of promotional activities should I include in my plan?
- How will I measure the success of my campaign?
- Which particular type of promotional activity should I produce?

Do

- I have produced a plan for a promotional campaign.
- I have devised promotional activities to get my product or service to the market.
- I know which of my promotional activities I am going to produce.

Review

- I can explain how my promotional campaign reaches my target market.
- I can explain how I would measure the success of my promotional campaign.
- I have a promotional activity or piece of material which looks professional.

Further reading and resources

Websites

Abta.com
ABTA code of conduct and Travel Trends Reports

Corporate.Easyjet.com
Their corporate website contains their annual review and corporate strategy.

VisitEngland: www.visitengland.com/plan-your-visit/visitengland-quality-schemes#/ Star ratings.

VisitBritain: www.visitbritain.org/markets
Inbound visitors market data.

Coastal Tourism Academy: www.coastaltourismacademy.co.uk

Institute of Customer Service model of excellence 'ServiceMark': www.instituteofcustomerservice.com

Research reports into current issues affecting travel and tourism: https://research.skift.com/reports/b2b-insights/

THINK ▶FUTURE

Gerry Hamilton

Destination marketing manager

Gerry works for an organisation that promotes Northern Ireland to visitors. He has a degree in marketing and had four years' experience in marketing before taking this job. He manages a team of four marketing assistants, which means that he has to organise their workload as well as his own. Every year, Gerry develops the organisation's marketing communications plan, which the team then implements over the course of the following 12 months. This is based on the calendar of events taking place throughout the year. For example, in 2019, they promoted a Christmas market, a food festival and the MAC International arts exhibition as well as other events. For each event, the team plans the type of promotion, such as advertising in newspapers or on local television, printing leaflets and distributing marketing materials such as posters. This is all planned well in advance and the costs have to be within the team's marketing budget. At the same time, the team also promotes visitor attractions, activities and destinations in Northern Ireland. Everything they do is branded with the organisation's logo.

Another aspect of Gerry's work is dealing with press enquiries and hosting press visits. A member of his team will accompany press visitors to events, places or attractions to show them all of the details. The resulting articles are great free publicity for Northern Ireland and its tourism industry.

The organisation works with key partners such as hotel chains, local restaurants and businesses to share marketing activities and costs. One member of the team is a social media and digital marketing expert, and she is responsible for placing promotional content on social media platforms and ensuring that internet searches rank the organisation highly. While Gerry isn't a social media specialist, he still has to have a good understanding of it to manage his team.

Focusing your skills

Think about the role of destination marketing manager.
- What types of personal skills would you need to do Gerry's job?
- How could you develop your organisational skills so that you could manage several different projects at the same time?
- What qualifications do you think you would need? Do you think a degree is always necessary?

- Learn to be creative in your approach to problem solving. Gerry's team has to think of new ideas to get people's attention, and you can practise this by thinking about ways of presenting your work in a unique but professional manner.
- How important is it to be reliable and stick to deadlines?
- How could you improve your knowledge of how to use social media for marketing purposes?

Getting ready for assessment

Suzanne is working towards a BTEC National Certificate in Travel and Tourism. She was given an assignment to report on the marketing activities of two different travel and tourism organisations and to present her findings to the editor of a travel marketing journal, *Getting Ahead in Travel*. Her presentation had to include:

▶ an explanation of how marketing activities are carried out to help each organisation achieve its objectives, taking into account internal and external factors

▶ an evaluation of how well her chosen organisations plan marketing activities to contribute to growth and build customer relationships

▶ an evaluation of how marketing activities used by both organisations contribute to their success, taking into account both internal and external factors

▶ recommendations for improvements to future marketing activities with justification.

Suzanne shares her experience below.

How I got started

First, I read the text two or three times to make sure I understood exactly what was required. Then I chose my two organisations, making sure they had different approaches to marketing. I chose a business travel centre and a local hotel. I wanted to think about internal and external factors affecting my chosen organisations, so I carried out an analysis of each of them. I think I will be able to talk this through at a meeting with the hotel manager. At the same time, I can ask him about their marketing plans and what internal factors affect them. I will make notes on each element of the marketing mix for each of the organisations. The advertising is easy as it's all in the public domain. I need to determine the business objectives of the organisations, so I am looking for their annual reports on the internet, although the local hotel is unlikely to have an annual report. If I can talk to the managers as well, I will get more of an insight. I made a list of questions for my meetings, but I also made sure I had done as much research as possible beforehand. Once I had all done all my research and had assessed my findings, I planned the article carefully and then wrote it up.

How I brought it all together

▶ I made notes on the internal and external factors affecting marketing for my chosen organisations.

▶ I made separate notes on each organisation's business objectives.

▶ I thought about each element of the marketing mix

and how each organisation addressed them.

▶ I discussed my findings with one of my colleagues, trying to decide what was working well in the company's marketing and what needed to be improved.

▶ I had to decide how to deliver my presentation and what to call it.

▶ I allowed myself plenty of time for preparation and asked my dad to listen to my presentation.

What I learned from the experience

I know a lot more about how to find information about companies, including detailed information from their annual reports. I realised that preparing questions for meetings is really important.

Discussing my work with my colleagues helped me see where the marketing plans were going well and where they were supporting organisational success.

Think about it

▶ Have you written a plan with timings so you can complete your assignment by the agreed submission date?

▶ Have you used the text to start you off with a list of research elements?

▶ Have you thought about what you can find on the internet or whether you will need to have face-to-face meetings?

▶ Have you thought about how to present your work?

▶ How will you reference your work and ensure the presentation looks professional?

Managing the Customer Experience in Travel and Tourism

4

Getting to know your unit

Providing excellent customer service is an essential part of remaining competitive in the travel and tourism industry. When your products and services are often not physical, it is the quality of the customer service that helps the customer choose the right product to meet their needs. This unit will develop your understanding of what excellent customer service means and give you the opportunity to develop practical skills.

How you will be assessed

This unit will be assessed by a series of internally assessed tasks set by your tutor. Throughout this unit you will find assessment activities that will help you work towards your assessment. Completing these activities will not mean that you have achieved a particular grade, but you will have carried out useful research or preparation that will be relevant when it comes to your final assignment.

In order to achieve the tasks in your assignment, it is important to check that you have met all of the Pass grading criteria. You can do this as you work your way through the assignment.

If you are hoping to gain a Merit or Distinction, you should also make sure that you present the information in your assignment in the style that is required by the relevant assessment criterion. For example, Merit criteria require you to analyse, assess and demonstrate, and Distinction criteria require you to evaluate and consistently demonstrate.

The assignment set by your tutor will consist of a number of tasks designed to meet the criteria in the table. These may include:

▸ producing a report evaluating the significance of excellent customer service in a chosen travel and tourism organisation

▸ demonstrating customer service skills in different travel and tourism situations

▸ evaluating your own customer service skills and producing an action plan to develop your skills further.

Assessment criteria

This table shows what you must do to achieve a **Pass**, **Merit** or **Distinction** grade, and where you can find activities to help you.

Pass	Merit	Distinction
Learning aim **A** Explore how effective customer service contributes to organisational success		
A.P1 Explain the factors that influence customer decisions in the travel and tourism industry. Assessment activity 4.1	**A.M1** Analyse the potential impacts of a travel and tourism organisation not responding effectively to a customer. Assessment activity 4.1	**A.D1** Evaluate the importance for a travel and tourism organisation of providing excellent customer service that complies with UK regulations and increases customer loyalty. Assessment activity 4.1
A.P2 Explain the potential positive impacts of delivering excellent customer service. Assessment activity 4.1		
A.P3 Explain the importance of managing customer expectations. Assessment activity 4.1		
Learning aim **B** Demonstrate customer service in different travel and tourism situations		
B.P4 Competently demonstrate communication and interpersonal skills appropriate to meet customer needs in two different situations. Assessment activity 4.2	**B.M2** Confidently and effectively demonstrate communication and interpersonal skills appropriate to meet customer needs in two different situations. Assessment activity 4.2	**BC.D2** Consistently demonstrate initiative, responsibility and professionalism in using communication and interpersonal skills to successfully meet customer needs in two different situations, evaluating the importance of the personal development plan in contributing to the development of own skills and to the potential business success of travel and tourism organisations. Assessment activity 4.2
Learning aim **C** Review effectiveness of own performance in customer service to add value to travel and tourism organisations		
C.P5 Review own customer service skills and produce an action plan to address areas where improvements could be made and explain how development of skills will add value to travel and tourism organisations. Assessment activity 4.2	**C.M3** Assess how the personal development plan could improve own performance of customer service and help travel and tourism organisations achieve their business goals. Assessment activity 4.2	
Learning aim **D** Plan to monitor and improve customer service to achieve organisation objectives		
D.P6 Present a basic plan explaining how a selected organisation could use monitoring methods and use data to improve customer service in line with its organisational objectives. Assessment activity 4.3	**D.M4** Present a detailed plan analysing how a selected organisation could develop its monitoring methods and use data to improve customer service in line with its organisational objectives. Assessment activity 4.3	**D.D3** Present a comprehensive plan with recommendations of how a selected organisation could develop its monitoring methods and use data to improve customer service in line with organisational objectives. Assessment activity 4.3

Getting started

Choose a travel and tourism organisation that you will be able to use as a basis for your research for all aspects of this unit. You could do this by asking your tutor to arrange for one local travel and tourism business to talk to the whole group about their organisation and its customer service. Alternatively, you could choose a local travel and tourism organisation and visit them to find out about their customer service. If neither of these options is possible, choose a national travel and tourism organisation that provide lots of online information about their customer service.

A Explore how effective customer service contributes to organisational success

An organisation's attitude towards its customers is key to its success. All communications and interactions with the organisation's customers must convey a consistently positive attitude that recognises the importance of the customer and their value to the organisation.

Customer service in travel and tourism

Customer service is the assistance and advice given by a business or organisation to its customers. In this section you will consider what makes excellent customer service in the travel and tourism industry.

The needs and expectations of internal and external customers

A business or organisation has two different types of customer.
▶ **Internal customers** – these customers are colleagues and other members of staff who work within the same organisation to provide products and services. They may also be suppliers or colleagues from a partner organisation.
▶ **External customers** – these customers are people from outside the organisation who buy its products and services.

It is very important when delivering customer service that you think about who the customers are and how well you know and understand their needs.

Internal customers are colleagues who need service and support from other colleagues. For example, cleaners and maintenance staff in a hotel make sure that the environment is clean, safe and secure for other staff members as well as for external customers. In return, cleaners and maintenance staff also require service from others. They need their managers to give them clear information about their tasks and rotas and they may need to work with administration staff to order supplies.

Thinking about the way in which customer service interconnects like this within an organisation also requires you to think about the impact of your work on the organisation's culture, aims and objectives. Providing good service to internal customers can lead to external customer satisfaction, because happy employees who can do their jobs effectively are more productive, creative and loyal to their organisation.

External customers are the people who buy products and services, and organisations are obviously dependent on their external customers. Without customers, a business will not be able to continue to operate. Treating customers with respect and giving excellent service ensures that they continue to buy from that business.

1 In Table 4.1, give an example of what each of these internal customers might need from a colleague or supplier. Say which colleague, department or supplier they would ask for the service.

▶ **Table 4.1:** Internal customers and their needs

Internal customer	Needs
A new starter wants to use a PC but can't log in	
Janice has not been paid her overtime for the month	
Ali needs to check some flight details for a customer	
Sally wants to send an invoice to a customer	
Garima has received a customer complaint and she needs to escalate the telephone call to her manager	

2 How do you think the needs that you have identified differ from the needs of the customers interacting with Ali, Sally and Garima?

First impressions

It can take seconds for a customer to form their first impressions of a business or organisation, so it is important that these first impressions are positive. Once a negative first impression has been formed, it is very difficult to change customers' minds, so it is worth making sure that customers will form a good first impression.

First impressions could relate to:

▶ **the visual appearance of the business** – for example, a poor first impression might be formed if staff look scruffy and are chewing gum, whereas a good impression would be given by well-dressed staff who have a professional appearance

▶ **staff behaviour** – for example, a poor impression would be created by staff slouching over desks, talking to each other and ignoring their customers, whereas a good impression would result from positive behaviour and body language, such as greeting customers with a smile

▶ **communication** – for example, a poorly written letter that is not personalised or being kept waiting for long periods on the telephone can create a bad impression, whereas a good impression can be created by a well-written letter or by having a telephone query dealt with promptly and efficiently

▶ **the product display** – a customer is more likely to buy from a business whose products are arranged in an appealing display than a business whose products and services are badly presented or out of date

▶ **the appearance and usability of the website or mobile app** – is it clear and easy to use with reliable content, or is it cluttered and difficult to navigate?

An organisation's goals

The basic customer service goal of any customer-focused organisation should be to provide consistent customer service that exceeds its customers' expectations. This should apply at all points at which the customer may encounter the organisation, not just at the point of making a sale. An organisation that does this will demonstrate that it is customer focused.

An organisation's goals emerge from its business strategy. However, because business strategies are not often made public, it can be difficult to assess how much an individual organisation's strategy focuses on customers. Organisations usually publicise statements that embody their strategies, such as their vision and mission, which are explained in Table 4.2. Many organisations also publicise a set of values, which they use to summarise their working culture and the way in which their organisation operates. In travel and tourism these values should show a strong customer focus, reflecting the importance of the customer to the organisation.

▶ **Table 4.2:** Examples of organisations' public strategy statements

Key term	Definition	Example
Vision statement	A longer-term vision or picture of where the organisation wants to go or what it wants to achieve	easyJet: 'Our Purpose: Seamlessly connecting Europe with the warmest welcome in the sky'
Mission statement	A short statement of what the organisation does and why it does this	UNIGLOBE Travel: 'The mission of UNIGLOBE Travel is to be the leading and most dependable travel management company in the world that sets the standard for professionalism and reliability to its customers'
Values	Principles that guide how a company will behave in order to further its mission	'IT'S Norwegian: 'Innovation, Teamwork, Simplicity'

In practice, it is not always clear whether a statement is a vision statement or a mission statement. Sometimes it can be difficult to work out what a set of values really means within the daily life of the organisation. The best way to find out about the strategic goals of an organisation is by looking at its annual report or by asking a contact within the company to share their business plan with you.

Case study

Royal Caribbean vision

Royal Caribbean International is a cruise company. On its website it states the following customer service principles and vision statement.

Anchored in Excellence
- We always provide service with a friendly greeting and a smile.
- We anticipate the needs of our customers.
- We make all effort to exceed our customers' expectations.
- We take ownership of any problem that is brought to our attention.
- We engage in conduct that enhances our corporate reputation and employee morale.
- We are committed to act in the highest ethical manner and respect the rights and dignity of others.
- We are loyal to Royal Caribbean and Celebrity Cruises, and strive for continuous improvement in everything we do.

Vision
Generate superior returns for our shareholders by empowering and enabling our employees to deliver the best holiday experience and enhancing the well-being of our communities.

Check your knowledge

Read through the principles and vision stated by Royal Caribbean International. Now match the following customer-focused goals, numbered 1–5, with examples from the vision and principles of Royal Caribbean International.

1 All customers are valued and respected in an equal way.

2 Individual needs are sensitively accommodated.

3 All problems are resolved efficiently and calmly.

4 Initiative and creativity are used to cater for customer needs.

5 Consistent service provided to all customers.

Factors in customer decision-making

What makes a customer choose a particular product, service or supplier? Every travel and tourism organisation needs to understand how different aspects of their service can influence their customers to make a purchase. Examples of different factors that influence customers' decisions are shown in Table 4.3.

▶ **Table 4.3:** Factors that influence customers' decisions

Factors	Example of poor service	Example of good service
Product knowledge	A customer is looking for an adventure holiday in Peru. The travel agent asks a few questions and then starts an internet search for possible holidays. The customer decides not to use the travel agency because they could search the internet themselves	A customer is looking for an adventure holiday in Peru. The advisor asks lots of questions, suggests suitable holidays and shows videos and photos on the internet of the suggestions. She then advises about vaccinations, visas and currency exchange
Assurance of the company's reliability and ability to meet expectations	A customer ordered theatre tickets from a travel agency, but the tickets have not been delivered. The play is in two days' time and the customer cannot get through on the phone to find out where the tickets are	The organisation's **customer charter** lays down the timescale in which documents should be delivered and the organisation sticks to this timescale
Empathy and listening	A customer misses their flight due to a road traffic accident, but there is no one available to advise them. Instead, they sit in the departure lounge to search the internet for another flight from a different airport that they then book and pay for, getting a taxi to their new departure airport	A customer misses their flight due to a road traffic accident. The customer service advisor at the airport desk listens sympathetically, transfers the customer to an evening flight and the customer pays the difference in price of the higher fare
Effectiveness of communication	A customer is booking a holiday for a special anniversary and wants to ask the agency a question. It is difficult to find contact details, but he eventually finds an email address and emails them. In response, he receives a badly written email containing mistakes and spelling errors, and feels upset and let down	A customer has a question about booking. He looks on the website for contact details, easily finds a telephone number and speaks to a friendly and efficient advisor who answers his query immediately
Credibility of the organisation	A customer is booking a hotel in Oxford. When she checks its TripAdvisor reviews, she sees some negative reviews that have not been answered by the hotel and decides to book a different hotel	A customer is booking a hotel in Oxford. When she checks its TripAdvisor reviews, she sees mostly good reviews, though there are a couple of negative reviews. However, these have responses from the hotel which address the points raised by the reviewers in a friendly and competent way
Perception of value for money	A customer books a train journey through an agent and then discovers that they could have purchased a much cheaper ticket	A customer books a train journey through an agent who takes time to find the cheapest fare for the customer. The customer feels that they have received good service and value for money

Key terms

Customer charter – a written statement of the rights of the organisation's customers.

Empathy – being able to understand and share the emotions or feelings of another person.

easyJet customer charter

Read easyJet's customer charter.

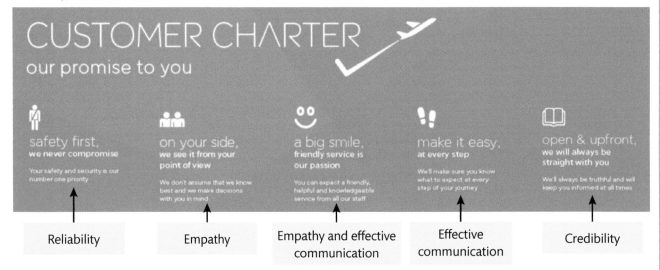

Check your knowledge

1 How does easyJet ensure that its customer charter is communicated to its customers?

2 How does easyJet make sure that its staff know about the customer charter?

3 Identify three ways in which easyJet can ensure that staff implement and comply with the charter.

Importance of teamwork in ensuring excellent customer service

All work in the travel industry involves some kind of teamwork. If a team works well together it is more likely to provide an excellent service. Imagine how you would feel as a customer if you arrived at your holiday resort and found that there was no one there to greet you and direct you to where you needed to go, because someone in the resort team had failed to tell the transfer rep that the flight was going to be early.

When a team works well together to provide excellent service, the team members will feel job satisfaction and a sense of well-being. However, working as a team can also present difficulties, and you may have experienced this yourself on school projects or organising events with friends.

A good team will:
▶   be motivated to achieve the same goals
▶   have a leader who delegates tasks appropriately
▶   know the lines of authority
▶   understand their own and others' team roles
▶   be confident and have self-esteem
▶   communicate well with each other
▶   make clear decisions
▶   pay attention to detail
▶   respect and trust each other
▶   have clear roles and responsibilities
▶   support each other
▶   have a 'can do' approach.

All travel and tourism organisations will try to ensure that their staff work well as a team. A happy team not only helps to create a positive image of the company, but is also more likely to be efficient and maximise the organisation's commercial success by satisfying its customers.

Customer-facing roles

A customer-facing role is one that requires the staff member to interact directly with customers. Customers have expectations of the travel and tourism professionals with whom they interact, although these expectations may vary from customer to customer. Their expectations will also vary depending on the role of the staff member.

▶ When interacting with cabin crew, customers expect a friendly welcome onto the aircraft and prompt, efficient service of any drinks or food. They do not expect to be hassled by the sale of products throughout their flight. The most important expectation that customers have of the cabin crew is that the crew is highly trained and knows what to do in the event of an emergency.

▶ When interacting with a hotel receptionist, customers expect a friendly welcome without having to queue. They expect the receptionist to give information about the hotel and facilities. They also expect any requests, such as restaurant bookings, room issues or upgrades, to be dealt with immediately.

▶ When interacting with a travel agent, customers expect the agent to have knowledge of the products that they are selling and to be able to make recommendations about potential holidays and transport methods. They expect the agent to be efficient, to take all relevant details accurately and to calculate costs correctly.

▶ Friendly professionalism is a vital part of any customer-facing role in travel and tourism

Theory into practice

Imagine you are a customer. Identify the expectations that you would have of each of the following roles and make notes about each expectation.
- Hotel manager
- Tour guide
- Tourist information assistant
- Children's resort rep

⏸ PAUSE POINT

Define the terms 'mission', 'vision' and 'values'.

Hint   Look back at Table 4.2 on page 188 if you can't remember, then write the definitions in your own words.

Extend   Explain how an organisation's values can support good customer service.

Customer communication, expectations and satisfaction

Identifying the customer

In order to provide excellent customer service, organisations must identify their customers, recognise their differing needs and provide products and services that meet their requirements. For example, a tour operator will provide different holidays and ranges of excursions for a group of students who want to go clubbing and a middle-aged couple who want to escape the British climate in January. Similarly, on a day trip to a theme park, a young couple will have different needs to those of a family with two children. The tour operator and the theme park need to ensure that their products and services can cater for all of their customer groups.

Theory into practice

Read through the different customer types in Table 4.4.

▶ **Table 4.4:** Different types of customer

Type of customer	Specific need
An individual	A single room
A family group of two adults and two teenagers	
A wedding party	
An organised tour group	
A regular traveller	
An inexperienced traveller	
A customer who regularly visits the hotel	

Identify one particular need that each type of customer might have when staying in a hotel.

Understanding disability

Some customers may have special needs, which may mean that they require additional and sensitive customer service. This may be because they have:

▶ mobility problems, for example, wheelchair users
▶ a hearing impairment
▶ a visual impairment
▶ speech difficulties
▶ intellectual or cognitive impairments
▶ mental health or emotional problems.

You should not make assumptions about disabilities or special needs. Remember that they may not be visible and they are sometimes temporary.

There are many reasons why an organisation must provide accessibility and a high standard of service to customers with disabilities. One reason is that they have a legal responsibility to do so under the Equality Act 2010. This Act requires businesses to anticipate, as far as they are able, the needs of customers with disabilities.

Another reason is that customers with disabilities have the right to the same standards of customer service as other customers. According to the disability charity Scope, there are an estimated 13.3 million people with a disability in the UK. These people require customer service, just like other people, and are also an important source of business.

The reputation of an organisation hinges on the service offered to all customers. The rise of social media and review sites such as TripAdvisor means that customers can share bad experiences more widely than ever before.

It is important to ensure that staff know how to interact with people with disabilities. Many people are unsure how to communicate with people who have special needs, and this can result in customers feeling insulted or patronised. Staff must feel confident that they can use appropriate communication to suit the individual, and places of businesses must be accessible to people with a range of disabilities.

Staff training courses might cover:

▶ the provisions of the Equality Act
▶ why accessibility is important to businesses
▶ how to produce an accessibility statement and action plan
▶ effective communication
▶ guidance on helping customers with different disabilities.

Tourism for All UK (TFA) is a charity that aims to raise standards of accessibility in tourism by working with the government and with the travel and tourism industry. TFA also provides an information service for people with disabilities. The charity offers training courses for employees in travel and tourism, which are officially endorsed by the Institute of Hospitality and the British Hospitality Association. TFA offers a general course called 'First contact with disabled customers', which is then followed up with role-specific courses such as 'Hotel Receptionist' and 'Amusement, Themed Parks and Attractions staff'.

Organisations like Tourism for All can advise organisations on how to provide an accessible environment. This might mean making physical changes for access such as wheelchair ramps but can include other provision; for example, training staff on the understanding and particular needs of dementia sufferers. The UK government provides advice and examples of good practice on the 'Accessible Britain' website. The case studies include easy walking trails, specially adapted bicycles for people with disabilities on cycling tours and accessible restaurants.

Communicating clearly and respectfully

Your communication and interpersonal skills need to be of the highest standard, especially when you work in customer-facing roles. These skills include your written and verbal communication skills.

Verbal communication

Most of us use face-to-face verbal communication many times a day: when shopping, getting on a bus, greeting friends or working in a team. However, it is important to know how to use verbal communication to its full advantage when dealing with customers. For example, personal presentation is a very important element of your interpersonal skills, because this will make as much of an impression as what you say and do. You must also consider your tone of voice and be aware of your body language, because these things will also communicate to your customer, perhaps even more than what you say.

The advantage of face-to-face communication is that you can read your customer's body language to understand how they feel. You can also use brochures, leaflets and other materials to help you communicate with your customer, and you can answer any questions easily as they arise. Face-to-face communication is often on a one-to-one basis, such as between a travel agent and a customer. However, it can also involve groups of people, such as at a welcome talk in a resort.

Verbal communication also takes place over the telephone. To be able to communicate well on the telephone you need good listening skills. Remember that you must listen to the tone of voice as well as the words being said. It is particularly important to speak clearly and check understanding when on the phone – as you cannot read the body language or any other non-verbal information such as gestures and facial expressions.

Active listening is a crucial skill to develop. It means that you demonstrate through your words and your actions or body language that you understand what is being said to you. For example, you can make appropriate responses, such as 'I see' or 'Oh dear', and ask questions such as 'So are you saying that he shouted at you?' This demonstrates to the customer that you are listening and that they can trust you.

Body language, or non-verbal communication, is an important way in which people communicate to others how they feel, although they may not be aware of the message that their body language is giving. Body language includes the way in which you stand, use eye contact, hold your head, **gesticulate** and use facial expressions. It is essential that you are aware of your body language and can use it to convey a positive message and build **rapport** with your customers.

▶ How do you think each of these people are feeling? What makes you come to that conclusion?

An important aspect of providing good customer service is recognising your customers' feelings from their behaviour. Watching their body language and listening to their tone of voice are the best ways of working out what your customer is really feeling.

Theory into practice

Work in pairs. Take it in turns to choose one of the feelings listed below and act it out without speaking, so that your partner can identify the feeling from your body language. You can use facial expressions, gestures and movement, but you must not speak.

- Anger
- Exhaustion
- Confusion
- Excitement
- Sadness
- Happiness
- Boredom

How successful is your partner at interpreting your body language?

Another verbal communication skill is the use of questions. Asking the right questions is a key to good communication and, whatever job you choose to do, you will have to ask questions of your colleagues and customers. In some situations, the type of question that you ask is as important as the words that you use to ask it. This is especially true when selling products and services or dealing with a difficult situation.

Table 4.5 lists the different types of question and gives examples, and the uses and limitations of each type of question.

▶ **Table 4.5:** Types of question and their uses

Type of question	Explanation	Examples	Use	Limitation
Closed	A question that prompts a 'yes' or 'no' answer	• Have you sent in your booking form? • Will you be staying for dinner? • Have you received your tickets?	To clarify facts rather than to gather information	Closed questions will not provide further information for discussion
Open	A question that cannot be answered with a 'yes' or 'no'. They usually start with words like 'what', 'when', 'how', 'who', 'why', 'where' or 'which'	• What did you enjoy most about your holiday? • Why are you upset? • How can I help you solve this problem? • Where have you been on holiday before?	To start a discussion or conversation and to gather information	A talkative person may answer at length or in an unfocused way, and may take up a lot of your time
Reflective	A question that checks understanding and gives people a chance to think about what has been discussed	• So you feel the hotel staff were unfriendly? • So you want somewhere sunny, but you are not looking for a beach holiday?	To check that you understand and to allow the customer to add to what has been discussed	The answers may take up time, and you may lose the thread of the previous discussion
Leading	A question that suggests what the answer should be, or leads the person into answering in a certain way	• So you feel that if the flight had not been delayed you would have had a nice holiday?	Try to avoid using leading questions	The question indicates what you are thinking and is unlikely to obtain a full or true answer. It may also make the customer feel that you are misrepresenting what they have said

In most situations, such as when establishing a customer's needs, you need to ask open questions. In some cases, reflective questions may be useful, particularly when dealing with a complaint or making a sale. Table 4.6 on page 196 shows you how to rephrase some closed or leading questions as open questions.

Theory into practice

1 Rephrase the following closed questions so that they become open questions.
   - Can I help you?
   - Are you okay today?
   - Do you like the view from your balcony?
   - Would you like to go to Greece again this year?

2 Rephrase the following closed questions so that they become reflective questions.
   - Is your budget £400 per person?
   - You don't want to go to Spain?
   - Was it the airline's fault?

Key terms

Slang – informal language, often used by a particular group of people, such as teenagers.

Jargon – special words or terms used only by people in a particular profession, such as in aviation.

Acronym – an abbreviation made up of the initial letters of a phrase and spoken as a word, such as NASA.

Research

Do you know what these common travel and tourism terms mean? Find out what they are and write your own definition for each one.
- Blackout dates
- ETA
- PRM
- Layover
- Offloading
- Red eye

▶ **Table 4.6:** Rephrasing questions to provide better customer service

Do not use	Do use
Did you enjoy your holiday?	How was your holiday? Tell me what you enjoyed about your holiday.
Did you learn a lot at the welcome meeting?	What sort of things did the resort representative tell you at the welcome meeting?
Do you want to go to Ibiza because of the nightlife?	What is it that makes you want to go to Ibiza?
You've been to Spain a lot, haven't you?	What destinations have you been to before?

When communicating with customers, you also need to be aware of the language that you use. It is very important to avoid using **slang**, sarcasm and inappropriate humour, as these will make you and your organisation seem unprofessional and it may offend customers. In addition, you also need to avoid using **jargon** and **acronyms**. This sounds obvious, but it can be very easy to forget that customers may not understand the terms that you use with colleagues.

Written communication

Although most of your written communication will be done using a computer, there are occasions when you will need to write information by hand. Examples include:
▶ completing an enquiry form
▶ taking a telephone message
▶ leaving a message for a colleague.

This means that you need to ensure that your handwriting is clear and easy to read, otherwise people may misunderstand what you have written.

When filling in any document, bear in mind that it could potentially be used in a court of law. This means that you should:
▶ take your time over it
▶ write in professional language
▶ make sure that the information provided is complete and accurate
▶ include all relevant times and dates
▶ give facts, not opinions.

Remember that written communication is more formal than verbal communication. This means that it is sometimes used to confirm decisions that have previously been discussed over the telephone or in person.

It is important that the correct form of written communication is used, usually by responding to a customer in the format in which they contacted you. For example, if they have sent an email, you should respond by email. No matter what form of written communication you use, it should be written in a professional manner and well presented, using correct spellings and appropriate language. This applies to handwritten notes, typed letters, emails and even comments on social media.

When handling your organisation's social media presence, you should always be careful about what is stated in public. It is usually best to deal with complaints and discussions offline.

Some written communications will be produced professionally, such as brochures, maps, leaflets, websites and questionnaires. However, you will still need to check that the content in these documents is accurate, such as destination names, prices and dates. Customer itineraries and cost quotes also need to be checked carefully, and should follow a common format. Your organisation should have a specific template for these documents, and it is important that you use these templates.

Theory into practice

Work in small groups. Copy and complete Table 4.7 explaining which method of communication you would use for each message.

▶ **Table 4.7:** Methods of communication

Message	Method of communication
The manager of a travel agency wants to advise a customer of a change of hotel	
A resort rep wants to let head office know that a customer has made a serious complaint about the hotel. She thinks that other customers may also complain	
Two hotel receptionists have agreed to swap shifts. They want to tell their manager	
An airline has decided to make 20 airline staff redundant and needs to inform the whole workforce about this decision	
A customer has had a great holiday and wants to spread the word about her chosen tour operator	
A visitor to a museum has been overcharged. He realises this only when he gets home	
After spending two weeks reading about two potential destinations, Jamal wants to confirm a holiday with the travel agent	

Compare your answers with other members of your group and discuss the reasons for your choice.

Understanding key areas of customer expectations and satisfaction

An organisation might know who its customers are and understand the principles of clear communication, but it also needs to know what its customers expect from the organisation. You have already seen in this unit that there is a huge range of customers, all of whom have different needs and expectations.

Anticipation of good service

Customers form an idea of service to expect from an organisation even before they use it. The organisation's image will influence whether or not customers choose to buy their products and services. Customers' impressions of an organisation may be influenced by the organisation's advertising or sales materials, and it is important that businesses can fulfil the customer expectations created by their marketing campaigns. Customers' impressions may also be influenced by the reputation of the company, which is usually based on reviews and word-of-mouth recommendations from other people.

Responding to needs and exceeding expectations

To understand customer expectations you will need to:
▶ ask questions that allow you to gather information about the stated needs of your customers
▶ use this information to try to identify any **unstated needs**
▶ find available options to meet these needs.

If the enquiry is straightforward, because the customer knows exactly what they want, this can be done quite easily. However, if the customer's needs are less clear, they will rely on your product knowledge to determine whether you can meet their needs.

Discussion

Work with a partner and discuss your impressions of the following organisations and destinations. What do you think has helped to form your impressions?
• Virgin
• Manchester United
• Ibiza
• Venice
• Ayia Napa in Cyprus
• Australia
• A local hotel
• Hilton

Once you have discussed with your partner, discuss your ideas with the whole group.

Key term

Unstated needs – those which the customer does not mention outright but are implied from other things they say or do.

When presenting customers with the available options, you must identify the three or four options that best meet the needs of the client and describe how this product or service matches these needs. For example, you might introduce the **features** of a holiday and turn them into **benefits** for the customer: 'I have just found a holiday in Tenerife that might be suitable. It is available for when you want to travel. I know that you want hot weather, and the temperatures in Tenerife will be high at that time of year. There is five-star accommodation available and it has a pool, which you particularly requested'. This description of the holiday is accurate, but it could be presented in a way that makes it even more appealing to the customer. Table 4.8 shows some examples of ways in which features can be described as benefits.

▶ **Table 4.8:** Examples of benefit statements

Feature of holiday	Your benefit statement
The hotel has a large swimming pool and a children's pool	'This hotel has a really large pool. There will be plenty of room for you to swim and you won't be disturbed by children's games'
The hotel is isolated	'It is a wonderfully quiet location – no neighbouring hotels to share the beach with. You will also have great views from all rooms'
The hotel is in the middle of a town	'You will be right in the middle of things. You can stroll out each evening and really get involved in local life'
Excursions included	'You have two excursions included in the price, both of which are guided, so you will certainly learn a lot about the local area'
Representative available	'A representative will be on hand if you have any queries while you are in the resort. They will be able to advise you where to go and they can arrange local excursions and car hire if you decide to explore while on holiday'

It is important to ensure that the information you provide is reliable and accurate. For example, if you told a customer that the weather in Saint Lucia is predictably good in September and October, you would be incorrect unless you added that there is a possibility of hurricanes during this period.

Many travel products and services like flights and holidays are booked a long time in advance. This means that customers have parted with their money but have not yet felt the benefit of their purchase. Travel and tourism organisations must keep these customers happy up to the point at which they take their flight or return from their holiday. They can do this by keeping in touch with the customer and reassuring them that everything is on track. For example, an airline might send reminder texts or emails about the flight or inform the customer of any extra services that they can purchase. Similarly, tour operators or travel agents send out information to help the customer plan their holiday. This might include destination information and advice or details of any excursions on offer.

Recognising implied or unstated needs will help you respond appropriately to a customer's needs. You should aim to exceed customers' expectations. You can do this by providing exceptional help for customers with special needs, by dealing promptly with any problems that occur and by offering additional products or services.

Excellent customer service also aims to 'delight' the customer. This might involve providing a bottle of champagne in a hotel room booked for an anniversary celebration or offering a discount on a repeat booking, but it does not have to involve money or gifts. For example, if customers return to a restaurant and are recognised and welcomed by the manager and staff, this really improves the customers' impression of the restaurant and its staff without costing the business anything.

Managing customer complaints

Customers usually appreciate that problems may arise and understand that these problems may sometimes be out of the control of the company involved. For example, a taxi strike in a destination will disrupt customers' travel arrangements, but it is beyond the control of the tour operator. The company can still deliver great service by dealing with the problem efficiently and satisfying the customer despite the problem.

Even the most successful travel and tourism organisations receive complaints. Some may be justified complaints and some may not be justified but, either way, your knowledge of policies and procedures will help you to deal with the situation calmly and without taking the complaint personally.

Some organisations reassure customers in advance that their problems will be dealt with by publishing a complaints policy. Complaints should be viewed as opportunities to demonstrate excellent service recovery and to leave a customer even more satisfied than if the complaint had not arisen. However, it is particularly important to know when the complaint should be escalated to a senior member of staff because it is outside your **remit**.

It is important that, throughout the complaints procedure, the customer is kept up to date with the progress of their complaint. This will reassure them that their complaint is being taken seriously and will be addressed.

> **Key term**
>
> **Remit** – the extent of the activities or responsibilities of a person's job.

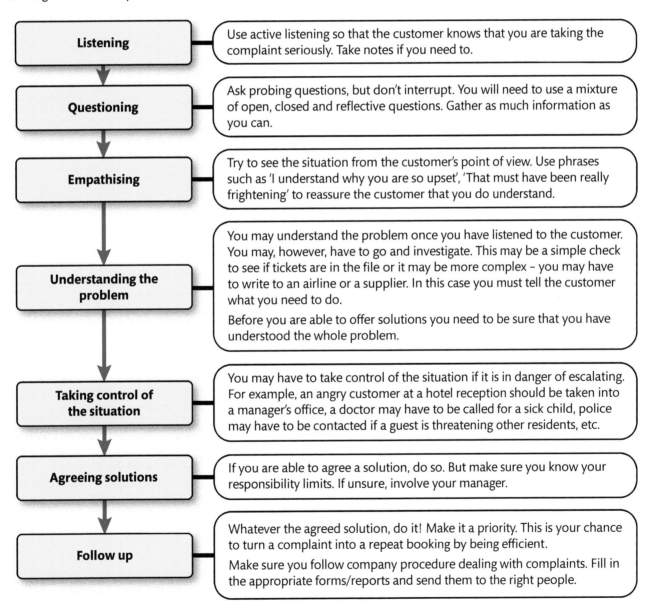

Listening — Use active listening so that the customer knows that you are taking the complaint seriously. Take notes if you need to.

Questioning — Ask probing questions, but don't interrupt. You will need to use a mixture of open, closed and reflective questions. Gather as much information as you can.

Empathising — Try to see the situation from the customer's point of view. Use phrases such as 'I understand why you are so upset', 'That must have been really frightening' to reassure the customer that you do understand.

Understanding the problem — You may understand the problem once you have listened to the customer. You may, however, have to go and investigate. This may be a simple check to see if tickets are in the file or it may be more complex – you may have to write to an airline or a supplier. In this case you must tell the customer what you need to do.

Before you are able to offer solutions you need to be sure that you have understood the whole problem.

Taking control of the situation — You may have to take control of the situation if it is in danger of escalating. For example, an angry customer at a hotel reception should be taken into a manager's office, a doctor may have to be called for a sick child, police may have to be contacted if a guest is threatening other residents, etc.

Agreeing solutions — If you are able to agree a solution, do so. But make sure you know your responsibility limits. If unsure, involve your manager.

Follow up — Whatever the agreed solution, do it! Make it a priority. This is your chance to turn a complaint into a repeat booking by being efficient.

Make sure you follow company procedure dealing with complaints. Fill in the appropriate forms/reports and send them to the right people.

▶ **Figure 4.1:** Dealing with complaints

A complaints procedure

A national organisation includes a comprehensive complaints procedure on its website.

'Unhappy with the service you have received? We are always glad to receive comments, feedback and suggestions.

As part of our complaints procedure, we will:

- treat complaints seriously and deal with them properly
- resolve complaints promptly and informally whenever possible
- learn from complaints and take action to improve our service
- ensure that complaints are treated in confidence.

What to do if you have a complaint

It's always better if you can let us know immediately. Most complaints can be sorted out quickly, and our staff will welcome the opportunity to do this if at all possible.

If you are unable to complain at the time you can contact us by email, in writing or by telephone.

What happens next?

Should you have cause to complain over the phone, we will try to resolve the issue straight away. If you complain by email or in writing, we will do everything we can to resolve it within 14 days. If this is not possible, we will explain why and give a new resolution date.

What if the complaint is not resolved?

If you are not happy with our response, then you can get back in touch with us by writing to the organisation's Customer Services department. Your complaint will be reviewed, and our response will be sent in writing within 14 days.

If you are still unhappy having received a reply, then you can write to our Managing Director, who will ensure you receive a response to your complaint.

Check your knowledge

1 Explain how the organisation escalates complaints if necessary.

2 How do you think the organisation ensures that they learn from complaints?

3 How do you think customer complaints should be dealt with?

4 What do you think would happen if a complaint against the organisation were made on social media?

5 What is your opinion about the organisation's timescale for responding to complaints?

6 What do you think would happen if a complaint were ignored?

The implications and potential risks of not addressing complaints

The most obvious consequence of failing to resolve a complaint is that the customer will remain dissatisfied. This customer is very unlikely to return and they are also likely to tell other people about their negative experience. This could be a serious risk to the organisation, as a loss of customers will mean a loss of revenue. The harm to a business's reputation is equally damaging, as customers whose complaints are ignored or dealt with badly will publicise their dissatisfaction, especially on social media.

> **Key term**
>
> **Reasonable skill and care** – the level of expertise and care that you would expect from a professional or a business.

Organisations who do not deal with complaints also risk breaking the law. A key piece of legislation that protects customers is the Consumer Rights Act 2015. This Act replaced various pieces of existing consumer legislation and brought them all together into one Act. It applies to products and services, including digital content. The Act states that services must be carried out with **reasonable skill and care**, and it applies to information given verbally or in writing to the consumer, which is legally binding where the consumer relies on it in order to make decisions. From October 2016 air, sea and other travel organisations had to begin complying with the Act, and passengers whose travel service was delivered without reasonable skill and care can apply for compensation.

The Act also sets out what should happen in other circumstances, including:

▶ when a product (including digital content) is faulty
▶ when services do not match up to what was sold or agreed by the business
▶ when a contract contains unfair terms.

Package holidays are protected by the Package Travel and Linked Travel Arrangements Regulations 2018, and the Civil Aviation (Air Travel Organisers' Licensing) (Amendment) Regulations 2012. If you booked accommodation that was not part of a package, you would be protected under the Consumer Rights Act, and the owner would be required to provide the accommodation with reasonable care and skill and ensure that it was as promised and described to you when you booked it.

Balancing customer satisfaction with organisational objectives

Many organisations list customer satisfaction as one of their organisational objectives, alongside more commercial objectives relating to business growth and profitability. However, there may be times when customer expectations are unrealistic, unsafe or too costly to meet. In these situations, the only solution is to explain respectfully and clearly why the customer demand cannot be satisfied.

Discussion

A family on holiday were waiting for a taxi to take them to catch an easyJet flight to London. Their taxi was held up by a road accident. While they were waiting in the hotel reception, they realised that other holidaymakers waiting for taxis were also hoping to catch the easyJet flight and a British Airways flight. Eventually, all of the passengers arrived at the airport and were 30 minutes late for both flights.

The British Airways and easyJet pilots had both been informed of the problem. The British Airways pilot chose to wait for the 12 passengers who were late for the BA flight, whereas the easyJet pilot chose not to wait for the 11 passengers who were late for the easyJet flight.

Which pilot was right? What were the considerations that they had to take into account? What might be the repercussions of their actions?

PAUSE POINT   Explain the different steps of the complaints process.

> **Hint**   You will find these in the text or you can refer to the complaints procedure of the company you are researching.

> **Extend**   Why do organisations publish their complaints policies and procedures?

The potential impact of customer service for the organisation

Positive or negative effects

The customer service provided to customers can have positive and negative effects on travel and tourism organisations. These potential effects include:

▶ feedback from customers, particularly to other customers
▶ the business's reputation or public image
▶ the business's sales
▶ the number and types of customers that the business attracts
▶ customer confidence in the business
▶ employees' job satisfaction.

Table 4.9 examines the potential positive and negative impacts of customer service.

Table 4.9: Potential positive and negative impacts of customer service on travel organisations

Area affected by customer service	Positive effects	Negative effects
The number and types of customers	• Loyal customers come back to the organisation providing 'repeat business' • Satisfied customers recommend the organisation to people who then buy from the organisation. These new customers are needed even when a business has a loyal customer base. For example, cruise companies have made efforts to attract younger customers	• Poor service makes people unlikely to return to the business • Poor service also makes it difficult to attract new customers, who often rely on reviews and the recommendations of friends and family
Sales	• Repeat business and new customers should increase sales and profits	• The loss of customers may cause sales and profits to fall
Business reputation or image	• Good customer service provided by sales consultants, good customer experiences of the product or service and positive experiences of after-sales service all have a positive impact on reputation • Satisfied customers may recommend the business to other people, and this can improve the business's public image	• People who receive poor service will talk about it: they will tell their friends and family and they may also bring it up on social media. This can damage the organisation's reputation and public image
Employee job satisfaction	• Providing excellent service and dealing with satisfied customers is very rewarding for employees • Positive feedback from customers provides job satisfaction and a feeling of well-being among employees	• If employees cannot provide good customer service or meet customers' needs, they are likely to feel unhappy about their work and are unlikely to talk about their company with pride • Unhappy employees are also more likely to leave to work elsewhere, and recruiting and training replacements can cost the business a lot of money
Feedback	• Organisations often use good feedback in their PR. This can have a positive impact on employees and on the organisation's reputation	• Poor feedback is harmful to the reputation of the company and often upsets employees

Key term

Competitive advantage – something that puts a business in a favourable position in comparison with its competitors.

Providing excellent customer service is the best way for an organisation to gain a **competitive advantage**. Staff training must be provided in order to maintain excellent levels of customer service. In addition, the business's products have to be up to date, the company's premises must be well-maintained and levels of customer service regularly monitored and evaluated.

The importance of job satisfaction is exemplified by the service-profit chain, a basic version of which is shown in Figure 4.2. The chain links profitability with other benefits to an organisation, including customer satisfaction and employee satisfaction.

Figure 4.2: The service-profit chain

Theory into practice

1 Think about a time when you received excellent customer service. Describe it to a partner. What aspects of the customer service made it excellent? How did it make you feel?

2 Discuss with your partner whether you have ever used a particular organisation or bought a product simply because it was recommended to you.

Regulatory and organisational requirements

You have already seen that organisations must comply with the Consumer Rights Act and the Package Travel Regulations. In addition, there are other examples of standards or regulations that might apply to an organisation.

Service standards

These are measures of quality that organisations decide to work towards in order to demonstrate their commitment to quality. One quality management standard is ISO 9001, published by the **International Organization for Standardization (ISO)**. ISO 9001 (Customer Satisfaction) is based on the following seven quality management principles.

1 Customer focus
2 Leadership
3 Engagement of people
4 Process approach
5 Improvement
6 Evidence-based decision making
7 Relationship management

These principles help to provide guidance and tools for organisations who want to ensure that their products and services consistently meet customers' requirements, and that quality is consistently improved. ISO also publishes other standards.

▶ ISO 1002 (Customer Satisfaction and Complaints Handling) focuses on complaints handling

▶ ISO 1004 (Measuring Customer Satisfaction) provides guidelines for measuring and monitoring customer satisfaction

▶ ISO 9004 (Managing for Sustained Success in an Organisation) is another quality management system that is designed to help businesses to meet the needs and expectations of customers in the long term.

Statutes and regulations

A statute is a written law passed by Parliament. Parliament also passes regulations, such as building regulations. Compliance with statutes and regulations is a legal requirement, and customers could sue if an organisation failed to comply with them. For example, the Data Protection Act 2018 sets out the rights of people whose personal data is held by businesses in their filing systems, and a customer would have the right to complain if a business released their personal data to a third party without the person's permission.

The Development of Tourism Act 1969 established a British Tourist Authority and Tourist Boards for England, Scotland and Wales with responsibility for promoting the development of tourism to and within Great Britain. This impacted on customer service in that these boards were able to co-ordinate activities across the industry and promote standards of service and provide insightful research.

Key term

International Organization for Standardization (ISO) – develops and publishes international standards. The standards are requirements or guidelines that organisations comply with in order to be awarded the standard.

Link

You will learn about the Data Protection Act 2018 in Unit 5: Travel and Tourism Enterprises, Section B.

Other guidelines

Other guidelines may be introduced by industry bodies. For example, in December 2016 the Civil Aviation Authority (CAA) introduced guidelines to help UK airports provide better support for passengers with hidden disabilities and more effective communication ahead of travel. One of the suggestions is to make information available in a range of formats, including clear pictogram images and audio messages. Airports should consider providing quiet routes and quiet areas, and must ensure employees, including security staff, are given enhanced hidden disability training.

Obtaining and interpreting feedback and identifying improvements

One impact of customer service is the collection of feedback from customers and employees. For example, customers will discuss their experiences of good and bad service on social media sites and review sites. The way in which feedback can be used to improve service is explored in Section B.

PAUSE POINT Explain the potential positive and negative effects of customer service on sales and employee satisfaction.

Hint Refer to Table 4.9 on page 202 if you are not sure.

Extend How does employee satisfaction lead to customer loyalty?

Assessment activity 4.1   A.P1 A.P2 A.P3 A.M1 A.D1

You are working as an intern for a customer service consultant who provides customer service advice and training. For the last few weeks you have been involved in a 'deep discovery' exercise at a travel and tourism organisation. This means you have been working closely with employees to find out what their job entails and how they deliver customer service both internally and externally. You have also been looking closely at the organisation's policies and procedures for delivering customer service.

You are now ready to produce a report on your findings that evaluates the importance of excellent customer service, that complies with UK regulations, to the organisation. You should include:

- the goals of customer service in the travel and tourism organisation
- the significance and potential positive impacts of delivering excellent customer service that complies with UK regulations
- the potential impact of not responding effectively to a customer
- the importance of managing customer expectations.

Give reasons and examples that justify your evaluation and give clear conclusions.

Present your report to your line manager at the consultancy and to the managers of the travel and tourism organisation. You might present it orally with explanatory notes or submit a written report.

Plan
- What is the task? What am I being asked to do?
- What information do I need to gather from my selected travel and tourism organisation?
- What information do I need from other resources?

Do
- I have made a plan to carry out the research needed with a timescale and deadlines.
- I have decided the form my presentation will take.

Review
- I can explain what the task was and how I approached the task.
- I can see what I would do differently next time.

B Demonstrate customer service in different travel and tourism situations

Customer service skills and behaviours

Some people are naturally good at providing excellent service. They have an outgoing personality, appear to be always positive and are not intimidated by difficult situations. Other people have to learn these skills.

Communication and interpersonal skills

Verbal skills

The situations in which you need to demonstrate verbal skills could include face-to-face customer service, such as serving a customer in a travel agent, and over the telephone, such as dealing with a booking enquiry about a holiday. You may also need to use verbal skills to communicate with larger audiences, such as in resort welcome meetings and when giving presentations. Welcome meetings normally take place the morning after guests have arrived at a resort. They will have recovered from their journey and will want to learn about the resort's facilities, the local area and any planned excursions. The meeting usually takes place in a hotel lounge or bar and complimentary drinks are usually served, though this will depend on the time of day. It is important to be well prepared for this meeting. Table 4.10 lists effective verbal communication skills that should be used in different situations.

▶ Remember to smile when speaking on the telephone as it will improve your tone of voice

▶ **Table 4.10:** Effective verbal communication skills

Face-to-face	On the telephone	Welcome meeting	Presentation
• Create rapport by smiling, greeting the customer and asking some questions to put them at ease • Maintain eye contact, but do not stare! • Show empathy by thinking about how you would feel if you were in the customer's place • Focus on providing helpful and friendly service • Choose your language carefully • Practise active listening techniques • Ask open questions to gather necessary information • Be aware of your body language and the body language of the person to whom you are speaking	• Use an appropriate greeting • Ask the caller's name and use it as you talk to them • Speak slowly and clearly, using short sentences and phrases • Avoid using jargon and acronyms • Vary your tone of voice so that it does not come across as monotone • Check that the person on the other end of the line understands what you have said • Ensure that there is minimal background noise around you • Smile, as this will affect the tone of your voice and make it sound friendly • Ask if you can give them any further help and thank them for calling before ending the call	• Give out invitations to the meeting on the transfer bus from the airport to the resort • Arrive at the meeting location in good time and in the correct uniform • Make sure that the room has a suitable layout and enough chairs • Take promotional materials and documentation, such as booking forms • Ensure that any drinks are ready to be served • Know which guests to expect and their names • Introduce yourself and welcome the guests • Distribute information sheets about excursions, facilities and safety • Tell guests about location of notice board and information file, as well as representative's visiting times and contact details • Take bookings for excursions, car hire and other additional services • Thank guests before they leave • Answer individual questions	• Adapt your presentation style (formal or informal) depending on the audience • Introduce your topic clearly • Use cue cards to help you remember points rather than using a long script • Keep your presentation slides brief and to the point • Be aware of your body language and the body language of your audience • Maintain eye contact with the audience, but not just one person! • Focus on talking to the audience rather than reading from your cards • Conclude by summarising the points that you have made • Ask if there are any questions and answer them

Non-verbal communication

Non-verbal communication is usually written communication. The situations in which you need to demonstrate non-verbal skills could include writing or checking the content of brochures, maps, websites, letters, emails, reports, advertisements, text messages and digital media such as social media platforms and apps.

When practising your non-verbal communication:

▶ decide which type of communication is appropriate, remembering that you should answer an enquiry in the same medium in which the enquiry was received

▶ think carefully about what you want to say before you press send, because once the communication is sent it cannot be unsent

▶ check your spelling and grammar

▶ use an appropriate style for the type of communication. You might use a formal style in a letter but a more relaxed style that is friendly but still professional on social media

▶ use company templates if they are provided.

Overcoming barriers to communication

In all forms of communication, use your interpersonal skills to recognise and overcome barriers to communication. The barriers may be from you or from your customer. Barriers may include:

▶ closed questions, so make sure that you avoid them
▶ failing to empathise, so show understanding and sensitivity, especially in difficult situations
▶ choosing inappropriate language, so think about your language choices carefully
▶ anger or aggression from customers, so stay calm and maintain a positive, professional attitude
▶ poor body language, so practise active listening
▶ tone of voice, so vary the pitch and tone of your voice to maintain customers' interest and to ensure that you do not sound bored
▶ inconsistent customer service, so make sure that you respond to different customers in the same way.

Key behaviours

As you saw in the previous section, the training programme at Jet2.com focuses on employee behaviours that sum up the business's values. In your professional life you should think about your own behaviour and make sure that it is appropriate and professional. For example, no matter what role you take in the travel and tourism industry, you will need to be able to problem solve, show respect to your customers and colleagues and be assertive enough to say no in a polite and respectful manner when necessary.

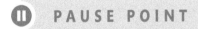 **PAUSE POINT**   A new colleague is trying to respond to an email from a customer who is asking about the weather in their chosen holiday destination. Give your colleague some guidance on the non-verbal skills that they should use in this situation.

> Hint   An email is a written form of communication, but it is less formal than a letter.
> Extend   Write the email. The destination is Tenerife and the customer is going in May.

Dealing effectively with customer service requests and complaints

Customer service situations

In this section you will practise the skills that you have learned about in this unit. This will include verbal communication, both face-to-face and over the telephone, and non-verbal or written communication.

Theory into practice

In this task, you will practise your face-to-face communication skills.

Prepare and carry out a welcome meeting for a resort of your choice. Make sure you:

• include correct and appropriate information about the products and services on offer
• promote excursions and other additional services
• relay any messages about the facilities or safety issues.

You should deliver your welcome talk to one or more of the others in your group, and your audience should critically evaluate your skills. Then you should swap roles and repeat the exercise.

Theory into practice

In this task you will demonstrate that you can deal with a problem and complete the necessary records in line with organisational policy.

You are a holiday representative in Fuengirola, Spain. You are visiting a hotel when an accident occurs and you are called to the scene. A child slipped while running near the pool and fell into the water. The child was rescued from the water by Jo, the lifeguard, and seemed to have slight concussion and a broken leg. The lifeguard called an ambulance and the child went to hospital, escorted by her parents.

Allocate the characters described above and carry out a role play of the accident, taking turns to play the representative. As the representative, make notes on what you will do and whom you need to inform. Complete the accident form provided in Figure 4.7.

Dealing with customer service requests and complaints

Difficult situations can test your customer service skills to the limit, so you need to consider some additional points when dealing with problems and complaints. For example, you need to know the limits of your own authority and understand when you should escalate a problem to your manager. As an employee, you will be empowered to deal with some situations, such as authorising a small amount of compensation for a problem with a customer's room, but you must be able to direct problems to your line manager and follow the company procedure for this.

Sometimes, especially in difficult situations, you will be required to keep a record of what was said and done to document what happened and why it happened. This is particularly important in case of any future enquiries or complaints. You may have to complete forms and ensure that you comply with legal requirements.

FABULOUS
Holidays

REPORT OF AN ACCIDENT OR DANGEROUS OCCURRENCE

Notes on how to use this form are included at the end of this form

A. Person making the report **Property** ______

Name ______

Your role on the property ______

B. Date, time and place at which the accident took place. It is important that you are as precise as possible in completing this section.

Date of accident ______ Time ______

Address where the accident took place ______

Specific location where the accident took place ______

Was a photograph of the location taken? **YES/NO** ______

Normal activity carried out at this place ______

Why was the injured person there at the time? ______

C. The injured person

Name ______ Ref. No. ______ Pitch No. ______

Address ______

Nature of injury and condition and part of the body affected ______

D. Witnesses

Name ______ Name ______

Address ______ Address ______

E. Describe the event and how it happened. Please refer to the note. Draw a sketch if appropriate.

______

______

______

______

______

______

NOTES ON HOW TO COMPLETE THIS FORM

1. Please be as clear and precise as possible when completing this form.
2. In section E, you are asked to state only the facts relating to the incident, not opinions as to who is at fault. Details you must include are: what happened; information relating to any police involvement in the matter; and action taken by yourself or any other person involved in this matter. You should also include a sketch of what happened.
3. Fax one copy **immediately** to the Operations Department and one copy to your Area Manager.

Figure 4.3: An example of an accident form

Handling complaints can be difficult but, if they are handled well, they can provide you with an opportunity to give excellent customer service and turn the complainant into a very happy, loyal customer. The following are tips for handling complaints.

▶ Listen to the complaint, remembering to use your active listening techniques.
▶ Do not take the complaint personally.
▶ Summarise and repeat the complaint to the customer to check that you have understood their complaint.
▶ Empathise with the customer's situation without admitting any liability for the complaint.
▶ Tell the customer what you are going to do about their complaint and when you will do it, and clearly agree the solution with the customer.
▶ Stay calm and professional at all times.
▶ Keep appropriate records of the complaint, your dealings with the customer and the solution to the problem.

Case study

Dealing with a complaint

HOTEL FACILITIES COMPLAINT FORM

- Please complete this form AS SOON AS POSSIBLE following customer complaint regarding the facilities.
- It is essential you bring the matter to the attention of the hotel management with a note of any action to be taken.
- The hotel management must sign this form in acknowledgement of the complaint.

Property [_____] Date [_____]

Brief summary of complaint: _____

Customer name: _____ Ref No: _____

Reported to member of hotel management: _____

Action to be taken with agreed timescale: _____

Signed on behalf of the hotel: _____

Signed staff member: _____ Date: _____

Figure 4.4: An example of a complaints form

'I won't go into the exact details. What I will say is that the service was appalling and one of the restaurant "specials" was spam in gravy! Anyway, after about four days of horrible food and terrible service, I complained to the rep in our resort. She was very helpful and said that she would sort things out with the restaurant manager. In spite of that, the restaurant situation still didn't improve. We then wrote out a customer complaints form and got the rep to sign it.'

Check your knowledge

1 Could the holiday representative have resolved this complaint so that it was not pursued on return to the UK? If you think she could, explain how.

2 What would the representative do if she thought that the customer's complaint was not valid?

3 Complete the complaints form provided in Figure 4.4.

Theory into practice

1 In this task you will practise giving correct information and advice on the phone.

Mrs Huang calls you at the retail agency where you work. She wants to fly from Gatwick to Brussels tomorrow morning to get to an afternoon meeting. She also wants to know the price of a taxi into Brussels city centre from the airport. Find out possible flight times and prices and call her back with the information.

2 In this task you will practise giving correct information and advice face-to-face.

Zuzanna Fisher is taking a gap year before university. She has booked a world ticket with you and will spend part of her year away in Australia, and she will also visit Thailand. She is hoping to get some work in Australia and needs advice about visas. She is in your office so you need to find out and tell her straight away. You also need to tell her about any vaccinations that she might need in order to visit Thailand.

3 In this task you will practise dealing with a problem face-to-face, ensuring that you comply with relevant legislation.

You work in the customer service department at your nearest airport. A customer in a wheelchair has arrived but doesn't know what the procedure is for booking assistance to the aircraft. Explain the procedure to the customer and how you will be able to help them. Make sure that you comply with legislation and regulations such as the Equality Act 2010.

4 In this task you will practise dealing with a problem, responding by letter, and practise saying no.

You work in the customer service department at British Airways. You have to reply to a letter of complaint about a flight delay. The delay was due to unexpectedly severe weather conditions, meaning that it is not covered by Denied Boarding Regulations. Write a letter to the complainant, Mr M Moran, explaining that there is no case for compensation and apologising for the delay. The delay was on 20 February and it was a two-hour delay on a flight from Heathrow to Geneva.

5 In this task you will practise following protocol in an emergency situation.

You work as a holiday representative on a campsite. Explain to a new colleague why campers are not allowed to use candles in their tent. Describe to the colleague what they should do if a fire broke out in a tent.

PAUSE POINT   Describe the points to remember when dealing with complaints.

Hint   Look back at the previous pages or research the complaints procedure used by the organisation you are researching.

Extend   Explain how complaints can be useful to a business.

210   Managing the Customer Experience in Travel and Tourism

Review effectiveness of own performance in customer service to add value to travel and tourism organisations

Evaluate individual performance

After practising your customer service skills using the activities provided in the previous section, in your class or workplace, you should carry out an **audit** of your own customer service skills and produce an action plan to develop them further.

Key term

Audit – a thorough review or assessment.

Skills audit

A skills audit is a simple self-assessment of the skills that you have demonstrated in customer service situations.

Theory into practice

Look at the skills listed in Table 4.11 and, for each one, give yourself a score between 1 and 5, where 1 is excellent and 5 is poor.

Once you have completed the table, discuss your self-assessment with a partner. Do they agree with your scores? Think about what you can do to improve your skills.

▶ **Table 4.11**: A skills audit

Skill	1	2	3	4	5
Spelling					
Grammar					
Greeting people and building rapport					
Using open questions					
Positive body language					
Tone of voice					
Active listening					
Problem solving					
Handling complaints					
Assertion – saying no when necessary					
Teamworking					

Personal SWOT

You have already seen how businesses and organisations can use SWOT analysis. You can also use SWOT analysis to assess yourself, looking at your existing strengths and weaknesses, as well as any threats posed by gaps in your skillset and opportunities to develop those missing skills.

Table 4.12 is an example of a personal SWOT analysis of communication and interpersonal skills.

▶ **Table 4.12**: An example of a personal SWOT analysis

Strengths	Weaknesses
• I am very good at English, with accurate grammar and good spelling skills, so I can write letters and emails quickly and correctly • I am a good listener and do not interrupt people but listen carefully and check that I have understood using questions • I am creative and have had some good ideas to solve customers' problems • I understand how to read body language and have become quite good at reading it to guess someone's mood • My appearance is smart • I have a good work ethic – I want to succeed	• I am shy and dislike giving presentations as I am nervous. I find it difficult to make eye contact with the audience • I tend to read my notes, which spoils the presentation • I dislike confrontation and to avoid it I accept complaints easily and overcompensate people • I need to practise using open questions • I have got the procedure for dealing with an aspect of service wrong because I didn't know enough about it • I find it difficult to chat to people who I don't know well
Opportunities	**Threats**
• I can get to know procedures and policies at work by researching more and asking my manager • I could volunteer to do some charity work or visit old people so that I get used to meeting new people and chatting • I can practise giving presentations and ask for feedback	• My shyness may prevent me having a customer-facing role • People may bring complaints to me and I will give them whatever they want because I am not assertive enough • I will make mistakes because my knowledge of company policy is not good enough

(**Theory into practice**)

Using the template used in Table 4.12, carry out a SWOT analysis of your own interpersonal and communication skills.

Action plan

Once you have carried out your skills audit and SWOT analysis, you should use the results to develop an action plan. The action plan should be based on SMART targets:

▶ **Specific** – the objective is explained clearly and contains specific details that will be achieved
▶ **Measurable** – it will be easy to see when the objective has been achieved
▶ **Achievable** – the objective is realistic
▶ **Relevant** – the objective will help you to achieve what you set out to achieve
▶ **Time-bound** – the objective has a specified end point.

The action plan should:

▶ address any weaknesses, which should remove or reduce any threats
▶ list the resources that you will need in order to meet your targets
▶ include review dates for each target
▶ show how you will monitor your progress towards achieving your targets
▶ be based on SMART targets.

Table 4.13 is Sam's action plan, based on her SWOT analysis in Table 4.12.

▶ **Table 4.13:** Sam's action plan

Target	Tasks	Resources	Progress	Review date
Develop presentation skills	• Complete online tutorial in presentation skills	• Library	• Tutorial complete	31 Jan
	• Develop a welcome meeting presentation	• Internet • Brochures on destination • Feedback from two classmates	• Positive feedback from classmates	14 Feb
	• Develop a presentation for my Customer Service assignment	• Assignment resources from research and the internet and my chosen organisation • Feedback from two classmates and my tutor	• Positive feedback from classmates and my tutor	28 Feb

Theory into practice

Develop your own action plan, making sure that it includes SMART targets based on your skills audit and SWOT analysis. You can use Sam's example in Table 4.13 to help you.

PAUSE POINT Explain how a personal SWOT analysis can help someone to develop an action plan to improve their skills.

Hint Think about how it finds the gaps in someone's skillset.

Extend How can you monitor your progress using an action plan?

Adding value

Developing your customer service skills will contribute to the success of your organisation because your actions and behaviours will have a huge impact. If you can do your job well, the organisation will benefit. Fulfilling your role well will have positive impacts on:

▶ the customer
▶ the organisation as a whole
▶ your colleagues
▶ your own personal development.

Figure 4.5 shows how these four areas interact and have an impact on each other.

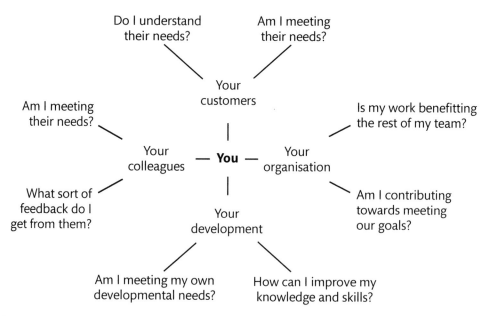

Do I understand
their needs?

Am I meeting
their needs?

Your
customers

Am I meeting
their needs?

Is my work benefitting
the rest of my team?

Your
colleagues

— **You** —

Your
organisation

What sort of
feedback do I
get from them?

Your
development

Am I contributing
towards meeting
our goals?

Am I meeting my own
developmental needs?

How can I improve my
knowledge and skills?

▶ **Figure 4.5:** The impact of improving your customer service skills

It is possible to assess the impact of customer service improvements on a business by analysing its performance indicators. For example, you could use surveys or any changes in the business's Net Promoter Score to monitor whether there is any improvement in customer satisfaction.

Case study

BA Beyond the Flight Deck

In 2012, British Airways (BA) launched the Beyond the Flight Deck (BFD) programme with the aim of improving customers' experience by allowing them to interact with their pilots. As part of the BFD programme, pilots go through a two-day training course to learn about customer needs and expectations and to learn the customer service skills needed to provide a great customer experience.

The pilots use what they learn from this training course as part of their day-to-day role, such as updating passengers about turbulence and providing flight information over the aircraft's public address system. The BFD programme also equips aircraft crew with customer feedback data about the route that they are about to fly, allowing them to learn from previous experience.

According to the Peer Awards for Excellence, BA reported a 10 per cent increase in customer satisfaction ratings from BA customers who interacted with their pilot before, during or after the flight. They also saw an 11 per cent increase in customers' likelihood to recommend BA to others, and an 11 per cent increase in customers' likelihood to travel with BA again.

Check your knowledge

1   Why do you think that pilots used to be excluded from traditional customer service training?

2   Why do you think this programme has had such a positive impact on customer satisfaction?

3   Give examples of how an individual pilot who participates in the BFD programme would add value to BA as an organisation.

 **PAUSE POINT**   What are the four areas of impact of customer service delivery?

Hint   One area is you and your personal development.

Extend   Why do you need to think about all four of these areas when delivering customer service?

Assessment activity 4.2

Part 1

Your internship manager wants you to start carrying out short training sessions in customer service with clients in travel and tourism organisations. Before you are given this responsibility, your manager wants you to practise your skills with her to demonstrate that you are competent to train others. She has presented you with the following situations to assess your delivery of excellent customer service. In each situation you should respond to the customer who will be played by another person in your group or a tutor. You should deal with each situation as confidently and effectively as you can. You will be assessed on your ability to consistently demonstrate initiative, responsibility and professionalism.

1   You work on the information desk for a low-cost airline at London Stansted Airport. You are confronted by a very angry passenger who has missed his flight to Milan because he was late. He is only carrying hand baggage but he arrived at the departure gate five minutes after it closed. He is in a particularly bad mood because staff would not let him through even though he could see that the plane was still sitting by the gate. To make matters worse, the information board has just shown that this flight is delayed by 30 minutes.

Decide what to do and respond to the customer in an appropriate way.

2   You work for a tour operator in their call centre. You receive a telephone call from Mrs Flanagan, a disappointed customer who has just returned from a city break in Venice. Her husband had booked the weekend to celebrate their anniversary. She tells you that the flights and transfer went very smoothly but everything went wrong at the hotel.

   - They had booked the honeymoon suite but were allocated another room.
   - They were unable to swim in the hotel pool as it was closed for repairs.
   - The first night they had aperitifs in the hotel bar but the second night it was restricted to a private party and they could not go in.

She says she is going to write a poor review on TripAdvisor about your organisation and has already tweeted about the hotel.

You cannot understand why these issues were not resolved during the stay. You also think that customers were informed about the pool closure at the time of booking and received a discount off the price of their holiday because of the inconvenience. Now you need to:

   - respond to the customer's complaint on the phone
   - explain you need to look into it further
   - phone the hotel in Venice for further information
   - email your manager to check whether customers were notified of the pool closure.

The manager replies to say the pool closure was notified and a discount already given.

The hotel manager remembers the couple and says it is true they did not get their booked room but that they did not complain at the time. He agreed that the bar was sometimes closed because of functions but he did not realise that they were unhappy about it.

Decide how to resolve this complaint and call Mrs Flanagan to tell her what you intend to do and to get her agreement. Follow up your phone call with a letter to Mrs Flanagan confirming what you have agreed.

Plan

   - What are the different scenarios? What am I being asked to do?
   - What customer service skills do I need to respond to these complaints?
   - What reviews have I carried out before? How can I use these to support this review?
   - What format should I use for my review and action plan?
   - How will I evaluate the usefulness of my plan?

Do

   - I have decided what the resolution should be in each case.
   - I have decided how I will respond to the customers to calmly bring about my proposed resolution.
   - I have considered how to present the written communication.
   - I have carried out a review and developed an action plan.
   - I have discussed ways of evaluating the plan with my group.
   - I have included SMART targets in my action plan.

Review

   - I can see how some of my skills can be developed and I will put these developments in my action plan.
   - I have listened to the feedback and will act on it in the future.

Part 2

Your manager has asked you to complete a review of your own customer service skills and produce an action plan to address areas for improvement, as well as an explanation of how developing your skills will add value to the travel and tourism organisations with which you work.

You should:

- review your customer service skills using a suitable tool such as SWOT analysis
- produce a personal action plan that addresses areas where improvements could be made
- assess how developing your skills will both improve your own performance and help travel and tourism organisations achieve their goals
- evaluate the usefulness of your action plan in developing your own skills and in contributing to the potential success of travel and tourism organisations.

Plan to monitor and improve customer service to achieve organisational objectives

How organisations research, monitor and analyse customer service

It is essential that travel and tourism organisations continuously monitor and evaluate the service they provide in order to maintain high levels of customer service. This monitoring process will provide them with information and data about their customer service levels.

In order to monitor customer service, a business must first know exactly what they are trying to achieve and how they are trying to achieve it.

Organisations gather a great deal of information from their customers using a variety of different sources:

▶ **Data analysis** – visitor numbers, for example to a visitor attraction. These numbers can be benchmarked year-on-year to analyse trends. Occupancy rates are measured in hotels to analyse whether the hotel is reaching capacity and whether promotions are needed to encourage trade. Prices fluctuate according to estimated occupancy rates.

▶ **Social media and online reviews** – price comparison websites and online review sites give customer ratings and reviews. This is useful for travel and tourism organisations as it provides them with free market research: it tells them how they and their competitors are performing. TripAdvisor is the best known review website, but there are others. Businesses can also use social media as a way of gathering customer reviews. For example, Let's Go Cambridge is a travel and tourism business that encourages its customers to leave reviews on TripAdvisor by handing out cards that the customer can scan with their smartphone. This means that leaving a review is easy and can be done immediately, resulting in Let's Go Cambridge being the number one punting attraction in their city.

▶ **Community forums** – provide a business with a way of inviting customers to share their experience with the business. This makes customers feel privileged and enables them to give feedback. For example, Hilton used a forum to gather customer feedback on their new room selection feature. This feedback suggested that customers also wanted information about the locations of facilities outside the hotel, such as attractions and restaurants, as well as facilities provided in the hotel. This led Hilton to change the feature to include the information that customers wanted.

▶ **Instant feedback** – some organisations give customers instant incentives to collect feedback from them while they are still interacting with the organisation. For example, a restaurant could give customers a free cocktail or dessert in exchange for answering some on-the-spot questions.

▶ **Mystery shopper** – used by many companies to assess the performance of their staff or to assess the competition. The mystery shopper is someone who is employed to visit shops or make telephone and internet enquiries, and will pretend to be a customer who is interested in making a purchase or a booking. The mystery shopper assesses the customer service provided and gives a detailed report to the business. This method is commonly used by tour operators, travel agents and call centres.

> **Link**
>
> You will learn more about mystery shoppers in Unit 5: Travel and Tourism Enterprises, Section A.

Information from loyalty programmes

It is crucial that the organisation finds out whether their loyalty programme and other strategies work.

Loyalty programmes provide extensive data on customers, because members give the business a lot of personal information when they join the programme. They are allocated a membership number, which they present at every transaction with the business, so all their buying behaviour is monitored. This allows the organisation to personalise product offerings to their loyalty programme members based on their previous behaviour. Other strategies to encourage customer loyalty that can be monitored in this way include branded credit cards, such as British Airways' American Express® credit card, and pre-paid cards, such as Thomas Cook's Travel Money Card.

However, if everyone has a loyalty programme, do they continue to work? Critics say that it is doubtful that the programmes encourage loyalty. They say the main drivers for loyalty are trust and quality of service and if these are not in place, the loyalty programme will be wasted effort. Successful businesses like Hilton understand the importance of personalising the customer's experience and 'delighting' their customers, which results in customer loyalty. For example, when a member of Honors stays at a Hilton Hotel or property, their personal preferences are updated on the programme's system, and this information is made available to staff at all hotels and properties. This allows staff to personalise the guest's experience and is also likely to improve customer satisfaction ratings.

Analysing the competition

Travel and tourism organisations constantly monitor their competitors to make sure that they are not being left behind in any aspect of their customer service. They do this by looking at review sites, by conducting mystery shopping and by analysing competitive marketing campaigns. The travel and tourism industry changes constantly as customers' needs change, as new products are developed and as new competitors emerge into the market. It is essential that organisations continuously monitor and evaluate the service that their competitors provide as well as monitoring their own service provision. This will help them to keep their customers and maintain high levels of customer satisfaction.

Performance indicators

Performance indicators are the benchmarks used by businesses to measure their performance over time. Customer service teams usually have weekly, monthly, quarterly and annual performance targets that are based on performance indicators. Examples of performance indicators include:

▶ revenue and profits
▶ number of sales – many businesses set fixed sales targets and staff may be paid bonuses when targets are exceeded
▶ customer satisfaction surveys – some businesses aim to attain a fixed percentage rating for their customer service
▶ number of complaints – many businesses have a target level of complaints that is as low as realistically possible
▶ the number of loyal repeat customers
▶ the number of new customers
▶ the number of good independent reviews from review sites or on social media
▶ the business's Net Promoter Score (NPS), which is based on customers' ratings on a scale of 1–10
▶ social media activity – the **reach** of a post on social media and the number of posts, likes and shares.

Key term

Reach – how many people a post or advertisement reaches.

Performance indicators can be efficiency measures, such as how many customers are being served and how quickly customers are serviced, or effectiveness measures, such as whether customers are receiving the right type of service and are satisfied.

Net Promoter Score is a tool that allows businesses to understand their customers' perception of their customer service provision. Customers are asked a single question: How likely is it that you would recommend our company/product/service to a friend or colleague? The scoring for this answer is based on a 0 to 10 scale. Figure 4.6 shows how the scale works. 'Promoters' are customers who score 9–10: loyal customers who will keep buying from the business and will recommend it to others. 'Passives' are customers who score 7–8: satisfied customers who do not have particular loyalty to the business or its brands. 'Detractors' are customers who score 0–6: unhappy customers who will tell other people about their negative experience.

The Net Promoter Score is arrived at by subtracting the percentage of detractors from the percentage of promoters. A score over 80% such as achieved by Jet2 is thought to be a very good score.

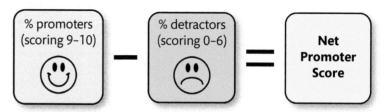

▶ **Figure 4.6:** Calculating the Net Promoter Score

These performance measures and targets are usually used because they are:
▶ derived from the best organisations in the travel and tourism industry
▶ developed through 'best practice' research
▶ based on historic data from within an organisation
▶ based on published standards or regulations
▶ a combination of the above.

Although performance monitoring helps to identify gaps and opportunities for improvement, it is of limited use if no action is taken to make improvements or if no one can decide what form the improvement should take.

PAUSE POINT   Explain at least four ways of monitoring customer service in travel and tourism.

    Look again at the examples you have just read or think about the travel and tourism organisation you are researching.

    Explain the drawbacks of informal feedback from customers.

The role of technology in the customer experience

Comparison sites

The internet allows customers to compare information about the prices of hotels, destinations, package holidays, car hire and many other travel arrangements. It has become an essential marketing tool in travel and tourism.

A comparison site allows a customer to compare many products on one site. There are lots of examples and some specialise in different sectors. For example, someone looking for a hotel might look at trivago or Booking.com, whereas a customer wanting to compare deals on travel insurance could use comparethemarket.com or confused. com. If a customer would like to compare their options for a complete holiday, they might use lastminute.com or Expedia, which allow them to add on all the elements of a trip, such as flights, transfers and hotel rooms.

These sites are incredibly helpful: they give customers an overview of what is available in the market and allow them to compare prices. In that way, they have had a positive effect on the customer experience.

However, customers do not like comparison websites if they:
▶ do not seem trustworthy, for example, if the information they provide seems unreliable and inaccurate, or if customers doubt that they will keep their personal data secure
▶ are difficult to navigate
▶ include a lot of add-on costs, for example, booking fees
▶ have poor customer or user ratings.

Travel and tourism organisations are under pressure to use comparison sites to advertise their products to customers. This is because customers use comparison sites as a virtual shop window, and businesses cannot afford to be left out. They also need to monitor what is on offer on these sites to find out what their competitors are offering and what prices they are charging.

Customers often assume that using a price comparison site is going to get them the lowest price. However, a 2016 survey carried out by the hotel group IHG found that this was not always the case. The survey found that:

▶ 75 per cent of Britains were unaware that they could be charged more by booking through a price comparison site
▶ nearly 80 per cent of Britains falsely believe that price comparison sites offer the best rates and a further three-quarters believe that all available rates are shown
▶ 76 per cent of customers would not use price comparison sites if they thought they could be overcharged
▶ under 10 per cent of Londoners book directly with a hotel company, while the savviest shoppers are in the south-west with nearly 2 in 10 (18 per cent) always booking directly.

Reviews and review sites

Review sites are another way in which technology has had an impact on customer service. Sites like TripAdvisor are very popular as they allow people to read and post reviews about a number of travel and tourism businesses. Comparison sites also often provide customer reviews to help people make decisions. One downside is that these reviews may not be completely reliable as people's opinions are **subjective**. Sometimes, customers give very poor ratings even if only one small thing went wrong, which can seriously impact a business, as even one bad review can affect customer choice. However, if a customer finds that there are numerous reviews all saying similar things, they are more likely to trust these reviewers' judgements.

Mobile apps

Mobile apps have become a standard part of customer service for many travel and tourism businesses. For example, in 2012 Thomson (now TUI) launched the MyThomson app, which allows customers to book excursions and access discounts while on holiday.

Some businesses encourage customers to use their mobile app by offering app-only deals. For example, when Voyage Privé launched their free iPhone app, they offered holiday add-ons that could only be booked through the app, such as exclusive car rental discounts. Rail company apps allow customers to book and download train tickets, while festivals provide apps to help customers plan their visit. For example, the Glastonbury app provides users with an interactive map.

Most holiday apps include features such as:

▶ booking management, such as accessing the booking details and making changes
▶ mobile boarding passes
▶ hotel information
▶ destination guides
▶ destination weather forecasts
▶ currency converter
▶ 'find my car' functionality to help people find their car at the airport car park
▶ postcards.

Theory into practice

1 Choose a price comparison site that focuses on hotels. Make sure that you all choose different sites to use. Once you have chosen your site, research a two-night stay in the Novotel in Greenwich for two people, for 23–25 of next month. Then research a stay at the Cragwood Country House Hotel in Windermere for the same number of people and the same dates.

2 Now compare your findings with how much it would cost to book these same trips using the hotel's own website.

3 Discuss your conclusions with your group.

Key term

Subjective – based only on someone's personal taste or judgement.

Research

Choose a free travel app provided by a travel and tourism business. Evaluate the app and its usefulness to customers, including a description of its features and a judgement as to the usefulness of each feature. Do you think it is worth a customer using this particular app? Or do you think that the customer could find other more useful apps for weather forecasts, travel information and destination guides?

Technology has also been used in innovative ways to enhance the customer experience at attractions. Virtual reality (VR) technology has been used to great effect by theme parks to enhance the experience of roller coasters. At Thorpe Park, Derren Brown's Ghost Train incorporates VR footage to produce a convincingly scary experience for customers. At the Natural History Museum in London, on-site VR experiences include a Great Barrier Reef Dive guided by David Attenborough.

Role of social media

Organisations use social media platforms to promote their products and services. Examples include Facebook, Instagram, Twitter and YouTube, where new and existing customers can 'follow' the organisation, and blogging platforms such as Blogger and WordPress. The emergence of these platforms has created new distribution channels for businesses to promote their brand, and they allow greater communication between businesses and customers.

Using social media, businesses can:

- engage with their customers
- increase the number of visitors visiting their website by linking to it from social media platforms
- run competitions and promotions, especially with partner organisations
- promote products and services
- create interest in their brand and build a reputation
- encourage and monitor customer feedback, as well as dealing with negative feedback.

> **Link**
>
> You learned about distribution channels in Unit 1: The World of Travel and Tourism, Section B.

Case study

Cumbria Tourism

 Cumbria Tourism
11 August ·

Enter our photography competition for the chance to have your image on the front cover of The Lake District, Cumbria Holiday Guide!

Show us how you've captured our stunning county as #theplacetobe.

> One of the competitions on Cumbria Tourism's Facebook page

This campaign won Cumbria Tourism 'Best Campaign by a Destination Management Organisation using Social Media' at the Social Travel Britain Awards. The campaign aimed to promote the county as a place for tourists to visit, using stunning photography in combination with catchy taglines.

Cumbria Tourism uses its Facebook page to promote the beautiful scenery and the travel and tourism businesses in the Lake District. One way in which they do this is by running competitions.

Check your knowledge

1 Explain how Cumbria Tourism engaged with their customers by running this competition.

2 How did they use this competition to attract new users?

3 What products are they promoting in this competition?

Social media allows customers to share their own thoughts and ideas. Because of this, travel and tourism organisations such as Cumbria Tourism can encourage people to share their memories and photographs of good holidays in a particular destination. This acts as a virtual word-of-mouth recommendation and may encourage others to visit the destination as well.

However, this also means that customers can share their frustrations and their negative experiences on social media. For example, imagine that an airline fails to update its customers to notify them that they can now reserve their seats, and a large group travelling together arrives at the airport only to find out that they have not been allocated seats together because they did not reserve seats. These customers are very likely to complain about the airline's failure on Facebook, Twitter or other social media sites. As a result of this, it is very important that businesses monitor their social media sites carefully and respond to customer complaints in a professional and friendly way.

Impact on customers who have difficulty accessing technology

The products and services offered by travel and tourism organisations are increasingly dependent on the use of technology, such as customer relations software, to manage their customer data. In addition, the way in which these organisations require customers to use technology is increasing. For example, many transport businesses are introducing the use of **eticketing** and **mticketing**.

However, customers without smartphones or access to the internet may find it difficult to access these technology-based products and services. This can cause problems when booking products such as airline seats, especially with low cost airlines, where customers are directed to book online rather than over the telephone or face-to-face. People who prefer a face-to-face service can use travel agents who will book and print documents on their behalf. However, this takes time. For holiday bookings, companies like TUI will still send tickets and documents through the post, but this takes 14 days and so cannot be done at the last minute.

Airlines in particular have worked hard to persuade customers to book online rather than by phone, as this is the cheapest way for a business to take bookings. This change in customer behaviour is known as **channel shift**. However, some businesses are concerned that this drive to move online may ignore the needs of those people who are not internet savvy. Sections of the older demographic use the internet but, according to the Office for National Statistics (ONS), in 2018 almost 5 million older people (over 75) in the UK had still never used the internet. Travel and tourism organisations could reach out to older people and provide help to use digital technology and social media. Older people on holiday spend more money on restaurants and hotels than any other demographic, but marketing tends to target younger age groups.

Discussion

The high street bank Barclays trained more than 12,000 Barclays Digital Eagles to help customers, particularly those over 65, to use the internet. The bank introduced Tea and Teach workshops for customers who wanted to learn how to use mobile devices.

Discuss ways in which travel and tourism organisations could help older people to use digital technology to plan and book their trips and holidays.

Reliability and validity of information or data

When using technologies such as social media and apps, organisations have to ensure that these channels are continually updated and that the information provided there is as **reliable** and **valid** as the information in their printed brochure. Customers will be frustrated if they look at a business's website or an app and find that it provides information that is out of date or inaccurate.

Link

You learned about eticketing and mticketing in Unit 1: The World of Travel and Tourism, Section B.

Key terms

eticketing – tickets are sent by email and printed by the customer.

mticketing – tickets are sent to a mobile number and the customer presents them on their phone screen.

Channel shift – the process by which organisations persuade customers to use different distribution channels to those that they would usually choose.

Reliable – reliable information remains the same and does not change, no matter how and where customers look for it.

Valid – valid information is accurate and represents what it is supposed to represent.

Hint   Think about when you have used technology to research your travel arrangements.

Extend   How do travel and tourism organisations ensure that the information they provide through their website and social media pages is up to date?

How organisations improve the customer experience

Improvements in customer experience should be based on the analysis of current service and an excellent knowledge of the current position and aims of the organisation.

Leaders should have a clear understanding of the current status before making any change. They should know:

▶ the organisation's vision, mission and core values

▶ the range and diversity of products

▶ suitability for customer needs

▶ partnerships with other brands

▶ current marketing and promotion.

You will now consider each of these points using the hotel chain Hilton Worldwide as an example.

The vision, mission and core values

You looked at examples of goals, vision statements and mission statements earlier in this unit. However, simply having these things is not enough: employees need to know what they are and how to implement them. Anyone working for an organisation should know its vision, its mission and its core values to help achieve these things. Table 4.14 lists Hilton's vision, mission and values.

▶ **Table 4.14:** The vision, mission and values of Hilton

Vision statement	To fill the earth with the light and warmth of hospitality
Mission statement	We will be the pre-eminent global hospitality company and the first choice of guests, Team Members and owners alike
Core values	(Note how the values spell out HILTON) • **H**ospitality – we're passionate about delivering exceptional guest experiences • **I**ntegrity – we do the right thing, all the time • **L**eadership – we're leaders in our industry and in our communities • **T**eamwork – we're team players in everything we do • **O**wnership – we're the owners of our actions and decisions • **N**ow – we operate with a sense of urgency and discipline

Discussion

How do you think that knowing the Hilton values would help an employee working on the front desk in a Hilton hotel? Imagine that they are dealing with a customer who has arrived at 10 p.m. to find that their reservation has been lost and the hotel is full.

The range and diversity of products

Employees must know all of the products and services offered by the organisation so that they are able to meet the needs of their customers. For example, Hilton operates a broad portfolio of different brands, including:

▶ their flagship full service Hilton Hotels & Resorts brand

▶ their luxury and lifestyle hotel brands – Waldorf Astoria Hotels & Resorts, Conrad Hotels & Resorts and Canopy by Hilton

▶ their full service hotel brands – Hilton Hotels & Resorts, Curio – A Collection by Hilton, DoubleTree by Hilton and Embassy Suites by Hilton

▶ their focused service hotel brands – Hilton Garden Inn, Hampton by Hilton, Homewood Suites by Hilton and Home2 Suites by Hilton

▶ their timeshare brand – Hilton Grand Vacations

▶ their focused service midscale brand – Tru by Hilton.

It is necessary for employees to know about all the business's hotels and their target markets, even if they only work in one particular brand of Hilton hotel. This is because this product knowledge will allow them to advise guests on future stays with Hilton worldwide.

Suitability of products and services

Businesses like Hilton have a variety of brands because each can be tailored to meet the needs of particular sections of their market. For example, a guest choosing to stay in a Tru by Hilton hotel is likely to have different needs to a guest who stays in a Waldorf Astoria hotel, and customers will have different **perceptions** of the different brands. Staff need to monitor customers' perceptions of products by implementing the organisation's chosen feedback methods.

Analysis of the feedback will result in change and improvement to brands. In January 2019, a Hilton brand, the Waldorf Astoria, introduced a new concierge service, based on responses to a global study of their luxury travellers.

Over one-third of respondents wanted a 'jet lag' concierge to anticipate and cater for their needs. Services included a 'bath master' who will run your milk and honey bath or taking the guest's dog for 'personal pooch training'.

Partnerships with other well-known brands

Partnerships benefit both parties if they are successful. Some of Hilton's brands are involved in a partnership with Clean the World, a global health organisation, dedicated to sustainability, water and health. Owners and employees are challenged to collect bars of soap by Global Handwashing Day for Clean the World to distribute to communities in need.

The campaign aligns with Hilton's Travel with Purpose initiative, the company's corporate responsibility strategy.

Marketing and promotion

Companies can put together and trial specific packages to help them to identify customer needs and preferences. For example, a tour operator could offer a package that includes a new type of excursion and then measure sales to see if customers are choosing to buy it. Sometimes, businesses will run promotions that require customers to answer questions in exchange for discounts.

Technology such as apps can make it quite easy for businesses to trial new ideas and packages. For example, Hilton trialled the popularity of an app that allows guests to check-in, select their preferred room and use their smartphone as a digital key to their room. This kind of trial can be easily monitored by reviewing customers' usage data. If it works well, the promotion can be implemented more widely.

Creating a customer-focused organisation and implementing service standards

A customer-focused organisation prioritises providing excellent customer service as a means of generating a profit. In order to develop as a customer-focused organisation, a business must:

▶ develop an organisational culture that values and rewards excellent customer service

▶ develop customer service standards and metrics that measure those standards.

Key term

Perception – the way in which people regard or think about something.

Theory into practice

Imagine that you are a customer service manager working at Hilton's Renwick Hotel in New York. What products and services do you think employees need to know about in order to work in this specific hotel and its environment? How would you find out about what customers think about this information?

Prepare notes for a training session on this subject for a group of junior employees.

Discussion

How does the Hilton/Clean the World partnership enhance the customer experience?

A customer-focused organisation should also be committed to a continuous improvement process, which will ensure that it does not get left behind and maintains its competitive advantage.

Reviewing mission statements and core values to include customer service

Organisations usually have a long-term business strategy, setting out their aims for the next five years, and this is often supplemented by a one year short-term business plan. When the business strategy is reviewed, it creates an opportunity to make sure that the organisation's vision, mission and core values really focus on customer service.

The strategic plan will usually cover:
▸ a vision of where the organisation intends to be in the future
▸ a mission statement that captures the core purpose of the organisation
▸ a statement of corporate values that drives the way in which the organisation operates
▸ key objectives such as increasing sales or improving customer satisfaction ratings
▸ short-term goals, which are a breakdown of the objectives

Theory into practice

Read the following vision and mission statements, which are taken from the York Museums Trust.

- Vision: our vision is for York Museums Trust to play a major part in positioning York as a world class cultural centre.
- Mission: our vision is to cherish the collections, buildings and gardens entrusted to us, presenting and interpreting them ass a stimulus for learning, a provocation to curiosity and a source of inspiration and enjoyment for all.

Now amend the vision and mission statements to include a focus on the customer experience.

Case study

Even corporate away days like to be beside the seaside, says Butlin's boss

Once the domain of knobbly knee and glamorous granny contests, Butlin's, now celebrating its 80th year, has changed with the times. The holiday company's boss isn't shy about showing off those alterations.

Butlin's has shrunk from ten 'camps' – including one in Ireland and one in the Bahamas – in its heyday in the 1960s to just three modern resorts today. Redcoat-in-chief Dermot King is adamant that the leisure business is more than just the faded glory of seaside entertainers and crazy golf.

'Families remain our core market – with "Just for Tots" breaks for parents with children under five growing in popularity,' he explains. 'There's a trend towards larger family groups which often includes grandparents.

But we also reach out to couples, groups and single people of all ages. Our live music weekends for adults featuring music from past decades are always in demand.'

Tapping into the corporate market for conferences, product launches and company 'away days' is another success story. Since being launched in 2012, this business has grown by 147 per cent, with some 10,000 delegates each year from companies including AstraZeneca, Argos and Greene King.

'We can host a boardroom meeting for 12 or a product launch for thousands – along with a variety of team-building exercises including treasure hunts and even exclusive access to the fun-fair,' he reveals.

'Our highly-developed values and culture of doing everything possible to meet the needs of holidaymakers – to 'delight' them by working as a team – is shared as an approach that can be applied to customers of any organisation or business.'

Check your knowledge

1   How successful has Butlin's been in breaking into the corporate market?

2   How do you think Butlin's achieves its values and delights its customers?

3   Why do you think Butlin's needed to review its strategy?

4   Research the Butlins' mission statement. What does it focus on? Does it include customer service?

Analysing the customer journey

Fáilte Ireland's model of excellence showed that analysing the customer journey is one of the steps in creating customer service standards. This means identifying every step in the customer's journey through a business's customer service provision. This is done to ensure that the business understands the customer's viewpoint and to ensure that all points of contact between business and customer are covered by the business's service standards. Another name for this analysis is perceptual blueprinting. This should give a view of how customers currently experience the service provided, how the service needs to improve in the future and what needs to change in order to make the change happen.

Model of excellence

Whether a business is reviewing its customer service delivery or just starting up, it may need support in setting up and reviewing its customer service standards. Some businesses use a model to help them get started. The Irish tourist board, Fáilte Ireland, published the following model of excellence. You can see how it provides steps that a business can follow when setting up its standards. One of the most important steps is to identify the key 'contact points' between the customer and the business, which make up the different parts of the customer journey.

Case study

Fáilte Ireland's model of excellence

Standards of performance

Achieving consistency of service is perhaps the **holy grail** for any tourism business and that goal can only be achieved if you:

- identify key contact points and interactions with your customers
- devise standards of performance (SOPs) to guide how service should be delivered across all those interactions
- train and regularly coach all your employees on how to deliver the standards
- constantly monitor and measure your ability to deliver the standards of performance consistently across the service experience
- devise mechanisms which enable you to continuously improve.

Communicating core values and identifying training for employees

Once a strategy has been developed by senior management, or in consultation with employees, it must then be communicated to all employees. In addition, team and individual plans should be developed so that they can help to achieve the organisation's vision, mission, values and objectives.

A business's mission and values are only useful when they are implemented by employees. They should summarise the culture of the organisation and everyone should live up to them. Employees should be reminded of these statements in the following ways:

▶ discussions at regular business conferences
▶ training sessions
▶ meetings to discuss achievement
▶ team and personal objectives being linked to the mission and values
▶ visual reminders of the values in the working environment.

For example, a good training scheme for a new starter should help to embed the business's mission and values in their professional behaviour. During their first week, they should be given an induction session to explain the mission and values, among other things. One of the other members in their team should be assigned to act as their mentor to give them ongoing support. After six weeks, the new starter should then go on a full day's training about the business, its customers and its values. They should have regular one-to-ones with their line manager, assessing their performance against targets that are consistent with the business's values and mission, and they should have six-monthly or annual appraisals to check that they are meeting their targets.

Training may be delivered face-to-face or online. For example, many tour operators use online training courses to deliver destination training. Customer service training may be provided in-house or by sending staff to an external specialist such as Welcome to Excellence. The disadvantage of external courses is that, although they might give good training, they may not be able to reinforce the mission and values of the employee's organisation.

Jet2.com is a low-cost airline which delivers its own customer service training programme in-house. Its training programme, Take Me There, is designed to ensure that all employees deliver the business's values in their everyday life at work. Take Me There is delivered to all Jet2.com employees and is based on four key behaviours that represent the brand's values:

▶ create memories

▶ be present

▶ work as one team

▶ take responsibility.

Listening and acting on feedback

Gathering feedback from customers is very important in monitoring customer service and finding out what needs to be improved. It can be formal, such as sales transaction data or website tracking data, or it can be more informal, collected by listening to and observing customers.

Only a minority of customers give feedback or complain, while most dissatisfied customers simply leave and do not come back. If an organisation asks customers about its customer service, it is important that it acts on what they say. For example, it is common now for waiters to ask whether a customer's meal is satisfactory. If the customer says no, it is important that the waiter does something about this feedback rather than just carrying on and ignoring the information that they have been given. Body language can also be used to identify whether a customer is satisfied or dissatisfied, which is useful when observing customers.

One problem with capturing informal feedback is that customers do not always give an honest answer to a question because they may be shy or do not want to be rude. For example, someone may be dissatisfied with their food but will not say so to the waiter when they ask if it is all right. Alternatively, it may be that staff are not asking the right questions, so they may not receive complete or accurate feedback. In addition, the staff member receiving the feedback may misunderstand what the customer meant, meaning that they may not pass on exactly what was said. For these reasons, businesses use more formal methods of gathering feedback.

▶ **Questionnaires and comment cards** – commonly used for monitoring customer service levels. They are a formal method of gathering information and provide extensive data which can be analysed to draw conclusions about customer views. Questionnaires should be well laid out and easy to complete, and should reassure customers that any information they give will be treated in confidence. Some organisations offer an incentive, such as a gift or entry into a prize draw, to customers who complete their questionnaire. The questions should be phrased carefully, as they should be easy to understand and unambiguous, and should mean the same thing to the customer and to the organisation. Figure 4.7 is an example of a customer questionnaire.

> **Link**
>
> Look again at Table 4.6 on page 196 to consider the importance of phrasing questions correctly.

Interpreting a questionnaire

Read the questionnaire, then answer the questions that follow.

UNBEATEN TRACK TRAVEL

We love to know what our customers think so that we can improve our tours. Complete our short customer survey and be in with a chance to **win £500 of travel vouchers**.

		Poor	Satisfactory	Good	Excellent
1	How would you rate your booking experience?	○	○	○	○
2	How would you rate the quality of the travel advice that you were given before booking?	○	○	○	○
3	How would you rate the service provided by your guide?	○	○	○	○
4	How would you rate the cleanliness of your hotel?	○	○	○	○
5	How would you rate the food provided during your stay?	○	○	○	○
6	How would you rate the service of the staff at your hotel?	○	○	○	○
7	How would you rate the quality of your excursions?	○	○	○	○
8	How would you rate your holiday overall?	○	○	○	○
9	Would you consider taking another tour with Unbeaten Track Travel?	○	○	○	○
	Do you have any other comments?				

▶ **Figure 4.7:** A questionnaire that could be used to monitor the customer experience

Check your knowledge

1 Explain how this questionnaire monitors the customer experience.
2 How are customers encouraged to complete the survey?
3 What kind of improvements do you think the company could make following analysis of the responses?

Review sites

Review sites include Trip advisor, trust pilot and many others already discussed. Organisations should constantly monitor any reviews posted and respond appropriately.

Ryanair has a function in its app so that passengers can give immediate feedback. They rank their overall experience, boarding, crew friendliness, service onboard and range of food and drink, on a 5-star rating system, ranging from 1 star for Very Poor, to 3 stars for OK, to 5 stars for Very Good.

Case study

92 per cent of Ryanair customers satisfied with their experience

January 2019

Ryanair releases its 'Rate My Flight' statistics every month. In January 2019, they showed that 92 per cent of surveyed customers were happy with their overall flight experience.

Some 92 per cent of respondents rated their overall trip 'Very Good /Good/ OK', recording similar ratings for boarding (87 per cent), crew friendliness (94 per cent), service onboard (93 per cent) and range of food & drink (82 per cent).

'Rate My Flight' is available in Dutch, English, French, German, Italian, Polish and Spanish, via the Ryanair app, which can be downloaded from the iTunes and Google Play stores.

Ryanair's Robin Kiely said:
'Rate My Flight is a digital initiative launched under Year 3 of our "Always Getting Better" customer experience improvement programme, which allows customers to provide real-time reviews on their flights via the

Ryanair app, from the moment they land. We welcome all customer feedback so that we can continue to improve all aspects of the Ryanair customer experience. Customers who want to rate their flight should download the Ryanair app, allow for push notifications, and will be sent the survey through the app upon landing'.

Check your knowledge

1 As a group, carry out a SWOT analysis on customer service at Ryanair. Use the information in the case study as well as asking the opinions of people you know who have been Ryanair passengers. You could also research Ryanair's customer experience improvement programme.

2 Following your SWOT analysis, suggest some improvements that Ryanair could make to their customer service.

3 Comment on the reliability of the data in the satisfaction survey.

▶ **Table 4.15:** Ryanair customer satisfaction survey

Category	Very good/ Good/OK	Very good	Good	OK	Poor	Very poor
Overall experience	96%	40%	37%	19%	2%	2%
Boarding	88%	45%	19%	24%	9%	3%
Crew courtesy	94%	54%	31%	9%	4%	2%
Onboard service	89%	50%	22%	17%	7%	4%
Food and drink choice	75%	20%	18%	37%	20%	5%

Service level agreements

Service level agreements are performance standards for delivery of customer service.

They state the level of service the organisation expects to provide to its customers. They include criteria such as response times, quality of service and complaints procedures.

SLAs are used to monitor performance.

Theory into practice

Choose a travel and tourism organisation and find out what service level agreements are in place.
- Describe the key performance indicators or metrics that are used to measure whether service level agreements are met.
- Evaluate their effectiveness in measuring performance against the agreements (i.e. how well do they work?)

Explain why employees need to know the mission statement and core values of their organisation.

Hint   Think about how employees deliver customer service.

Extend   Explain three ways in which employees can learn the mission and values of an organisation.

Assessment activity 4.3   D.P6   D.M4   D.D3

As an intern for a customer service consultant who provides customer service advice and training, you recently carried out a 'deep discovery' exercise at a travel and tourism organisation. You produced a report on your findings that evaluated the importance of excellent customer service to the organisation. Your manager has asked you to return to the same organisation and produce a plan to improve customer service in that organisation, considering how it can improve levels of service and increase customer loyalty.

You should include:

- the effectiveness of the methods used to improve the quality of customer service and loyalty
- recommendations on the most effective methods to improve customer service and increase customer loyalty.

Present your report to your line manager at the consultancy and to the managers of the travel and tourism organisation. You might present it orally with explanatory notes or submit a written report.

Plan
- What is the task? What am I being asked to do?
- What information do I need to gather from my selected travel and tourism organisation?
- What information do I need from other resources?

Do
- I have made a plan to carry out the research needed with a timescale and deadlines.
- I have decided the form my presentation will take.
- I have thought about the gaps in service in the organisation which will help form my recommendations.

Review
- I can explain what the task was and how I approached the task.
- I can see what I would do differently next time.
- I have thought about the feedback on the presentation of my report and will act on it in the future.

Further reading and resources

Chahal, M. (2016) 'Are loyalty schemes broken?' *Marketing Week*, 13 July 2016.

Fitzpatrick, K. (2015) *Travel and Technology: Digital Trends for the Travel Industry in 2015 and Beyond*, London: e3.

Magnini, V.P., Crotts, J.C., Zehrer, A. (2011) 'Understanding customer delight: an application of travel blog analysis', *Journal of Travel Research* 50, 5: 535–545.

Tourism for All UK: www.tourismforall.org.uk
Information and advice about sustainable tourism.

Gov.uk: www.gov.uk/government/publications/accessible-britainchallenge-good-practice-examples/

accessible-britain-challenge-goodpractice-examples
A government website providing information about accessibility.

International Organization for Standardization: www.iso.org
Information about different international standards.

Citizens Advice: www.citizensadvice.org.uk
A consumer information website.

Institute of Customer Service case studies: www.instituteofcustomerservice.com/membership/case-studies
Information about good practice in customer service.

THINK ▶FUTURE

Cathy Farrell

Head of Accommodation for Butlin's (Bourne Leisure Group)

Cathy joined Butlin's in 2015. She had a lot of experience in managing customer service so she went straight into a senior role at the business. Part of her job description is to enhance guests' experience, 'ensuring that they are at the heart of everything we do'. She also has to 'improve accommodation standards so that they are recognised as best in class' in the travel and tourism industry. When she started in the role, she also had to oversee the development of IT systems to underpin the guest experience and look after internal customers as well as guests.

Her primary role is to support the teams in Butlin's three resorts who have to implement the business's accommodation strategies. The team's aspiration is to deliver 'clean and fault-free accommodation for our guests – every time'. The aim is that this contributes to the business's financial success by delighting their guests and therefore encouraging them to book again and tell their friends what a great time they had at Butlin's.

Cathy's job is not office based. In fact, it is quite the opposite. She visits each of the three resorts at least once a month, spending two or three days with the accommodation teams during each visit. She spends the time looking at what the team does, how they do it and how it contributes to the guest experience. Cathy spends time considering what could be improved if she and her teams had unlimited time and money to spend on improvements, and then she has to decide what they can do to improve within their resources.

Focusing on skills

If you want to become a manager or work in customer service, what do you need to do?

- Think about whether you like to be out and about or in an office.
- Develop the organisational skills that you will need to deal with the paperwork and time management that are part of being a manager.
- Learn about leadership and take any training opportunities that will help you to be a great manager.
- Consider whether you enjoy interacting with people. As part of her job, Cathy talks to a lot of people every day, including housekeepers, gardeners, senior marketing staff and the managing director.

- Think about whether you can create and nurture relationships. This is important in management as well as in customer service, because managers must nurture good relationships with their team members. Get lots of practice in building relationships through face-to-face customer service.
- Do you believe that people are the most important resource to a business? For managers like Cathy, taking care of their team will help them to take care of their guests and provide the best possible service.
- Do you have a problem-solving attitude? You can develop your problem-solving skills by volunteering to deal with difficult situations.

Getting ready for assessment

Greg is working towards a BTEC National in Travel and Tourism. He was given an assignment to produce a report on the delivery of customer service in a travel and tourism organisation and evaluate the significance of excellent customer service to the organisation. At a later date he had a further assignment to produce a plan for improving customer service in the same organisation. He could choose to give either an oral presentation or a written report/plan for both assignments.

Greg shares his experience below.

How I got started

I work part time in the local travel agency where I had done a work experience placement. By the time I was given this assignment, I already had quite a lot of customer service experience, so I could draw on my own experiences. I'd also been collecting information for my customer service unit for a couple of months, so I knew that I could use this information in my assignment.

How I brought it all together

▶ I made a plan that included all the headings from the assignment brief.

▶ I want to get a Distinction, so I worked out what I needed to do in order to cover all of the Pass, Merit and Distinction criteria.

▶ I collected together all of my notes from this unit and from working at the travel agency and I matched them up with the sections on my plan, so that I knew which resources supported each section of my plan.

▶ I decided to submit a written report rather than give a presentation.

▶ I added review dates to my plan so that I knew what I had to do and when I had to do it, all the way up to the date of my submission

▶ I asked staff in the agency what they knew about the organisation's mission and values.

▶ I allowed myself plenty of time for writing and asked my brother to proofread my finished report.

What I learned from the experience

I found that the hardest part was evaluating the effectiveness of the methods used for monitoring.

I found it difficult to know what to look at to help me come to a decision, and I had to ask my manager at the travel agency to help with this. He had loads of information and data on the number of complaints, the business's revenue and the number of repeat customers. He also gave me some information about staff retention.

Obviously I couldn't get information about other employees' targets and performance, because that sort of information is private, but I could use my own targets as an example.

I also found it hard to find information about the use of social media, because my travel agency doesn't really do much on social media. In my report, I made a recommendation that I could contribute to this and make a Facebook page, so I'm looking forward to doing this soon.

Think about it

▶ Do you know what the assignment brief is asking you to do?

▶ Have you chosen a travel and tourism organisation that will be prepared to provide you with information or that publishes all of the information that you will need?

▶ Have you gathered together all your notes from this unit?

▶ Have you contacted people at your chosen organisation so that you can talk to them and get advice?

▶ Do you have some examples of how they use technology to help them deliver their customer service?

▶ Have you found examples of how they manage their social media presence?

▶ How will you present your work and make sure that it looks professional?

Travel and Tourism Enterprises

5

Getting to know your unit

Assessment
This unit is internally assessed using a series of assignments set by your tutor.

In this unit you will have the opportunity to demonstrate your entrepreneurial and promotional skills. You will research potential travel and tourism enterprises and develop your own start-up plan and marketing strategy, which you could use to launch your own new enterprise. You will also learn how to prepare a pitch to promote your plan to interested parties. All of these skills will be of great help in your future employment.

How you will be assessed

This unit will be assessed by a series of internally assessed tasks set by your tutor. Throughout this unit you will find assessment activities that will help you work towards your assessment. Completing these activities will not mean that you have achieved a particular grade, but you will have carried out useful research or preparation that will be relevant when it comes to your final assignment.

In order to achieve the tasks in your assignment, it is important to check that you have met all of the Pass grading criteria. You can do this as you work your way through the assignment.

If you are hoping to gain a Merit or Distinction, you should also make sure that you present the information in your assignment in the style that is required by the relevant assessment criterion. For example, Merit criteria require you to analyse, assess and discuss, and Distinction criteria require you to evaluate.

The assignment set by your tutor will consist of a number of tasks designed to meet the criteria in the table. These may include:

▶ carrying out market research to investigate opportunities for a new travel and tourism enterprise

▶ producing a start-up plan for a new travel and tourism enterprise

▶ preparing a marketing strategy to raise awareness of a new travel and tourism enterprise

▶ presenting a pitch to generate interest in the new travel and tourism enterprise.

Assessment criteria

This table shows what you must do in order to achieve a **Pass**, **Merit** or **Distinction** grade, and where you can find activities to help you.

Pass	Merit	Distinction
Learning aim A Carry out market research to identify a new travel and tourism enterprise idea to meet the changing needs of consumers		
A.P1 Explain the different types of market research that can be used to identify a new travel and tourism enterprise idea. Assessment activity 5.1	**A.M1** Analyse research information to inform a start-up plan for a new travel and tourism enterprise idea. Assessment activity 5.1	**A.D1** Evaluate the importance of carrying out thorough and appropriate market research before embarking on a new travel and tourism enterprise. Assessment activity 5.1
A.P2 Carry out research for a new travel and tourism enterprise idea. Assessment activity 5.1		
Learning aim B Develop a start-up plan for a new travel and tourism enterprise to meet the changing needs of consumers		
B.P3 Explain the proposed travel and tourism enterprise. Assessment activity 5.2	**B.M2** Analyse the feasibility of the start-up plan for a new travel and tourism enterprise. Assessment activity 5.2	**BC.D2** Evaluate the feasibility of the start-up plan and marketing strategy, taking into account any constraints. Assessment activity 5.2
B.P4 Produce a start-up plan for the new travel and tourism enterprise. Assessment activity 5.2		
Learning aim C Prepare a marketing strategy to launch the new travel and tourism enterprise to raise consumer awareness		
C.P5 Explain why the elements of the marketing mix are important in raising awareness for the new travel and tourism enterprise. Assessment activity 5.2	**C.M3** Assess the potential effectiveness of the marketing strategy in raising awareness for the new travel and tourism enterprise. Assessment activity 5.2	
C.P6 Prepare a marketing strategy for the new travel and tourism enterprise. Assessment activity 5.2		
Learning aim D Carry out a pitch for the new travel and tourism enterprise start-up plan in order to generate interest in the new travel and tourism enterprise		
D.P7 Prepare the resources and documentation needed to present a pitch for the new travel and tourism enterprise to a selected audience. Assessment activity 5.3	**D.M4** Plan and present a pitch for the new travel and tourism enterprise, making recommendations for improvements. Assessment activity 5.3	**D.D3** Demonstrate individual self-management and initiative in the presentation of a high-quality, successful pitch that generates interest in the new travel and tourism enterprise. Assessment activity 5.3
D.P8 Present a pitch for the new travel and tourism enterprise to a selected audience. Assessment activity 5.3		

Getting started

Find out if there are any small travel and tourism businesses in your area that you can visit to discuss how they started. Before you arrange any visits, discuss potential businesses with the rest of your group and tutor, to make sure that not everyone goes to the same place!

A Carry out market research to identify a new travel and tourism enterprise idea to meet the changing needs of consumers

In this unit you are going to consider enterprise ideas that you could start up yourself. In order to do this you need to carry out some market research. It is very important to carry out thorough research before you set up a new enterprise. Starting your own business is a risky venture, as you will be investing time and money, so you need to have plenty of evidence that shows that there is a market for your idea.

Types of market research

There are two different types of research: primary and secondary. You will need to decide whether to do primary or secondary research, or a mix of both. Your research will help you to decide whether there is a market for your idea and what kind of enterprise you should start.

Primary research

Primary research produces information or results that are being collected for the first time. Collecting this information is sometimes called field research. Researchers do this type of research only when they are sure that the information they require has not been collected elsewhere by someone else. There is no point investing time and money to find out information that is already easily available.

Methods of collecting primary data include the following types of surveys:

- questionnaires
- observation
- focus groups
- consumer panels.

Surveys are often interviews carried out with customers or potential customers. They may be completed by post, email, telephone, face-to-face or online. They are usually based on a questionnaire asking fixed questions, rather than a free discussion.

Questionnaires

There are many examples of questionnaires used in travel and tourism, often to gather feedback on a product or service. For example, tour operators ask customers to fill them in at the end of a holiday and hotels leave them in rooms for guests to complete. The response rates are usually good for these types of surveys if they are carried out face-to-face. This is because the **respondents** are a captive audience and the interviewer can write down the responses immediately.

> **Key terms**
>
> **Primary research** – information or results that are being collected for the first time.
>
> **Respondent** – the person who is answering the questions.

You could draw up a questionnaire to find out what people think of your idea or to establish customer needs in a certain market. The following points are guidelines for writing a questionnaire.

▶ First, before you write any questions, make a list of what you want to find out.

▶ Go through the list and discard anything that is not absolutely essential.

▶ Go through the list again and try to organise the information you want to gather in a logical way.

▶ Write the questionnaire, asking general questions at the beginning and moving on to more specific questions.

▶ Never ask more than one thing in a question and try to use **closed questions** (requiring yes or no answers) as the responses are easier to analyse.

▶ Use a limited number of **open questions** (prompting free answers) if you want to find out the respondent's opinion.

▶ Avoid bias by asking questions in a neutral way. For example, 'What attractions did you visit?' rather than 'What nightclubs did you visit?'

▶ Use **filter questions** if the respondent does not need to answer every question. For example, 'If you answer no to question 5, go to question 11'.

Always request **classification data** at the end of a survey, such as how old the respondent is and what they do for a living. If you ask these questions at the beginning, they may feel that you are being intrusive and want to stop answering questions. The only exception to this rule is when you need to establish whether the respondent fits a **quota** before continuing with the questionnaire.

Key terms

Closed questions – questions that are answered with a 'yes' or 'no', such as 'Did you go on holiday this year?'

Open questions – questions that are answered with longer answers, such as 'Where did you go on holiday this year?'

Filter questions – questions that allow the respondent to omit certain questions which may not be applicable to them.

Classification data – the age, gender and occupation of the respondent, which is used to group respondents into categories.

Quota – a fixed or required number of something, such as the number of people in a particular age group to be questioned.

Theory into practice

Using the guidelines, design a short questionnaire to be given to your colleagues or friends and family. It could be about where they are going on holiday this year or their plans for future travel. Make sure that it asks no more than ten questions, only ask one open question and ask respondents for classification data.

Event debrief

Look at the questionnaire in Figure 5.1 and answer the questions that follow.

The Bryant Centre — Post-event Questionnaire

Name of event: _____

Room used: _____

Date of event: _____

Name of event organiser: _____

Booking your event:

Did you check room availability on our website?	Yes ☐	No ☐
Was the information we sent you accurate?	Yes ☐	No ☐
Did your account manager give you enough support?	Yes ☐	No ☐

Any other comments?

[ ]

Our facilities:

Did the meeting/conference room provide a positive atmosphere?	Yes ☐	No ☐
Did you find the audio-visual facilities easy to use?	Yes ☐	No ☐
Was the size and location of your meeting/conference room as you had expected?	Yes ☐	No ☐

Any other comments?

[ ]

Our service:

Was the room correct for your booking?	Yes ☐	No ☐
Did we provide services on time as specified in your schedule?	Yes ☐	No ☐
Was the service you received efficient and well-organised?	Yes ☐	No ☐
Did the catering meet your expectations?	Yes ☐	No ☐

Any other comments?

[ ]

Would you use the Bryant Centre again?	Yes ☐	No ☐

If you had to give us a score out of 10, what would it be? _____

Were any members of staff particularly helpful? If so, please name them. _____

▶ **Figure 5.1:** An example of a questionnaire

Check your knowledge

1 What type of question is mainly used in the questionnaire in Figure 5.1?

2 Give one advantage and one disadvantage of using this type of question.

3 Suggest two aspects of the service provided that could be changed if customers answer 'no'.

There are different forms of survey techniques and they have their advantages and disadvantages, as shown in Table 5.1.

▶ **Table 5.1:** Advantages and disadvantages of different survey techniques

Method	Advantages	Disadvantages
Face-to-face interview	• Interviewer can explain the questions if necessary • Response rate is usually good • Interviewer can use 'prompts' to aid recall, such as a hint like 'Have you heard of any of these brands: Thomson, Thomas Cook, etc.?'	• Interviewer may bias questions and therefore respondents' answers • Can be expensive to carry out because of interviewer's time • Can be difficult to recruit trained interviewers
Telephone interview	• Easy to carry out • Many calls can be carried out in a short time • Response rate is fairly good • Personal contact with respondent	• People can find telephone calls intrusive • Cannot give visual prompts
Mail/email questionnaire	• Cheap to carry out • Requires few staff	• Response rate is usually very low • Requires a list of appropriate addresses • Questions cannot be explained to respondents
Internet questionnaire	• Easy to carry out • Responses are instant	• Respondents limited to people who access that website so the sample is already biased • Questions cannot be explained to respondents

Observation

Observation is a very simple and yet effective research method. There are several ways of conducting observations. For example, one of the simplest ways of doing this is for an observer to watch customers, such as in a travel agency, and report on how they behave. The observer will use a checklist or take notes to aid later recall. Alternatively, cameras can be used instead of live observers and the footage can be analysed later.

Observation is not a cheap research method as you need either observers or cameras. It is also time-consuming. The observer can also bias the results simply by being there, unless they are completely unobtrusive. The results are also then analysed by the observer, who may not be completely objective and could create bias in the way in which they report their findings.

Mystery shoppers are a common form of observation that can be used in any sector. For example, in travel and tourism, someone might pretend to be a customer at a travel agency in order to report on the performance of the staff. Travel and tourism journalists often use this technique and report the results in publications such as *Travel Trade Gazette (TTG)*.

Mystery shopper plans trip to South-East Asia

Travel Trade Gazette publishes a weekly mystery shopper feature on its website. In September, the secret shopper went to Althams Travel Services in Halifax to book a tour in South-East Asia for two. They gave the agency and the travel agent a very positive score of 76 per cent, saying:

'The welcome was immediate and the consultant appeared interested and attentive from the outset. It felt as though they were experienced in this type of holiday and they asked questions to establish my needs. I stayed briefly in the agency and the consultant said they would call me the next day and email details. The quote included information about what I could do during the tour and the main sights for each destination were summarised with accompanying images. They suggested a tailor-made itinerary with Travelmood departing Heathrow and taking in multiple destinations for £5,545. The consultant phoned the next morning and again Tuesday. They were keen to secure the business in a friendly manner. I would have scored them even higher but I felt the sales process, although efficient, was a little hurried for my status as a first-time traveller to the area in need of reassurance.'

Check your knowledge

1 Give three examples of aspects of the customer service provided that led to the high score.

2 The mystery shopper felt that the process was a 'little hurried'. What would you recommend the travel agent could do differently to avoid this criticism?

3 What is a tailor-made itinerary?

Focus groups

A focus group is a group of people who are invited to participate in a group discussion about a certain topic. The discussion could take place in someone's home, a hotel or an office. Participants may be offered an incentive to attend, such as a voucher for flights. The discussion is held to find out people's attitudes towards a particular product or service. A group leader, who is often a psychologist, leads the discussion.

Consumer panels

A consumer panel is a group of consumers within a specific market who respond to regular questionnaires or meet for discussions at regular intervals. The panel is designed to represent the views and behaviours of the whole market for a product or service. They help researchers to understand the attitudes and behaviours of the target market. For example, the Civil Aviation Authority (CAA) Consumer Panel was established in 2012. The panel represents aviation consumers and examines the work of the CAA to ensure that the organisation keeps a focus on the rights and interests of consumers.

Secondary research

Secondary research finds information that has already been collected. A researcher has already collected the information and other people can access it through sources such as books, websites, journals and newspapers. Secondary research is sometimes called desk research as it can be done at a desk or computer or in a library. Secondary research is done before undertaking any primary research – if you cannot find everything that you need to know using secondary research, you may then want to conduct your own primary research.

Secondary research may be carried out into either internal sources or external sources.

Internal sources of secondary research are the business's own publications or datasets, including:

▶ customer databases

▶ business costs and profits

▶ passenger numbers (for transport principals such as airlines)

▶ business productivity.

It can be very difficult for anyone outside the business to access these sources of data without knowing people who work for that business. However, many travel and tourism businesses publish annual reports containing much of this information. They are useful sources and are usually available on the internet.

Key term

Secondary research – research into information that has already been collected.

Link

You have already learned about secondary research sources in Unit 3: Principles of Marketing in Travel and Tourism.

Case study

A strong performance

At the end of 2018, easyJet released an Annual Report celebrating a year of strong performance. That year, the business had carried a record 88.5 million passengers, increased revenue and increased pre-tax profits. The 2018 Annual Report explained these headline figures:

'Revenue increased to £5,898 million, with passenger volumes increasing by 10.2 per cent and revenue per seat was £63.09. Load factor for the full year grew to 92.9 per cent, reflecting easyJet's strong network positions.'

Profit before tax was £578 million despite disruption in the industry. Ancillary revenue amounted to £1,210 million. easyJet has also purchased part of Air Berlin's operations at Berlin Tegel airport and Berlin is now its second biggest city base after London.

Check your knowledge

1 Explain the following terms:
   • revenue per seat
   • load factors
   • revenue
   • profit
   • currency impact

2 What is meant by ancillary revenue?

3 Why do you think easyJet wanted a base in Berlin?

External sources of research are much easier to access. These sources are usually produced about the industry as a whole by organisations such as the government, market research companies and trade journals.

There are specialist companies that produce research reports on the travel and tourism industry. For example, Mintel is a global market intelligence agency that carries out research into markets and how these markets are changing. The company employs teams of specialist researchers and market analysts who collate trade, industry and government data, and then use this data to produce reports and forecasts across all industries, including travel and tourism. The business produces regular market reports about markets, including the:

- package holidays market
- independent holidays market
- specialist holidays market
- cruises market
- air travel market
- hotels and accommodation market
- domestic tourism market
- short/city breaks market
- business travel market.

These reports can be very expensive (about £300 each), but students can sometimes access them through a library that subscribes to them. A similar business, Keynotes, also provides market reports at a cost.

Other great sources of information include tourist boards, such as VisitBritain, and government departments and agencies, such as the Office for National Statistics (ONS) and the Department for Digital, Culture, Media & Sport (DCMS).

A more recent source of information is customer reviews available on businesses' websites or on sites such as TripAdvisor. However, if you choose to use these reviews as a source, always bear in mind that they could be biased.

PAUSE POINT

Explain why you would carry out secondary research before you do your primary research.

Secondary research is sometimes called desk research. Primary research is sometimes called field research.

VisitBritain conducts secondary and primary research. Find and explain an example of each from their website.

Quantitative data and qualitative data

Research data is often divided into two categories.

- **Quantitative data** consists of facts and figures which can be measured and illustrated through numbers. The number of people admitted to a museum in one day is an example of quantitative data.
- **Qualitative data** consists of opinions and judgements that represent an individual person's view of something. Qualitative research is more difficult to conduct and the data is more difficult to analyse, as it is about why people behave and think the way that they do. Sometimes customers themselves find it difficult to explain why they choose to buy certain things.

Theory into practice

1   Identify which of the following pieces of research are qualitative and which are quantitative.

- Research into the number of holidays taken in a year.
- Research into why people choose British Airways flights.
- Research into how much money Holiday Inn made over the last three years.
- Research into weather patterns in Jamaica.
- Research into the types of entertainment that visitors would like in a new venue.

2   Find your own examples of qualitative and quantitative research.

Purpose of market research

Market research is usually used to see whether a business idea is viable or to help an entrepreneur identify a new business idea in a particular sector. There are four main purposes:

▶ to identify or review the target market

▶ to establish customer needs

▶ to identify a gap in the market

▶ to identify competitors.

You need to think realistically about what kind of enterprise you would be able to undertake. You may want to plan a one-off event, such as a charity fundraiser, or you may want to work on planning a profit-making travel and tourism venture that you can start up when you finish your studies. Ideas could include selling tour-guiding services, setting up a cycling tour in your local area or setting up as an Airbnb location or a guest house.

Reviewing target market

Researching your target market will help you to identify a market or review an existing market to find out whether their needs have changed. This will affect the products and services that you would market to them. For example, you may want to aim your product or service at older people, so you might choose to conduct a survey on this group. If you are not sure who your target market is, research will help you to identify who is most interested in the idea, especially if it covers a number of people in lots of different groups, such as:

▶ couples

▶ young people

▶ families

▶ groups

▶ older people or seniors.

Having completed this research, you can then analyse the data to find out which group is most interested in your idea.

Establishing customer needs

If your idea is still in development, you can carry out research to find out what different groups need and how these needs may be changing. This will help you to find out about market trends and to identify which markets are growing. For example, if you are aiming to establish some kind of tour-guiding service in your local area, this kind of research could help you to identify whether people still want a traditional guided tour or whether they would prefer a digital tour that they can access through their smartphone.

Identifying gaps in the market

Entrepreneurs often set up businesses because they have spotted a need for a product or service that is not currently being met by existing businesses. This is known as a gap in the market. The aim of your research may be to find a gap in a particular travel and tourism market.

Identifying competitors

You may have a great idea for a business, but if lots of businesses are already doing it, you must decide whether it is worth going ahead with that idea. In order to beat the competition, you would have to ensure that the product or service has a **unique selling point (USP)**, which is something that makes your product or service stand out from the competition. Your USP might be that your product is better quality or that you provide a more personalised service. A USP should be something that is difficult for competitors to copy. For example, if you simply lowered the price of your product, competitors could also do this and remove your USP.

Market research is not just for start-up businesses. Even in an existing business, you have to conduct research to make the case for a new product or service. Businesses only want to invest money in new ideas that look like they have a good chance of succeeding, so you need to provide evidence that the idea has a chance of success.

The Prince's Trust is a useful source of funding for young people starting up their own business. The Trust's Enterprise Programme helps 18–30 year olds start their own businesses by providing financial support and business advice, and it operates in England, Wales and Northern Ireland.

PAUSE POINT
Explain what is meant by the term 'target market'. Choose a theme park and decide what its target market is.

Hint
Think about dividing up the market for theme parks into different groups with similar characteristics.

Extend
How will you determine the target market for your own idea?

Interpreting research findings

Presenting your findings

A key decision that you need to make is how you will present your findings. For example, you could choose to write up a formal report. However, it is important to consider your audience and how much time they have to consider your research findings. For example, if you have 10 minutes to pitch to a group of investors, you may choose to present your findings visually, using diagrams and charts, to help your audience understand the data quickly and easily.

Some of the different ways in which research can be presented include:
▸ a written report or high-level summary
▸ bar charts and line graphs
▸ a spreadsheet
▸ an infographic such as a pie chart (see Figure 5.2 on page 245)
▸ slides using presentation software such as Microsoft PowerPoint® or Prezi.

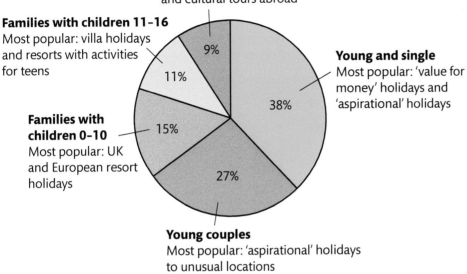

Older couples with no children
Most popular: UK countryside breaks and cultural tours abroad

Families with children 11–16
Most popular: villa holidays and resorts with activities for teens

Young and single
Most popular: 'value for money' holidays and 'aspirational' holidays

Families with children 0–10
Most popular: UK and European resort holidays

Young couples
Most popular: 'aspirational' holidays to unusual locations

9% · 11% · 38% · 15% · 27%

▶ **Figure 5.2:** An example of a tour operator's different market segments presented as a pie chart

2 out of 5 visitors to Britain watch live sport during their trip and... **73% choose live football**

Premier League　VisitBritain　FOOTBALL IS GREAT BRITAIN

#HomeofFootball

▶ A VisitBritain infographic about inbound visitor numbers

When you are deciding how to present your data, ask yourself the questions shown in Figure 5.3.

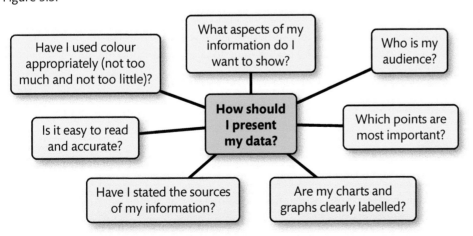

Have I used colour appropriately (not too much and not too little)?

What aspects of my information do I want to show?

Who is my audience?

Is it easy to read and accurate?

How should I present my data?

Which points are most important?

Have I stated the sources of my information?

Are my charts and graphs clearly labelled?

▶ **Figure 5.3:** Questions to ask when deciding how to present research findings

▸ **Table 5.2:** Visits to Cresta theme parks 2016–2019 (in thousands)

Year	Ghost Nights	Pelican	Jurassic	Mammoth	Future
2016	459	459	860	360	800
2017	556	459	958	250	800
2018	700	560	1045	250	750
2019	750	459	1067	200	400

Validity and reliability of research or data

It is important that any research material you produce is both valid and reliable. If research findings are valid, this means that the research has actually measured what it set out to measure. However, if the research methods are not well designed, this may lead to findings that are invalid. For example, a researcher may be using research findings to make claims about the general population, even though the research only used groups of 16–25 year olds.

If research findings are reliable, this means that the research could be repeated and would produce the same results every time.

Analysing research

It is possible to analyse data by hand, but this is time-consuming and difficult. Computer analysis is the most commonly used technique, especially with quantitative data, and it ensures **cross-tabulation** of data. It is more difficult to analyse qualitative data electronically because the responses will be more diverse than simple 'yes' and 'no' answers.

Once the findings have been produced and analysed, they must be interpreted and conclusions drawn from them. Recommendations based on the conclusions of the research can then be made so that the findings can be acted upon. The data, the conclusions and the recommendations should usually be presented in a written report.

Assessment activity 5.1

A.P1 A.P2 A.M1 A.D1

Your local council works closely with the tourist information centre to increase tourism in your area. You have been asked to find potential entrepreneurial ideas for development that could boost local tourism and the local economy.

1 Explain the different types of market research that you could use to identify a new travel and tourism enterprise idea.

2 Think of a specific travel and tourism enterprise idea and use some of the market research methods you have identified to carry out research into how much interest there is in your idea.

3 Analyse the findings of your market research and use this to decide whether your business idea is feasible. You will use this information in later assessments when you produce a start-up plan.

4 Evaluate why it is important to carry out thorough and appropriate market research before starting a new travel and tourism enterprise.

Plan
- What are the different stages of the assignment?
- Do I have enough knowledge and understanding of types of research in order to explain them?
- How will I get started?
- How will I present the types of research?
- How will I present the findings?

Do
- I know the different types of research.
- I have an idea and I have chosen my research methods.
- I know how to present my findings.

Review
- I can explain the steps that I took to complete my research and analyse my findings.
- I can explain how I would take this project forward to the next stage.
- Present all your work in a research portfolio.

B Develop a start-up plan for a new travel and tourism enterprise to meet the changing needs of consumers

Making a start-up plan is a very important step in the creation of a new business. In this learning aim, you will learn about the different parts of a start-up plan, including making legal decisions, calculating whether the business will be financially **viable** and what resources you will need to start and run the business.

> **Key term**
>
> **Viable** – able to work properly or be successful.

Legal aspects of the new enterprise

Legal form

There are different types of business, known as legal forms of business. When you are setting up your travel and tourism enterprise, the most likely forms of business will be:

▶ sole trader
▶ partnership
▶ private limited company.

> **Link**
>
> You have already learned about legal forms of ownership in Unit 1: The World of Travel and Tourism.

One of your early decisions will be which of these to choose for your enterprise. Each legal form has its own advantages and disadvantages, as shown in Table 5.3 on page 248.

Business	Advantages	Disadvantages
Sole trader/ partnership	• Simplest way of starting up as you just have to inform Her Majesty's Revenue and Customs (HMRC) that you are now self-employed • If you have a partner, you can share decision-making and have access to more **capital**	• Profits are subject to personal tax, which is higher than corporation tax • The person and the business are one **entity**, which means that you will be liable for the business's debts
Limited company	• Profits are subject to corporation tax, which is lower than personal tax (though you will still pay personal tax on your salary) • Separate entity from owners so you have limited liability, meaning that you will not be personally liable for any debts • Creates a more professional image than being a sole trader • Company name is protected once it is registered with **Companies House**, so no one else can use it	• More complex to set up, as you need to complete many documents and send them to Companies House • May require professional help such as from an accountant • Money cannot be easily withdrawn from the business without formally recording it as a salary, dividend or loan

Copyright and intellectual property

Your **intellectual property (IP)** is property that is the result of your own creative activity, including products, services and brands, inventions, designs and writing. You can protect your IP in various ways, as shown in Table 5.4.

▶ **Table 5.4:** Different ways of protecting intellectual property

Protection	Description
Copyright	Copyright is usually applied to artistic works such as music, books and software codes. If the work is original, copyright comes into being as soon as the work is created. You can show this by putting the copyright symbol (©) on your materials and website
Trademark	A trademark (™ or ®) protects a name or brand and gives the owner the exclusive right to use it. When you are deciding on your brand, make sure that it is not already being used by someone else, or too similar to an existing brand. You have to apply to the **Intellectual Property Office (IPO)** for trademark protection, but this process is straightforward and inexpensive
Registered design rights	Registered design rights protect designs that are new and unique in character. Registering gives the owner 15 years of exclusive use after the creation of the design

Key terms

Capital – money used to invest or start up a business.

Entity – a thing that exists (often legally).

Companies House – the government agency responsible for registering businesses and providing information about businesses to the public.

Intellectual property (IP) – property that is the result of creative activity.

Intellectual Property Office (IPO) – a government agency responsible for intellectual property rights.

Legislation

Your new enterprise must comply with all relevant legislation. This can be quite daunting for people setting up new businesses, but there are plenty of sources of support and advice. In addition, not all legislation will apply at first. For example, you don't need to comply with employment law until you employ staff.

Employment legislation

There are many different employment laws and directives that businesses must comply with. Larger organisations employ legal specialists or have a human resources (HR) department to ensure that they are compliant with this law.

Employees have statutory rights, including the right to:

▶ a written contract
▶ the national minimum wage or national living wage
▶ an itemised payslip that shows tax paid and employer contributions to a pension and other benefits
▶ at least 28 days' paid holiday including bank holidays
▶ sick pay after the fourth consecutive day of absence due to sickness.

By 2018, employers have to enrol any employees aged between 22 and pension age into a workplace pension scheme. In addition, employers must comply with laws on health and safety, discrimination, bullying and parental leave after the birth of a child. Employers also need to have liability insurance, as well as documented disciplinary and grievance procedures.

If you employ freelance workers, the rules are different because they are not classed as employees.

Health and safety legislation

The Health and Safety at Work Act 1974 requires businesses and organisations to have a health and safety policy and carry out risk assessments, and it lays out the employer's duty of care towards employees and members of the public.

The Management of Health and Safety at Work Regulations 1999 have specific requirements regarding risk assessment. When a risk assessment is conducted, a risk assessment form should be completed and kept for future reference. In addition, the points in Figure 5.4 should be considered when carrying out risk assessments.

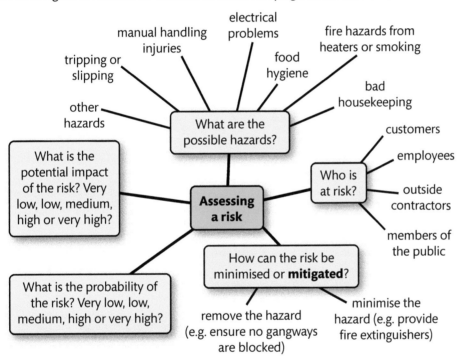

▶ **Figure 5.4:** Different aspects of risk assessment

> **Key term**
>
> **Mitigate** – make something less severe or less serious.

> **Theory into practice**
>
> Let's Go Cambridge organises tourist activities in Cambridge. Imagine that you are a manager at Let's Go Cambridge and have been asked to conduct a risk assessment for a 50-minute punting tour for eight customers from China, who do not speak English. Complete Table 5.5 (one example has already been provided for you) and then discuss your ideas with the rest of the group.

Table 5.5: A risk assessment for a punting trip

Description of hazard	Who is at risk?	Probability of risk	Potential impact of risk	Mitigation of risk
Slippery surfaces	• *Customers* • *Employees*	*Medium*	*High*	• *Ask customers to wear appropriate footwear* • *Put down non-slip mats where possible*

Data protection legislation

The Data Protection Act 2018 provides rights for people who have information held about them by businesses or organisations. This data may be held in electronic or other filing systems. The Act requires those who record and use personal information to follow the following basic data protection principles.

Discussion

Can you think of any organisations or businesses that hold information about you, such as your school or college? If you are happy to do so, discuss some of your examples with the rest of the group.

Everyone responsible for using personal data has to follow strict rules called 'data protection principles'. They must make sure the information is:
- used fairly, lawfully and transparently
- used for specified, explicit purposes
- used in a way that is adequate, relevant and limited to only what is necessary
- accurate and, where necessary, kept up to date
- kept for no longer than is necessary
- handled in a way that ensures appropriate security, including protection against unlawful or unauthorised processing, access, loss, destruction or damage.

Environmental protection legislation

There is a lot of environmental legislation in the UK and the extent to which you need to comply with this legislation depends on the nature of your business.

Broadly, the legislation covers:
- air emissions – for example, from machinery or dust
- land contamination – for example, from waste products or dangerous substances
- noise pollution – for example, from factories or bars and clubs
- waste disposal – for example, ensuring that dangerous substances are disposed of correctly
- waste discharge – for example, ensuring that sewage is processed and discharged safely.

If you think your enterprise might have responsibilities under one of these headings, you can visit the Environment Agency website (in England and Wales).

Consumer protection legislation

Link

You have already learned about consumer protection in Unit 4: Managing the Customer Experience in Travel and Tourism.

Consumer protection legislation refers to the laws, standards and codes of practice that protect customers from unfair trading. The main legislation that affects businesses is the Consumer Rights Act 2015, which covers issues such as the quality of a product, the process for returning products and the process for repairing or replacing faulty products.

  **PAUSE POINT**

Give two advantages of setting up a sole trader business and two advantages of setting up as a limited company.

Hint

Think about legal aspects such as debts, as well as how the customer will regard the business.

Extend

Your business has incurred some debts that it cannot pay. Which type of ownership is better in this situation? Why?

Financial feasibility of the new enterprise

Projected costs

Projected costs are the costs that you predict you will need to cover to set up and run your business.

Set-up costs

Before you can start your enterprise, you need money to cover your initial expenses (set-up costs). These might include:
- legal costs of setting up a company
- website development
- start-up promotions and leaflets
- premises and equipment (if needed).

Fixed and variable costs

Once your business is up and running, you will still have to cover its costs. There are two types of costs:

▶ **fixed costs** – these are costs that remain the same no matter how much of a product you sell (for example, rent)

▶ **variable costs** – these are costs that go up or down depending on how many sales you make (for example, the cost of raw materials to make the products that you sell).

For a business to be **feasible**, it must make enough **revenue** to cover its **total costs** and make a profit. At first, you may have to borrow money to cover these costs.

Determining the amount of finance required

Once you have calculated your projected costs, you can work out how much finance you will need to get the business started.

Most enterprises experience a period when their costs exceed their revenue as the business gets going. In this time, you will need sufficient cash reserves to cover costs until sales come in. If you are lucky, you might have some **working capital** to see you through this period. If not, you will have to borrow the money or sell some shares in your business to raise funds.

Payback period

The **payback period** is the length of time that it takes for a business to make back the amount of money that it invested in its set-up. Determining the payback period is very simple. For example, if your start-up costs are £10,000 and your repayments are £1000 per month, then the payback period will be 10 months. Working out how long it takes to cover your initial investment will give you an indication of when your business will start to break even.

Break-even point

The break-even point is the point at which a business's revenue from sales is exactly the same as its costs. Knowing when your business will break even will help you to plan your finances.

> ## Key terms
>
> **Fixed costs** – costs that remain the same no matter how many sales are made.
>
> **Variable costs** – costs that change with the number of sales that are made.
>
> **Feasible** – possible or practical.
>
> **Revenue** – income or money made from sales.
>
> **Total costs** – the sum of fixed and variable costs.
>
> **Working capital** – the capital or money that a business makes and uses to fund its day-to-day activities.
>
> **Payback period** – the number of months or years it takes for a business to recover its initial investment.

Worked Example

A souvenir t-shirt shop has fixed costs of £2,400 per week. Its t-shirts cost an average of £3 each. It sells each t-shirt for £15. Calculate the shop's break-even point.

The break-even point is calculated using the following formula:

$$\frac{\text{fixed costs}}{(\text{sales price} - \text{variable costs})}$$

Each t-shirt brings in £12 more revenue than it requires the business to pay out in variable costs:

£15 sales price – £3 variable costs = £12 revenue

So the break-even point can be calculated:

$$\frac{\text{fixed costs}}{(\text{sales price} - \text{variable costs})}$$
$$\frac{£2,400}{(£15 - £3)}$$
$$\frac{£2,400}{£12} = 200$$

This means that the break-even point occurs when 200 t-shirts are sold each week.

> ## Theory into practice
>
> A tour guide in York works on his own and charges £9 per person for a guided tour around the city. His fixed costs are his phone contract and website management, which come to £50 per week. His variable costs are £3 per tour for entry fees to various places of interest on the tour.
>
> How many tours does the tour guide need to sell every week to break even?

Projected profit or loss

Unless you calculate your projected profit or loss, you will not know how much – if any – profit you will make from your enterprise. This knowledge will help you to adjust your costs or selling prices so that you make a profit.

Projected profit or loss is calculated by:

1 working out your total projected revenue
2 working out your total projected costs
3 taking projected costs away from projected revenue.

> **Theory into practice**

Table 5.6 shows a projected profit and loss estimate for a one-day careers event.

1 Complete the calculations and decide if the event will make a profit or a loss.

▶ **Table 5.6:** A profit and loss estimate for a travel and tourism careers day

Careers in Travel and Tourism Event	
Projected revenue	
300 attendees (×£30 per person)	
20 stands (×£500 per stand)	
20 advertisements in programme (×£30 per advert)	
Total projected revenue	
Projected costs	
Cost of venue	£1,000
Three speakers' travel expenses and fees (×£200 each)	
Refreshments (×£3 per person)	
Administration costs	£250
Publicity materials	£500
Total projected costs	
Total projected profit/loss	

2 Can you think of any other sources of income?
3 Can you think of any additional costs?

Cash flow forecast

A cash flow forecast helps a business to see how much cash it will have coming into and leaving its accounts. Businesses may make a profit when everything that they are owed is finally paid, but if they do not have a steady inflow of cash then they may struggle to pay their suppliers. These problems can be significant in the travel sector. For example, a tour operator will book flights and hotels a long time before the customer pays for them, so the tour operator will need enough cash in its accounts to pay for these bookings.

Cash inflow includes:

▶ payments for sales from customers (receipts from sales and **value added tax (VAT)** on sales)
▶ the cash put aside to start up the business (start-up capital)
▶ interest paid on savings
▶ shareholder investments
▶ overdrafts or loans.

Cash outflow includes:

▶ payments to suppliers – for example, hoteliers and transport principals
▶ payments on fixed assets – for example, the rent on a company office

> **Key term**
>
> **Value added tax (VAT)** – a tax added to business sales.

- loan repayments
- overheads – for example, employees' wages, electricity bills and telephone contracts
- purchase of fixed assets – for example, computers or bicycles for a cycle hire company
- stock – for example, stationery or raw materials.

Net cash flow shows the difference between total payments and income.

The cash flow forecast can be divided into three parts, as shown in Table 5.7:
1 projected revenue (cash inflow)
2 projected costs (cash outflow)
3 net cash flow (the balance).

▶ **Table 5.7:** A cash flow forecast for a newly set-up website design business

	April	May	June	July	Aug	Sept	
Revenue (inflow)							Note that there is no revenue in the first month.
Sales		£5,500	£5,500	£5,500	£5,500	£5,500	
Costs (outflow)							
Rent	£1,000	£1,000	£1,000	£1,000	£1,000	£1,000	
Equipment	£250	£250	£250	£250	£250	£250	
Salary	£2,000	£2,000	£2,000	£2,000	£2,000	£2,000	Monthly sales – total cost.
Electricity	£0	£0	£75	£0	£0	£75	
Travelling	£200	£200	£200	£200	£200	£200	
Total costs	£3,450	£3,450	£3,525	£3,450	£3,450	£3,525	
Net cash flow	–£3,450	£2,050	£1,975	£2,050	£2,050	£1,975	The opening balance is always the same as the previous month's closing balance.
Opening balance	£3,000	–£450	£1,600	£3,575	£5,625	£7,675	
Closing balance	–£450	£1,600	£3,575	£5,625	£7,675	£9,650	The closing balance is the difference between the opening balance and the net cash flow.

Case study

Cash flow forecasting

Sunita and Rachael run a guest house business in Gloucester. The guest house has 12 bedrooms.

Sunita has been looking at the sales figures over the last few months and is worried that they are going to have to take out a loan. She knows that there is £1,000 in the business account. She is creating a cash flow forecast for the coming financial year starting in April.

1 Create a cash flow forecast for Sunita and Rachael using the following information.

Cash inflow

Room sales, which guests pay immediately:
- May to October £5,000 per month
- November and December £3,000
- January and February £3,500
- March and April £4,000.

Food and bar:
- May to October £1,000 per month
- Other months £500 per month.

Cash outflow
- Wages: £4,000 per month

- Repainting: £900 in May only
- Maintenance: £100 per month
- Heating and lighting: £50 per month
- Advertising: £20 per month.

Other expenses:
- May to October £200 per month
- Other months £150 per month.

2 Should Sunita and Rachael be concerned? Explain why you think problems may be occurring.

3 Make realistic recommendations to resolve the problems.

Sunita suggests to Rachael that they should apply to their bank for a £12,000 overdraft facility and use this money to refurbish three rooms that are not currently being used. This would increase monthly room sales by £800 and would provide another £120 in food sales.

4 Choose the best month in which Sunita and Rachael could undertake the refurbishment and then update the cash flow forecast for the month following the refurbishment.

Cash flow problems

Joe Larson was the managing director of a specialist tour operator called Safari Specials. Unfortunately, after 12 years with the business, he had to announce that it had failed. The business could not pay its bills and the banks were unwilling to lend it any more money.

About four years ago, the business was doing very well, so Joe decided to move the business into a bigger office and hire more staff. This meant that the business's annual overheads increased from £900,000 to £1.6 million. Just after the move one of the key managers left the business, taking some members of staff with her, and set up a rival business.

In response to these events, Joe cut the number of staff and the number of safari destinations on offer. However,

this came too late. A number of long-term accommodation contracts had to be paid for, as well as flights, and Safari Specials did not have enough cash to pay these bills. The business failed with debts of almost £4 million.

A competitor suggested that Safari Specials had probably overcommitted by buying too many airline tickets for May and June, many of which remained unsold.

Check your knowledge

1   Identify the cash flow problems experienced by Safari Specials.

2   Suggest how Joe could have better managed the cash flow problem.

PAUSE POINT   Define the following terms: break-even point, cash flow, payback period, fixed costs, variable costs.

> **Hint**   These terms are all related to the financial feasibility of an enterprise.

> **Extend**   Write a step-by-step explanation of how you would work out a cash flow forecast.

Resources required for the new enterprise

Resources are the things that a business needs to start up and function. These resources could be:

▶ physical resources
▶ financial resources
▶ human resources.

Physical resources

Physical resources are the physical things that you need to run your business. For example, you may need equipment, promotional materials such as business cards or simply a place to work.

You need to have your physical resources in place before you launch your enterprise. You will need a place to work even if, initially, this is just a desk in your bedroom. You will also need a computer (a laptop or PC) and a telephone. You will need some business cards and possibly also some leaflets about your business. After this, your physical resources depend entirely on the type of business.

Financial resources

Financial resources are the sources of funding that a business needs to function. Organisations of all sizes have to raise funds from time to time to finance their growth, new ventures or takeovers. Sources of finance include:

▶ grants
▶ bank loans and overdrafts
▶ investors (including shareholders, friends and family)
▶ crowdfunding.

> **Theory into practice**
>
> Gandys is a clothing brand and social enterprise founded by two brothers who were orphaned in the 2004 Boxing Day tsunami. Their core product is flip flops, but they have added other product ranges and expanded the company into a clothing brand. They have used their profits to build homes for orphans and continue to invest into their charity, the Gandys Foundation.
>
> 1   Imagine you are setting up a business making and selling flip flops. List the physical resources you will need and discuss them with the rest of your group.
>
> 2   How would you pay for these physical resources?

Grants

A grant is a sum of money given by the government or another organisation to deserving businesses in need of funding.

The government invests in many tourism enterprises. This is because an increase in tourism benefits the economy. There are strict criteria for eligibility when applying for grants, and a grant will not usually be given for the full cost of a project or venture.

The National Lottery is another source of grants. Figure 5.5 is an example of a grant from the Heritage Lottery Fund supporting the year of History, Heritage and Archaeology 2017.

Stories, Stones and Bones

As part of the Scotland-wide celebrations of the Year of History, Heritage and Archaeology 2017, we want to inspire people to get involved in learning about and enjoying their heritage for the first time.

Stories, Stones and Bones will encourage people in communities across Scotland to dig deeper into their past and to find out more about their local history, customs and traditions – resulting in often complex, sometimes quirky but always fascinating stories.

We are offering grants of £3,000 to £10,000 to projects which engage new people and a wider range of people with their history. From researching local historic landmarks, learning about natural heritage, unearthing the history beneath their feet to delving into archives, our grants will give everyone the chance to explore their heritage and celebrate and share what they learn with others.

▶ **Figure 5.5:** An example of a grant for heritage visitor attractions

Bank loans and overdrafts

Banks are an obvious source of funding. They can offer business loans for a set period of time with an agreed repayment schedule. The repayment amount will depend on the size of the loan and the **interest rate**.

Banks will only lend money if the money is guaranteed, which means that the bank has a guarantee that it will get its money back. For example, a loan could be secured against a house, meaning that the bank could take the house if the loan is not repaid. Alternatively, a family member could act as the borrower's guarantor, meaning that they agree to pay off the debt if the borrower cannot do so.

Banks will also probably ask to see a formal business plan before deciding whether or not to loan money to a business, especially a new business, as they want to make sure that the business will succeed and pay back the loan.

Another bank-based source of finance is an overdraft facility. This is more flexible than a loan, because an individual has an agreed overdraft amount and can borrow what they need up to that limit. It is very quick to arrange an overdraft and you don't need to provide as much security as for a loan. However, if you exceed the agreed limit, you will have to pay penalties, which can be expensive.

Investment from friends and family

Many small businesses are financed by the founders' families and they can grow to be huge family enterprises. Similarly, the founders' friends may wish to invest in the business to share in the profits without having to provide hands-on commitment.

Key term

Interest rate – the proportion of a loan that is charged as a fee for taking out a loan.

Link

You will learn more about formal business plans later in this section.

Investment from shareholders

Another way of raising funds is to issue shares in your company. By buying shares, individuals give the business money to invest in its activities. In return, shareholders become part-owners of the business with voting rights on some operational decisions. When profits are distributed, they are shared among the shareholders as dividends. If the company does not make any profit, there are no dividends.

Companies can issue shares to raise enough capital to start up and get running. If a company needs more money to expand or to undertake a new venture, it can issue new shares to raise the finance. Sometimes many shares are owned by the business's own employees. This gives them an incentive to help the company to succeed as they will receive dividends as well as their salary.

Crowdfunding

Traditional methods of funding for a business involve asking a small number of organisations for large sums of money. In comparison, crowdfunding invites large numbers of people to each donate a small amount. The entrepreneur sets up a profile on a crowdfunding website and spreads the word about their project, often through social media platforms. The profile on the crowdfunding website explains the idea and how much money is needed to fund the project. People who are interested can then donate in one of three ways.

1 Backers donate just because they like the business's idea and want to back it. Rewards may be offered, such as tickets to an event, but ultimately there is no financial return on the donation.
2 Backers fund a business as part of a peer-to-peer lending scheme, where the value of the investment is repaid with interest. However, there is no guarantee of any return on the investment.
3 Backers fund a business as part of an equity crowdfunding scheme, where the backer's investment buys them a share of the business. However, the value of shares can go down as well as up and there is no guarantee of any return on the investment.

Link

You have already learned about shares and shareholders in Unit 1: The World of Travel and Tourism.

Case study

Successful crowdfunding

> The Mathematical Bridge is a popular tourist attraction in Cambridge

The Mathematical Bridge in Cambridge is a well-known tourist attraction and feat of engineering. What if tourists, having seen the bridge, could then buy a model of it to take home and build for themselves?

This is how Ben came up with the idea of selling models of the bridge to tourists. He set up a business called Ponticulus Design and spent over a year designing the model, testing and retesting the design to make sure that it was a true replica of the bridge and could be

successfully built. Once he was happy with the design and had a prototype, he planned his product launch. His business planning showed that he needed an initial investment of £3,000 to start manufacturing and fund further marketing.

He set up on the crowdfunding website, Kickstarter, launching his enterprise with the aim of getting £3,000 within one month. In return for pledging money, backers would receive a variety of rewards depending on the size of their donation, from a 'thank you' on the business's website to an early model of the bridge.

By the end of the month, the project had attracted 491 backers and nearly £12,000 of investment.

Check your knowledge

1 Why do you think Ben spent so long designing and testing his product?
2 What other sources of funding might be useful for Ben? Why?
3 How could you use crowdfunding to help set up your enterprise?

Human resources

Human resources are the people that a business uses to function. Your human resources may just be the skills and abilities of you and any business partners. For example, you may set up a business with someone who is good at web design and who can take care of the business's website.

Your human resources include any people to whom you outsource work, such as an accountant. This is especially important if you have set up on your own because you have to be realistic about what you can do for yourself and what you need a professional to do. Be clear about what your strengths are and where your time is best spent.

Once you decide to employ people, employees also make up your human resources. At first, you might start by paying freelance staff rather than employing your own full-time staff. This will give you flexibility, as you only need to pay them for the amount of work you contract them to do, which will enable you to cover busy or seasonal times. Once your business is established and growing, you might need more staff to cover specialist functions.

Case study

Take a punt

▶ A punt is a flat-bottomed boat, popularly used in the university cities of Oxford and Cambridge

Let's Go Cambridge was originally started by two partners. Simon was responsible for the punts and delivering the tours, while Caroline was responsible for bookings and administration. As the business became more popular,

they found that they needed more chauffeurs to pilot the punts so they employed freelance chauffeurs, paying them well and offering incentives to chauffeurs when they received good reviews from tourists on TripAdvisor. Later on, once the business had moved into an office, Simon and Caroline employed an administrator to run the office. They outsourced their website design to a professional web designer and their accounts to a professional accountant.

Check your knowledge

1 What are the disadvantages of employing freelance staff?

2 What would happen if all the chauffeurs for the punts were full-time employees?

3 What other staff is a company like Let's Go Cambridge likely to need?

PAUSE POINT   Give three potential sources of funding for a start-up enterprise.

> Hint   Look back at the section about financial resources.

> Extend   Explain the benefits of crowdfunding to an investor. What are the disadvantages?

Documents to record the start-up plan for the new enterprise

Formal business plan

Once you have done your research and planned your resources, you have to record your start-up plan as a formal business plan.

A business plan is a detailed document, so it takes some time to create, but it helps you to evaluate your business planning and assess whether you have included everything

Research

Find out whether your bank offers business planning guidance. If it does not, do an internet search using the terms, 'Lloyds bank business planning' or 'Prince's trust business plan', and use the Lloyds Bank or Prince's Trust resources to help you.

that is needed. It also shows that you have done your research and have a good business case for your idea. This will be particularly useful if you need external financial support from investors or banks to whom you will be expected to show a formal business plan.

There are lots of templates available for business planning, so you can find and use one that you like. However, no matter what template you decide to use, your plan must include:

▸ your mission statement – your business's overall aim
▸ your objectives – how the business will achieve its mission
▸ your strategy – how the business will achieve its objectives
▸ your projected costs and income – your budget and cash flow forecast.

Many banks provide business plan templates and examples of business plans. Some organisations such as the Prince's Trust also provide help for business planning and they too provide a template for you.

Flowchart

A flowchart is a diagram showing a sequence of activities or events. You might choose to produce a flowchart to support your business plan. This provides a visual representation of your plan, which you can use to show to potential investors or business partners. Figure 5.6 is an example of a flowchart being used for a business plan.

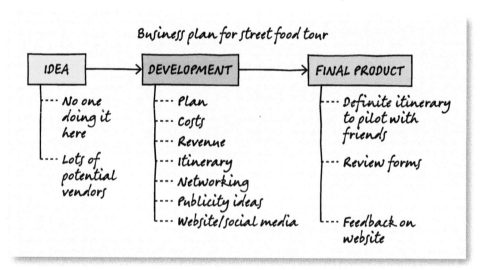

▸ **Figure 5.6:** An example of a flowchart

Report

Alternatively, you might decide to put your business plan into a report format. In this case, you could add your marketing strategy to the report. A report should also contain a high-level or executive summary, which provides an overview of the whole plan for anyone who doesn't have time to read the full report.

Research

Some local councils run programmes about starting up businesses. Search your local council's website for examples of any guidance or free courses that would help people wishing to set up their own enterprise.

Business basics workshop

The Business Basics one-day workshop is part of the Business Basics Programme backed by Wandsworth Council. It covers the three fundamental elements – money, marketing and management – required to start up and run a business.

In this workshop you will learn about the following.

1 Money:
- start-up costs to get going
- forecasting sales to make a profit
- business costs and keeping them under control
- starting up a business on a limited budget.

2 Marketing:
- who is your target market
- what is unique about your business that will make people buy

- who are your competitors and how to compete against them
- how to reach your customers and win their business.

3 Management:
- how to manage yourself and your time
- administration you will need to do in the business
- how to plan for success.

Lunch/light refreshments are provided and the service is free for young people aged 16–30.

Check your knowledge

1 Why do you think Wandsworth Council supports the Business Basics Programme?

2 What do you think are the benefits of attending this workshop?

3 Can you identify anything that you think is missing from the workshop?

 PAUSE POINT   What are the main elements of a business plan?

 Hint   Look at the business plan template from the Prince's Trust or Lloyds Bank to help you.

Extend   What do you think is the best way to present your business plan? Why do you think this?

 C   **Prepare a marketing strategy to launch the new travel and tourism enterprise to raise consumer awareness**

Marketing mix

The **marketing mix** is a combination of four key elements that a business or organisation uses to achieve its objectives and meet the needs of its customers. These elements make up the core of a business's marketing strategy and are commonly known as the 'four Ps'.

▶ **Product** – the thing that you are selling.
▶ **Price** – the price at which you sell it.
▶ **Promotion** – the way in which you market it.
▶ **Place** – the place where customers can buy it.

Businesses often develop separate strategies for each of the four Ps, but it is important to remember that these elements are interdependent and work together.

In the UK, marketing has been a high-profile aspect of business since the 1970s. Most travel and tourism businesses have a marketing department or a marketing manager. It is important that you devise a marketing strategy to launch your new travel and tourism enterprise idea, otherwise you are unlikely to attract enough customers to make it a success.

Key terms

Marketing mix – the combination of the four main elements of marketing: product, price, promotion and place.

Product – anything that can be offered for sale that can satisfy a customer need, including physical objects, services and ideas.

Products and services

According to Philip Kotler and Gary Armstrong, a product is:

> anything that can be offered to a market for attention, acquisition, use or consumption that might satisfy a want or a need. It includes physical objects, services, persons, places, organisations and ideas.

(Source: *Principles of Marketing*, 2016, 16th edition, Pearson)

Kotler and Armstrong's definition of product shows that a service is also considered to be part of a 'product' within the marketing mix. Most travel and tourism businesses market and sell services rather than physical products. The marketing for services may be different from that for a physical product. This is because the quality of the service is dependent on the people delivering the service and this must be taken into account.

Features of products

Products and services may be **tangible** or **intangible**. When you buy a product, it is usually tangible, like a book or a pair of shoes. However, buying a travel and tourism service is not like that because you cannot see it or touch it before you buy. You may be able to see pictures and brochure descriptions, but you can't often try out the real thing.

Travel and tourism products and services are also **perishable**, meaning that they can only be sold within a certain time period before they expire – like food going off in a supermarket. For example, once a flight has left an airport, it is too late for the airline to sell any more seats because they have 'perished'. This means that some transport principals, especially airlines, have to have a high **load factor** to ensure that their flights are as full as possible to make a profit.

The product features represent the core value of the product. For example, the features or core of a package holiday are the accommodation and transport that are provided as part of the package. There will be a whole range of additional features depending on the holiday chosen, such as food, sports facilities and entertainment.

Theory into practice

Find a printed holiday brochure or e-brochure and complete the following tasks.

1 Choose a holiday from the brochure and write down everything that is included in the price. You can choose to include items for which you must pay a supplement. Try to decide which aspects are tangible products and which are intangible services. For example, a free t-shirt is a tangible product, whereas the services of a holiday rep are intangible.

2 Make a table of your findings, then compare it with someone else's table and discuss any similarities or differences.

3 Discuss your ideas with the group.

Benefits of products

The features of a product convert into benefits for the consumer. For example, the features of a holiday will lead to benefits such as relaxation, the opportunity to go sightseeing or to learn a new skill.

Travel and tourism organisations are always looking for new features to add to their products and services. They want to give further benefits to their customers in order to maintain their competitive advantage. For example, theme parks introduce new rides every season to attract customers, and cinemas offer a wider range of foods and drinks, more comfortable seats and more leg room.

Unique selling point

Every product should aim to have a quality or feature that sets it apart from its competitors, known as the USP. The USP is a very useful element in the marketing strategy for a product, as it can be used as a focus for advertising and can be linked to the pricing strategy. For example, Responsible Travel is the first dedicated travel agent for responsible tourism, considering the impact of its customers on the environment and society, and attempting to minimise this impact.

⏸ **PAUSE POINT** Identify the features and benefits of a train ticket and journey from Leeds to Edinburgh.

> Hint Think about the distance between Leeds and Edinburgh. How would you feel if you had to stand all the way?

> Extend What are the features and benefits of the same journey for a customer who uses a wheelchair?

Pricing strategies

Price is the second element of the marketing mix. Travel and tourism businesses must use pricing as a means of achieving their objectives, because if they do not get their price right they will not make a profit. There are many different pricing strategies. A company will determine the strategy to be adopted by considering:

▸ the stage that the product has reached in the **product life cycle**
▸ competitors' activity
▸ the prices of other products sold by the same company.

Key term

Product life cycle – the sequence of the four stages in the life of a product from launch, through growth, into maturity and then decline.

Cost plus

The cost plus pricing strategy is one of the simplest pricing strategies. The business simply calculates the cost of producing the product and then adds a percentage to give the return it wants as profit. Although it is simple, it is not the most effective approach to pricing. If sales targets are not met, there will not be a profit. This approach also ignores the basic premise of marketing, which is that a business must identify and satisfy its customers' needs. Every approach to pricing should start with the questions: 'What is our customer prepared to pay?' and 'Are all of our customers going to pay the same price?'

Penetration

A penetration pricing strategy is useful for a new product, so it could apply to your travel and tourism enterprise idea. The aim is to start off with a very low price to gain market share quickly and attract interest from price-conscious customers. Once the customer base is established, the price can then be increased to normal market rate. The advantages and disadvantages of this pricing strategy are shown in Table 5.8.

▸ **Table 5.8:** Advantages and disadvantages of a penetration pricing strategy

Advantages	Disadvantages
Increases sales volume as a lot of customers are attracted by the low price	Customers may not buy because of concerns that the low price indicates poor quality or even a lack of safety
Lowers overall costs as the increased revenue results in economies of scale	Lowers profits if the sales volume is not high enough
Attracts new customers	New customers may leave when the price rises
Unsettles the competition	Can only be used for a limited period of time, otherwise the business will not make enough money

This strategy is usually applied to fast-moving consumer goods, which are household goods such as groceries and cleaning products. It is also used in travel and tourism, and has been used by the low-cost airline, Norwegian. In 2014, the airline started flying between London and several American cities, charging much cheaper prices than other transatlantic airlines.

Skimming

Skimming is another strategy that can be adopted for new products and services. Using this strategy, the business introduces its product at a very high price. It is costly to introduce a new product or service, so charging a high price helps a business to cover these costs. The high price also suggests exclusivity and quality, and products marketed using a skimming strategy often attract people who are keen to be first to try a new product (also known as 'innovators'). However, if the product does not achieve enough sales at the high introductory price, the price must be reduced.

Competitor-based pricing

Competitor-based pricing is used in highly competitive markets where companies keenly watch their competitors' prices and react quickly to lower their prices if anyone else lowers theirs. This happens constantly in the airline and tour operation sectors. This pricing strategy relies on a lack of brand loyalty among customers, who must be prepared to switch brands to get the best price. However, it can also be a dangerous strategy if prices drop so low that companies start to lose money or even fail.

Odd pricing

Odd pricing assumes that customers will feel that the price is cheaper because it is an odd number rather than the next highest round number, such as £499 rather than £500. This simple approach to pricing can be used in conjunction with any of the others, and it is based on the idea that, psychologically, £499 seems significantly less than £500.

Promotional pricing

A promotional pricing strategy links the product's price with a special promotion for a limited period of time. Sometimes the customer has to collect tokens to be eligible for the special price. This draws attention to the product and gains publicity, so it is especially useful for new products. Tourist attractions often use this pricing strategy.

Seasonal pricing

A seasonal pricing strategy changes the price depending on the time of year, and this is particularly important in the tourism industry. The whole year is divided into three seasons.

▶ **Peak** – the most popular season for a particular type of holiday, when prices are highest.
▶ **Shoulder** – the seasons either side of peak season.
▶ **Off-peak** – the least popular season for that type of holiday, when prices are lowest.

Peak season always coincides with school holidays. This can cause problems for parents, who have to pay the highest prices to go on holiday with their children. Some parents try to avoid this by taking their children on holiday during term-time to avoid peak-season holiday prices, though this can also cause problems.

It is not just tour operators who charge higher prices at times of high demand. Airlines charge more on Friday afternoons and at the end of weekends, and rail fares cost more during the rush hour.

Case study

An all-inclusive holiday

▶ One of First Choice's Premier hotels

Check your knowledge

1   Prices for holidays at Riu Montego Bay differ between peak (high) season and off-peak (low) season. Explain why this is.

2   Find this hotel on First Choice's website and calculate the price for a family of two parents and two children going on a week's holiday at Christmas.

3   Define the term 'all-inclusive'.

4   What other things would the family need to pay for, on top of the all-inclusive price?

⏸ PAUSE POINT   Skimming and penetration are both pricing strategies. Explain the difference between them.

         Hint   Both strategies are suitable for new products or services but may not attract the same customers.

         Extend   Find a real-life example of a skimming pricing strategy and a penetration pricing strategy.

Promotion

To achieve their marketing objectives, travel and tourism businesses must make sure that their customers are aware of their products and services. The tools they use to do this are collectively known as promotion and form part of the marketing mix.

Research

Some businesses' customers are consumers (members of the general public). Other businesses' customers are trade customers (other businesses, such as travel agencies). How do you think the marketing strategies for these two types of business will differ?

Advertising

Advertising is the use of public announcements or messages (advertisements) that are designed to influence people or attract their attention. Advertising is paid for and is placed in the **media**, such as television, newspapers, radio, magazines, directories, billboards and posters on transport. It is also used on the internet and social media platforms such as Twitter and Facebook.

▶ **Newspapers** – the UK has many daily newspapers and several Sunday newspapers, but *The Sun* has the biggest circulation of all the national daily newspapers. Advertising is sold by the page, half page or column. Prices vary according to the position and size of the advert. Spaces on the front and back pages are the most expensive because they are the most prominent. The newspapers with the highest **circulation** figures can charge the highest advertising rates, meaning that *The Sun* is the most expensive newspaper in which to advertise. There are also hundreds of regional newspapers, some of which are free. Circulations vary and some circulations are small, but these can be useful and inexpensive places to advertise for a company that wants to advertise its services in a particular area.

Key terms

Media (plural of 'medium') – the different means of public communication such as print newspapers, television and radio broadcasters, and the internet.

Circulation – how many copies of a particular publication are distributed.

Theory into practice

On one chosen day, make a note of every piece of advertising that you see and where you see it. Compare your list with a partner's and see if there are any similarities or differences.

- **Magazines** – these include consumer magazines, which are bought by the general public, and business and professional journals. There are over 3000 consumer magazine titles in the UK, so the advertiser can be precise about target audience. Women's magazines are the biggest category of consumer magazines in the UK. There are also several travel magazines that are aimed at consumers, especially people who want to buy or who own property abroad, including *Condé Nast Traveler*, *The Sunday Times Travel Magazine* and *Wanderlust*. Business and professional publications are aimed at people within particular industries, such as travel and tourism. *Travel Weekly* and *Travel Trade Gazette* are both professional journals.

▷ *Condé Nast Traveler* is one well-known travel magazine

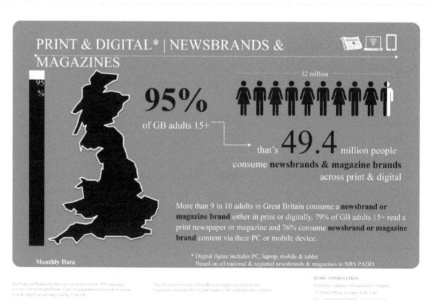

▷ The *National Readership Survey* provides estimates of the numbers of people who read Great Britain's newspapers and magazines

- **Television** – most television channels (other than the BBC) are commercial channels, which means that they are funded by the sale of advertising or sponsorship. Examples include ITV, Channel 4 and Sky. Advertising is sold in 'spots', with each spot being about 30 seconds long. The price of a spot varies according to time of day, with

Theory into practice

Choose one of Great Britain's newspapers. Find out the latest circulation and **readership** figures for that newspaper by looking at:

- the newspaper's website
- the *National Readership Survey* website.

Draw up a bar chart comparing the figures for the last three years.

Key term

Readership – an estimate of how many readers a publication has.

peak time occurring between 17.30 and 22.30 when most people are watching. The highest rates will be charged if a particularly popular programme is being shown, such as an important football match. Advertisers buy a package of spots, repeating the advertisement to ensure that the message reaches as many people as possible. However, television advertising is very expensive. Another form of advertising on television is sponsorship, where businesses pay to sponsor a particular programme. For example, Citroen sponsors Channel 4's *First Dates*.

▶ **Radio** – as with television, most radio stations are commercial stations that carry advertisements. Many businesses advertise on local commercial stations and you should note the ones in your locality, as these are the ones that you would most likely use for a new enterprise. There are also many national commercial stations, such as Absolute Radio. Spots are sold on radio in the same way as on television, with peak times costing more money.

▶ **Cinema** – cinema advertising can be a useful way of reaching a particular group of potential customers. As with any form of advertising, marketers will look at the audience profile of a film before deciding on whether to advertise at screenings of that film. Advertisers aiming to reach the 15–24 age group may choose cinema advertising over other forms of advertising as going to the cinema is the biggest leisure activity for this age group. They make up the largest proportion (29 per cent) of the UK cinema audience.

▶ **Online** – online advertisements can be linked to your internet searches, so if you search for 'low airfares', you will find that you are targeted by advertisements for travel sites. Businesses want to advertise on websites that are relevant to their product but that also receive high numbers of **unique users**. Advertisers usually pay for online advertising using a pay-per-click system, where the advertiser pays the host website every time a user clicks on their advert and is directed to their own website.

▶ **Skywriting** – this can be a useful advertising medium for one-off events such as exhibitions or club nights. They are often used over beaches where people are sitting or sunbathing and will see the advert. A one-off message can cost around £600 an hour.

▶ **Billboards** – billboards are found all over the UK, usually on roadsides. Businesses that specialise in outdoor advertising sell the space to advertisers. Advertisements can also be placed on taxis, buses, on the London Underground, at railway stations and at bus stops. Large and colourful posters are a good way for travel and tourism businesses to remind commuters that they can get away to sunnier places.

The advantages and disadvantages of the different forms of advertising are shown in Table 5.9.

Discussion

Find an example of travel television programme sponsorship. Why do you think the sponsor wants to be linked with that particular programme? What are the advantages to the business? What are the advantages to the television channel? Can you think of any disadvantages? Discuss your findings with the rest of the group.

Key term

Unique users – the number of individual people who visit a website during a given time period.

▶ **Table 5.9:** Advantages and disadvantages of different forms of advertising

Medium	Advantages	Disadvantages
Newspapers	• Can be print or online • Can target precise audience or readership • Can include detailed information in advertisements • Short lead time, so last-minute travel advertisements can be included at short notice	• Do not use much colour • Newspapers are soon thrown away • Advertising space can be cluttered
Magazines	• Can be print or online • Can contain colourful, glossy advertisements • Can target precise audience • Can include inserts (leaflets inside the magazine)	• Colour advertising is expensive • Most magazines are national so cannot target regional audiences • Long lead time so not suitable for last-minute travel offers
Radio	• Listeners are often loyal to a channel and will hear the advertisements • Cheaper than television • Can have an immediate impact, especially when promoting offers and events	• Advertisements cost more than print advertisements • Listeners may be doing something else at the same time so they may not be engaged by the advertisement

▶ **Table 5.9:** *Continued...*

Medium	Advantages	Disadvantages
Television	• Reaches a large number of people • Can target audiences by time and programme • Can have a high impact due to colour, moving images and audio	• Expensive to produce and place advertisements • Potential audience may be dispersed over several channels • People can avoid advertisements by channel-hopping or fast forwarding on catch up
Online	• Can have a high impact due to moving images and video embedded into websites • Are paid on a pay-per-click system so only pay for people who express an interest in the product	• Can require maintenance to keep up to date • Can take time to find the most suitable host websites • Advertising space can be limited
Cinema	• Can have high impact due to use of big screen • Has a captive audience	• Expensive to produce advertisements
Billboards	• Can allow regional targeting • Can be very eye-catching in public places • Low cost	• Usually static • Prime locations are expensive • People have short exposure to the message

Key terms

Digital marketing – advertising that uses digital media such as the internet, electronic billboards and mobile devices such as tablets and smartphones.

Social media – communication channels such as Facebook, Twitter and Instagram.

Email marketing – sending adverts and promotions directly to targeted groups by email.

Electronic billboards – computer-controlled billboards with changing messages.

Research

There are lots of examples of trade and consumer shows in travel and tourism. Research some of these shows when deciding on your marketing strategy.

Digital marketing

You have already learned about some of the ways in which the internet can be used for advertising, but **digital marketing** particularly makes use of social media platforms, such as Facebook, Twitter, LinkedIn and Instagram, which are crucial ways of reaching younger markets.

Social media can be cheap to use, which makes it attractive to businesses as a method of advertising. Organisations can set up Facebook pages allowing followers to engage with the business by sharing the business's tweets and Facebook posts with their friends and contacts. The way in which information is presented on social media differs from traditional advertising because it has to look like a conversation rather than an advertisement. Businesses have to manage their social media presence carefully, as negative comments can be posted online and these are not always easy to remove. Social media platforms are good places to promote your new enterprise as you are probably familiar with using them and they are cheap to use.

Email marketing is another element of digital marketing. It can be used to provide news or to provide offers. Customers are used to giving businesses their email addresses, so people can be persuaded very easily to sign up for emails to get a special offer or discount. Once you have a basic format for your marketing emails, they are quick to produce and to send. They can also be tracked, allowing businesses to measure the response. However, if a business sends too many emails, its customers may stop reading them.

Electronic billboards are usually placed in the same locations as more traditional static billboards, such as at bus stops or by the side of the road, but their advertisements usually rotate every 6 to 8 seconds. Because they are computer-controlled, they are flexible and can be changed instantly. Billboards often support other media campaigns.

Trade and consumer shows

Trade and consumer shows are large exhibitions attended by businesses in a particular industry. Most shows have the aim of promoting new sales and attracting potential customers. Consumer shows are holiday and travel shows held annually in large cities, aimed at potential holidaymakers. Some shows are only for travel and tourism professionals and are of no interest to the general public, such as the Travel and Technology Show, which appeals to trade customers who need to update their technology.

Brochures

Brochures are an effective sales tool and a traditional way of promoting tourism products. Many travel agencies are starting to use e-brochures as well as print brochures, as customers like to browse on the internet and e-brochures are cheaper to produce than print brochures. Leaflets or inserts can also be inserted into brochures to promote other businesses' products or services.

⏸ PAUSE POINT   Explain the difference between traditional and digital media, giving examples.

> **Hint**   Think about the kinds of advertising that are available on the internet and those that are not.

> **Extend**   List some of the potential drawbacks of using social media as an advertising channel.

Public relations and media liaison

Public relations (PR) is a major part of the promotional mix and can be important to travel and tourism companies with small marketing budgets. This is because PR activities are much cheaper than other forms of promotion. PR may be carried out in-house or contracted out to a specialist PR agency.

The responsibilities of the PR department may include:

▶ creating press releases for newspapers and magazines
▶ getting coverage on television and radio programmes such as breakfast news programmes or chat shows
▶ organising events, exhibitions and receptions
▶ publishing newsletters.

All of these PR activities are designed to present the company in the best possible way in the media or in a community.

Media liaison is part of PR and involves dealing with enquiries from the media and issuing press releases. You can find examples of press releases or news items on any tourism business's website. PR staff will also call their media contacts if they want to place a story in the press about their company.

Guerrilla marketing is a creative style of marketing, where promotions are placed in low-cost media and PR is then used to create a high degree of consumer interest in these promotions so that consumers talk about the campaign, especially on social media.

Place

Place is the element of the marketing mix that considers how to get the product or service to the customer. The means of getting the product to the customer is known as the distribution channel or distribution chain. In the travel and tourism industry, the distribution channel is complicated by the fact that there is often no tangible product to pass through the channel.

> **Link**
>
> You learned about distribution channels in Unit 1: The World of Travel and Tourism.

Distribution channels

▶ A **direct distribution channel** links directly from the supplier to the consumer, such as through the supplier's own website, telephone call centres or high street agencies.
▶ An **indirect distribution channel** is one in which there is a third party between the supplier and the consumer. In travel and tourism, the third party is usually a travel agent working on a commission basis, but may also be a travel wholesaler or inbound tour operator.

Direct distribution is becoming more and more popular. For example, tour operators advertise on television and social media platforms to attract direct sales. Some have even introduced sales channels on television, such as Thomas Cook TV. This means of distribution has been so successful that annual holiday sales through television channels have soared.

Direct distribution can help lower distribution costs for businesses such as airlines. For example, all bookings for low-cost airlines are taken through the airlines' websites, which keeps the costs low as airlines do not have to employ call centre staff or pay commission to travel agencies. Similarly, tour operators used to have to use travel agencies to distribute printed brochures to customers. These glossy brochures are

Key term

Marketing strategy – the detailed schedule of activities that are to be undertaken, where and when they are going to be undertaken, and the cost.

expensive to print and they need to be updated and reprinted regularly. The switch to e-brochures, which act as part of a direct distribution channel, has reduced costs for some tour operators.

In addition, indirect distribution channels have some significant disadvantages. For example, a tour operator selling through travel agencies will have to accept that:

▶ commission must be paid on every sale made through a travel agency
▶ independent travel agents decide how to rack the brochures and may not give prominence to a tour operator's product
▶ tour operators have little control over the quality or method of selling
▶ travel agents take add-on sales, such as car hire and insurance.

Businesses also use social media to market their products and services directly to consumers and encourage customers to buy directly from the business, rather than through a third party. A cheap way of getting new customers is through client referrals, where one happy customer refers their friend. This is particularly easy to do on social media, where customers may share businesses' tweets and posts with their friends.

Marketing strategy

A **marketing strategy** is a detailed plan of the activities that a business will undertake to market its products. This plan will include where and when these activities will take place and the cost of these activities. Figure 5.7 shows one way in which you could create a successful marketing strategy.

Identify the target market
• age and gender
• income
• location
• lifestyle
• attitudes

Define the message
• the product story
• the benefits of the product

Choose the media
• what media?
• where in each medium?
• when?

Create the marketing plan
• mission
• objectives
• marketing mix

Evaluate the campaign
• measures and metrics
• successes
• weaknesses

▶ **Figure 5.7:** A method for creating a successful marketing strategy

Content of the marketing message

The marketing message is what a business wants people to know about it and its products and services. For example, what are the business's products or services? What do they do? What are their features and benefits? Businesses must think carefully about their message and how it works as a USP to set them apart from anyone else in the market.

Selecting an appropriate marketing mix

To put together a marketing mix, a business first has to decide on the objectives of the marketing strategy. Potential objectives for travel and tourism businesses include:

▶ informing the public about a new product or service

▶ informing the public about a change to the product or company

▶ increasing sales

▶ increasing market share

▶ reassuring existing customers

▶ responding to competitors' promotions

▶ reminding consumers that the business is there and ready to take their custom

▶ reinforcing the business's public image.

These objectives will be achieved only if the company chooses the right marketing mix.

Your strategy needs to make potential customers aware of your new idea. Before you decide on your marketing mix, you must identify your target market for your new idea. This process is known as **market segmentation**. Identify their key demographic characteristics, such as age, gender, lifestyle, attitudes and behaviour, and then use this information to create a profile of your target customer.

There will be **constraints** on your marketing strategy, such as the available budget and the amount of available time. For example, you will need to work out how much money you can spend on your strategy. Do you have enough budget for traditional advertising, or will you concentrate instead on using social media platforms?

> **Key terms**
>
> **Market segmentation** – identifying different groups of customers with similar characteristics in order to aim a product or service at that group.
>
> **Constraint** – something that limits or restricts something else.

Selecting appropriate media

A business will waste its marketing budget if its promotional campaign does not reach the intended audience. Usually, the advertiser wishes to reach a particular group of people, so they will choose a medium that is used by an audience whose profile matches the profile of the business's intended customer. All media channels publish profiles of their audiences, including information such as their gender, age group and socio-economic group. These profiles help advertisers to select appropriate media. Media channels also often produce documents containing their advertising rates, known as rate cards, which can help you to determine what kind of advertisement you can afford to place.

Evaluating the strategy

A business must evaluate its marketing strategy to see whether it has been a success. One way of doing this is to measure its results against its original objectives. Were the objectives achieved?

You should consider how you can best evaluate the success of your own marketing strategy for your travel and tourism enterprise. For example, if your objective was to create interest in your product or service, do you have any evidence of that interest, such as an offer of funding from a potential investor?

The following are other forms of evidence.

▶ **Sales and/or return on investment** – if the objective of the strategy was to increase sales, the sales figures can be used as a measure of its success. Return on investment is also easy to measure at the end of the financial period: has the money invested in the marketing strategy resulted in a profit?

▶ **Feedback from customers** – organisations carry out surveys and include feedback forms or pop-ups on websites to encourage customers to give them feedback about their marketing. Customers may be asked where they heard about the product or service, and this can indicate which marketing campaign is driving customers to the product. Feedback may also be posted on social media.

▸ **Competition response** – if competing businesses rush to copy the idea or product being advertised, this also indicates that the marketing has been effective.

Case study

Screw it, let's do it: Virgin Holidays on the launch of its 'most ambitious campaign' yet

by Rachel Gee

Virgin Holidays is launching its first live ad in a bid to get more people to take long-haul holidays, as it says that Brexit has made people want their money to work harder than ever.

The 'most ambitious brand launch' in Virgin Holidays' history begins on Saturday when it will air its first live TV ad during The *X Factor*. The ad will showcase influencers across 18 different destinations, as the company hopes to demonstrate that normal people can make these destinations a reality, not just celebrities.

Despite concern for the travel industry following Brexit, Virgin Holidays has used this to its advantage and changed its marketing strategy to reflect the notion that customers now want their money to work harder than ever. The overall campaign, titled 'Seize the Holiday', runs for six weeks.

The new campaign will focus on all demographics, not just families, after Virgin Holidays saw a pickup in demand for **experiential** travel from millennials, cruise and honeymoon bookings.

Success will be measured through brand consideration preference, booking enquiry numbers, the number of appointments booked in retail stores and online, and engagement through social channels.

Although TV is a key element in the campaign, the live ad will also be pushed out on social media through Facebook Live and YouTube, while other social and outdoor methods will include press, radio, digital, mobile, Twitter and Instagram. The latter will involve competitions with the hashtag #SeizeTheHoliday.

Check your knowledge

1 Are there any other points that you would highlight because they tell you something about the way in which Virgin Holidays created this campaign?

2 Can you think of any other ways in which Virgin Holidays could evaluate the success of their campaign?

A live advertisement, filming 18 different scenes live from key Virgin Holidays' destinations.

Medium chosen to reach the right demographic

The kind of people that the target customers aspire to be like

Key term

Experiential – based on an experience.

Analysis of bookings is internal research

How the strategy will be evaluated

A range of media has been selected, combining digital and traditional channels to reach the target audience from all angles

Competitions support the campaign

Case study

UK's first new travel service allows luggage check-in from your front door

Press release 11 October

AirPortr, the London based travel technology start-up, in partnership with British Airways (BA), has today launched AirPortr + Bag Check-In. This 'game-changing' new service for passengers allows travellers to check-in their luggage remotely from anywhere in London to their destination airport.

From the doorstep of a passenger's home, the hotel lobby or desk in the city, the AirPortr + Bag Check-In service with BA enables passengers to travel completely luggage free until they reach baggage reclaim at their destination.

This new service is a step-change in the passenger air travel experience. BA passengers flying from London will, for the first time, have the opportunity to experience the next generation of seamless travel and a further step towards an end-to-end customer journey. Perfect for those who seek to avoid the conundrum faced by what to do with bags with a late flight or early hotel check-out and freeing up some

valuable time to make the most of the day by squeezing in that extra business meeting or doing some last minute sightseeing. Equally travellers can wave goodbye to the stress of dragging heavy luggage onto the tube, bus or train during rush hour and arrive at the airport calm, relaxed and ready to start their journey.

AirPortr will deliver any size or weight item of luggage to London Heathrow, London Gatwick and London City Airport with bags checked in from a London address. Prices start from £20 for pickup from a local airport area for the first bag, £30 from central London for the first bag and £40 for the first bag from outer London and 'Airport to Airport', with an additional cost of £10 per additional bag.

Check your knowledge

1 Who do you think is the target market for this service?

2 What is the pricing strategy?

3 Find out how the service is being promoted.

⏸ PAUSE POINT   Explain the different elements of a marketing strategy.

> Hint   Look back at Figure 5.7.

> Extend   How would you evaluate the success of a marketing strategy?

Assessment activity 5.2

B.P3 | B.P4 | B.M2 | C.P5 | C.P6 | C.M3 | BC.D2

Produce an individual start-up plan for your idea for a new travel and tourism enterprise. Make sure you include an explanation of the:
- legal aspects of the new enterprise
- financial feasibility
- resources required.

Record all your plans on relevant documents, such as a formal business plan.

Produce a marketing strategy to support your start-up plan, which can be used to launch the new enterprise. Make sure your strategy explains the importance of the different elements of the marketing mix and how you will use them to raise awareness of your idea.

Assess the potential effectiveness of the marketing strategy.

Analyse and evaluate the feasibility of your start-up plan and marketing strategy, saying how you will manage any constraints.

Plan
- What documents will I need to produce?
- How will I use my research from the previous assessment activity?
- How will I present my plan and strategy?
- How will I evaluate my plan and strategy?

Do
- I have a template to use for my business plan.
- I have all of my research findings from the previous assessment activity.
- I have gathered and organised all my notes and research on aspects of business planning and the marketing mix.

Review
- I can explain how my marketing strategy will raise awareness of my idea.
- I can evaluate my plan and strategy, and explain why it will work.
- I know what constraints will affect my plan.

D Carry out a pitch for the new travel and tourism enterprise start-up plan in order to generate interest in the new travel and tourism enterprise

Opportunities to present your pitch to an audience

Once you have completed your start-up plan and marketing strategy, you need to pitch your new enterprise. The purpose of the pitch will determine the method of presentation or venue. For example, you may be pitching to launch your product to potential trade customers or consumers. Alternatively, you may be pitching to an investor or organisation to secure funding or publicity to launch your idea.

Trade journals, newspapers, websites and social media

You could use trade journals and newspapers to generate interest in your new enterprise by pitching your idea as a great news item. You could choose to advertise, but most publications are expensive to advertise in, whereas an article or news item will have a greater impact and cost you nothing. If you do want to advertise, local publications will be cheaper than national newspapers or trade journals.

If you decide that advertising is too expensive, you will need to create a press release. You must find out who to send it to by studying the contacts list of the newspaper, magazine or website. Alternatively, you could pitch it in person if you think that your idea is newsworthy enough.

If you use a press release, you should:
- send it to the most suitable publication for your idea
- give it an attention-grabbing headline
- keep it concise but include all essential information
- include photographs if possible
- include contact details for further information.

Research

Find out the cost of a half page advertisement in *Travel Trade Gazette*, in *Condé Nast Traveller* and in a local newspaper or publication.

Assuming money is no object, which of these would be best suited to raising interest in your new idea? Explain why.

Case study

Eurostar launches e-vouchers for Christmas: a gift that's going places

25 October

Christmas shoppers looking for the ultimate gift can celebrate as Eurostar is launching e-vouchers just in time for the festive season. In just a few clicks, the gift can be easily sent to friends and family, whilst avoiding the hassle of the high street.

With a broad range of destinations to choose from, there's a city to appeal to every type of traveller. Whether you're looking to spoil a foodie friend with a trip to Lyon, a loved one in Paris or a wine enthusiast in Provence, the Eurostar e-voucher makes it easy to treat friends and family to the perfect Christmas gift.

From 14 November, shoppers simply log on to Eurostar.com, select the value of the voucher, add a personal message and send direct to their inbox. Once received, the recipient may choose to redeem the e-voucher to travel to any of Eurostar's destinations throughout the year.

Check your knowledge

1   Make a list of the key points in this press release.
- What is the product?
- When will the product be available?
- Where will customers buy the product?

2   How do Eurostar introduce the idea in the title and first paragraph?

3   What do you think is the point of the second paragraph?

Rate cards are usually available for advertising on websites as well as on print media. You can choose different types of banner adverts, usually for a month at a time. You can also pay-per-click for click-throughs to your own website. The advantage of this is that you can monitor how many people are looking at the advert by measuring how many click through onto your website.

Social media is a great way for you to pitch your idea as you can encourage your friends and contacts to share your idea with their friends and contacts. If you set up some interactive content, such as a competition, you may be able to engage followers in conversation about your idea.

Exhibitions and conferences

Exhibitions and conferences are held for many industries, including the travel and tourism industry. Exhibitors and speakers at these events aim to promote new sales and attract potential customers.

The World Travel Market is held every November in London and it is probably the best-known travel-related trade fair. It attracts visitors from overseas as well as from across the UK. It is held at ExCeL, a purpose-built exhibition venue in east London. It attracts over 50,000 visitors every year. Visitors have to be professionals working in the travel and tourism industry or related industries, so the exhibition is not for consumers. A stand at the World Travel Market has the potential to reach a lot of trade professionals, but it will be expensive.

▶ The World Travel Market in 2015

The British Tourism and Travel Show is dedicated to domestic tourism and is also held annually. It takes place at the NEC in Birmingham. The show attracts over 2000 visitors over two days and hosts more than 250 exhibitors. There are two ways of pitching goods and services at the show. Exhibitors can:

▶ hire a stand at around £300 per square metre
▶ take part in the seminar programme to discuss information that is useful to the audience, such as on a key issue facing the industry or new business opportunities.

Another example of a travel and tourism exhibition is Travel Technology Europe, held at Olympia in London. This would be useful to attend if your idea is related to travel technology. It is not of great interest to the public but it attracts potential trade customers.

Destinations is a holiday and travel show held annually at Olympia, which is mostly visited by potential holidaymakers from the general public. There are specialist shows too, such as the Holiday Park and Resort Show at the NEC and the London Boat Show at ExCeL.

Let's work together

One of the exhibitors at the London Boat Show is On the Water (www.onthewater.co.uk), an organisation that gives people advice on taking up water-based activities.

Ben Clifford set up his own surfing business with support from the Prince's Trust Enterprise programme. He had worked at a school helping young people with learning difficulties, but was left unemployed when his contract came to an end. He had the idea of combining his passion for surfing with doing more for young people and set up Surfability UK CIC, which helps people with disabilities and learning difficulties to surf and improve their confidence.

Check your knowledge

1 Explain why Ben might carry out a pitch for On the Water.

2 What would be the potential benefits for Ben and for On the Water of working together?

3 How might a stand at the London Boat Show help Surfability UK CIC reach a wider audience?

Reasons to attend the Holiday Park and Resort Show

1 **Keynote speakers**
   Key individuals and experts in their fields will share their knowledge, stories and advice.

2 **Networking**
   Share ideas with like-minded individuals and gain advice from their success stories and failures from diversifying, innovating and growing their business.

3 **Free advice**
   Under one roof, over two days this will be the only place in the UK a rural land or business owner can source information and advice on funding, grants, planning, new products, new services, new ideas, troubleshooting, business tips, marketing tools, networking, inspiring keynote sessions, like-minded professionals, potential partnerships and so much more. Visitors go into their next venture fully equipped!

4 **Niche sector specialities**
   Advice and ideas for every sector, whether it's tourism and leisure, renewable energy, farm attractions, land rental, alternative agriculture, diversified farm production, and the list goes on...

5 **150 seminar sessions**
   Our seminar sessions will cover all aspects of rural business, from inspiration to advice.

6 **Sourcing products and services**
   Attendees meet and do business with over 300 of the UK's top exhibiting companies, on hand to demonstrate their products and services.

7 **Rural business specialists**
   New ventures will require finance, insurance, planning and advice. Having rural business experts alongside suppliers means all the information and help you need is in one place, at one time.

Check your knowledge

1 Explain how you could pitch your idea for a new enterprise at this show.

2 Explain who your target market would be.

3 Find out the potential cost of doing this, including your transport costs for travel to the exhibition.

 **PAUSE POINT** Give four examples of travel and tourism shows that could be used to raise awareness of a new travel and tourism enterprise.

 Hint Look at the websites of exhibition venues like the NEC, Olympia and ExCeL to see what shows they are hosting in the next 12 months.

Extend Explain why some shows are only for trade visitors.

Factors to consider when choosing presentation method and venue

There are a number of factors that need to be taken into account when preparing for a presentation.

- **Size of venue** – if you are doing a personal pitch in a venue, consider how much space you need. This will depend on the size of your audience, the equipment you need and any physical products you are going to show. Venue rooms usually have maximum capacities, so make sure that you know how many people you are expecting.
- **Risk assessment** – you need to make sure that the room is safe and suitable for the number of people you are pitching to. Can the entrances, exits and reception areas cope with the number of expected visitors? Will everyone be able to get out in the event of an emergency? Are the exits and gangways clear and free from obstacles? Are the fire exits signposted?
- **Contingency planning** – you must also plan for other things that can go wrong. Make sure that you have a back-up plan in case your equipment fails. Check how far you need to travel to get to the venue and how long it will take. Research alternative methods of transport in case your planned method is cancelled. Check the weather forecast and ensure that you have organised your materials well in advance.
- **Insurance** – you should not need your own insurance at this stage, although you will do when your enterprise is set up. For your presentation, you just need to check that your venue has suitable insurance covering public liability.
- **Available budget** – this can be a significant constraint on your pitch as well as on marketing activities. If you need a venue, you might be able to use your contacts to find a free or cheap venue. However, you need to achieve a balance between spending what you can afford and ensuring that your pitch reaches the right audience.
- **Visual impact** – provide professional-looking signage and directions to help visitors find your presentation room or venue. You should also think about the visual impact of your presentation and how you will use visuals to engage your audience.

Appropriate resources

If your pitch is a presentation, you will need to set up your equipment in good time and ensure that the environment sets the scene for your idea.

Some of the resources that you may need include:

- multimedia equipment
- shelving or literature racks
- panel display boards
- posters

- flags and bunting or other decorations
- a whiteboard.

Appropriate supporting documents

During your preparation for your pitch or presentation, make sure that you have created the essential documents that will support your pitch. These may include:

- posters
- handouts or flyers
- an executive summary of your plan
- a brochure
- business cards.

In addition, your materials need to include documents that show that you have considered and anticipated any questions that potential customers or investors may ask. These could include:

- contingency plans
- a cash flow forecast
- potential sales forecasts
- manufacturing costs
- a marketing strategy.

Theory into practice

Ben is the founder of Ponticulus Design (see earlier case study on page 256). Part of his business model is to give talks about his project to schools with the aim of encouraging entrepreneurship and an interest in engineering and science. His talk lasts 40 minutes, including time for questions from children.

1 What resources could Ben use to set the scene for his talk?

2 What supporting documents or materials should Ben use to support his talk?

3 Draw up a contingency plan for the talk, including potential travel issues and preparation for questions.

Appropriate presentation skills

It is important that you present your pitch in an appropriate and professional manner. This includes your own presentation and attitude, the amount of preparation that you have done and your communication skills.

Personal presentation, conduct and attitude

If you look the part, you will feel more confident and instil confidence in your audience. Pay attention to your body language during your presentation – try to appear relaxed and open, even if you are feeling nervous. Leaning forward slightly shows you are alert and interested, and maintaining eye contact (without staring) shows you are confident and willing to engage with the audience.

Other points to consider are outlined below.

▶ Wear clothes appropriate for a business meeting – make sure every item of clothing is clean and free from creases, and ensure that you are also clean and well-presented.

▶ Smile and shake hands when you are introduced to a smaller audience or introducing yourself in a confident, professional manner to a larger group.

▶ Think before answering audience questions – if you are not sure of the answer, take a few moments to gather your thoughts rather than rushing straight into an answer.

▶ Show a positive attitude by listening attentively to, and showing interest in, questions and comments from members of your audience.

▶ Avoid habits such as fiddling with your hair or tapping your foot.

▶ Make eye contact with everyone in the audience rather than fixing on just one person.

Preparation and subject knowledge

The success of your pitch is dependent on the amount of time you invest in preparing, planning and designing your presentation.

Below are some guidelines for creating and organising the content of your presentation.

▶ Make sure that your presentation has a logical structure and an informative title.

▶ Introduce your presentation with a brief summary of your idea and what you are going to cover.

▶ Describe key points such as who the customers are, the size of your potential market, how your idea meets the customers' needs and where your income will come from.

▶ Outline any successes so far, such as market research that proves that your potential market exists.

▶ Explain your marketing strategy.

▶ Describe your competitors and explain why your enterprise will be more successful than theirs.

▶ Explain what you want from your audience.

▶ Briefly summarise the points that you have made.

▶ Take questions from the audience.

Guidelines for the design of your presentation are summarised below.

▶ Keep written text on slides to a minimum – use headlines to indicate the content to your audience and use your notes and knowledge to talk about these headlines.

▶ Only make one point on a slide, otherwise you may confuse your audience.

▶ Use font, colour and photographs appropriately to make the presentation visually appealing.

▶ Add your business's logo (if you have one) to the presentation slides.

▶ Consider all possible questions and prepare answers to these questions.

You could watch *Dragons' Den* or similar programmes for examples of possible questions that you may be asked. Above all, keep practising and ask for feedback on your practice presentations.

Using resources and equipment safely and effectively

Misusing resources such as visual aids and technology will ruin your presentation. Make sure that you have thought of all possible problems and created an appropriate contingency plan. For example, what would you do if there is no internet connection or no sound coming from the speakers?

You might have the option to use some of the pieces of equipment listed in Figure 5.8 on page 277. Only use them if they enhance your presentation and engage the audience.

Communication skills

The way in which you communicate with your audience will have an impact on the way they feel about your pitch, so it is important to get it right.

Explain your ideas convincingly

You have to be able to convey your passion for and interest in your subject to your audience. You are much more likely to be able to do this if you are knowledgeable about the subject, have done plenty of research and planning, and have practised your presentation.

Engage your audience

You should always begin by making sure that everyone can hear you. It is important to speak clearly and consider the tone of your voice to ensure that it is not monotonous. You should also make sure that the pace of your speech is neither too slow nor too fast. Feedback from practice presentations will help you get this right. Do not worry if you need to pause to think of your next point.

Listen to your audience

Your audience may wish to ask questions or make comments. You will need to decide and let the audience know whether questions can be asked at any point during the presentation or should be saved until the end. When you are listening to questions, focus on the speaker and make eye contact with them. Practise active listening by using your body language to show that you are listening, such as nodding in appropriate places.

Resources and equipment

Microphone

- Make sure you know how to turn it on and off.
- Speak normally into it – you shouldn't have to project your voice.
- Check that the microphone is off when you don't want the audience to hear what you are saying.

Whiteboard/flip chart

- Write up key points beforehand (writing takes time and requires you to turn your back on your audience).
- Make sure your writing is clear, readable and large enough to be seen from the back of the room.
- If you are using an interactive whiteboard, practise in advance.

Handouts

- Do not give out handouts during your presentation.
- If people need the information in the handouts during the presentation, give them out before you speak. Otherwise, give them at the end.

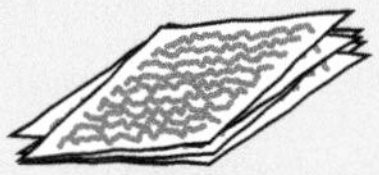

Digital presentation resources

- If you are using Microsoft PowerPoint®, Apple Keynote or Prezi, make sure that you arrive early and can check that your presentation works on the provided PC or laptop.
- If you are using videos, check that there is a working internet connection or that the video is loaded, that the sound works and that the speakers are loud enough.

▶ **Figure 5.8:** Choosing the resources that you should use for your presentation

Take and answer questions

First, it is important that everyone can hear the question that has been asked. If the speaker is quiet or the question is quite long, you can lose the attention of the rest of your audience. Politely cut off long questions and summarise them for the rest of the group. Make sure everyone has heard and understood the question before you respond. Give a brief, clear and accurate answer. If you do not know the answer, be honest about this but say that you will find out and get back to them.

Present information in a persuasive manner

Use the guidelines that you have already read to create your presentation. Make sure that the communication method you choose is appropriate for your audience, and use simple clear English in your written and oral presentation. In particular, you should avoid using acronyms and jargon, as this can leave your audience confused or unengaged.

One important thing you can do is to prepare an **elevator pitch**, just in case you meet someone and have the opportunity to tell them quickly about your idea. An elevator pitch should take no more than 30 seconds, and it should:

- say what your idea is
- state the benefits
- state the USP
- ask an open-ended question to engage the listener, such as 'How would you feel about being the first travel agent to...?'.

Key term

Elevator pitch – a brief 30-second summary of your business or idea (so-called because it could be delivered in the time it takes to go up or down in an elevator or lift).

Theory into practice

Think of any presentations that you have been to. These can include lessons.

1 List all the aspects of the presentation that you found really effective or engaging.

2 List the aspects that were not so effective or engaging.

Which points would you try to use in your own presentations? Which would you avoid?

Prepare some guidelines for someone in your group to help them prepare for their pitch. Talk through the guidelines with them.

Hint   First, find out what their presentation is about and whether it is going to be read or listened to.

Extend   Practise your own presentation and ask a partner to read or listen to it and provide constructive feedback.

Assessment activity 5.3

D.P7   D.P8   D.M4   D.D3

Your local council has invited people to pitch potential ideas for travel and tourism enterprises that they would like to support. You have already produced your business plan and developed your marketing strategy. You may also consider including recommendations for improvements to these documents, based on any additional research you have done.

You must now plan, prepare and deliver a presentation in your chosen form to generate interest in your new idea.

Make sure that you have created or sourced a venue and appropriate resources and documents for your pitch, including a log of how you managed your time and resources to produce your presentation.

Plan
- How will I present my pitch?
- What considerations should I think about when deciding how to do my presentation?
- How do I incorporate my business plan and marketing strategy into my pitch?
- What resources will I need?

Do
- I have prepared my presentation.
- I have created and prepared all the resources I need to support the presentation.
- I have all the supporting documents I need.
- I have practised my presentation.
- I have considered my personal presentation.

Review
- I can explain what went well and what was less successful.
- I have feedback from the audience on my presentation.

Further reading and resources

Levinson, J. C. (2007) *Guerrilla Marketing* (4th ed.), New York: Houghton Mifflin.

Condé Nast Traveller magazine: **www.cntraveller.com/uk**
A consumer travel magazine online.

Wanderlust Travel magazine: **www.wanderlust-magazine.co.uk**
A consumer travel magazine online.

Travel Trade Gazette (TTG): **www.ttgmedia.com**
A publication for the travel trade.

Mintel market research: **www.store.mintel.com/industries/holidays-and-travel**
Reports on consumer research (may be free through your library).

Radio Joint Audience Research (RAJAR): **www.rajar.co.uk**
Statistics and information about radio audiences.

UK Cinema Association: **www.cinemauk.org.uk**
Facts and figures about film and audiences.

Advisory, Conciliation and Arbitration Service (ACAS): **www.acas.org.uk**
Help and advice for employers and employees to help prevent or resolve workplace problems.

THINK ▶▶FUTURE

Simon Godfrey and **Caroline Robinson**

Let's Go Punting (part of Let's Go Cambridge Limited)

Simon and Caroline started Let's Go Punting in Cambridge in 2010. The business sells punting tours to tourists through their website. Customers who book in advance pay a lower price than customers who just turn up. Advance bookings allow Simon and Caroline to plan how many punts and punt chauffeurs they need. Selling through the internet is key to their success, as it allows them to reach a much larger audience than simply relying on people seeing their punts when walking by the river. Customers who have booked the 45-minute tour meet Simon or one of the punt chauffeurs on the riverside.

The couple also run Cambridge Hen Party, Cambridge Corporate Events and Tours of Cambridge. Each of these companies has its own website linked to the home website. The company can run 200 hen parties every year, and these are also booked through their website. To offer hen parties and corporate events, they work with partners such as local bars and restaurants. Developing these networks has helped them as they can now negotiate good prices with suppliers and extend the product that they offer their customers.

A typical tour includes punting, a scavenger hunt of the city on foot (looking for key attractions and buildings from a set of provided clues) and a picnic prepared by one of their partner businesses. Hen parties might also include activities such as cocktail making at a local bar. Although they have competition from national companies that run hen parties and events, Simon and Caroline have an advantage because they have built up personal relationships with local suppliers, meaning that they have a better knowledge of the available products.

The business has grown a lot since it was set up. It now has an office and, at the busiest times of year, they have eight large punts, ten punt chauffeurs, a manager and two salespeople on riverside for drop-in sales.

Focusing on skills

If you want to set up your own business, what do you need to do?

- If your business is web based, you need to invest in the best website you can afford or have excellent web development skills yourself.
- Develop your organisational skills – you need to pay attention to detail and be good at administration. You can practise these skills by planning your assignments carefully.
- Be prepared to work long and unsocial hours – you will only succeed by putting in a lot of hard work.

- Be motivated and passionate about your idea, and know your product inside out.
- Understand finances and how to keep to a budget. You can practise this by budgeting your own personal finances.
- Develop networking skills – get to know people in the industry in your local area by attending networking events or through your assignment work.
- Research the resources available to help small businesses, such as tax workshops run for free by Her Majesty's Revenue and Customs (HMRC).

Getting ready for assessment

Suvarn is working towards a BTEC National Foundation Diploma in Travel and Tourism. He was given an assignment to prepare a start-up plan and marketing strategy for a new travel and tourism enterprise including:

- legal aspects of the new enterprise
- financial feasibility
- resources required.

Suvarn had already done his research and so he knew what travel and tourism enterprise idea he wanted to develop.

How I got started

I decided to run a French food market in my local town. I had seen this in other towns and I had been to French markets on holiday. I thought it was something that would work in my local area – not as a regular weekly market but once or twice a year.

In my first assignment for this unit, I did lots of research to see if local people would be interested in the idea and to find out if they would go to such a market. I also went to one that was happening in a town about an hour away, to get some more ideas about the stalls and who they were run by. This was a great help as I talked to some of the stallholders and got their business cards. I was also able to talk to them afterwards on Facebook, and seeing their business cards made me decide to create some of my own.

Once I was sure about doing the market, I was ready to start creating my plan. I had a lot to think about. I needed to consider all the legal aspects, the finance, and the resources that I would need, such as a venue and stalls. I knew where to find a business plan template that I could use, but I still had to think about what to charge stallholders and whether there would be an entry fee for visitors. I also needed to work out how to advertise the event without spending too much money. There was so much to do!

How I brought it all together

- I made a mind map showing all aspects of the enterprise.
- I collected all my notes from the unit and matched them up with the aspects listed in the mind map.
- I made a plan of what to do when leading up to the submission of my assignment.
- I decided to present the information in a portfolio with the business plan first, followed by the marketing strategy in sections. I had examples of my press release and Facebook page for the market in the portfolio.
- I allowed myself plenty of time to write up my plan and strategy, and asked my dad to proofread them for me.

What I learned from the experience

I should have shared my first mind map with someone, just to discuss it and check that I hadn't missed anything – then I might have remembered that I would need insurance.

I learned a lot about funding. I knew that my market would make a profit if it succeeded but I still needed money upfront to hire the venue and the stalls.

You can get free publicity. I spoke to someone at my local newspaper and they were interested in doing a small article on my project.

Think about it

- Is your idea for a new travel and tourism enterprise clear in your mind?
- Have you considered everything that needs to go into your business plan and marketing strategy?
- Have you gathered together all your notes and the results of your market research?
- Have you thought about how to present your work?
- How will you make sure that it looks professional?

Mapping grid: BTEC Nationals Travel and Tourism (2010)

The following grid maps the contents of this book against the 2010 specification of the BTEC Nationals in Travel and Tourism. This indicates where content relating to this earlier specification can be found in this student book.

2010 Specification		2019 Student Book	
Unit	**Learning Outcome**	**Unit**	**Pages**
1. Investigating the Travel and Tourism Sector	1. Know the travel and tourism component industries and their organisations	1. The World of Travel and Tourism	11–24
	2. Understand the role of travel and tourism organisations and their interrelationships	1. The World of Travel and Tourism	8–10 25–28
	3. Know the developments that have shaped the present day travel and tourism sector	1. The World of Travel and Tourism	29–33
	4. Understand how trends and factors are currently affecting the travel and tourism sector.	1. The World of Travel and Tourism	45–60
2. The Business of Travel and Tourism	1. Know the different types of organisations operating in the travel and tourism business environment	1. The World of Travel and Tourism	8–10
	2. Know the characteristics of different types of travel and tourism organisations	1. The World of Travel and Tourism	8–10
	3. Understand how travel and tourism organisations gain competitive advantage to achieve business aims	4. Managing the Customer Experience in Travel and Tourism	202
	4. Be able to produce a business case for a travel and tourism enterprise within financial constraints.	5. Travel and Tourism Enterprises	247– 259
4. Customer Service in Travel and Tourism	1. Understand the importance of providing excellent customer service in travel and tourism organisations	4. Managing the Customer Experience in Travel and Tourism	186– 191 201–204
	2. Know how travel and tourism organisations adapt customer service to meet the individual needs of customers	4. Managing the Customer Experience in Travel and Tourism	216–217 222–229
	3. Know the customer service skills required to meet customer needs in travel and tourism contexts	4. Managing the Customer Experience in Travel and Tourism	192– 200
	4. Be able to apply customer service and selling skills in travel and tourism situations.	4. Managing the Customer Experience in Travel and Tourism	205–210 215 –216

2010 Specification		2019 Student Book	
Unit	**Learning Outcome**	**Unit**	**Pages**
5. Marketing Travel and Tourism Products and Services	1. Understand the factors influencing marketing in travel and tourism	3. Principles of Marketing in Travel and Tourism	146–153
	2. Know the marketing mix (the 4 Ps) of a travel and tourism organisation	3. Principles of Marketing in Travel and Tourism	163–171
		5. Travel and Tourism Enterprises	259– 268
	3. Be able to conduct a market research activity for a travel and tourism organisation	3. Principles of Marketing in Travel and Tourism	154–162
		5. Travel and Tourism Enterprises	236–246
	4. Be able to organise a promotional campaign for a travel and tourism organisation.	3. Principles of Marketing in Travel and Tourism	142
7. European Destinations	1. Be able to locate gateways and leisure destinations within the European travel market	2. Global Destinations	70, 84–91
	2. Know types of holidays available in Europe to meet differing visitor motivations	2. Global Destinations	78–83
	3. Know factors and features determining the appeal of leisure destinations in the European travel market for UK visitors	2. Global Destinations	69–76
	4. Understand how factors affect the development and decline of the European travel market.	2. Global Destinations	103–115
8. Long–haul Travel Destinations	1. Be able to locate major long–haul destinations of the world	2. Global Destinations	68–69
	2. Know the types of holidays offered within long–haul destinations that meet different visitor motivations	2. Global Destinations	78–83
	3. Understand how factors can affect travel to long–haul destinations	2. Global Destinations	103–115
	4. Know the features and facilities that contribute to the appeal of long–haul destinations for different types of visitors	2. Global Destinations	69–76
	5. Be able to plan a long–haul tour	2. Global Destinations	92–102

Index